Inscribed to Hugh Knapp
with warm regards and sincere good wishes.
                    Chester C. Maxey

Oct. 24, 1971

THE WORLD
I LIVED IN

A Personal Story

by

Chester C. Maxey

i

Dorrance & Company
Philadelphia

This book tries to tell the story of my life in relation to the world I lived in. I have chosen to omit much that is purely personal and to include much that tells of the institutions with which my life has been chiefly associated. These include mainly Whitman College, the University of Wisconsin, Columbia University, Western Reserve University, and the New York Bureau of Municipal Research. So many years of my life have been identified with Whitman College that certain parts of this narrative may seem like a topical history of that distinguished institution, and it of necessity is a partial history of Whitman College as seen through my eyes.

It would not be true for me to declare that everything has been objectively told. No man writing the story of his own life can be detached enough to do that. Although I will not claim to have been objective, I can honestly say that I have tried to be authentic. In all instances where documentation has been available I have used it and respected it. When I have had to depend on memory alone, I have tried not to forget that memory is rarely the equivalent of total and exact recall. I have tried to tell what I actually remember and nothing more, leaving retrospective embroidery to the reader's own imagination.

In rereading the manuscript I have been unavoidably impressed by the many times I have used the first person singular. No doubt I have succumbed to the temptation to overwork that seductive pronoun, and my only apology is that I sought to achieve a narrative style that would be less stilted than third person locutions usually accomplish. It seemed better to me to lean heavily on the pronoun "I" than to burden the discourse with verbiage simulating modesty at the expense of fluency and lucidity. If this offends, I beg the reader to remember that if

I were speaking instead of writing these memoirs, I would be speaking mostly in the first person singular. He would be the first to expect that.

I am indebted to my wife and to my daughter Marilyn for critical reading of the entire manuscript; to Dr. Louis B. Perry, my successor as president of Whitman College, for a similar service on those chapters specially dealing with that office; and to Mrs. Louise Humphrey for meticulous care in the typing of the manuscript.

CHESTER C. MAXEY

March, 1966

CONTENTS

PART I, ELLENSBURG, WASHINGTON, 1890–1908

PART II, WHITMAN COLLEGE, 1908–1912

PART III, UP TO THIRTY-FIVE

PART V, PRESIDENT OF WHITMAN COLLEGE,
1948–1959

PART VI. RETIREMENT, 1959–?

PART I
ELLENSBURG, WASHINGTON, 1890-1908

I. FAMILY BACKGROUND

May 30 or 31, 1890

I was not born in a hospital, a fact which brands me as a child of the nineteenth century. I have no birth certificate, another hallmark of nineteenth century nativity. When I was thirty-six years of age I had to prove the time and place of my birth to the satisfaction of the Passport Office of the Department of State. I was able to do this rather easily because my mother and the attending physician were still living and, at my request, deposed on oath before a notary public that I was Chester Collins Maxey, born at Ellensburg, Washington, on May 31, 1890. This and the passport issued thereafter are the only proofs of identity that I have, and I have kept them in my safety deposit box ever since.

Thus the date of my birth was legally attested, but if my father had been living he probably would have dissented to the extent of one day. He always maintained that I was born on May 30 instead of May 31. It seems that I was born shortly before or shortly after midnight, and nobody happened to be keeping close tab on the time. Father was positive that I made my earthly debut before midnight and Mother was equally positive that it was after midnight. She entered her version of it in the family Bible, the school records, the baptismal papers, and elsewhere that the date was required. Father let her have her way, but always reminded her in a joking way, when my birthday came around, that she was a day late. That is why I remember the matter so clearly.

How I chanced to be born in a small white cottage on the southwest slope of Craig's Hill, Ellensburg, the first child of Morton M. Maxey, a pioneer of that little community, and his recent bride, Leota M. Collins of Mt. Vernon, Illinois, is a circumstance of which I, naturally, have no personal knowledge. As I have reconstructed the facts from family hearsay, my

3

advent in the world was incidental to a series of Maxey migrations.

My paternal grandfather, Simeon W. Maxey, and his family, migrated from the vicinity of Mt. Vernon, Illinois, to Ellensburg, Washington Territory, in 1882. My father, then twenty-two years of age and unmarried, came along with the rest of the family. Seven years later, in the summer of 1889, he returned to Mt. Vernon and there, on the 15th of August, as I recall the entry in the family Bible, was married to Miss Leota M. Collins, The relationship between my father and mother during his seven years "out West" has always been a mystery to me. My father died when I was seven years old, long before I had any curiosity about parentage. When I was old enough to ask questions about such matters, my mother proved very reticent about the seven-year interlude. She simply did not want to talk about it, and I never could pry anything out of her.

I am sure that my father and mother were not engaged when he set out for Washington Territory in 1882. He was then a grown man on his own in the world, while she was just a schoolgirl of fifteen. I am equally sure that no correspondence passed between them and that neither made the slightest effort to keep in touch with the other. Ultimately I came to the conclusion that Mother's reason for not wanting to talk about the years between 1882 and 1889 was that, so far as she and my father were concerned there was simply nothing to say.

But Morton Maxey and Leota Collins were far from strangers. They knew each other very well. Not only had they been born and raised in the same community, belonged to the same church, attended the same country school; they knew each other as blood kin—second cousins. They had the same great-grandfather—William Maxey—and the father of Morton Maxey and the mother of Leota Collins were first cousins. Susan Maxey Collins, Leota's mother, was "Cousin Sue" to Morton, and Simeon W. Maxey, Morton's father, was "Cousin Sim" to all the Collinses. The brothers who sired these two lines of cousins were Charles H. Maxey and William M. A. Maxey, both of whom are my great-grandfathers.

4

My guess is that when Morton Maxey trekked westward in 1882 he had no romantic interest in Leota Collins, nor she in him. She was just a kid cousin, one of a score or more with whom he passed the time of day and sometimes played around with when the various Maxey and Collins families visited back and forth. But when he returned in 1889 she was a full grown woman and the belle of Pleasant Hill. I don't believe he went back to Illinois that summer of 1889 with any thought of marrying Leota Collins or anyone else. I believe he just went back for a general visit with kinfolk, friends, and neighbors. After all, he had been away seven years, and he could have been homesick for the sight of old scenes and faces. But—and this is my own guess—after he saw Leota at twenty-two years of age, the idea of matrimony hit him so hard that he staged a whirlwind campaign and swept her off her feet. As a matter of fact I believe those two had such a pell mell courtship that they hardly realized they were married until the ceremony was over and they were on their way to Ellensburg.

One thing I do know for sure. "Cousin Sue" was not at all happy about the match. She made no bones about her disapproval, then or later. Back in 1882 she had thought and said that "Cousin Sim" was foolish at his age (then fifty) to pull up stakes and move to the Wild and Wooly West, and she had no doubt that her daughter Leota was now headed for the jumping-off place. Nor did she regard Morton Maxey as a preferred "catch." She had known him since birth, knew him almost as well as her own children, and she was well aware of his great success in *not* settling down and accumulating property and other species of this world's goods. She did not believe most of the tales he told about the wonders of Washington Territory, and could not imagine why he was so eager to get back there and take Leota with him. Now that he was back home in Illinois, why on earth couldn't he settle down and stay?

But, if "Cousin Sue" took a dim view of the marriage "Cousin Sim" and his family were correspondingly delighted. Leota Collins was a favorite niece and cousin, almost as close as a sister to "Cousin Sim's" daughters, Franceska and Sina. Morton could not have brought back a bride that the Ellensburg Maxeys would welcome more cordially or love more deeply. And I know, as a matter of fact, that my mother came to have warmer affections and more durable relations with the Maxeys of Ellensburg than with the Collinses of Mt. Vernon, who were also Maxeys on the distaff side.

So much for the marriage by which I was destined to emerge on the planet Earth. It did not last long, for my father died in 1897, but it was a good union for me to be born of. It gave me a remarkable physical heritage, a thoroughly competent mental heritage, and a salutary enviroment in which to grow up.

The Maxey Clan

The Maxeys who migrated to Ellensburg, Washington Territory, in 1882 were descended from a certain Jesse Maxey (1750–1808), who was born in the Som's Creek district of Maryland, later moved to New River, Virginia, and finally settled in Sumner County, Tennessee. Jesse Maxey had four sons and one daughter, and our branch of the clan stems from his eldest son, William, who was born in Virginia in 1770, migrated with his father to Tennessee, and then, in April 1818, moved to Jefferson County, Illinois, where he made his permanent home. Our little family tree appears thus:

Jesse Maxey, 1750-1808
Elizabeth Luvoins (dates unknown)

William Maxey, 1770-1838
Mary Emily Allen, ?-1837

Charles H. Maxey, 1805-1885	William M. A. Maxey, 1812-1885
Sally Bruce (dates unknown)	Edda Owens, 1811-1880
Susan Bruce Maxey, ?-1915	Simeon W. Maxey, 1832-1909
George A. Collins, ?-1878	Minerva Whittenberg, 1838-1902
Leota M. Collins, 1867-1953	Morton M. Maxey, 1860-1897
Morton M. Maxey, 1860-1897	Leota M. Collins, 1867-1953
Chester Collins Maxey, 1890-	Chester Collins Maxey, 1890-
Elnora Campbell, 1890-	Elnora Campbell, 1890-

6

As family trees go, the foregoing is decidedly on the short side, but it contains every name and date of which I am sure. In trying to trace my ancestry further back than Jesse Maxey, I have consulted several Maxey genealogies and found them in total disagreement. One, for example, traces Jesse Maxey to Walter Maxey, a rug weaver, who was said to have migrated from Wales to France in the year 1600, married a French woman, and raised a family there. Another takes Jesse back to an Edward Maxey who was said to have come from Wales to America around 1725 and settled in Maryland. Still another says that the first Maxey to come to America was an Alexander Maxey, who settled at Wenham, Massachusetts, in 1659. A fourth says that Jesse's father was Justinian Maxey, and that Justinian's father was named Edward. I have assumed that none of these folk tales can be fully trusted.

Jesse Maxey, however, is a documented person, and that is why I prefer to start with him. He is recorded as having been on the payroll of the Virginia militia during the American Revolution, and he is further recorded as having been buried in the Douglas Cemetery, some three miles north of Gallatin, Tennessee. It is also a matter of record in the historical annals of Tennessee that one day in 1788 "he wandered too far away from the fort, was shot by the Indians, scalped, and left for dead, but recovered and lived twenty years thereafter." My grandfather, Simeon W. Maxey, had juicier tales to tell than that. He told me that his grandfather told him that Jesse was scalped all right, but not because he wandered too far from the fort. Grandfather said Jesse was too good a woodsman to wander away from the fort and let himself be ambushed by the Indians. What really happened, said my grandfather, was that Jesse was outside the stockade in the adjacent woods when he was forced to answer an urgent call of nature. While he was squatted down in a defenseless posture, the Indians sneaked up on him from behind. But he did recover and live twenty years thereafter, and was looked upon as quite a hero.

Jesse's son, William, is also a documented person. The records of Jefferson County, Illinois, disclose that in 1820 he established

7

the first grist mill in that county; that in 1821 he was appointed a justice of the peace and in that capacity, on July 6, 1821, performed the first marriage ceremony in Jefferson County. The records also show that William and Mary Emily Allen, his wife, had seven sons and four daughters. I am descended from two of William Maxey's sons, Charles H. Maxey and William M. A. Maxey, which, I suppose, makes me a double-dyed, inbred Maxey. My father and mother, having a common great-grand-father (William Maxey), were, according to the rule of the English common law, second cousins, which meant, of course, that my sister Aurel and I were third cousins as well as brother and sister.

Perhaps it was because of such genealogical convolutions that I never took much interest in family history. I know little more than hearsay. My grandfather Maxey thought that the Maxeys who first came to America were French Hugenots who had been driven out of their native land by the revocation of the Edict of Nantes. I am willing to accept this, but I can offer no proof that it is true. However if it *were* true, it would be more likely that the Maxey migrants went from France to Wales rather than the other way around. My doubts about the reliability of Maxey folklore were considerably strengthened by reading a French treatise on the origin of family names. This I found one day while browsing in the New York Public Library —the main library at 42nd Street and Fifth Avenue. In those years I could read French almost as rapidly as English, and I was curious to see what a French scholar might have to say about the origin of the Maxey name. The author of this treatise said that Maxey is one of several family names derived from varied pronunciations of the Roman praenomen Marcus. For several centuries Roman legions were stationed all over Western Europe, and one of the commonest first names among the Romans was Marcus. There must have been thousands of Romans named Marcus in all parts of the empire. In the tongues of the Franks, Germans, Celts, Britons, and so on, Marcus was given different pronunciations. We cannot be ab-solutely sure of the original Latin pronunciation, for classical

8

scholars are not agreed as to whether Latin was spoken with a hard or a soft "C" or with an open or a closed "U." It could have been, as in the United States today, that pronunciations differed according to locality. Hence, it is entirely possible that natives in different parts of the Roman Empire might have heard Marcus rendered as Mar-koos, Mar-kee, Mar-soos, or Mar-sees, and in their own languages they might very easily convert it into such adaptations as Marx, Marks, Marquis, Markey, Marcy, Maxcy, Maxey, Maxse, Macksey, McSee, or Maxon. Derived from the Latin as praenomens, such names could very easily be transformed into both cognomens and place names and thus become attached to families all over the Roman world. That is why, in my opinion, it is unlikely that the various Maxey families in the United States stem from a common ancestor any more than the various Smiths, Joneses, and Browns.

Therefore, I say that I am not sure of anything more than that my particular clan of Maxeys was sired by the Jesse Maxey mentioned previously. He and his wife, so far as I know, begot the Maxey men and women who became early-day settlers of Jefferson County, Illinois. I believe I have a pretty fair idea what sort of people these Jefferson County progenitors of mine were. My grandfather, Simeon W. Maxey, knew a great deal about them, and, as a small boy, knew them all directly, including the original William Maxey. From things he told me and from impressions gained from other sources, I believe the Maxey clan of Jefferson County was composed of two sharply contrasting types of kinfolk—the migrants and the habitants. The migrants were perennial frontiersmen, afflicted with itchy feet and forever in quest of a better land beyond some far horizon. The habitants were settled-down people, who clung to the old locales and old homesteads and had little desire to see beyond the horizon. William Maxey was one of the migrants, as his father Jesse had been. My grandfather, Simeon, was a migrant, as were two of his four brothers. All of Simeon's three sons were migrants, and my father was the most migrant of the three. Why all of William Maxey's children became habitants, while almost all of his grandchildren reverted to type and became migrants, I cannot explain, for they all lived in unsettled times.

Whether migrants or habitants, most of William Maxey's children and grandchildren considered themselves farmers, but not many of them actually were genuine farmers. They lived on farms rather than in cities, like William Maxey, and, also like him, most of them had too many sidelines to be dedicated dirt farmers. William Maxey was a farmer-miller-justice of the peace; William M. A., my great grandfather, was a farmer-physician-preacher; Simeon, my grandfather, was a farmer and county and state officeholder; Morton, my father, was a farmer, railroad man, restaurant operator, teamster, and cattleman. None of them really ever made a living out of farming alone or would have been content to do so. In later life most of them moved to town and made farming a sideline. They liked variety and they had versatility.

The elders of the Maxey clan, though short of schooling themselves, were strong supporters of education. Before there were public schools, they sent their children to "subscription" schools, so named because they were financed by sums annually subscribed by the patrons. Many of the elder-generation Maxeys were sufficiently intellectual and sufficiently ambitious to undertake private reading and study to qualify for learned professions. Some became teachers, some lawyers, some ministers, and some physicians. Very few ever went into business, except as an adjunct of farming. I was the first of my direct line to graduate from college, but not the first to have a good education.

My clan of Maxeys were Methodists through and through—always had been, so far as I know. Several became ordained Methodist ministers and others became lay preachers. Our Methodism, in a way, confirms my grandfather's belief that our particular line of Maxeys were of French Huguenot derivation. I have encountered Maxeys who were not Methodists, but I have never known a Jefferson County Maxey whose heredity, if not current church affiliation, was anything but Methodist. There is some documentary proof that an Edward Maxey, who lived on Soms Creek, Maryland, was one of the group who in

10

1760 assisted Robert Strawbridge in building a log meeting-house for the first Methodist society founded in America. Methodist documented history confirms that there was such a Robert Strawbridge, a local preacher, who had been spreading Wesley's "Arminian" theology in Maryland and Virginia for ten or more years before the great Francis Asbury was sent over from England in 1771. Our shadowy Edward Maxey could have been one of Strawbridge converts and assistants, and he could have been the father of Jesse Maxey, though proof of both seems to be wholly lacking.

However, if there were Maxeys in Maryland and Virginia in Strawbridge's time—and there is plenty of proof that there were—and if they were Huguenot exiles, as they well might have been, nothing would have been more natural than for them to fall in with John Wesley's version of the anti-Calvinistic, anti-Catholic ideology preached by the great Dutch theologian, Arminius. Jacobus Arminius had affirmed and Wesley had proclaimed that every sincere and honest Christian could be assured of his own personal salvation. All he had to do was to repent his sins, seek the assistance of divine grace, and experience the ecstasy of conversion and spiritual rebirth. This free-will doctrine was abhorrent to both Calvinists and Catholics, but, to exiled Huguenots, who had been persecuted by both, it must have sounded like an angelic message.

In political affiliation, the Jefferson County Maxeys, prior to the Civil War, were Democrats—fervid followers of Andrew Jackson and Stephen A. Douglas. The war between the states transformed some of them into equally ardent Republicans. My grandfather, Simeon W. Maxey, was one of these. Once he told me that he had voted for Douglas in 1860 and then joined a secret organization known as the Knights of the Golden Circle, which he soon realized was not a patriot organization but part of the Copperhead underground. Democrat that he was, Sim Maxey stood shoulder to shoulder with the Little Giant of Illinois politics in being uncompromisingly pro-Union. He promptly withdrew from the Knights of the Golden Circle and enlisted in Company B of the 110th Illinois infantry. This regiment won fame and glory by reason of its participation in several of the toughest campaigns of the war. Grandfather, a first sergeant in Company B, took part in the terribly bloody battles of Perryville, Stone's River, Chickamauga, Missionary Ridge, Lookout Mountain, and Atlanta. He marched with Sherman "from Atlanta to the sea," was in the final grand review of the Union armies in Washington in April, 1865, and then was sent to Chicago for mustering out.

One of the many thousands of soldiers in the field who voted for Lincoln and the National Union ticket in 1864, he found it impossible to return to the Democratic Party in 1868. Thereafter he called himself a Republican and brought up his children and grandchildren too, as far as he could, to associate Democrats with treason and secession. He never could quite forgive two of his brothers who stayed with the Democratic Party, and never would admit that they had any justification for not changing parties as he had. But they had. All of the Maxey antecedents were in the slave states, and some of the older members of the clan had been slaveowners before moving to the free state of Illinois. Even though of Unionist persuasion, they were Southern sympathizers on the question of abolition. But my grandfather's generation had become Westerners rather than Southerners, and Westerners could stand together in fighting for the Union and differ entirely on slavery and emancipation. I remember Grandma Collins telling how she went to live with her parents, Mr. and Mrs. Charles H. Maxey, while her husband was serving in the Union armies. Her sister Martha was also staying with Papa and Mamma for the duration of the war, for her husband had gone South and enlisted in the Confederate forces. The old folks were Democrats and Southern sympathizers. So news of a Confederate victory always brought rejoicing for all except Sue, and news of a Union victory could not be much enjoyed by Sue because of the general gloom throughout the household.

The reason I have written at some length about my Maxey progenitors and made little mention of the Allens, Bruces, Owenses, Collinses, Whittenbergs, and other ancestors in my family tree is that my knowledge of any but the Maxeys is just about nil. I know that my maternal grandfather, George A. Collins, was born in Virginia and migrated to Jefferson County in early life. I know that by occupation he was a school teacher and farmer. I know that he served in the Union forces throughout the Civil War. I know that he died when my mother was eleven years old. Beyond these fragments of information about one person, I have never learned anything about the Collins family. I know that my paternal grandmother was born Minerva T. Whittenberg. She died when I was twelve years of age, and though I have a few memories of her, they are rather dim. Of her family I knew one sister and one brother. The sister, Aunt Polly Livesay, was a longtime resident of Ellensburg. I think she and her husband migrated with the Maxeys in 1882. Her husband died when I was very young, but one of his brothers, whom we called Uncle Jim, lived in Ellensburg several years and I got to know him quite well. Aunt Polly was more a grandmother to me in many ways than my own grandmother, because she loved me and fussed over me from the time of my birth until I was a grown man. This is all I know of the Whittenbergs. Of the other progenitor families mentioned above, I know absolutely nothing.

II. EARLY ENVIRONMENT

Frontier Town

When Grandpa Maxey and family arrived in Ellensburg, Washington Territory, they found a tiny frontier town of four or five hundred inhabitants. If there had been any possibility of its being rawer or raggeder than it was, it would have been, for it was that kind of a town. If "Cousin Sue" could have seen it, she would have said at once that her gravest doubts about "Cousin Sim's" good sense were well founded. She still had those doubts and thought them well founded a quarter of a century later, when she finally yielded to persuasions and

13

entreaties and came to Ellensburg for a visit. "The Burg" by that time had grown into a fairly presentable municipality of five or six thousand people, but it was still too rough and tumble for Sue.

In 1882, when the Maxeys came, Ellensburg was about as near to the jumping-off place as one could go. Seattle, then a mud-spattered logging camp of 3,500 people, was the *ultima Thule;* farther by land it was not possible to go, and farther by sea was not easy. Between Ellensburg and Seattle there was nothing but mountain wilderness—no settlements, no railroads, no highways, nothing but a footpath across the Cascade Mountains. Ellensburg was in very truth the end of the line for overland transportation in the Pacific Northwest.

To reach Ellensburg in 1882, the Maxey family had journeyed from their home in Illinois to San Francisco by rail, thence to Portland, Oregon, by ocean steamer, from Portland up the Columbia to the Dalles by river boat, then had crossed the river by ferry and staged in overland via Satus Pass to Yakima City (now Union Gap), and from there, also by stage by way of the Wenas Pass, to Ellensburg. It had taken nearly two months to make the trip, and all but Grandpa were seeing the West for the first time. He had been out once before, on a scouting trip he said; had been to Ellensburg and had hiked across the mountains to Seattle where he caught a boat back to San Francisco.

Looking backward from my present vantage point in time, it seems appropriate to raise and try to answer the question of why, with the whole Northwest to choose from, Grandpa Maxey should have picked Ellensburg as the best place to locate. He once told me that his attention was first directed to Ellensburg by an old army comrade named Swasey, and, if I remember correctly, he said also that he and Swasey had traveled on the earlier scouting trip to the Pacific Northwest. He explained his decision to leave Illinois by saying that after a cyclone had ruined his prize orchard, he up and decided in a moment's time that he would not live in such a climate any longer. So he made up his mind to move to some part of the country where cyclones did not occur and find a place where he could grow an orchard without the risk of violent devastation. That was why he and Swasey made the scouting trip, so he said.

I am sure that Grandfather was telling the truth just as he remembered it, but I felt equally sure that his memory of the truth involved a certain amount of retrospective rationalization. He did not remember, in his old age, the foot-loose fever which had motivated his middle years. Like thousands of other Civil War veterans, "Sim" Maxey, the far-marching soldier of '62-'65, could not stand being bivouacked very long. Returning to his Jefferson County farm after his discharge from the army, he had gone along in his former ways and become a sufficiently substantial citizen to be named a highway commissioner and superintendent of the county fair, but his heart was beyond the horizon. No doubt a cyclone did damage his precious orchard, but what was a forty-acre orchard in Jefferson County to compare with a possible 160-acre orchard in some fair valley of the West? He had owned the Jefferson County place since 1853, which meant that most of the trees were past their prime. Of course he could replant and make a comeback, and that might have been the safe thing to do. But, out beyond the Great Divide, there must be abundant opportunities not merely to get back in the orchard business, but also to start a new life and possibly realize fantastic gains.

In the 1880's Ellensburg impressed many an emigrant as a likely place to find the pot of gold at the end of the western rainbow. Grandpa Maxey was not the only one who concluded that this was the best place to settle down and exercise his homesteading rights. Many another judged that the Northern Pacific would promote the development of a very considerable metropolis in the Kittitas Valley. It is easy nowadays to forget that the Northern Pacific Railroad once loomed as large in the public mind as the Union Pacific, which had been pushed across the country immediately after the Civil War. As a matter of fact, there had been a time when it seemed that the Northern Pacific might beat the Union Pacific to tidewater, but one mischance after another postponed largescale construction on the northern route until 1879. Then it became a daily headline feature in the news all over the nation. The whole country was made familiar with the surveys indicating where the main line was to go and where many of the division points would be. It is my guess that Grandpa Maxey and his comrade Swasey, who went to Ellensburg on their scouting trip, both had looked long and hard at the maps of the Northern Pacific's projected route through to the Puget Sound and seen something more at Ellensburg than a shabby little trading post.

Ellensburg was the place where the Northern Pacific had to gird itself for a climb over or a bore through the Cascade Mountains. Ellensburg was the gateway to the Snoqualmie Pass, was sure to be an active center of railroad construction, and had every expectation of becoming a major division point on the completed railway line. Moreover, there were credible rumors to the effect that, if and when Washington Territory were admitted to the Union, Ellensburg would become the capital of the state. The future of Ellensburg looked as bright as any place along the line, and Grandpa Maxey proposed to be there in ample time to be in on the big harvest that was to come. Not only had the Northern Pacific smiled upon the town and given it a big boost; it had become the seat of a newly organized county (1883) named Kittitas; gold had been discovered in the Sauk district, some twenty miles to the northwest large deposits of coal had been found in the nearby Cle-Elum and Roslyn districts; extensive lumbering operations were already a-foot; there was abundant waterpower for milling; and there was a beautiful valley of the lushest farm land that one could ever hope to set a plow in.

The Northern Pacific main line was built into and through Ellensburg in 1886, and from the family talk in later years I deduced that the three Maxey boys had been extensively employed in the construction activities. Grandpa was otherwise engaged. He had taken up a homestead and was growing an orchard, and thereby hangs a little tale which illustrates some aspects of the settlement of the West. Grandpa could have

16

homesteaded almost anywhere in the Kittitas Valley, but he turned up his nose at the sagebrush areas, which eventually were to produce the finest farms in the Valley, and picked 160 acres of river-bottom land for his dream farm. Why? He wanted to be sure of getting land that would grow fruit trees, and he feared that the sagebrush soil never would, even with irrigation. So he chose land that was already growing trees. It was good land and he had no trouble getting a good orchard started. But he kept this property only seven years—just about long enough to bring his new orchard into bearing. In the fall of 1889 he sold the farm and used the proceeds to erect a brick business building on Pine Street, between Third and Fourth, in downtown Ellensburg. After a few years he sold this building and began dabbling in other things.

Soon after he moved to town Grandpa Maxey also built the residence at the corner of Fifth and Sampson Streets which was his home as long as he lived. Because of various family exigencies, I lived there almost as much as with my own parents. Grandpa Maxey's next property venture was the acquisition of a tract of land in the Menastash Canyon, some ten miles west of Ellensburg. Here he developed a showplace orchard which he owned until his death in 1909. My clearest memories of him span the years from 1895 to 1909. Some time before 1895—I think about 1890—Grandfather was appointed a state commissioner of horticulture as well as horticultural inspector for Kittitas County. These two jobs kept him traveling a good deal of the time, but called for very little office work. Thus he found time to carry forward the Menastash project and at the same time attend to his official duties. My impression was that he gave about half of his time to public responsibilities and half to his private affairs.

On the Menastash place he first built a one-room cabin and later a modest three-room cottage. I never understood altogether why, but he never made any attempt to move his family to the Menastash farm. One reason, no doubt, was that his official duties necessitated his having a home in town, but I am also rather certain that another reason was that the womenfolk balked. They had no intention of being isolated on a farm ten miles from town, with him away from home half the time. Since he had to go it alone in the Menastash, and since he loved company, he drafted me for a companion as often as possible. And I was a willing and enthusiastic draftee. I loved the place and loved the bachelor life that he and I had there. Time after time, especially during school vacations, Grandpa and I would take off for three or four days in "the Canyon" and forget the rest of the world. From the time I was six until I was past fourteen, I saw more of my grandfather than any other member of our family. Not only did I often go with him to the Menastash, but many times I rode with him on inspection trips around the county. During my father's long illness and after his death, Grandpa was a substitute father for me, and I don't suppose I could have had a better one. He always talked to me as though I were an adult, and he had the patience to answer all of my fool questions as honestly and amply as he could. Naturally, he filled me to the brim with Civil War tales as well as accounts of his other travels and adventures. He did his best to transmit to me much of his accumulated lore about horticulture. He told me most of what I know about our family history. And he stocked my mind with his own pet ideas of politics and religion. If I owe a debt of gratitude to one person above all others, my grandfather, Simeon W. Maxey, is that person.

The Ellensburg of my earliest memories (*circa* 1895 onward) had a newly hatched look that resulted from a monotony of fresh-burned brick and green-sawed lumber. The town was not old enough yet to be deemed adolescent. Counting from 1875, when the first trading post was established, Ellensburg was only twenty years of age in 1895. Counting from 1881, the date of its first municipal charter, it was only fourteen years old in 1895. But counting by the age of most of its business and residential structures, it was only six years old in 1895. For there had been a terrible fire on July 4, 1889, which had wiped out most of the original town. Ten brick blocks and more than two hundred frame houses went up in flames on that hot and windy day, and these were just beginning to be well replaced when I was a little squirt running around the village streets.

As a little kid roving around town, I loved the raw newness of Ellensburg. It seemed to me that there was always something new and different to watch. Little did I, or could I, realize then that the new town which was rising so quickly from the ashes of the old was to reflect the nineteenth century far more faithfully than the twentieth, which was approaching just around the corner. It could not boast a single paved street, nor even one surfaced with crushed stone. Sidewalks, where they existed, were of plank construction which was fastened to bed timbers with four-inch spikes. These gory instruments of crucifixion were as savage as ever they had been in the time of Christ. With a confirmed habit of working loose and protruding a half-inch or so above the surface of the boards, they were murder on shoecaps and no small peril to life and limb. Crosswalks consisted of twin two-by-twelves laid parallel on four-by-four bed sills and nailed down with six-inch spikes, which had all of the vices of the four-inchers and some of their own to boot. The crosswalks were supposed to stand high enough above the street grade to be free of mud and dust, but this was just a hypothesis. Actually, they had a magnetic attraction for anything hostile to clean and unscuffed shoes. Street lighting was limited to a few sputtering arc lights in the business district. People thought these were wonderful and boasted about them, but prudent citizens going forth after dark always took pains to equip themselves with a dependable kerosene lantern. A municipal electric light plant had been established in 1890, but was slow to garner customers. The Maxeys did not become patrons of the city lighting system until I was almost grown. They held to a widely prevalent opinion that electric lights were harder on the eyes than kerosene lamps. And I am not so sure they were wrong, in 1890.

A municipal water system had been established in 1892, and, like the light plant, it had a hard time getting business. The Maxeys in common with scores of other self-reliant burghers preferred to rely on their own backyard wells and cisterns.

19

All knew that the city water was alive with every species of worms, frogs, minnows, and sedimentation. If they had known anything about bacteria, they could have justly pilloried the city waterworks. The H_2O drawn from the backyard wells was more transparent and probably more sterile than the city water, which was taken from an entirely unprotected open stream and was not treated by filtration or chlorination. The concept of sanitation had not yet reached Ellensburg. Following the big fire of 1889, sewers had been constructed in the business district, but many years were to elapse before they were extended to the residential portions of the town. Standing atop Craig's Hill on a clear day one could quickly get a panoramic view of the town's sanitary system. Looming in monumental eminence at the rear of every residence was a facility denominated by common idiom as the "backhouse" or "privy." Most of these cubic conveniences were two-holers, but the eye could readily note some which made more generous concessions to the principle of togetherness. Septic tanks had not yet been invented, and consequently each household had the reponsibility for disposing of its own accumulations of "night soil." When the sewer lines finally were extended over the whole town, most families (the Maxeys included) met the new challenge by replacing the dual throne of the "privy" with a water-flushed toilet and let the privy continue in its backhouse status at the rear of the lot. To have such a feculent cubicle inside the house would have been unthinkably vulgar.

Also situated at the rear of most of the residences the panoramic viewer would have espied a barn, a woodshed, and perhaps a chickenhouse. Most people kept a team of horses and one or more cows, and it was not unusual for a family to keep enough chickens to consume the table scraps and supply meat and eggs for the larder. "Dunging" out the stable, currying the horses, milking the cow, and feeding all of the livestock were a part of the daily rhythm of life. Equally a part of the daily routine was getting in the fuel (always wood or coal, or both) to supply the battery of voracious stoves which were the common instrumentalities of cooking and heating. Capacious woodboxes were a feature of all the Maxey homes and also a goodly selection of king-size coal scuttles.

Mindful of the down-to-earth needs of the citizenry, the founding fathers of the town had provided not only a plenitude of wide streets but also a parallel system of back alleys. Midway between every set of parallel streets ran an alley which carried a type and volume of traffic not permitted on the streets. The alley supplied direct access on both sides to abutting barns, woodsheds, chickenhouses, and privies, and therefore was the channel through which delivery of feed and fuel was made and wastes carted away. The alley also served as a lawful repository of mountainous piles of manure, ashes, trash, and garbage of which each household must daily disburden itself. When, by daily accretion, these mounds of wastage reached blockade proportions, the city authorities might intervene and require them to be hauled away, at the householder's expense. On windy days, which often occurred, aromas of wondrous variety were let loose upon the long-suffering populace. And insect life, especially of the winged species, found in the alleys of the town a stimulus to miracles of procreation.

In my boyhood, livery stables flourished in Ellensburg much as service stations do now, but provided distractions to the special relish of the male inhabitants which no present-day super-service station could possibly match. The next most flourishing line of business was running a saloon. Small boys were not supposed to hang around livery stables or saloons, but small boys then as now had a natural genius for being where they should not. There was also a red-light district which small boys were supposed to know nothing about.

The foresight of Ellensburg's founding fathers had limits. It did not extend to parks, playgrounds, swimming pools, and other facilities for public recreation. This was not because the founding fathers would have balked at such things, but simply because they could not visualize them at all. As far as they could perceive, almost the whole outdoors was and always would be available to the people of Ellensburg for recreational uses. Within the city were plenty of wide streets and alleys,

21

also innumerable vacant lots for the kids to use as playfields, and in every direction beyond the city limits were open spaces galore for picnicking, hunting, fishing, and other sports. As a measure of economy, the public school grounds were covered with a layer of cinders two inches deep. Children were not thought to need the school grounds for purposes of play; they had the whole countryside to play in, and it was their business to get to and from school in double quick time. A cinder cover would save the cost of watering and caring for a lawn and would not make mud for the children to track into the building.

For many years, ball games, horse races, foot races, and other sporting events were staged on the streets or vacant lots of the town. When I was about ten years old some kind of local syndicate built an athletic field with a partly covered grandstand, running track, baseball diamond, and football gridiron in the south part of town. This was used by the school teams, town teams, and other athletic groups. Both as a player and as a spectator I put in many absorbing hours at this field. I can't remember that it ever had any name other than the "ball grounds."

Whether health conditions were better or worse in Ellensburg at the turn of the century than in other western towns, I don't know. I do clearly remember that we had our annual scourges of typhoid, polio, diphtheria, pneumonia, scarlet fever, jaundice, and influenza. Tuberculosis was rampant all the time, and there were years when we were pretty badly ravaged with smallpox. Compared with most kids, I was phenomenally healthy. Mild seizures of mumps, measles, chickenpox, and scarlet fever came my way, but my one and only serious illness was jaundice, now called hepatitis. Of course, I had a cold with a runny nose all winter, but so did every other kid in town. That was normal and nobody thought or tried to do anything much about it. Ellensburg sanitation, as I have already pointed out, was akin to mediaeval, and preventive medicine was limited to vaccination against smallpox, which was always delayed until after an epidemic had broken out. The town had no hospitals, clinics, dispensaries, or public health services of any kind. The sick were taken care of at home, and mostly by members of their own family. Such surgery as could not be performed in the doctor's office was performed at the patient's home with whatever apparatus could be rigged up for the occasion. In the medical profession there was a guerilla war between the homeopaths, allopaths, and osetopaths. The Maxeys, like most other families, switched from one to the other without the faintest conception of what they were warring about or whether any of them had proper qualifications for the practice of medicine. We chose our doctors according to our prejudices. My mother had a prejudice against tobacco, so we never, if she could avoid it, had a doctor who smoked or chewed. Needless to say, Mother's range of choice was a bit circumscribed.

Several of the twentieth century conveniences were slow to reach Ellensburg. One of these was the telephone, possibly because of the shortage of local risk capital for promotion purposes. The first telephone was installed in our home after I had gone away to college, and I actually never spoke over a telephone until I was past sixteen years of age. The first telephones in Ellensburg were placed in business firms, professional offices, schools, the railway depot, the police station, the fire station, the court house and other focal centers. My folks could see the advantage of a telephone in those places, but not in a private home. Ellensburg had scores of families which felt the same way. You called a person on the telephone only in dire emergency or when there was no other way to reach him. It always seemed better, if possible, to see him in person or write him. In my time I have done a great deal of high-wide-and-handsome telephoning all over this country and to foreign parts, but I must frankly confess that the no-telephone habits of my youth were so firmly implanted that I have never felt at ease in using the telephone. My children and grandchildren use a telephone as though they were born with the instrument in their hands, and they almost were, for a telephone is standard equipment in every hospital delivery room today.

Door-to-door mail delivery was also slow in coming to Ellensburg. I was a big boy going to high school when this occurred.

From the time I had been first allowed to go down town alone, one of my regular chores had been to go to the post office and bring home the mail. I generally went once a day and sometimes twice. Some of the more affluent or more secretive gentry rented private boxes at the post office, but not the Maxeys. I had to stand in line at the general delivery window and take my turn, but I didn't mind because, though the line was usually long, that meant just so much more gossip to garner. One of the controversial issues in church circles was whether the post office should be open on Sunday. The goodie-goodies wanted it closed and the more worldly thought it no desecration of the Sabbath to collect their mail on Sunday, especially if they were box renters. The town got so steamed up over this momentous issue that it was a blessing when free delivery came. Of course, nobody in Ellensburg had authority to decide whether the post office should be open on Sunday, but they could argue themselves blue in the face and fire off letters to their congressman about it.

In my pinfeather years Ellensburg was what would now be called a wide open town. It had twice as many saloons as grocery stores and more whorehouses than churches, and the emporiums of vice ran seven days and nights a week. Both the gin parlors and the sex dispensaries ran extensive gambling operations on the side—poker, roulette, faro, and all the rest. Such was the prevalent pattern all over the West in that era. Being a railroad town, a cattle town, a mining town, and a lumber town as well as the trading center of a good-sized farming area, Ellensburg was always a seller's market for the vice trade. On Saturdays especially, everybody who was so inclined was welcome to come to "the Burg" and cut loose, and cut they did, with such verve and violence that small boys roaming the streets had plenty of opportunity to behold fights and other exciting sights. Short of mayhem and murder, the local constabulary were inclined to be indulgent, and seldom bothered much when things that started indoors were settled outside.

The first big battle in local politics that I remember was over the question of whether the saloons should be closed on Sundays. Similar restriction of the bawdy-houses was not even

24

considered. My recollection is that the Barleycorn Brigade won the first skirmishes very handily, but that the Christian Soldiers finally rallied enough votes to force the city council to enact a Sunday closing ordinance. My memories of these matters are sharpened by certain gambits that we kids thought funnier than a circus. Just for the heck of it, on Sunday afternoons or evenings, a gang of mischievous imps would go sneaking through the alleys trying the back doors of saloons. If one were found unlocked, the imps would throw it wide open, yell like Comanches, and then streak it for safer parts of town. Days of belly-laughs could be wrought out of a few episodes of that kind. The big idea was to throw a scare into the saloonkeepers. It never occurred to us that if a saloon door was unlocked on Sunday, the proprieter no doubt had made discreet arrangements in just the right places.

But new, raw, and rough though it was in my boyhood years, Ellensburg was not without uplifting influences, not bare of all refinement, not utterly barbarous. It had a public school system good enough to atone for many deficiencies; few western towns had schools half as good. Ellensburg also was the seat of a state normal school (now Central Washington College) which maintained a high level of academic excellence for that day and age. The town also had a remarkably fine theater building and an annual series of theatrical performances which were as good as many large cities could boast. It had good church buildings (for that period) and these were often served by ministers of superior education and ability. It had also strong local lodges of most of the great fraternal orders of the nation—Masons, Odd Fellows, Elks, Moose, Eagles, Red Men, Woodmen of the World, Knights of Pythias, and so on. There were also art clubs, reading clubs, and lecture series of various sorts. When I was about ten years of age a public reading room was established, and this later evolved into a Carnegie Library.

If I were to essay a summation of the Ellensburg influences, apart from the Maxey family, which most largely shaped my life, it would not be far amiss for me to say that I was a fortuitous product of the streets, alleys, vacant lots, ball grounds, railroad yards, stockyards, livery stables, swimming holes, fishing streams, public schools, Normal School, theater, reading room, boy's gangs and the Methodist Church. Those were the principal avenues through which I made contact with community life.

The Family Circle

The Maxeys lived on a scale which I would say was about average, maybe a little above average, for Ellensburg. They were not well-to-do enough to indulge many luxuries, but neither were they by any means poor folks. I recall hearing in my youth a great deal of talk about the terrible Panic of 1893 and the hardships it caused—the great railway strike, Coxey's Army, bread lines, and the like—but my folks seemed to have weathered this economic typhoon in pretty good shape. In 1892 Grandfather Maxey was appointed superintendent of the Washington State forestry and horticultural exhibits for the World's Columbian Exposition to be held in Chicago the following year. He spent most of 1892 gathering material for the exhibits and most of 1893 in Chicago setting up and supervising them. That he had an ample expense account I am sure, and I also believe that he received a substantial official stipend in compensation for his personal services. In 1892 my father and his partners, a brother and the brother's brother-in-law, were running a large herd of cattle on the ranges in the area of the present towns of Twisp and Winthrop. I don't know much of the financial affairs of this partnership, but my father had the means, in cash, to send Mother and their two children back to Mt. Vernon for a visit in 1893. There may have been occasions during the troubles of 1893-94 when some of the Maxeys, maybe all of them, were hard-up for ready cash—so was everybody else—but they never were in need of food, clothing, and shelter.

Food was one commodity the Maxeys always had in abundance—groaning abundance, I would say. Financial ups and downs did not keep the Maxeys from eating high on the hog. Meat three times a day was common fare; unlimited quantities of milk and butter were on the table at every meal; of home-grown fruits and vegetables there was always more than we could eat;

26

bread and pastries also constituted a large part of every meal. Maxey cooking was "Southern style" and we always had the necessary butter, lard, and other cholesterol building fats to do it up brown. In middle life most of the Maxey men and women grew plump; some could have been called portly; but none ever died of a cancer, a coronary, or a kidney or liver ailment. There was a family saying that if a Maxey lived past thirty, he would live past eighty. Not all exemplified this rule, but the great majority did. They were active people who burned up a lot of calories every day and did not worry about their weight or digestion. Although they knew nothing of proteins, carbohydrates, vitamins, enzymes, and the other dietary mystiques of modern times, every meal they served was a balanced meal, and in quantity.

The Maxeys always owned their own homes, my father being the conspicuous exception. The housing which the Maxeys provided for themselves never was elegant, but by their own standards it was as good as they had enjoyed "back in Illinois" and that was as good as they thought necessary. Inside plumbing was not for them; they had never had it and did not want it. Running water in the house was another convenience they resisted for a long time; all they thought necessary was a hand pump in the kitchen or on the back porch to raise water from the well. They did not use water in large quantities. The weekly bath was taken in a galvanized iron washtub, the water being lifted from the nearby kitchen range where it had been heated in a wash boiler. Since this had to do for the whole family, each member, as his turn came, was doled out no more than two or three gallons, to be cooled by water drawn from the pump. The kitchen range usually was a voracious woodburner which served as a sort of central heating plant as well as a cookstove. Some of the more sophisticated ranges had a reservoir for water on one side, and this was so connected with the firebox that four or five gallons of water could be kept warm all the time. Scalding hot water was generally available on short notice from the steaming teakettle which was always billeted on one of the rear lids of the stove. The weekly wash was done in the kitchen in bad weather, but otherwise was taken to the back porch or even the back yard. Standard laundry equipment included a copper-bottomed wash boiler, two or more galvanized wash tubs, a corrugated washboard, and a hand-operated wringer consisting of two rubber rolls turning against one another by engaging gears operated by a hand crank. Washing was woman's work, and the males of the household were supposed to be scarce around the kitchen on wash day. Ironing was done with the old-fashioned one-piece sad-irons heated on the kitchen range. These in my early youth were displaced by lighter irons with detachable handles.

The kitchen was the heart of the household, and not alone by reason of any close association of hearts and stomachs. In addition to being a cookery, the kitchen served as a dining room, living room, and general utility room. The large, extensible table in the kitchen was a multiple-duty artifact. At meal time it was a dining table; at other times it might serve as a library table, a sewing table, a conference table, a game board, or writing desk. Between meals the kitchen table was anything the family wanted it to be, for it was the general custom, when only family members were present, for all to sit together in the kitchen for conversation, games, reading, business, or what have you. Very few people of our acquaintance had a dining room, wouldn't have used it if they had, couldn't see any sense in it. I was fifteen years old before we lived in a house with a dining room.

By curious contrast, however, everybody had a parlor, and the Maxey parlors would have been classed as tending toward elegance—Victorian elegance, that is. We did not overdo the elegance, but had enough to embellish the parlor as definitely a room for special occasions. One of these embellishments was, almost invariably, an over-sized heating stove ornately trimmed with nickeled trappings. Another was a reed organ ornamented with fancy wood-carvings and operated with a pedal-worked bellows. Pianos were a rarity in early Ellensburg, both because of their cost and their weight. Two men could readily hoist a reed organ into the bed of a farm wagon and take it anywhere, and the womenfolk could move one around the room with ease, but a piano required special handling. Keeping company with the stove and the organ were the inevitable humpbacked sofa, oaken center table, and platform rocking chair. There might be several smaller rockers and a few windsor-type straight-back chairs. A large and ornate kerosense lamp always stood on the table or depended from the ceiling. Rag-woven throw-rugs might be used as floor coverings, but wall-to-wall carpeting (preferably Brussels) underlaid with newspapers or building paper was more usually seen. Drapes, curtains, hangings, and pictures adorned the room like foliage.

As remarked above, the parlor was not for everyday use. You never lounged around in the parlor or entertained close friends there. The parlor was for formal occasions. Distinguished guests were welcomed in the parlor; funerals and weddings were held there; solemn family occasions, such as the reading of a will or the conduct of family prayer by the visiting minister, took place in the parlor; and large parties, including many guests outside the family circle, were given in the parlor. Most people felt that the priest or pastor, the family lawyer, or the principal of the school should be received in the parlor, but not the family doctor; he went straight to the sickbed or sat with the family in the kitchen. In short, the parlor was for social space, not living space.

In my boyhood days, Ellensburg had no funeral homes or morticians. There was one man who was called an undertaker because he sold caskets as a sideline in his furniture business, but he was not a licensed embalmer and did not pretend to be a funeral director. Bodies were prepared for burial by the loving kinfolk and neighbors of the deceased, almost always women. The body was placed in its coffin and kept in the family parlor until the funeral, which was held either in the parlor or a church. There was nowhere else to have a funeral. All of the Maxey funerals that I remember, save one, were held in the family parlor. The one exception was my father's funeral, which was conducted by the Masonic order and held in the Methodist Church. Without a parlor to serve as cloister, chapel, reception room, assembly hall, and social center, I don't believe communal life would have been possible in the little Western village of my youth.

My recollection is that the Maxeys were never short of beds and bedrooms. On some occasions there might be an overflow of overnight company, but the emergency was always quickly met by making a pallet on the floor for the children. I recall many times when a half dozen or more young Maxey siblings were laid out on the floor like so many sticks of cordwood, a few quilts underneath and a blanket or two on top for cover. We just loved it; it was barrels of fun, and who cared about sleep? We did not—until our exasperated elders cracked down and scared the snickers and snorts of us. If not artistically furnished, the Maxey bedrooms certainly were never short of basic equipment, which always included high wooden bedsteads with webbed or woven springs on which were laid straw or cotton mattresses bearing featherbeds at least eight inches deep. Reference to one's downy couch of ease was no empty locution in those days.

Other bedroom furniture included a dresser or bureau, a clothes press, and a commode equipped with water pitcher and washbowl above and the indispensable slop jar or chamber pot (we kids called them "thunder mugs") underneath. Outdoor plumbing was for daytime use; according to the prevalent mores no self-respecting Maxey would arise at night and sally forth to the backyard privy. It would be absurd to light a lamp or lantern, carry it downstairs, and make an undress parade clear to the backhouse. Next morning it would be the talk of the neighborhood. The chamber pot was invented to avert just such exigencies, and could be easily used without even so much as striking a match. Since we had no hired help, the women of the household were the chambermaids. The menfolk did not mind working in muck and manure out of doors, but to suggest that they carry chamber pots indoors was an insult to their dignity. This seemed to be an accepted principle for the division of labor, and I never heard any of the women complain about it.

As a rule, our bedroms were unheated in the winter, though an occasional sybarite might take a footwarmer to bed or a heated brick wrapped in newspaper. The cooling of bedrooms in summer was impossible. Even if electric fans had been available, we had no electricity. Air conditioning was as yet an undreamed dream. We sweltered through the hot summer nights dressed in outing flannel nightclothes and did not even have sense enough to discard the feather beds. We could not, or did not, imagine any right and proper sleeping usages which would be more comfortable. I think, perhaps we did not shun discomfort as much as people do today. We had been on intimate terms with a lot of discomfort from infancy onward, were in the habit of taking it in stride.

Such, in brief summary, were the living standards and conditions of my youthful years, up to about the age of fifteen or sixteen. My folks thought they were good and so did I. Nobody in that time thought them sub-standard, and they were not. There were people who lived more luxuriously than we, but they did not have enough more either in quantity or quality to make us envious. Some people put on more "side," than we did, but this was amusing more than irritating because we knew pretty generally how little the "swells" had to be puffed up about. There were very few financial secrets in little old Ellensburg. We were perfectly, I would almost say smugly, satisfied with our own circle of kinfolks, friends, fellow Methodists, lodge brothers and sisters, and near-by neighbors. We had no incentive to be social climbers, because it never occurred to us that we could gain anything either materially or psychologically by such antics.

The Maxey clan in and around Ellensburg consisted of Simeon W. and Minerva T. Maxey, their three sons (Brova, Morton, and Cromwell), their two daughters (Franceska and Sina), their eleven grandchildren, their cousins Henry Maxey and Eliza Maxey Maddox and their several sons and daughters, and an almost equal or greater number of in-laws. Grandpa Maxey had bad luck with wives. His first wife, the only one by whom he had children, died after less than a week's illness in 1902.

Double pneumonia, the wickedest bacterial assassin of the time, took her off. Grandfather's second wife was a woman from Illinois whom I rather suspect was a correspondence bride. I never knew the true facts of the matter, but I knew they did not hit it off well and was not surprised when they were divorced after about two years of marriage. The third wife was also an Illinois woman of whose antecedents I knew nothing and learned nothing. She made a good impression on me and on all the rest of the Maxeys, I believe, but the marriage bed was scarcely warm before she, too, was snatched away by pneumonia.

Grandpa's eldest child was B. A. Maxey (we called him Uncle Brovy) whose name is recorded in the annals of Ellensburg as having been at various times city marshal, fire chief, and street superintendent. When not on the city payroll, he engaged in contracting work (mostly sidewalk and sewer construction) which usually came from the city. His first wife was Ella Hestwood of Mt. Vernon, Illinois, whom he married before the family moved to Ellensburg. Their children were Nellie, Alzora, Oscar (deceased in infancy), Clifton, Katherine, and Evelyn. Clifton was about my age and we played together a great deal as young boys. The other children were either so much older or so much younger that I never got to know them very well.

Morton M. Maxey, my father, was the second child. He was born on the 4th of July, 1860, a fact of which he was inordinately proud. I have already told a good deal about him and my mother, and as to my father I cannot add very much. He died when I was seven, and I am not sure that what I think I remember of him is from direct impression or from hearsay. He seems to have been the family favorite, the smooth operator who could always get around his parents and wheedle his brothers and sisters into doing as he wished. The thing I remember most vividly about him is that he played games with me, joshed with me, and seemed to have fun entertaining me. Most fathers of that period did not unbend with their children; none of my uncles did, and as a result my cousins thought I had it easy. I suppose, but of course don't know, that my life would have been quite different if my father had lived. He was a restless man, a born risk-taker and adventurer, but not systematic and persistent enough to succeed in most of the adventures he undertook. He probably would have been off to the Klondike in the gold rush, off somewhere else following an oil boom, and so on for the duration of his life. If my life had been cast in that sort of mold, I might have become a different sort of Chester Maxey.

So far I have made only indirect mention of my sister Aurel, who was born November 24, 1891, and died just a few weeks before her sixteenth birthday, in late September, 1907. Because Aurel died so young and had suffered frequent illnesses there grew up a sort of family legend that she was a fragile and sickly thing with an otherwordly nature. Nothing could be farther from the truth. Aurel had the misfortune to be born with low resistance to the many acute infections which ran rampant those days. Whatever was going the rounds usually bowled her over. I either did not catch the infection at all or had a mild attack, but she caught almost everything and was desperately sick. However, between these virulent seizures of contagion, she was as sturdy, vigorous, and lovely a specimen of feminity as one would ever hope to see. She was in her second year of high school and had already established herself as one of the popular personalities of the school, when an epidemic of meningitis swept through the town. Aurel was one of the unfortunates who caught it and died. I was one of the "natural immunity" lucksters who went unscathed. Had there been any technique of antitoxins or antibiotics, Aurel's life might have been saved and indefinitely prolonged. If so, I am sure that my life would have been different in many ways.

The third child of the S. W. Maxeys was a daughter, Franceska (Aunt Secca). She never married and lived with her parents to the end of their days. Aunt Secca also was a second mother to several of the grandchildren, of whom I was one. Truth to tell, I have as many early boyhood memories of Aunt Secca as of my own mother.

The fourth child and third son was William Cromwell

(Uncle Cromie) Maxey. He married an Ellensburg girl named Ella Frisbie, and they had two children. He lost all three in a diphtheria epidemic during my infancy. Uncle Cromie never remarried. From middle life until his retirement he was an employee of the signal department of the Northern Pacific Railway. He lived to be nearly ninety years of age. The fifth child was a daughter named Sina, who was about the same age as my mother. After the family moved to Ellensburg, Sina married a gentleman named George D. Hogue. The Hogues had four children—Maxey, Letah, Glenn, and Rhea. The Hogue children were my closest cousins, particularly Letah and Glenn, who were in the same age bracket as my sister Aurel and I. The Hogue children, like Aurel and me, spent a great deal of time with our grandparents and thus became more or less regular playmates.

It is difficult, looking back sixty years or more, to be sure which of one's memories are real and which come from hearsay. One reason I feel moderately sure of most of my memories from the age of five onward is that I entered the first grade of the Ellensburg public schools in September, 1895, being just five years and three months old. Going to school greatly speeded up my mental development, and I am sure that it also sharpened my memory. As to events which took place before that, I do not feel entirely sure, but there are a few occurences which loomed so large in the family saga that they must have made some impression on my mind directly and, later, an even stronger indirect impression through repetition in family conversations. I shall briefly relate what I can of these events.

Some time in late 1891 or early 1892, my father, Uncle Cromie and Walter Frisbie (Uncle Cromie's brother-in-law) took a headlong plunge in the cattle business, putting all of their savings into the purchase of herds which they decided to run on the Methow River ranges in the vicinity of the present towns of Twisp and Winthrop. Compared with Ellensburg country, the Methow area in the nineties was primitive wilderness. It was something over a hundred miles north of Ellensburg, and since the Great Northern was as yet unbuilt, Ellensburg was its closest shipping point. Despite its remoteness from civilization, Father decided to take his family with him to the Methow country. The trip was made by horseback and covered wagon. I cannot say that I remember, but I carry in my mind an impression of having ridden many miles on the same horse with my father. Being around two years of age, I was plenty large enough, according to the standards of that period, to sit astride a horse behind my dad and hang on to the saddle strings. Maybe I didn't, but I rather feel that my father saw to it that I did, despite my mother's protests that I was too small. On arriving at our destination, we had to live in a two-room log cabin with packed-earth floors. It seems to me that I remember something about this, too—particularly the disciplinary measures employed to keep me from digging holes in the cabin floor. I also seem to remember being staked out in front of the cabin, with a rope securely tied both to the stake and to me, so that I could not wander away and possibly fall into a nearby stream. Possibly these shadowy memories are not memories at all of things that happened, but only imaginings based on hearsay around the family circle. But it took no imagination to be keenly aware of my mother's feelings about our four years on the Methow. She never spoke of them without bitterness and resentment.

Another early memory, which might be as much hearsay as direct memory, relates to our visit in and around Mt. Vernon, Illinois, in the fall and winter of 1893-94. The trip was real, however imaginary my recollections. Father stayed on in the Methow while Mother took Aurel and me "back home" to visit all the kinfolk and connections. We trekked overland to Ellensburg, there took the Northern Pacific through to Chicago and thence downstate to Mt. Vernon, by which line I know not. En route there was one incident which I believe I definitely remember. That was a layover at St. Paul, Minnesota. The second or third day out, Aurel became violently ill and began to have convulsions. Mother was obliged to detrain at St. Paul and find a doctor. This took a day or two, during which time I was parked with people who were strangers to me. I believe

I remember this. In fact, I think I remember it better than anything else that happened on the trip. I do remember that Aurel was desperately sick for many weeks— the trouble was typhoid fever—lost all her hair and had to learn to walk all over again. In the spring of 1894 we returned to Ellensburg and went back to the Methow. On the return trip, also via Northern Pacific, our train was marooned for a day or so somewhere in Montana on account of washouts on the line. I seem to have a stray memory or two of our standing out there in the middle of nowhere, waiting to be rescued.

In the winter of 1894-95, one of the severest on record in the Methow country, my father and his partners lost their entire herd of cattle. They thought they had stocked enough hay and other feed to carry the herd from pasture time to pasture time, but this winter was so long as well as cold that their reserves proved insufficient. There was no possible way to ship feed into the country—no railroads, no wagon roads, no river transportation up the Methow—so they had to stand by helplessly and watch their cattle starve to death. Father was now flat broke and sick, to boot. There was nothing to do but return to Ellensburg and look for a job. Father, being the adventurer type, had no doubt of his ability to make a comeback, and if his health had not failed, he probably would have done it with ease. His talent for winning and his talent for losing were about equal. It was easy for him to ride high and just as easy to fall flat; in between he was less gifted.

Of course Father did not know it at the time, nor did any of the doctors who treated him, that his illness was as undiagnosable as it proved to be incurable. The first diagnosis was stone in the bladder, and he underwent surgery for that. No stone was found, nor anything to suggest that there ever had been such a condition. The next diagnosis was catarrh of the kidneys, which assumed that there was some kind of inflammation of the inner membranes of the kidneys. All of the prescribed treatments of this supposed catarrh failed. Then the doctors decided that he must have some sort of rare blood disease. For three years Father was a semi-invalid—up a while, then down, up again, then finally down, until his death on September 24, 1897. There was no post mortem examination, but I doubt if dissection would have disclosed anything that the medical profession of that day would have recognized. My own personal guess after all these years is that my father's death was due to complications incidental to undulant fever, a disease utterly unknown at that time. Medical science now is aware that undulant fever is transmitted to humans through organisms associated with infected cattle and goats. The disease is a great simulator and even now is difficult to diagnose without the assistance of laboratory analysis. During the terrible winter of 1894-95 my father must have had countless exposures to the causative germs of undulant fever.

III. GROWING UP

Boyhood Memories

Of the years 1894-97 I have some rather vivid memories which have little to do with my father's illness and death. In truth, until near the end I was not aware that he was gravely ill. Memory may not be wholly correct, but I have almost as many recollections of my mother's illnesses during that period as of my father's. Time and again she was laid up with what the doctors called inflammatory rheumatism, and when that happened, Aurel or I, or both of us, would be bundled over to Grandpa Maxey's to stay until Mother could get around again. Being the older, and also more of a problem about the home, I usually got the nod for a prolonged visit with my grandparents, and Aunt Secca was the one who usually took over *in loco parentis*—loved me, spanked me, and tried to convert me from a pest into a sufferable being.

I got so that I really enjoyed these enforced visits with my grandparents, especially after I started to school, in September, 1895. The school was only two blocks from where my grandparents lived, and that enabled me to be early at school and to linger after school was out, thus giving me more playtime than most other kids. The first two or three months I attended school I was with my grandparents; then I was trundled back home again. Father and Mother were then living on the Shiflet place, about a mile and a half northwest of town. Here I came to realize that school was not going to be all beer and skittles. I had to walk both ways, and this meant starting early and getting home late, and making do with a cold lunch at noon, which my mother packed and I carried with me. School buses? Such things had not yet been imagined. I did not feel sorry for myself, because all the boys and girls who lived a distance from the school had to use "Shank's mare" just as much as I, some even more. It was pretty tough going sometimes because of the snow and cold, but we made it and probably were the better for it. The next spring my parents moved to a place only three-quarters of a mile from the school, and this shortened my daily jaunt by half.

I have some vivid memories of the next two years. In August, 1895, there had been a two-ply lynching bee in Ellensburg. The two victims had been strung up on a cottonwood tree which I had to pass twice daily on my way to and from school. Naturally, this kept the lynching episode in the forefront of my mind, and the talk I heard at home made it even more vivid. Although they did not condone lynching, my folks were of the opinion that few could have deserved it more than the victims of this outburst of mob wrath. The two had commmitted a double homicide in one of the downtown saloons, without any justification, legal or moral. In short, they had been guilty of cold-blooded, malicious, and premeditated slaughter. This was the culmination of a long series of murders and robberies whose perpetrators had gone scot free because of hung juries. Public opinion had reached a boiling point, and a self- constituted vigilante group in town decided that this should not happen again. The vigilantes organized the mob which yanked the villains out of the county jail and hanged them on the big cottonwood tree north of town. Nothing was ever done to prosecute the lynchers, which indicated that public opinion must have been on their side. This was my first lesson in frontier justice.

An even more vivid memory is the election of 1896, which was my first political experience. Historians say that the election of 1896 was one of the most exciting and bitterly contested in the annals of the republic. For the Ellensburg Maxeys, this certainly was true. As I have already said, they were staunch Republicans but in 1896 they were stauncher than ever before, because William Jennings Bryan was the Democratic and Populist nominee. The Maxeys had known the Bryans from way back, and did not like anything about them. William Jennings Bryan was born and raised at Salem, Illinois, some twenty miles from Mt. Vernon, and was almost exactly the same age as my father. Salem was the county seat of Marion County, just north of Jefferson County. Both the Bryans and the Jenningses were well-known Marion County families, and Jefferson County folks had opportunity to see and hear a great deal of them. Silas Bryan, W. J.'s father, was a circuit judge in that district for more than thirty years, and both he and his family were frequently in Mt. Vernon and Jefferson County. My grandfather's dislike of both the Bryans and the Jenningses was due not only to their being Democrats but also to his belief that they had been Copperheads during the Civil War. As to that, Grandpa may have known whereof he spoke, for he had traveled somewhat in Southern sympathizer circles before he enlisted in the Union Army. So it was his vehemently declared opinion in 1896 that a vote for Bryan was worse than merely voting for such heresies as free trade and free silver; it was a vote for treason and disunion. All of the political talk I heard at home and in other Maxey homes was rabid, and I listened with big ears to every word of it.

My excitement rose to fever pitch when the state convention of Democrats, Populists, and Silver Republicans was held in Ellensburg in August of 1896. The purpose of this gathering was to unite these three groups in what came to be known as the Fusionist Party, and to nominate a statewide Fusionist ticket. Some 1,200 delegates attended the convention, and most of them took part not only in the convention proceedings but also in the many parades and street demonstrations which were a daily occurrence. These were unforgettable sights for a boy of six going on seven, who knew, having been well instructed at home, that all of the noise and fanfare was the work of Satan's personal emissaries on earth. I was dead sure, and often trembled at the thought, that if Bryan won the election, the United States of America would soon be headed straight for hell on a handcar.

When school opened that fall, I discovered right away that I had to fight for my political convictions. Being a Republican, I went to school with both coat lapels generously adorned with McKinley buttons, of which my father and grandfather had procured an ample supply. To my surprise (how could there be so many wrongheaded people in the world?), there were just as many kids wearing Bryan buttons as McKinley buttons. It was deemed a great coup and was supposed to prove something important if you could snatch and throw away the buttons worn by kids of the opposite political party. This became the principal sport on the school grounds, and, of course, led to fist fights, which, being against the rules, were stopped by the principal or teachers. But stopping the fights on the school grounds merely led to their being adjourned to a convenient vacant lot after school hours. If I ever fought and bled for my party, it was when I was a boy of six. Never since have I put so much punch into a political campaign.

By the summer of 1897 my father's health had so far deteriorated and his income had fallen so low that we had to move in with Grandpa and Grandma Maxey. Father was bedridden most of the time and needed constant attention. Grandma, Aunt Secca and Mother divided the work of caring for him, keeping house, and raising the children. Much bothered by the summer weather, Father thought he would feel better on the Menastash farm, where the higher altitude made the weather uniformly cooler. So Mother and he and Aurel and I were moved out there and lived in Grandpa's three-room cottage for several weeks. One night in late August Mother awakened Aurel and me and said that Father had suddenly taken a bad turn for the worse and therefore we must return to town at once. She hitched up the buggy, propped Father up in the front seat, bundled Aurel and me up in blankets on the floor of the carriage, and headed for town as fast as she could drive. In less than a month Father was gone.

Just how the expenses of my father's illness and death were met, I have never known. He had no insurance (did not believe in it) and had lost all of his property. Since becoming ill in 1895, he had not been able to work regularly and was unable to work at all the last year of his life. Father was a Mason in good standing, and I know that the members of that order, both individually and collectively, gave him financial assistance. How much, I do not know. Grandpa and Grandma Maxey helped as much as they could, and so did his two brothers and brother-in-law. There may have been others.

Since there was no public assistance in those days, I am sure that whatever help we received came from private sources. The amount must have been adequate, for we were not reduced to beggary or distress. Of course, the costs of illness and death in 1897 were much less than now. There were no hospital bills because there was not a hospital in town. There were no nursing charges because all nursing was done at home by members of the family or by close friends. There were no laboratory charges, no X-ray charges, no ambulance charges, no embalming charges, because none of those existed in Ellensburg. Father's illness and death involved surgery, house calls by the doctors, and medicines. What the surgery cost, I am not sure, but I think I heard fifty dollars mentioned in the family talk about such matters. Physicians at that time charged a dollar for an office call and a dollar and a half for a house call, and I suppose Father had a goodly number of these, probably two or three dozen. The medicine bills probably were the heaviest of all, for the doctors of that era were lavish prescribers of pharmaceutical concoctions which had to be specially compounded. I well remember that Father always had on hand several bottles of medicine, patent and prescribed, from which he imbibed a heavy dosage several times a day. The funeral expenses were met by the Masonic order, which conducted the services both

41

at the church and the grave. My guess would be that although Mother was indeed a poor and bereaved widow, she was not left with a millstone of debt to weigh her down. My further guess is that most of our expenses were taken care of by the generosity of our family and friends. That sort of thing was customary in the nineties. Judged by modern concepts, its short-comings were many, but it did solidify families as none of the present-day welfare programs can do.

A few weeks after Father's death, Mother decided that we should not stay with his parents any longer. There was a two-room house not far distant, and this could be rented at a rate she thought she could afford. We moved into that house around the middle of October and stayed there during the winter of 1897-98. Our possessions consisted of household furniture and equipment, two cows, a dog, and a cat. There was enough of everything for our simple needs. The two cows were our most important possession, because they were our only source of income. Steinman's grocery store gave Mother drawing credit in exchange for her homemade butter, and she was able to sell the surplus milk to neighbor families who did not keep a cow. I was the delivery boy for both commodities. Mother milked the cows, because she thought my hands were too small to do a good job, but it was my job to churn the butter (using the primitive plunger-type churn). Other jobs assigned to me were to chop and carry in the wood and kindling needed to keep our two stoves going, carry out the ashes every day, clean out the stable, and run miscellaneous errands all over town. All this and keeping abreast of school work made me a busy seven-year-old boy. I had a real job to do, and a responsible one too. I was keenly aware that if I failed to do my job well we might be cold and hungry.

I doubt if the butter and milk sales were sufficient for all of our needs that winter. I can remember gifts of clothing, firewood, homecured hams, bags of potatoes, and other produce from kindly friends and relatives. We accepted these gratefully and without humiliation. We were on our own, trying to make our way, and we regarded these gifts as tokens of confidence and love rather than of eleemosynary pity. They were exactly what we would do, and fully expected to do, if and when the circumstances should be reversed. But with all the help we received, there were some unavoidable privations and hardships. My sharpest memory of that winter is chilblains. It seems to me I had chilblains all winter, and nobody who has not suffered that constant and terrible burning and itching of half frozen feet can realize what agony it can bring. Every night before I went to bed Mother would rub my feet with turpentine, vaseline, or melted tallow in the hope that this would relieve me enough to sleep through the night. None of these home remedies worked very well. I had to live with my chilblains most of the winter —for the simple and sufficient reason that we did not have the money to buy rubbers or overshoes. I had to be out of doors in all kinds of weather, and as a result my shoes were water-soaked much of the time and my toes frostbitten over and over again. At night Mother would put my shoes in the oven of the cookstove to dry them out, and next morning they would be so stiff and hard that my tender toes would writhe in agony as I forced my swollen feet into those shrunken shoes. When warm weather came, all these tribulations quickly vanished, but they were indelibly stamped on my memory just the same.

In the spring of 1898 we moved into a larger and better house, where Mother thought she could add to our income by taking boarders and roomers. The State Normal School at that time had no dormitories or dining halls of its own, and the non-resident students were therefore obliged to make shift as well as they could among the people of the town. Dozens of Ellensburg families were accustomed to "take in" one or more "Normals" as roomers or boarders or both. Mother thought this spelled opportunity for her, and it did. She was able to get two young ladies—Florence Abbott and Lucy Goodman—and their payments for room and board, added to our milk and butter income, eased our financial stringency a great deal. But we continued to operate the home dairy, and I continued to be the delivery boy, churn operator, and stable man, and began to do some of the milking. Mother now had several customers

43

for both butter and milk, and my job included collecting money as well as delivering these products. Mother held me to strict accountability down to the last penny, and thus at the age of eight I gained my first experience in sales of merchandise and financial accountability.

On account of the Spanish-American War, the year 1898-99 was one of tremendous excitement for me. Over this picayune war the whole American people lost their heads, and small fry such as I were thrown into transports of patriotic lunacy. I was a warmonger from the word "go." I wanted to shoulder a musket and march off to battle as Grandpa had done in '62, and mourned because I was too young for that. It all seems a little silly now, but I well remember how the spinetingling slogan "Remember the Maine" was splashed in banner headlines in all the newspapers, not once but time and time again. I remember how the war fever raged even more fiercely after Spain had met all the terms of President McKinley's ultimatum, how the local citizenry burst forth with pro-war meetings, street rallies, and other public demonstrations, and how the crowds gathered every day in front of the telegraph office to hear the latest news. Ellensburg had a militia company which immediately offered its services to the governor of the state and the President of the United States. This offer was promptly accepted, and then the town really did go off its rocker in an orgy of patriotic fervor in honor of "our boys in blue."

To me, the "boys in blue" were demigods. I had a direct personal interest in several of them. The captain of the company was Alfred C. Steinman, an old family friend, superintendent of the Methodist Sunday School, and co-owner of the grocery store where we did all of our trading. Since Captain Steinman was leading "our boys in blue," I hadn't the slightest doubt but that they were off to a holy war. John Charlton, Bill McDowell, and Jim Putman were other members of Company A who were close family friends and fellow Methodists. If the Spanish-Amercan affray had been a feudistic affair of Hatfields and McCoys, it could not have been more personal to me. I had to go through all the pretenses of being a soldier. I made me a wooden sword, had Mother sew white stripes down the legs of my blue denim jeans, and along with the other kids in the neighborhood went through boyish imitations of Company A at drill.

The war was over before Company A could be sent to Cuba, but it was among the troops sent to the Philippines to quell the Aguinaldo insurrection. For Ellensburg folks, this prolonged the war neurosis one more year, with the result that when Company A got back home in November, 1899, the town went into a frenzy of welcome, which afforded small boys like Chester Maxey a golden opportunity to yell their heads off as the train rolled into the station and carry banners or torchlights in the big parade. Just about this time the Boer War in South Africa came along to keep me in a red hot state of belligerency. I don't remember now the particular reasons why American opinion became so inflamed about this petty colonial conflict, but it did, and American sentiment was nearly a hundred per cent anti-British. In our press the Boers were depicted as doughty colonials, like our Revolutionary forefathers, fighting for independence as they had done and against the same enemy. I believed this a hundred per cent, so the Boer War for me was just about as much a personal cause as the Spanish-American War had been. And this fervor was intensified by the fact certain members of Boer military missions to the United States came to Ellensburg—for reasons, I believe, connected with the purchase of horses—and made some imflammatory speeches. I contrived to gain admission to some of those meetings and joyfully worked my hatred of the British up to the pop-off point.

The Boarding House Years

In the summer of 1899 my mother made a decision which entirely changed the pattern of my existence and decisively shaped my future. She decided to open a boarding house near the downtown business section of the city. Our cows had reached the age of diminishing returns, and income from two Normal students was not enough to carry us. Mother thought, correctly, that if she had a larger house, convenient to the business district, she could keep her Normal students and in addition secure enough day boarders to make things go. So we moved to a place on Ruby Street on the east side of the street between Fourth and Fifth. There were no house numbers in those days, but we were smack in the middle of the block. This location now is part of the business district.

Mother had guessed right, righter than she realized. Almost immediately she had more business than she could handle. A home-style boarding house was something new in Ellensburg, and there was a large population of unmarried men, of all professions and occupations, who had long been yearning for a place where they could get the kind of food that "Mother used to cook." The only public eating houses in town at that time were Chinese-operated restaurants, and the fare they offered was not specially toothsome. Mother was not a fancy cook, though if need be she could turn a trick or two in that department, but everything she served was top quality, palatable, and wholesome. Having learned to cook at the apron strings of a Maxey mother, she was well grounded in the Southern style of cookery, which meant that everything was hearty, appetizing, and well seasoned. This was specially appealing to the male animal, and Ellensburg at that time was a typical Western town in having a surplus of hungry male animals without wives. These flocked to Mother's boarding house—lawyers, doctors, dentists, merchants, bankers, railway conductors, locomotive engineers, Normal School professors, city and county officials, in short, a cross-section of the community. Before she realized it, Mother was in business in a large way, and had to hire help for both kitchen and dining room service.

Around the boarding house I was a good deal more than a mere hanger-on. Since there were no telephones in the town and no errand services of any kind, I had to be the chief of communications and transportation. In other words I had to serve as errand boy, delivery boy, messenger boy, and common carrier in general and particular. At a moment's notice I had to be ready to hop on my bike and whizz to town for some item of meat, groceries, or other merchandise that Mother needed "right now." I had to fetch and deliver notes, word-of-mouth messages, and all sorts of matter received or sent through the mails. In addition I was handy man and chore boy around the boarding house. These duties included keeping the coal hods and wood bins filled, carrying out the ashes daily, raking leaves, shoveling snow, sawing and splitting wood disposing of trash and garbage, and acting as chief chicken butcher for the boarding house. Chicken dinner was one of Mothers Sunday specials, and each Sunday dinner called for six or more carcasses. Since it was impossible in those days to buy dressed chickens at any meat market or grocery store, it was up to the individual householder to kill and dress his own. Mother was perfectly willing to dress out the carcasses but could not bring herself to wring a chicken's neck or chop its head off. So she cast me in the role of executioner. As a headsman I developed enough skill to decaptitate a chicken with one neat stroke of the hatchet. I did not relish the job, but it was mine to do. The Maxey boarding house had to make good on the Sunday special, and that meant a Saturday afternoon decimation of the fowl population by little Chester.

Mother made good money in the boarding house, and soon it became possible for Aurel and me to have a few luxuries as well as all of the basic necessities. We were never given allowances; no children, rich or poor, were given allowances in the nineties. Such a thing was unheard of. Mother generally gave us some spending money for special occasions such as Christmas and the Fourth of July, and if perchance one of us had conceived an irrespressible longing for something she did not consider too foolish, she might give us the money to buy it. But I never had any money of my very own until I was able to earn it myself. I soon learned, as every Ellensburg boy did in those days, that there were various, even devious ways of annexing pocket money independently of one's parents. My first venture in boyhood capitalism was selling table scraps, of which we had a never-ending supply, to certain of our boarders who owned hunting dogs. Canned or packaged pet foods were non-existent then, and the butcher shops did not cater to the pet trade. It was not easy for single men who were dog owners to find suitable food for their animals. I found myself operating in a seller's market, and often cleaned up as much as fifty cents a week (big money for a kid in that period) as a dog-food merchant.

Another business venture in which I participated, along with two or three close cronies, was scavenging the alleys of the town. The heaping trash piles of Ellensburg's alleys were treasure troves of articles which could be sold somewhere down town for a nickel or a dime, maybe more. The saloons were always in the market for empty beer bottles and whiskey flasks, which they would refill and relabel with their own brands or blends. The hardware stores were always ready to buy empty kerosene cans, syrup cans, and other such containers which could be used in retailing kerosene and machine oil. And you just might happen on to a piece of scrap iron or brass for which the junk man would gladly part with a shekel or two; empty jute bags and flour sacks were similarly marketable at the feed stores. Two or three boys working together could amass and sell enormous quantities of such loot. There was no city dump, no public or private collection service, nowhere for a householder to get rid of unwanted objects except to heave them into the alley. In my particular "firm" each boy had his own little hand wagon and his own special customers for certain articles. We would all pitch in and work together and then divide the profits at the end of the day.

I seem to have wandered somewhat afar from the boarding house, but not so far actually, for the Maxey trash pile was always one of the biggest in town, thanks to the boarding house, and I had squatters rights on that, which put me in a good position in dealing with the other members of our "firm." So I learned the rudiments of economics early, through practical experience. Through the boarding house I also picked up at an early age, other rudiments which were to be of great value to me in later life. Through the boarding house, I, as a small boy, became intimately acquainted with men in all walks of life, men who made up the community leadership in all fields of activity. Not only did I see and talk with them when they came to the boarding house; in my many and various errands around town I not only met them, but often, in my mother's name, transacted business with them. I probably knew more business and professional people and was in turn known by more than any other boy in Ellensburg. I got around more than most of the other boys, had more contacts. Some of our boarders took a special interest in me, gave me encouragement, were ever available with friendly counsel and advice, and often remembered me with birthday and Christmas gifts. As a matter of fact several of the leading citizens of the town came to be sort of substitute fathers for me. Of course I did not realize it at the time, but through these associations I was getting the rudiments of a broad education.

I am sure that these boarding house contacts with many different kinds of men and women had much to do with my dawning realization that there was a good deal more to education than the celebrated Three R's. Going to school had always been a thing I liked to do. Just how it came about I am not sure, but I had learned how to read before I went to school. Perhaps I was born with eye-brain coordination which made reading easy and a perpetual delight. I cannot recall the time when I had any trouble with reading. Going through page after page of printed matter was about as difficult for me as cutting melted butter. Naturally, therefore, school was a breeze I sailed through the elementary grades with little output of effort and could not understand why so many kids moaned and groaned about their studies. It never occurred to me that reading might be so difficult for them that even the simplest lessons meant hard work. It never occurred to me that tests and examinations could be unrelieved torture for anyone. To me, tests and examinations were games in which I matched my wits against the teacher's just as I would in checkers or any similar contest. I had no fear of failure and generally had the feeling that the odds were in my favor.

However, prior to the boarding-house period of my life, all of my outside-of-school associations and contacts had been

49

bounded by our family circle. I made no particular friends at school, ran with no gang, and seldom met anyone, old or young, who was alien to our little clan of kinfolk and close friends. The boarding house quickly changed all that. It was located in a neighborhood well populated with boys about my own age. Now that I lived in the neighborhood I was eligible to run with the neighborhood gang of kids, provided I could meet the acid test of fistic prowess, which meant that I had to prove my worthiness by fighting my way in. One of the boys was egged on to pick a fight with me. If I licked him, the gang would welcome me with open arms, but if he licked me, I would always be an outcast. I managed to make the grade and thus became one of the insiders.

With gang membership came social efflorescence. Our gang covered the town in its roamings, knew the alleys in the red-light district as well as those behind the churches, was intimately familiar with the geography of the railroad yards, kept tab on current events in the various livery stables, knew who was in the city and county jails, could tell an inquirer in which saloon to look for various prominent citizens, gate-crashed ball games and circuses together, and accumulated scores of dark secrets, as we thought, which we would never tell a soul outside our little tong. Our gang taught me facts of life that the Maxeys never discussed in the presence of children. Our gang taught me that a boy did not have to be a Methodist and a Republican to be as good in every way as I thought I was. Our gang made me familiar, on a low intellectual plane, with what Catholics, Episcopalians, Campbellites, Presbyterians, and other "unsaved" sectarians believed. I regretted that none but the Methodists would go to heaven, but it seemed that God had ordained things that way. Our gang taught me that not all Democrats were Confederates and that many Populists were nativeborn Americans. To put it in a nutshell, our gang of ratty little reprobates taught me for the first time in my life to look on the other side of things. And that lesson was doubly underscored by the more elevated associations I had with some of the wonderful men who came to our house three times a day for meals. From them I gleaned knowledge and insights which gave me glimpses of horizons the Maxeys had not seen.

Of course, I cannot prove that this social growth had any direct bearing on my school work, but I strongly suspect that it did. When I got into the upper grades I was introduced, through the school curriculum and the teacher's supplementations, to various dilutions of literature, history, and science in addition to the hard-core subjects such as grammar, arithmetic, and spelling. I feel sure it was then that I began dimly to perceive the outlines of those realms of intellectual adventure and achievement which could be opened by higher education. Not all of Mother's boarders were college graduates, but most of them were men of better than average education for that time. From listening in on the conversations among the boarders, I picked up thoughts which gave more abundant meaning to the things I was learning in school. From my associations with boys whose truths and values greatly differed from mine, I gained not only a measure of tolerance but a much greater measure of curiosity. Perhaps I am just imagining all this retrospectively, but it is still a fact that by the time I finished the eighth grade my mind was made up: I was going to get as much education as it would be possible for me to obtain.

At the turn of the century very few students went beyond the eighth grade. By then they were supposed to have had all the fundamentals. Public high schools were just beginning to be generally established, but were not as yet widely patronized. Ellensburg began with a two-year high school in 1890 and stepped up to a four-year program around 1902, and Ellensburg also had the Normal School, which could take one two years beyond high school. That much education I resolved that I would have by all means.

As I have already said, school work was easy for me. Not until I got to college did I run into any studies that made me sweat. In the Ellensburg schools, because I made such high grades with such apparent ease, I was often accused of being the teacher's pet, though I must confess that I was sometimes petted with a ruler, a strap, or a switch, for corporal punishment was then in high vogue. I broke the rules and "took my medicine," as the saying was, right along with the other kids. I deserved all I got; it could have been that I deserved more. Though I was not the meanest kid in school, I was far from the best. However, I did have one virtue that may have spared me punishments that otherwise would have been inflicted. I always had my lessons. Having myself been a teacher for nearly fifty years, I now realize how hard it is to mete out stern justice to a pupil who never fails in recitations and passes every examination with flying colors. Somehow the mischiefs and misdoings of the top-drawer students seem more pardonable than those of the dullards. It shouldn't be so, but teachers also are human and cannot help liking what they like.

Boy Life at the Turn of the Century

When I recall my boyhood, the boarding house period in particular, I cannot resist the temptation to make comparisons. In the Ellensburg of the 1890's and 1900's there were no Boy Scouts, no Y.M.C.A., no boys' clubs, and no youth organizations of any kind save the young people's societies in the churches, and the last named were primarily concerned with the inculcation of piety. The only directed or supervised activities a boy of that era could have were at school and at home. Everywhere else the boy and his gang, if there was one, were entirely on their own. In my case, which I believe was fairly typical, the school activities had to do only with the courses of study and the home activities with the daily round of duties and chores. Practically all of my play activities were in a world apart— the world of boydom, which was *terra prohibita* to all but boys. All of our games and other activities were self-planned, self-directed, and self-executed. We had no big brothers, Dutch uncles, counselors, sponsors, or any other species of adult oversight or assistance. We did not want any such thing, did not know what we were missing, and may have been just as well off for having missed it.

Our only team games were baseball and football. We played a

dozen varieties of baseball from "One Old Cat" and "Work-up" to full scale nineman team games with other neighborhood gangs. We had no school teams and no little league. All of our baseball was boy-organized, boy-managed, and boy-financed. Every boy provided his own ball, glove, and other equipment. Any boy who had money enough to buy a catcher's mitt was pretty sure to be made catcher by common consent. Nearly every kid wanted a turn at pitching, and got it, but none lasted long unless they were hard throwers or could throw a pretty good curve. The other positions were usually filled by argumentation, boy variety; which meant that the loudest and most scurrilous arguers usually won out. Sometimes we would resort to fists, but this was avoided as much as possible because it always delayed the game. We made our own rules as we went along, and these were usually our versions of the rules followed in the games played by the town team. But, as is characteristic of boydom, once a rule or form of procedure was accepted, sacred usage took over and made it well nigh inviolable.

Football did not begin to rank with baseball as a popular game among small boys. We played baseball from early spring till snowfall, but football was strictly an autumn sport. Nor did it accomodate itself as readily as baseball to the town's streets and vacant lots, and required more expensive equipment. You could buy a dozen baseballs for the price of one football. We used to substitute bean bags, small cushions, and other objects which could be conveniently carried under one arm for footballs. We seldom played football according to any rules, and our kind of football really was a beefed-up game of tag with tackling taking the place of tagging.

Basketball we did not play at all. It was just then being introduced throughout the country. In Ellensburg the only place basketball could be played was in the Normal School gymnasium, which was not open to the small fry of the community. There were no tennis courts in Ellensburg then, either public or private. There was a game called lawn tennis, from the fact that it was played on lawns, but it was in about the same category as croquet. Small boys hooted at those games because they were played by women as well as men. Golf? Nobody had ever heard of such a game. I am sure there was not a golf course in the entire state of Washington, perhaps not in the whole Pacific Northwest.

The games most commonly played on the school grounds or adjacent vacant lots were dare-base, leap-frog, fox-and-geese, baseball (all varieties), and marbles. These were the boys' games. The only girl's game that I distinctly remember was rope-jumping. None of these was an exclusively Ellensburg game; kids all over the country played them. However, we Ellensburg brats showed some originality in adapting them to our particular environs and tastes, and most of our adaptations were modifications in the direction of roughness. We liked rough games. For example, there was a version of leap-frog which we called "spats" that was one of the most violent and tricky games I ever played. In this game it was the privilege of the "leaper" as he hopped over the "stooper" to whack him on the rump as hard as possible. But it was the counter-privilege of the "stooper" to avoid this "spat" by dropping flat, rolling over, rising up, spinning around, or using any other evasive trick he could imagine. A dozen husky boys playing this kind of leap-frog could enjoy about as much violence as their physiques could endure. Another violent game was "shinny," a rough-hewn version of hockey. This, of course, was a skating game. Each boy provided his own shinny stick, which usually was as big a bludgeon as he could swing easily with two hands. In place of a rubber puck a small rock was always used. The object of course was for each side (and there could be as many on a side as wanted to play) to drive the rock to its goal and keep the other side from doing likewise. The only rule was to choose sides and lay to, whacking away at the rock and the opponents' sticks. There were no penalties, no times-out, no substitutions, no fouls, no officials. The game went on until everybody was exhausted or too banged-up to play any more. I always supposed that the game got its name from the fact that during skating season every player sported bruised shins from ankle to knee. How we did not brain each other I don't know.

We had many other games that were equally rough; in fact about the only game of skill that I remember was marbles. The marbles games that I best remember were bull ring, fish ring, squares (sometimes called "fats"), and lagging the line. Each had its own special rules and called for different skills. To be a good marbles player one had to have power, accuracy and control of the spins. Though modesty forbids, I will record the fact that I got to be a better than average marbles player at all kinds of games. If I had been challenged, way back then, to prove this boast, I could easily have done so by exhibiting the pocket full of marbles that I always carried with me. These were my winnings. If my mother had known this, she would have made me give them all back. She had forbidden me to play for keeps because, under our Methodist code, that was gambling, one of the blackest of sins. The sin aspect of the thing did not trouble me very much because under the code of boydom, which was more mandatory than that of Methodism, if you did not play for keeps, you did not play at all. But I did take discreet pains not to let Mother catch sight of my big hoard of marbles. She would have asked embarrassing questions, because she knew I did not have money to buy any such quantity of marbles. In fact, I became a sort of banker in marbles, staking other kids and collecting principal and interest in marbles.

Hide-and-seek we played both day and night, but run-sheep-run, a variant of hide-and-seek, we played only at night. These were mixed games, meaning that boys and girls played together. Our elders thought hide-and-seek quite innocent and run-sheep-run just the opposite. Reasons? The former was an individualized game in which each player hid out by himself; the latter was a collectivized game, played at night, in which the two sexes hid out in mixed groups. Ergo, there must be some sexy goings-on when run-sheep-run was played. Unless I missed something, run-sheep-run was about as antiseptic and asexual as a kids' game could be. Both time and circumstances were unpropitious for sexual dallying, and there were other and far more opportune occasions for sexual reconnaissance.

We did not play cops and robbers in my boyhood, nor did we daily feed upon criminal violence as a source of entertainment. We were violent ourselves, but we did not relish vicarious violence. Cowboys were real people, not celluloid shadows, to us. We saw them on the streets every day, and saw little in them to admire. Gamblers, marshalls, and alleged outlaws were also commonplace characters to us. We witnessed street fights, both with and without guns, and there was nothing romantic about them. Nor was there anything specially romantic or exciting about horses. For most of us, horses meant dirty work every day, and riding horseback or driving a team was no mark of social status. Any livery stable lout could do that. The kind of Indians and frontiersmen whom I thought heroic were not those I saw on the streets of Ellensburg every day but those I read about in the *Leatherstocking Tales* of James Fenimore Cooper. Daniel Boone was a great hero to me, but Jim Bridger was just a filthy old trapper, and Billy the Kid rated about as much esteem as a rattlesnake. The glorious years of the Old West as now depicted on TV and in the movies did not seem that way at all to boys like me, who lived in the closing years of that era. Nick Carter, the detective, Frank Merriwell, the peerless athlete, and Ralph, the boy corporal of Company K, were my beau ideals of fiction.

In my boyhood swimming was something the big kids taught the little kids, or the little kids did not get taught at all. In Ellensburg there was no such thing as a swimming pool, public or private, nor any near-by lakes or beaches. We swam in the rivers, creeks, and irrigation canals. The Town Ditch was the favorite swimming place of the gang I ran with. It was an irrigation canal which ran about a mile north of town, in a sparsely inhabited area. We swam in the nude there, because none of us had bathing suits or knew where to get them. Little did we care anyhow.

I had my first swimming lesson in the Town Ditch. The lesson consisted of being heaved into the water by four bigger boys who then stood on the bank and yelled instructions to me. The instructions consisted mainly of profane adjurations to kick my feet and paddle with my arms and hands. By so doing, I managed to get myself ashore, and the big kids then said I had learned enough to take care of myself in the water. Thus by trial and error, I learned to swim "dog-fashion" and later acquired more proficient techniques. The time eventually came, when I was twelve or thirteen, when I passed the supreme test, which was to swim across the Yakima River and back. This was a foolhardy thing to do, but I did not know it nor did any of the other kids who were along that day and dared me to try it. We were on our own that day, and none of our parents had the faintest idea where we were or what we were doing.

Nearly all of the male population of Ellensburg, except the Maxeys, hunted and fished. Game of all kinds was abundant from the city limits to as far back in the mountains as one might want to go, and nearly every stream abounded with trout. I never figured out why the Maxey men abstained. They all kept firearms and knew how to use them but never went hunting. Fishing tackle they seemed to know nothing about and did not care to. It was largely by accident that I became the fisherman of the family. As I have heretofore mentioned, we spent the last summer of my father's life on Grandfather's place in the Menastash Canyon. It so happened that the Menastash Creek was one of the best trout streams in the whole countryside, and many of the fisherman who worked this stream were friends of my father. Often, as they were fishing the portion of the stream which ran through our place, they would stop and visit a while with Father. By listening in on their conversations, tagging along behind and watching them in action, I became so interested in fishing that I cut myself a willow pole, found a piece of cotton twine to use for a line, made hooks out of bent pins, baited them with fat "pennywinkles," and went off fishing. I was actually lucky enough to catch two or three small ones, and this pleased my father so much that he said, "If the boy wants to fish that much, he should have some decent equipment." By means I never learned about, he got me a few plain hooks, two or three fly hooks, four or five yards of genuine fish line, and a cheap bamboo pole. That put me in business, and I kept the table supplied with fish the rest of the summer. I continued to be an enthusiastic and quite successful fisherman until I went away to college. Thereafter, my opportunities for fishing dwindled to the point that I finally got out of the habit and gave it up.

I was very eager to become a hunter, but Mother discouraged me in every way she could. However, I made and saved enough money to buy a pretty good air rifle, and with this weapon tried, with small success, to bring down various kinds of small game. When I was about twelve years old, Uncle Cromie gave me a Winchester .22 caliber rifle, and I was sure I would soon realize my dreams as a hunter. I took this with me on some trips to Menastash, but Grandpa objected to my going off alone with the gun, fearing I would either kill myself or somebody else, and Mother nearly had a conniption every time I left the house with the rifle. So, to keep peace in the family circle, I finally gave it up.

It was as a small boy in Ellensburg that I got my first experience in boxing and learned a bit about the finesse of the sport. Back in my time boys seemed to be born with a love of fist-fighting. At least I was, and so were all the kids I played with. The last whipping I got at school was for fighting on the school grounds, and, as I recall it, that was a let-off-steam fight rather than a bloody-nose fight. Another kid dared me to knock a chip off his shoulder. I did, and we started slugging toe to toe, not because we had anything against each other, but because we were both living up to the code. The school authorities did not see it that way, however, and we both got our pants dusted.

There were some fathers in Ellensburg who thought their boys ought to be taught to "use their dooks" efficiently, and hence provided the young hopefuls with boxing gloves and certain basic instructions. I did not have a father after I was seven, but I had friends with fathers of the kind mentioned above and I was always welcome as a sparring partner. Some of these fathers were pretty good coaches and loved to impart their knowledge of the "manly art of self-defense" to youngsters. I was fortunate enough to get in on enough of these sessions to learn what to do with my left and my right and how to manage my feet so as to make the proper moves. I never became much of a boxer, but I got good exercise out of "throwing the leather," gained confidence, and acquired a little more than a casual spectator's interest in professional boxing matches.

As yet I have made no mention of parlor games, and there is a good reason for this. Parlor games had little place in my young life. During the boarding house years, our parlor was a public reception room, and in the earlier years, the moves to and from the Methow together with my father's long illness precluded the use of our home for any recreational purposes. My mother's chronic ill health had the same effect in later years. I left home for college when I was eighteen, and I have raked my memory to see if I can recall any party or social affair that was held in our house before then. No such memory comes to the surface, and I am sure that none ever will. About the only parlor games that went on at our house were those that Aurel and I contrived for ourselves. She and I used to play checkers, crokinole (snap-finger pool), and tiddly-winks. Cards were forbidden to Methodists, except in such denatured versions as Authors and Flinch. Both were dull as dishwater. Learning to play with worldly cards was to be part of my college education; likewise dancing, which also was taboo for Methodists. At parties in Methodist homes or under church auspices we played such games as charades, clap-in-and-clap-out, blind man's buff, and musical chairs. Though I participated in these, I never went wild over them.

When viewers-with-alarm sound off about the sex obsession of modern youth, I wonder if they have any idea of the sex obsession of youth in those puritanical days of yore. As compared with the turn of the century, the young people of today are but mildly interested in sex, and actually know little about it. They have no chance to be sexually precocious. My generation did not have to be told about the birds and the bees; we did not need any sex instruction at school; we had no use for printed manuals on sex made explicit by drawings and illustrations. From our toddling years, we not only were exposed to sex, we had it thrust upon us. We could not avoid witnessing copulation almost daily in our own barnyards and chicken runs, and more exciting versions were available at the nearest livery stable. The newspapers and billboards carried large-scale display "ads" telling exactly where various pedigreed stallions and registered bulls would be standing for "service." We not only knew what that meant, but knew where the performances could be witnessed. It was like carrying coals to Newcastle for our parents or any one else to tell us how women got pregnant or where babies came from. And the truth is that parents seldom saw any need to offer such instruction.

Big kids instructed little kids about the "facts of life" so far as humans were concerned, but the little kids already had learned enough by observation to be apt pupils. Perhaps my generation would have turned out better if it could have had the benefit of sterilized sex instruction, though I cannot recall that any of us ever suffered psychological traumas or got tangled up in sex complexes because of what we learned from the big kids. Indeed, I think the big kids were more proficient teachers than our parents would have been. Although their information was not always perfect, the big kids did not preach or threaten, and I know of no evidence that learning from them left the learners any more susceptible to sex offenses or sex deviations than modern methods of sex intruction. The current theory, as I understand it, is that coldly scientific instruction about sex tends to abate prurient interest. Though I am not prepared to engage in any argument on that point, I reserve the right to be skeptical. In my youth, just the opposite theory prevailed, i.e., the less candor there was about sex, the less curiosity there would be. That theory never was even close to the truth. The conspiracy of silence and the suppression of sex information did not change the natural sex concerns and predilections of the youth one particle. We gabbled about sex constantly, and some went a good deal farther than talk. In this respect I think we were like all generations of boys and girls since human beings have inhabited this planet.

I do believe, however, that in one respect sex was played down far more in my youth than it is today. In the turn-of-the-century years there was almost no pairing off of boys and girls as "going steady" or "keeping company" or any such relation as that. There was very little "dating," as it is now called. Right up through our teens, except in one's own family circle, contacts with members of the opposite sex were largely limited to such affairs as church socials and school parties. A boy might walk a girl home from one of these parties, but did not thereby create or acquire any special status in her social life. There were no moving pictures, no corner hangouts, no public dance halls, no parks or playgrounds, no institutions of any kind which would throw boys and girl together in repeated social contacts. As a result, individual boys and individual girls did not have many chances to meet except at large and more or less formal parties. And most of the sex prattle was just as unilateral as the sex association. I do not mean to say that there were not exceptions—cases in which there was a special pairing off which might even go as far as illicit intercourse—but these definitely were far outside the regular pattern of boy and girl affairs.

Church and religion played a large part in my youthful associations and experiences. As I have already said, the Maxeys were devout Methodists. It was routine, therefore, that I should be baptized in infancy in the presence of the whole congregation of the Ellensburg Methodist Church. In Methodist practice that did not *ipso facto* make me a member of the church. Methodists believed that one had to repent and be converted in order to be qualified for church membership, and infants could not do that. So I did not join the church until I was fifteen years old, but at that time I went through the motions of being converted and saved. Not being technically a member of the church until I was fifteen did not keep me from being a regular attendant of the Sunday school and church services. I joined the Epworth League (young people's society) as soon

61

as I was old enough and worked my way up through the ranks until I became president. It was then the Methodist custom to have two or three weeks of revival meetings each year, usually in the winter season, and during these "protracted" services, as they were often styled, an extra special effort was made to lead sinners to the altar for conversion and salvation. I regularly attended these meetings and sometimes took part.

By all signs and tokens I should have become a lifelong Methodist or confirmed churchman of some species. But I did not, and in retrospect I find it difficult to explain why not. I went through all of the motions and made all of the professions conscientiously and sincerely. With all my being I tried to "catch fire" as most of my fellow Methodists seemed to do; I wanted to have the experience of being "snatched from the burning" and being assured of everlasting life. But the "still, small voice" never spoke to me. Despite all the terrors of hell as described by the evangelists, I never was thoroughly scared about where I was going to spend eternity, and I never had any devastating conviction of sin. Maybe I was born a skeptic— I wonder?

In college I was introduced to what then was known as "higher criticism" and did a great deal of reading in that fascinating field of study. I never could reconcile the knowledge acquired through my immersion in the literature of higher criticism with the creed of any church or sect. As I will relate at the proper chronological stage of this narrative, I never left the Methodist church or sought affiliation with any other. I simply became an inactivist. Nevertheless, I am glad that I went through the Methodist mill, for I believe that Methodism made some priceless contributions to my intellectual, cultural, and social development. Methodism's finest gift to me was the inculcation of a thorough familiarity with the King James translation of the Bible. In those days Methodism laid heavy stress on the "preached Word." Sunday school instruction was Bible teaching pure and undiluted; the morning and evening church services were at least half devoted to Bible readings; and the Epworth League meetings were largely devoted to

Bible study. During my active Methodist years I read the Bible through and through, not once but many times. Being an omnivorous reader, I also read every collateral commentary on the Bible that I could lay my hands on. Having a quick and tenacious memory, I absorbed as permanent intellectual property many vivid passages of Bible text which I could recite like poems or orations. Thus, unconsciously, I acquired an Elizabethan vocabulary and a feeling for Elizabethan rhetoric. It was a short step from the Bible to Shakespeare, Marlowe, Johnson, even Milton, and I was fully ready for them when the time came for me to read Elizabethan and Restoration literature.

I also credit Methodism with giving me invaluable instruction and experience in the art of public speaking. Methodists not only exalted the Bible, but demanded high-powered preaching based on the Book of Books. The first qualification for a Methodist minister was to be a good speaker, for preaching was the most important part of his job. During my boyhood many able and eloquent preachers were assigned to our Methodist church, and there were also frequent visits from the higher clergy, such as presiding elders and bishops. Some of these were brilliant orators, excellent models for a young boy with a talent for public speaking. The Methodist church, especially the Epworth League, supplied me a wonderful forum in which to practice the oratorical techniques I observed in the clergy. At every meeting there was an invitation to "testify," which was no more than a call to any individual who wanted to make an extemporaneous talk on religious or Biblical topics to stand on his feet and sound off. I always did, and undoubtedly spouted a lot of nonsense, but also learned a lot of tricks about the art of speaking in public.

Methodist theology did not grip me very strongly in the long run, but Methodist ethics did. Perhaps I should not speak of Methodist ethics as a distinct species of Christian ethics, but I believe there is much justification for so doing. Though I would not deny the existence of a generalized code of Christian ethics, I believe the distribution of emphasis is not the same in any two Christian sects. The Methodist emphasis in my youth was heavily laid on simple personal integrity and decency plus a specially strong antipathy to sins reflecting personal greed. The worst sin that Methodism could conceive was the unrighteous exploitation of one's fellow men. I have always been proud that I had that drilled into me from infancy to manhood.

Cultural Influences

Methodism certainly was a major cultural influence in my life, but there were others of equal, possibly greater, force. One of these undoubtedly was the reading habit which I acquired at a very tender age. As I have already mentioned, reading for me has almost always been as effortless as breathing, and I read as regularly every day as though it were a well nigh automatic bodily function. Of course, I had an insatiable curiosity; of course, I thirsted for information; of course, I wanted to be entertained; but much of the time I read just for the sake of reading. It gave me a glow of satisfaction to read anything that came to hand. Seldom in my boyhood and not often in later life have I had enough reading material on hand to snow me under.

Books were not easy to come by in the Ellensburg of my boyhood days. The only library in town was at the Normal School, and it was not open to the public. In the public schools the only books were a dictionary in each classroom and one or two stray reference books kept on the teacher's desk. If there were any private libraries other than the professional collections of lawyers and doctors, I never heard of them. Among my personal kinfolk and friends there were none from whom I could borrow books. They did not own as many as we. In my home, in addition to the Bible, there were eight books, namely, my mother's copy of McGuffey's *Fifth Reader,* her copy of Steele's *Natural History,* a copy of *Uncle Tom's Cabin,* a pirated edition of Thomas Moore's *Annotated Poetical Works of Lord Byron,* a medical adviser by Dr. Pierce of "Golden Medical Discovery" fame (he was about on a par with Lydia

Pinkham), a collection of prose and verse entitled *Golden Links in the Chain that Connects Mother, Home and Heaven,* a pietistical novel by one E. P. Roe, and one of the *Little Prudy* series of children's books. How do I remember them so clearly? Because I read them forwards and backwards—virtually memorized them.

Because I had my nose in a book so much of the time, folks began to call me a bookworm. They didn't know the half of it. Mother sympathized with my zest for the printed page and did her best to keep me supplied, but the problem was too big for her. It was a piece of rare good fortune that she could turn for help to Lucy Goodman and Flossie Abbott, the two Normal students who were living with us. They were delighted to take over, and I owe them a debt which I can acknowledge but never repay. In connection with their preparations for teacher certification both of these young ladies were taking a course on how to teach reading and literature to grade-school children. As a guinea pig, I was just what the doctor ordered for them. My reading pace was so rapid and my span of interests so broad that they got real excited about me, gave me special help, and borrowed many books from the Normal Library for me to use. They also urged Mother to buy me books for birthday and Christmas presents and advised her in making selections. It was at their suggestion that Mother gave me, at Christmas, 1899, the two-volume set of Beach's *Student's Encyclopedia.* This was a well-edited reference work designed for high schools and colleges, and proved to be exactly what I needed. Not only did it serve me as an authentic work of reference, the first I had ever seen; I read both volumes from cover to cover just for the sheer pleasure of reading and thinking. I became a sort of walking encyclopedia myself, because I committed to memory so much of what I read in those two volumes. I still have those books and treasure them beyond words. I suspect that their influence more than any other led me in the direction of collegiate education.

On the suggestion of Lucy and Flossie, Mother also gave me Mark Twain's *Tom Sawyer, Huckleberry Finn,* and *Tom Saw-*

yer Abroad. I simply reveled in these—so much so that Mother sometimes wondered if she had not made a mistake in giving them to me. In Methodist circles at that time Mark Twain's works were thought to be irreligious, and I suppose they were. But I loved them and Mother never bothered to read them, and so I was allowed to read them until I had nearly absorbed them verbatim. Little did I know then that I was reading books that were destined to become classics of American Literature and models of narrative style. To my taste, no American writer has ever equalled Mark Twain in making language come alive.

Other books which fascinated me between my ninth and twelfth years were G. A. Henty's *Life of Daniel Boone,* A. R. White's *The Blue and the Gray,* and Governor George Peck's *Peck's Bad Boy.* The last named was the "Dennis the Menace" of that genteel era and was thought to be the last word in juvenile delinquency, though I cannot see how it could have contributed to anything but a little rough horse-play at the expense of the older generation. Children's books such as *Black Beauty, Beautiful Joe, Little Men, Under the Lilacs,* and the Horatio Alger series I took at a gulp and never returned for a second taste. But I lingered over Washington Irving's *Astoria* and redigested page after page, for that was my first introduction to Northwest history. Among the so-called penny dreadfuls or dime novels of the era my favorites were the tales of the Merriwell brothers, Frank and Dick, and the Nick Carter detective yarns. Most of these paperback books were supposed to be corrupting, so I had to read them in the woodshed or hayloft.

In addition to what I have already said, I must give a special paragraph to the Bible. I was an absorbed and inveterate, if not always sanctimonius reader of the Holy Word. As a wedding present Mother had been given a large family-type Bible which was lavishly illustrated by Gustav Doré. This book was my special dish. I would spread it out on the floor and, lying flat on my belly, would pore through it by the hour. This pleased my mother very much, for she took it as a sign that I might one day have a "call" to the Methodist ministry. If the poor dear could have understood the real reasons for my fascination with the family Bible, she would have been shocked. With the aid of Doré's dramatic illustrations, I had discovered that the Bible could be as murderous as *Gunsmoke,* as gamey as *Rabelais,* as salacious as the *Decameron,* as sentimental as *East Lynne,* as martial as *Soldiers Three,* as full of derring-do as *The Three Musketeers,* as heroic as the *Illiad,* as tragic as *King Lear,* as poetic as *The Lay of the Last Minstrel.* In short, I had discovered, although I could not have explained it then, that the Bible is much more than a book, much more than a great masterpiece. What I found in the Bible was a whole literature—history, adventure, drama, poetry, philosophy, erotica, satire, and every other conceivable form of literary expression. I read the Bible not for the good of my soul, but because it was so exciting and entertaining that I could not let it alone. It may not have been good for my soul to read the Bible this way, but I think it was good for my mind and for my taste in literature.

Now a special word about my introduction to the Greek and Roman classics. This I owe to the Misses Goodman and Abbott. In their Normal School curriculum they had a course in story-telling to childern, and the material used in this course included a good deal of Greek and Roman mythology. For practice, those dear young ladies tried out a lot of this material on Aurel and me. I developed such an insatiable appetite for more of the same that they borrowed from the Normal library several books of Greek and Roman myths for me to read. For me, these were almost as fascinating as the Bible, and for similar reasons. So I proceeded to pack my skull with many stories of the Greek and Roman gods and goddesses, of the Trojan War, the journeys of Ulysses, and all the rest. In addition to equipping my imagination with a magnificent literary tapestry, this reading of the classical mythology certainly influenced me later on to elect courses in Greek and Latin as opportunity offered both in high school and college. I believe it also did much to stimulate my interest in the study of history. I doubt if I ever would have taken any courses in ancient history if it had not been for my boyhood introduction to the Greek and Roman folk tales.

When I could get them, I read newspapers and magazines as avidly as anything else. We subscribed to the weekly Ellensburg *Capital,* mainly because it was a Republican sheet and a purveyor of local news. Except for a page or two of boiler plate, it contained nothing but local items. For reasons I could only guess, my mother also subscribed to the weekly edition of the Toledo (Ohio) *Blade.* This, too, was a staunchly Republican paper, and during the Civil War it had played a role in the Middle West comparable to that of Horace Greeley's New York *Tribune* in the East. I presume the family got started with the weekly *Blade* during the war and kept it up through force of habit. The weekly edition which came to us, way out in Ellensburg, was made up for the most part of condensed reprints of the leading articles which had appeared in the daily editions of the *Blade.* These were well written and selected for a national audience. I read every issue eagerly and thoroughly, often saved them for weeks at a time to have opportunities to re-read them. The time eventually came when I was the only one around the house who read the weekly *Blade,* so Mother discontinued it and took on in its place the twice-a-week editions of the Seattle *Post-Intelligencer* and the Spokane *Spokesman-Review.* These were better than the *Blade* for Pacific Northwest news but inferior as to national and international news. There was no daily newspaper in Ellensburg until I was far up in my teens. The daily papers from Seattle and Spokane were delivered in Ellensburg from twenty-four to forty-eight hours late, but we did not subscribe to them, partly, I imagine, because the subscription rates were too high. I never got a look at a real metropolitan daily until I was in college.

I must have been ten or twelve years of age before any magazines, except the give-aways that I got at Sunday school, came into our home. I read the Sunday school magazines with the same voracity as everything else, but they supplied no nutriment for my mind. I remember nothing distinctive about them, not even their piety. One day—I don't remember exactly how or when—I came across a copy of the *Youth's Companion*, then published in Boston, Massachusetts. Instantly I recognized this as something I could not live without. Having saved up enough money to pay the subscription charge, I promptly hied myself to the post office and wrote out my very first money order to pay for this attractive magazine. I renewed that subscription every year as long as I lived at home. The *Youth's Companion* was right down my alley. Its stories were perfectly tailored to a boy's taste; its information articles dealt with subjects of uppermost interest for boys; and its special departments included such things as collecting and do-it-yourself methods. From the *Youth's Companion* a boy could learn how to make his own toys, build a rabbit trap, carve a wooden boat, salt and cure a fish, and a dozen and one other things of peculiar interest to boys. There were also most enthralling continued stories to keep one on tip toe from week to week.

As I got farther along in school there was increasing attention to current events, and I accordingly used some of my hoardings to subscribe to the *Review of Reviews*, a national magazine that specialized in doing a precis of the whole field of journalism. Each month it published a summary of current events with excerpts and condensations of news stories and editorials, and the whole was liberally illustrated with halftones and cartoons. The *Review of Reviews* opened doors for me that nothing else could have done. For the first time I could feel that I was not only in touch with what was going on in the world, but also knew what the leading minds of the day were thinking and saying about what was taking place. Later—when I was a teenager—I subscribed to the *World's Work*, that era's equivalent of the present-day *Fortune*. It is a good thing I did not know that twenty years later I would be contributing articles to the *World's Work*. I would have strutted around Ellensburg with my chest puffed out like a pouter pigeon.

Among the other cultural influences which I would credit with important increments to my social and intellectual growth I would mention church entertainment programs, Friday afternoon programs at school, public performances at the Normal School, circuses, medicine shows, street carnivals, and, extra specially, the Ellensburg Theater. It was the custom in Ellensburg Methodist Church for the Sunday school, the Epworth League, and some of the other auxiliary organizations to put on special entertainment programs at Christmas, Thanksgiving, Easter, and other special occasions. These included tinkling cantatas, pietistic plays, recitations, musical renditions, and other such fare. Now I would regard all of them as dull, even banal, but then I liked them and looked forward to them, especially if I had a chance to participate in some way, which I nearly always did. If I did not get a part in a play or get to sing in a chorus, I was almost sure to be asked to "speak a piece." And I was always ready to oblige. I absolutely loved to hear myself talk and always wanted to be before the public if I could. Had I been the backward kind, I would have missed a great opportunity. It was good for me to have frequent opportunities to appear and perform in public. I'll bet half of the audience laughed up their sleeves when I recited such gems of poesy as "Curfew Shall Not Ring Tonight," but it was doing that sort of stuff over and over again that taught me much of what I know about holding the attention of an audience.

I was also an eager volunteer for the Friday afternoon programs in my room at school. What educational theory, if any, lay behind the practice of using the last class period on Friday afternoons for a program put on by the pupils, I do not know. But I do know that it added an extra dimension to my education. These Friday programs were worked out in advance by the teacher; pupils were invited to take part and parents were often asked to attend, particularly those whose dear darlings were appearing in the program.

Come the last period on Friday afternoon, all desks were cleared of slates, tablets, papers, books, pencils, and other such paraphernalia; the pupils sat in the posture of "attention" while the teacher, as master of ceremonies, took charge of the program. The numbers usually consisted of recitations in prose, verse, or dialogues; pantomimes, sometimes involving two or more kids; renditions of popular songs by solo, duet, etc. Many of the youngsters never would take part in these programs, but I was always the eager beaver. If the teachers had allowed it, I would have been on every Friday afternoon program year in and year out. Lordy, how I loved standing before the class and declaiming such glorious (to me) verse as "Sheridan's Ride!" Being always ready, I got more than my share of invitations to perform, which probably was not too good for my ego but gave me wonderful basic experience in achieving self-possession before an audience. In later life, when public speaking became of vital importance to me, I never had to worry about what to do with my hands, how to keep my eyes beamed straight into those of my hearers, how to project my voice so that all could hear me, and many of the other trade secrets of the art of public speaking. Those things I learned as a kid in the churches and public schools of Ellensburg—learned by doing, which, if one is sufficiently self-critical to recognize his mistakes, is the very best way of learning.

The programs at the Normal School were of two general kinds. First were the public programs put on by the literary societies, and second, the public lectures. The public was generally invited to the literary society programs, admission free, and this, naturally, rendered them quite appealing to an impecunious kid. The lectures were not always free, and there was a lecture series of the lyceum type which cost about five dollars for the year. The literary society performances, entirely staged with student talent, took the place of movies, radio, and television for me. If any of those modern forms of diverting the youthful mind had been in existence, I probably would have thought the student performances pretty "corny," but as it was I found them highly entertaining. They supplied intellectual entertainment, a commodity of which Ellensburg did not enjoy an oversupply. I could have spent my evenings, and did spend some of them, playing simple games with the other kids, haunting the streets and alleys, hanging around the fringes in the pool halls, and in other brainless activities; but I had a hunger for something more, and the literary programs helped satisfy that hunger. Moreover, I found in most of those programs some idea, item of knowledge, or point of view that I could turn over in my mind again and again, and read up on, if I were sufficiently interested. I think, through attendance at these programs, I first began to get a dim conception of what higher education was about.

Occasional lectures without admission charge were offered by members of the Normal School faculty and other prominent personages, and I made a point of attending every one of these I could. But it was the annual lyceum series that really enthralled me. This usually consisted of six to eight lectures sold to the public as a package. The lecturers were always persons of national eminence in their respective fields, which, through a year's course of lectures, might comprehend such diverse subjects as science, travel, literature, history, art, music, and dramatic readings. The annual charge, as I have pointed out, was not prohibitive even to a small lad who had to make it by such back-alley business enterprises as I have previously described in this narrative. I could always scrape up five dollars if I had to, and I always did scrape up five dollars for the lyceum lecture series. I drank in those lectures like ambrosia from the gods. Time and again, after a lecture, I would go to my little encyclopedia and read up on it from every angle I could, and then I was alerted to be on the lookout for any supplementary reading on the subject which might come along in the newspapers and magazines.

My stock of information and ideas was enriched by various other forms of entertainment available in frontier Ellensburg. One of the most thrilling of these was the traveling circus. The "biggest and best" shows on the road played Ellensburg regularly year after year, and I saw them all—Sells and Forepaugh, Barnum and Bailey, Ringling Brothers, and all the rest. Usually I had no difficulty in getting tickets to the circus. Some one of Mother's boarders almost always, because of his official or professional status, had a supply of "comps" from which I could wheedle at least one. But if no "comps" were forthcoming, there was always a chance of getting a job as a roustabout, and by this means one could not only see the circus but aspects of circus life behind the scenes which were even more entertaining. Let a good-sized boy show up at the circus grounds at unloading time in the morning and one of the bosses was almost certain to put him to work, for they were always shorthanded. From the circus I got not only eye-opening entertainment but also an intellectual residue which was worthwhile. In that respect the menageries did more for me than any other feature of the circus. I was a grown man before I ever had a chance to visit a city with a zoo. When I saw the menagerie at the circus it was my habit to go home and read up as much as I could on all the animals I had seen, and that was good education.

Educative in a somewhat different way were the medicine shows and street carnivals which visited our town every season. The medicine shows were always free and therefore always assured of a full house, except that there was no house to be filled. A "Quaker" doctor, Indian herb healer, or snake oil vendor, having made due arrangements with the city fathers, would set up shop on a prominent street corner by erecting a platform four or five feet high and perhaps six feet square. The platform was always gaily decorated with bunting and lighted by kerosene torches. On this stage the nightly medicine show took place. The show was always put on by assistants of the great doctor who were made up as Irishmen, Dutchmen, Negroes, clowns, or other characters thought likely to jerk a laugh out of the hicks. The performance usually consisted of comic monologues (always as close to obscenity as they dared to skate), dialogues between two or more of the characters, a few tricks of legerdemain, a juggling act, some vile ventriloquism, and an indecent Punch and Judy show. In other words, it was low-grade vaudeville designed only to drum up a crowd of gawking standees.

As soon as the show had pulled in a large enough crowd, the Great Healer would take over and make a pitch for the sale of his nostrums. One who has never heard an old-fashioned medicine man make his pitch has never heard bathos at its best. Opening his speech with graphic and fearsome descriptions of

the worst ills human flesh is heir to, always dwelling insinu-
atingly on the venereal, then enumerating enough dangerous
symptoms to scare every member of the audience, the doctor
would ascend to his climax by predicting dire consequences for
the victims of these ailments unless they began treatments with
his universal panacea immediately. In tragic tones he would
explain how all other doctors and all other remedies had failed,
but his wonderful potion, thanks to its miraculous properties,
would not fail. Time and time again it had snatched sufferers
from the very brink of the grave. Then he would sink his
harpoon deep in the hides of his hearers. Ellensburg, he would
confidentially disclose, was a specially favored town. He had
been reluctant to come to so small a place, but hearing of its
desperate needs, he had condescended to come for just this
one week. So it was now or never, if you wanted to possess
his marvelous elixir of life. Thereupon, the assistants, laden
with bottles of medicine at fifty cents or a dollar apiece, would
begin to work the crowd, and when they had sold as many
bottles as they could soft-soap the yokels into buying, the great
doctor would arise and announce that tomorrow night a bigger
and better show would be given, so please tell all your friends
not to miss it.

Tomorrow night's show was always the same as last night's,
but I was always on hand along with all the rest of my gang of
buddies. To us, most of the jokes, especially the dirty ones,
were funnier and most of the stunts more amusing the second
or third time around. We knew what was coming and were
all set for the big guffaws. And I may as well confess that I,
along with the rest of the yokels, shelled out an occasional fifty
cent piece for the eloquent doctors' beautifully bottled elixir
of life. Moreover, I took it according to directions and waited
for miracles to happen, and, of course, they never did. Not in
one summer, but after several such letdowns, I learned my
lesson. Finally it dawned on my juvenile mind that the world
is full of suckers, and of fakers who prey upon the suckers.
That was a lesson worth learning.

The street carnivals were just as phony as the medicine shows but usually gave the sucker more of a run for his money. Ordinarily they drifted into town shortly after harvest, when everybody was supposed to be flush with money. On a vacant lot not too far from the center of town they would set up with such attractions as a merry-go-round, a Ferris wheel, a shooting gallery, various games of skill or chance that were always rigged against the customer, and always two or three tent shows of the strip-tease variety. For each attraction there was a charge, ranging usually from a dime to a dollar, and the carnival folks knew all the tricks of separating simpletons from dimes and dollars. Like most of the boys in my crowd, I seldom had much money to spend at the carnivals. The merry-go-round and other rides were usually within my reach, also the shooting gallery; but on most of the gambling games and tent shows the tariff was more than I could manage. But I always hung around the grounds, whether I was in funds or not, because it was such fun to watch the assorted cowpokes, sheepherders, railroad men, and so forth throw their money away. And what I saw and heard in these gamey environs helped fill out certain gaps in my education which home, church, and school had by-passed.

I am persuaded that in one respect uncouth little Ellensburg opened doors of culture to me that today's young people are entirely denied. I refer to what is colloquially called the legitimate theater, a term which originated, I suppose, to distinguish the traditional type of theater from the motion picture theater. Motion picture theaters were just getting started in Ellensburg when I left for college and played no part in my early development. Not so the legitimate; I was immersed in that from the time I was big enough to be allowed to stay up after 9 p.m. Ellensburg's first theater was known as Lloyd's Opera House, from the fact that it occupied the second floor of a building at the corner of Third and Pine Streets which was owned by a man named Lloyd. Here it was that I saw my first stage show— *Uncle Tom's Cabin*. Ellensburg was a good show town, and Lloyd's Opera House soon proved inadequate. Around 1900 a stock company of local citizens was formed to build a new theater. After considering several possibilities, this company bought the Lloyd Building, tore out its insides, and converted it into a first-class theater. There were few better anywhere at the time.

Almost every road show that toured the Pacific Northwest (and this was the heyday of touring companies) gave one or more performances in the Ellensburg Theater. Being halfway between Seattle and Spokane, blessed with good payrolls, good hotels, and an institution of higher education, Ellensburg could command the best theatrical fare there was. Year after year you could see in Ellensburg the best the country had to offer. Invariably there was a generous helping of Shakespeare, two or three crack minstrel shows, a scattering of musical comedies, several popular farces, and enough high-brow drama to satisfy all tastes. My taste ran specially to Shakespeare, minstrel shows, screaming farces, and the so-called problem plays.

Minstrel shows were universal favorites, and such famous companies as Christy's, Dockstadter's, and Primrose's are among those I heard in Ellensburg. Those born too late for the era of minstrel shows are to be pitied, I feel. I know that the music was "corny," the singing "soupy," the humor "square," and the dancing "jiggy." These things I know because people of elegant taste have told me so, and I must repect their opinions. But to me, as a small boy and later a teenager, a minstrel show was all wonder and delight. I knew, as all the audience did, that white men in blackface were not true replicas of the American Negro, but represented a romanticized Negro who was far more loved by the whites than the real Negro. But it never occured to me that these imaginary Negroes were caricatures insulting and demeaning to the Negro race. I don't think they were ever conceived as such by the whites, and, if they made any difference at all in our attitude toward the Negro people, it was to enhance our affection for our black brethren.

The same could be said of the "Tom" shows—show-biz slang for *Uncle Tom's Cabin*. These were minstrel shows with melodrama added and brought to its highest pitch. Despite the Methodist ban on the theater, my folks always made an exception of *Uncle Tom's Cabin*. Harriet Beecher Stowe's fictional

76

polemic against slavery was one book they had all read. In their affections it stood next to the Bible. They had no more idea of the liberties the popular dramatizations had taken with Harriet's original novel than the modern moviegoer has of what Hollywood does to the Bible when it films a *King of Kings* or comparable Scriptural extravaganza. Civil War veterans were numerous in every audience then, and Civil War emotions were still close to the surface. The "Tom" shows gave Northern and Western audiences exactly the version of slavery they believed and enlivened it with a potpourri of vaudeville and minstrel acts. This formula was unbeatable, and the "Tom" shows always packed the house. I attended every one that came to town, and never ceased to quake with fear when the bloodhounds almost nabbed Eliza when she crossed the Ohio River on floating cakes of ice, never failed to cackle at the antics of Lawyer Marks or snicker at his off-color remarks, always burned with indignation at the severities of Miss Ophelia, was delighted by the odd-sayings of Topsy, fumed with hate of Simon Legree, and always had tears to shed over the death of Little Eva and the sad fate of Uncle Tom. I loved every moment of it, and I believe I would again if I should ever have the chance.

In the case of the Shakespearean plays my mother also waived her objections to the theater. She knew nothing about Shakespeare, but the teachers at school always urged the students to ask their parents to let them attend the Shakespeare plays, and that removed the curse as far as Mother was concerned. Almost always when a Shakespeare company came to town there were special matinees for students, with lowered prices of admission. This also helped in removing the curse. As time went on her tolerance stretched enough to include the evening performances, and from then on I had it made. I managed to take in about all the Shakespeare that came to Ellensburg in my time. Some of this was ordinary, but much of it was superb—played by leading actors such as Frederick Warde, Ben Greet, Robert Mantell, and Sir Henry Irving. The plays I remember best were *Julius Caeser, The Merchant of Venice, Midsummer*

Night's Dream, and *Merry Wives of Windsor.* In addition to Shakespeare, Mother gave ground on such semireligious plays as *Quo Vadis* and *Ben Hur.* After I got to be big enough, I, in common with other adolescent louts around town, was often in demand as an extra for street scenes, mob scenes, and the like. This further removed the curse—because I was admitted free, might even be paid a quarter. I got to be a fairly proficient spear-bearer, street-rioter, beggar, or what you will.

I found it not too difficult as I grew older to push the theater doors apart oftener and oftener, and finally became a pretty regular attendant, but "nigger heaven," the topmost gallery in the house, was commonly my roost. It was the best I could afford most of the time. I wish I had kept a file of theater programs or a diary of theater attendance. Memory recaptures a great deal, but not as much as I would like. Among the plays I clearly recall having seen (and heard) as a boy in Ellensburg (in addition to those already mentioned) were: *The Rivals, The School for Scandal, She Stoops to Conquer, Rip Van Winkle, Way Down East, East Lynne, When Knighthood Was in Flower, The County Fair, Peter Pan, The Second Mrs. Tanquerary, The Old Homestead, The Playboy of the Western World, Shore Acres, The Great Divide, The Witching Hour, The Passing of the Second Floor Back,* and *Hedda Gabler.* The actors and actresses I most vividly remember were David Warfield, May Irwin, Richard Mansfield, Maude Adams, Mrs. Leslie Carter, John Drew, Chauncey Olcott, William Gillette, Nat Goodwin, Minnie Maddern Fiske, Willie Collier, Blanche Bates, May Robson, Julia Marlowe, and James K. Hackett.

Although my interest in the theater did not inspire any ambitions toward an acting career, attending so many productions of all sorts and qualities added much to my store of intellectual riches and also furnished me with many magnificent examples of the proper use of voice, gesture, posture, and physique on stage. By imitation, I learned how to convert some of those examples into assets for myself. Fortunate, indeed, is the boy who has good models to imitate, and I think mine were far better than the average for that era and possibly better than most youngsters have today.

Our family was not specially musical, yet I should not say that my musical education was wholly neglected. When I was about twelve years old my mother decided that it would be a nice social accomplishment if I could learn to play the guitar. Her deceased brother, Orval Collins, had been quite adept on this instrument, and she hoped I might do likewise. Mother bought a very good guitar and arranged for me to have lessons from a teacher who was a very competent professional. I was interested enough to cooperate quite readily, and for nearly two years I took lessons on the guitar. But I never became a good performer. I learned how to read music fairly well, learned how to play well enough to take part in group performances, and soloed once or twice in recitals; but I did not have any genuine musical talent. I had no desire to accomplish anything musically, not even entertain myself.

IV. TRANSITION

Back to Illinois

In my thirteenth year Mother decided to return to Illinois to live. She still spoke of Mt. Vernon as home, and had a feeling that things might work out better there, among her own folks, than in Ellensburg. Although she had prospered in the boarding house, and could have prospered even more, she got panicky about her health and came to the conclusion that running the boarding house was too hard for her. In a way it was, for, though Mother was able to hire and did hire enough help, she was not a good delegator. Having two women as helpers, instead of reducing, often increased her worries. Therefore, she was much attracted by a proposal from her youngest sister, Anna Collins, that Mother go in with her in the operation of a photographic studio. Anna had been a professional photographer for some years and was then employed in the leading studio in Mt. Vernon. But she was ambitious to have her own business and had learned of one that was for sale, at what seemed a bargain price, in the city of Urbana in northern Illinois.

Urbana and its twin municipality, Champaign, were the site of the University of Illinois, and this enhanced the prospect that a flourishing business in photography could be built up there. Not having enough capital to swing the deal alone, Aunt Anna proposed that she and Mother form a partnership, sharing alike in both the investment and the profits. Aunt Anna would take care of the technical side of the business and Mother would handle the commercial side. Mother was so eager to get out of the boarding house that she said yes without taking a second look. She thought the commercial side of a photographic business was essentially the same as the commercial side of the boarding house operation, and was certain it would be much easier on her health. I never knew how much money Mother put into this deal, but it must have been a substantial portion of her savings. The Balchen Studio, which she and Aunt Anna purchased, was located on the second floor of a pre-Civil War building in the heart of Urbana's business district, and the buyers had to take possession on July 1, 1903.

In March of that year Mother closed the boarding house, sold off most of her furnishings and equipment, packed the remainder for later shipment, and set off (with Aurel and me, of course) for Urbana, but she chose to go the long way around, via Denver and Pueblo, in Colorado, thence to St. Louis, Missouri, from there to Mt. Vernon, her home town, and from there on to Urbana. The reason for the roundabout trip was to visit relatives and friends. Naturally, Aurel and I were much excited about the trip. Once before we had been to Mt. Vernon and back, but that was ten years ago, when we were too young to remember much about it. Just the same, the thought of leaving Ellensburg for good was a little hard to take. The "Burg" had always been our home, and our best-loved kinfolks and friends lived there.

We were routed on the Northen Pacific Railway from Ellensburg to Billings, Montana, and from there on the Burlington Route to Denver. We went from Denver to Pueblo on the Denver and Rio Grande, took the Santa Fe from there to St. Louis, and then by Louisville and Nashville we went on to Mt. Vernon. The reason I remember this routing so clearly is that as a boy I almost lived and breathed railroads. Several of Mother's boarders were locomotive engineers or train conductors, and I loved to talk railroading with them. As much as I could I hung around the Northen Pacific depot and roundhouse, had the Northern Pacific trains and time-tables pretty well committed to memory, and knew where all the terminals and chief connections were located. Nothing could have fired my imagination more than this trip to Illinois over five or six different railroads.

Our reason for going to Denver was that Mother's sister Sally lived there. Sally had married a man named Walker W. Coffee, who was then employed as an express messenger on the Denver and Rio Grande Railroad. Aunt Sally was what Denver people in those days called a "lunger." Some years before, she had contracted tuberculosis, and she and her husband had moved to Denver in the hope that the high altitude and dry climate might benefit her health. There was a widely held medical theory at that time that "consumption," as it was then commonly called, was worsened, if not caused by climatic conditions. The Denver climate was supposed to be the most salubrious in the United States for "lungers," and thousands flocked there for the cure. Aunt Sally was temporarily benefited, though in her case the improvement did not result in a cure. She seemed to be on a rising curve at the time of our visit, and I remember her as a beautiful and adorable woman—the only blue-eyed blonde of the four Collins girls. Having no children of her own, she lavished great affection on Aurel and me. It seems that she was Mother's favorite sister and her husband Mother's favorite brother-in-law. Naturally, therefore, we had a wonderful time in Denver—went to all places of interest, saw some plays, and visited many friends and neighbors of Aunt Sally and Uncle Walker. Denver was the first big town I had been in since I was three years old and served as a great eye-opener for me. There I saw my first trolley car, my first automobile, and my first amusement park (Ellitch Gardens). I had read about such things but had never seen them with my own eyes. One day, shortly before our departure, Aunt Sally took Aurel and me to town on a shopping tour, saying she wanted to buy each of us a present to remember her by. She bought Aurel a lovely gold locket and me a gold ring, both suitably engraved. Both are now cherished as heirlooms in our family. Aunt Sally no doubt had a premonition that she would not win her fight against TB and wanted us children to have some keepsake gifts from her. We never visited her again, and about three years later she passed away.

Our stopover in Pueblo was one of the strangest episodes of my boyhood years. The people Mother visited there were friends she had made while living in the Methow country. They had left the Methow about the same time we did and had moved to the vicinity of Pueblo. "Vicinity" is putting it conservatively. The Dunkels (which was their name) had continued in the cattle business, and their present base of operations was a ranch way back in the mountains some forty miles from Pueblo. The nearest railway station was Graneros, but we had to detrain at Pueblo because there was no passenger service at the Graneros station. Jason Dunkel met us in Pueblo and drove us out to his ranch in a springless farm wagon. Mr. and Mrs. Dunkel had one child, a boy named Harry, who was three or four years my senior and much pleased to enlist me as a helper in his many cattleranch chores. We must have stayed there two or three weeks. I don't think Mother and Aurel had much fun, but I did. Harry let me ride with him in a cattle roundup, taught me how to "skin" a four-horse team, and put me on good terms with several Colorado natives of the genus burro.

The stop at St. Louis evokes only one sharp memory—the Union Station. This was the first structure of its kind I had ever seen, and, because I was something of a "sharpie" in railroad matters, I drank in everything I saw and put it on file in my repository of memories. My other recollection of the St.

Louis stop is that the people Mother visited there were named Smith and that they were people Mother had lived with or worked for, or both, just prior to her marriage. It seems that she was with the Smiths in St. Louis for several weeks or months and was home for a brief visit when my father returned to Mt. Vernon in the summer of 1889. The Smith's themselves have entirely faded from my memory.

To the best of my recollection, we reached Mt. Vernon some time in the early part of May, 1903. The plan was to stay with Grandma Collins, long a widow, and visit around among the many Maxey and Collins connections until the first of July, when Mother and Aunt Anna were to take possession of the studio in Urbana. Grandma Collins had a spacious and comfortable home in one of the better residential sections of Mt. Vernon. Following the death of her husband some twenty-five years earlier, she had sold the family farm and moved into Mt. Vernon, where she lived quite unpretentiously on a Civil War widow's pension and a moderate income from investments. Aunt Anna was her only child still living at home. After graduation from high school Aunt Anna had become an apprentice in a Mt. Vernon photographic studio and in that way had learned the relatively new profession of photography. Apprenticeship was the only means of learning that profession in those days. Aunt Anna had been a very precocious apprentice and now had a good position in one of the leading studios of Mt. Vernon. But, as I have already said, she wanted to be on her own and was so enthusiastic about the prospects at Urbana that she could hardly wait for the first of July to come. Neither could I, but for very different reasons.

We had not been long in Mt. Vernon when I became a problem child for my mother and all of her kith and kin that we had anything to do with. I was staging a rebellion, because for the first time in my life I was absolutely pinned down in a household of dear women who thought a boy's proper role in life was to behave like Little Lord Fauntleroy. For several years I had been living as un-Fauntleroy a kind of life as a boy could, and now I was imprisoned with Fauntleroy admirers as my jailers. There was no chance for me to break out of this prison, even for an hour or two at a time. I knew no boys my age in Mt. Vernon and had no chance to meet any. None of the many relatives and friends we visited had children of the right age. In Ellensburg, even when Mother tried to be hardboiled, there had been many outlets—school, chores, and kids waiting in the street or alley if perchance I could sneak away, which I often could. Now, in my early adolescence, I was penned up in a house with nothing to do, nothing to read that interested me at all, no games of any kind—just blank boredom day after day. My dear jailers were just as sweet to me as they knew how, and I was just as nasty as I knew how. Things finally came to such a pass that it was decided to send me into exile.

Mother's sister Lela and husband, Jesse Davis, were then living on a small farm four or five miles north of Urbana. It was through them, I believe, that Aunt Anna first learned that the Balchen Studio was for sale. The Davises were a childless couple who must have had no idea what it would mean to have a thirteen-year-old nephew around the place. Since all the arrangements were made without consulting me, I never knew what sort of understanding—or misunderstanding—was reached between them and my mother. I had the impression that I was to be more or less a guest of the Davises until the first of July, but the Davises had the notion that I was going to work for my board and room. Anyhow, around the end of May I was shipped off, via Illinois Central, to Urbana and the Davis farm, which proved to be about a fifty-acre corn-hog factory run somewhat as a sideline by Uncle Jesse, who was a carpenter by trade. I was pleased to go along with the deal, because I imagined nothing could be worse than Mt. Vernon and the Davis farm might be fun. That's where imagination played me false. The Davis farm proved to be an even more dismal prison than the Collins home in Mt. Vernon.

The Davises were solid, sincere, working people who had no children of their own and never, so far as I could ascertain, had had anything to do with children at all. They had no conception of what a boy of my age and rearing would like or dislike, and not enough imagination to care. They thought like peasants, worked like peasants, never had company, never went visiting, had no amusements, possessed no books, had no other reading material in the house (save mail-order catalogs), went to town only when absolutely necessary, and never even could find time to attend church on Sunday, though they deemed themselves religious people. From the first, their chief interest in me (as I saw it) was to get twelve hours of work out of me each day. I don't think I was any more or less lazy than most boys of thirteen, and I had done a good deal of manual labor for a lad of my years, but I just did not cotton to the idea of pulling weeds and swinging a hoe from dawn till dark.

So I became a bad boy again—sulked, dragged my heels, and slighted my work at every opportunity. When my aunt and uncle scolded me, I defied them. I was too big and tough to spank, so after a considerable amount of jawing back and forth, we settled on a sort of armed truce under which they put up with me and I with them until the first of July, when Mother and Aunt Anna arrived to take over the Balchen Studio. Mother's original intention had been that I would stay with the Davises until the opening of school in September, as this would give her time to find a house and get settled in Urbana. But when she heard what the Davises had to say about me, she knew that she had to get me out of their hair right away. This led to another makeshift in connection with which I continued to be a bad boy.

The Balchen Studio was located on the second floor of a decrepit downtown business building. Immediately underneath was an odoriferous Greek restaurant, from which the most variegated cooking smells ascended day and night. The studio consisted of three main rooms and several smaller ones. At the front, leading off the stairway from the street, was a large reception and display room; next came a combination work-and-stock-room; then came the dressing room, in which the customers did their primping before being "shot." At the rear was a skylighted gallery, where the shooting was done, and adjacent to it was the dark room, where the developing was done. A few small closets and cubbyholes completed the ensemble. There was no indoor plumbing and no running water, except in the dark room. Heating was supplied by hard-coal stoves in all three of the major rooms, though, of course, we had no need of these in July. To respond to the calls of nature, we had to go down an open stairway to a double privy at the back of the lot. This facility we shared with the proprietors and customers of the restaurant.

As a means of economy, Mother and Aunt Anna decided that the studio should serve not only as a place of business but as a residence for the four of us until such a time as other suitable housing could be found. They had it all figured out. Breakfasts would be prepared on a gasoline stove in the gallery; also other meals, as feasible; but if business interfered with meal preparation, there was an arrangement to have meals sent up from the restaurant below. Folding cots were obtained for beds, and Aunt Anna took the gallery for her bedroom while Mother, Aurel and I bivouaced in the reception room. Every morning, the first chore was to store the beds and bedding out of sight, then snatch a quick breakfast, and wait for business. This arrangement might have worked if there had been just the two adults, but with a boy of thirteen and a girl of eleven who had nothing to do but reel off time, it was impossible. I was more of a problem than Aurel, because there were little duties she could take on. She could be a sweet little receptionist and she could help out in the stock-room, but for a lummox like me there was nothing but ghastly idleness and loneliness.

If I happened to be in the studio when customers came in, it was up to me to make myself scarce immediately, and there were only two ways of doing this. One was to duck into the stock-room and hole up there until the coast was clear. The other was to go out and tramp the streets of Urbana and Champaign until I judged it safe to return. I would not have minded trudging the streets, for I had become quite accomplished at that in Ellensburg, but in Urbana and Champaign I was a total stranger. It was midsummer; the schools were closed; there were no public recreational facilities for kids my age—in short, there was simply no way of making contact with anybody my age. I might as well have been marooned on a desert island. At the studio there was nothing for me to read, and there was no public library or reading room that I could frequent. So I turned mean again, and I imagine my behavior was pretty beastly, because Mother became sort of frantic. There was no way she could punish or control me.

I don't know whether things would have worked out differently if the studio had made money, but it was soon evident that it would be a long time before it would support two families. The Balchen Studio was badly run down, probably had been losing money for a long time. Summer is always a dull time in the photography business, and the summer of 1903 was more than dull for the Collins Studio, its successor. There was hardly any business at all. How much of Mother's savings had gone into the purchase of the studio, I don't know, but I know she did not have enough left to carry us very long. Something had to give, and did. By mutual agreement between the partners, Mother stepped out. Aunt Anna did not have the means to pay cash, and I am not sure just how that aspect of the settlement was finally worked out. When Aunt Anna became sole proprietor, Grandma Collins decided to come to Urbana to live. She sold out in Mt. Vernon and purchased a home in Urbana. Whether she gave Aunt Anna any financial assistance, I never knew; but Aunt Anna survived two or three lean years and eventually developed the studio into a paying concern.

Back to Ellensburg

Now that there was no future for Mother in Urbana, she must have decided that Ellensburg had attractions after all. All of a sudden one day she asked Aurel and me how we would feel if she should remarry. We had no answer, because we had never thought of such a thing. So far as we knew, she had no fiance—had not even been keeping company with any gentleman of our acquaintance in Ellensburg or elsewhere. Then she told us that one of her former boarders, Mr. W. F. Doughty, had several times asked her to marry him, but she had put him off by saying she was not sure. Now she was thinking of accepting his proposal, but wanted us to approve. Both of us knew Mr. Doughty, though less well than most of the other boarders. He was a reserved and taciturn man, and had never made any attempt to get on friendly terms with us. We neither liked nor disliked him, but at the moment there was one strong point in his favor. If Mother should marry him, we would return to Ellensburg post haste, and that we wanted above all else. We were aware, of course, that Mr. Doughty was one of Ellensburg's leading business men. He owned and operated an ice and fuel business, also drayage concern, and had extensive farming interests besides. He was reputed to be rich, and by Ellensburg standards I suppose he was.

Though she would never admit it, I always thought that one reason Mother decided to remarry was the thought that I would be easier to manage if I had a firm step-father to keep me in line. If not that, at least she thought I might be more amenable to reason in Ellensburg than anywhere else. At any rate, around the first of September, 1903, we were back in Ellensburg. One Sunday evening after church services the Methodist minister came to Grandpa Maxey's home and there performed the ceremony which made Mother Mrs. Doughty for the remainder of her life. Immediately we moved into a rented house on Anderson Street just across from the public school. In a way, for us children, this was a good deal like getting back home again, for the house was largely furnished with articles which Mother had left in storage, and about the only new thing was our stepfather.

For me, however, more I think than for Aurel, it was also like stepping into a new world, because I had the problem of adjustment with a stepfather who was an unusually hard man to get to know. Aurel made the adjustment much more readily than I, because she had a more outgoing disposition than I. In retrospect I realize that the adjustment probably was just as difficult for Mr. Doughty as for me. He was a "no nonsense" type of fellow who had never had anything to do with youngsters and had not the faintest idea how to talk my language. I had been without a father since I was a boy of seven and saw no need of having one now. Besides, I had reached the age at which all boys tend toward insubordination. I could think of no reason why I should try to ingratiate myself with Mr. Doughty and gave him the silent treatment as much as possible. He did the same with me. We never quarreled, but we never found a common ground to stand on. Not until I was a grown man, with children of my own, and something of a success in worldly achievement, did Mr. Doughty and I come to be good friends.

With the opening of school in 1903, I entered the eighth grade. I had missed nearly a year of school on account of our Illinois safari, but the school authorities thought my past record good enough to risk letting me try the eighth grade without finishing the seventh. I found this easy to do. The teacher of the eighth grade, Mrs. Clara Greening, thought she saw academic possibilities in me and gave me special attention. She did not need to urge me to go on to high school, for my mind was already made up on that. But she did give me encouragement to believe that I could do well, not only in high school, but in college, too, if I had the ambition to go that far. Dimly and inarticulately, an ambition was growing in my mind—an ambition to be a professional man of some sort, a lawyer, a doctor, a teacher, or even perchance a minister.

V. TOWARDS HIGHER EDUCATION

High School Student

My stepfather thought and said that it would be a waste of time for me to go to high school. He thought the eighth grade was enough. If you were literate and well trained in arithmetic, that was all you needed for success in the business world. It was all he had; in fact, he had not even finished the eighth grade, and hence could not imagine any job I was not well enough educated to handle successfully. He was ready to put me to work in his own business and help me get a good start in the world. Naturally, when I refused, he felt rebuffed and unappreciated.

My mind had been made up for a long time that I was going to high school, and further if possible. Mr. Doughty's opinion to the contrary merely made me more bullheaded. We might have had a showdown on the matter if Mother had not very tactfully smoothed things out while at the same time taking my side. The younger Collins children (Orval, Sally, and Anna) all had graduated from high school, and Mother was quite proud of them. She wanted me to do as well, but I do not believe she ever looked upon high school as preparation for college. Mr. Doughty yielded gracefully, but I think he was of the same opinion still—that high school was all damned foolishness.

So, in September, 1904, I enrolled as a freshman in the Ellensburg High School, which had just been stepped up from a two-year to a four-year school and was busting its belt striving for accreditation by the state university and the state department of education. Going on to the Ellensburg High School on the surface did not appear to make any great changes in my way of life. I continued to go to school in the same building as before and have many of the same associations as before. The high school occupied most of the top floor of the one public school building in the town, but had a separate faculty and separate classrooms. Altogether there were about fifty students —approximately twenty-five freshmen, fifteen sophomores, ten juniors, and no seniors (because nobody had yet gone that far). We represented about 10 per cent of the total enrollment in the Ellensburg public school system—the fortunate few who were going to have a chance to prove ourselves equal to something more than the Three R's. It did not take me long to make the discovery that high school was going to be a bigger intellectual adventure than anything I had previously experienced. For the first time I was taking subjects which seemed to have boundless outer dimensions.

At the turn of the century there were few differences of

opinion as to the rightful function of a high school and no differences at all as to the subjects which should be taught. Everybody was supposed to understand, and it was taken for granted that everybody did understand that the sole business of a high school was to prepare students for college. Therefore, the high school curriculum bore down most heavily on those subjects which were required for college entrance. At the turn of the century this meant classics, modern languages, mathematics, science, English, and history. A high school which conducted a successful four-year course of instruction in those basic fields would be accredited by the state university and the state department of education, and this was an accolade that every high school sought. Ellensburg was determined to have it just as soon as possible, and so made an extra effort to set up a curriculum and hire a faculty that would meet the most critical standards.

So there is really nothing remarkable about the fact that the Ellensburg High School put me through four years of Latin, two years of German, four years of English, three and a half years of mathematics, three years of science, and four years of history. To have done less would have been to fall down on its job. But what is remarkable is the way in which the job was done. The high school faculty, for an enrollment that started at about fifty and never in my four years exceeded a hundred, consisted of one part-time and five full-time teachers. This meant that all classes were small, which was a great advantage to groping kids like myself. But a far greater advantage was the quality of the teachers, all of whom were good and some of whom were as good as any teachers I have known at any level of education. In those long departed days any college graduate could teach in high school without the necessity of taking a lot of special methods and teacher training courses. He did not even have to be certified as competent in a particular subject field, nor was he required to be a resident of the State of Washington or given any favors because he was a graduate of a Washington institution. In other words, the whole United States could serve as an unrestricted recruiting ground for faculty talent. The Ellensburg school board took full advantage of that opportunity. First, they appointed as superintendent of schools a Wisconsin man named J. W. Nesbit, and gave him a free hand in choosing teachers. Nesbit was an exceptional school man. Educated and long experienced in the great Wisconsin system, he brought to Ellensburg the kind of standards few frontier towns could boast, and he insisted that those standards be met and maintained. Moreover, he set an example by teaching alongside the people he supervised. Nesbit taught all of the history courses offered in the high school, and I took them all. I never had a better history teacher, either in college or in graduate school.

Nesbit ranged far and wide to find good teachers, and was successful. Every teacher that I had in the Ellensburg High School I would still rate as superior and several of them I would give top rating in any company. In the latter category, as I have already said, I would include Nesbit himself; and I would also accord the same high rank to Lulu M. Craig, who taught Latin; George M. Jenkins, who taught mathematics; and Heber H. Ryan, who taught German. The excellent teaching certainly helped keep me on my toes through all my four years in high school. I was deeply interested in every course I took and worked my head off for the sheer joy of it. None of the work was hard, but I was too interested to slough off and loaf. At the end of the four years I stood at the head of my class and was chosen valedictorian.

Save to point out a few contrasts between then and now, I am not going to enlarge upon characteristics of the Ellensburg High School from 1904-1908. In any modern official evaluation, it would be downgraded to the bottom of the list for one reason alone. It had no library whatever. In the study hall there was one copy of Webster's *Unabridged Dictionary* and one set of the *Encyclopedia Americana*. This was the sum total of the high school library, and I will say this much for it: it got a real workout every day. It is amazing how much can be learned from a few good reference works if the desire is there.

Our little old Ellensburg High School would be similarly ostracized today for its total lack of science laboratories or equipment. In one classroom there were two tables which could be used for demonstration and experiments, but equipment was limited to one small microscope, a pair of scales, and a few handpump burners. Any other equipment we wanted, we made ourselves or did not get at all. In my senior year a group of us decided we would like to study chemistry. We persuaded the school board to allow us to use a room in the attic, where we put in our own benches, supplied our own test tubes and other materials and supplies, bought our own textbooks and notebooks, and put up the money to rent pieces of apparatus we could not afford to buy. Believe me, we did our best to get value in return for our investment in that course.

There was no paternalism in those rugged days. No board of education or other school officer in Ellensburg ever gave me a handout in the shape of free textbooks, free equipment, or free supplies for any course of study that I took in the whole four years. From my own earnings, summer earnings mainly, I paid for every book, every sheet of paper, every drop of ink, every pencil, and every item of scientific material that I used. I was glad to do it then, and in retrospect I am glad that I had to do it. Every book that I bought became a prized personal possession, which I kept and read over again and again. I carried most of my high school textbooks to college with me and used them to brush up on fundamentals that had slipped my mind. Having few other books at hand, I thoroughly digested my high school textbooks, and I underscored lines, wrote in marginal comments, and otherwise desecrated the printed page as I wished. I have managed to hang on to several of those high school books and have them in my library today. As I page through them from time to time, I can retrace in sharp detail some of the most important phases of my educational development. For my money, free textbooks are for the birds, not for serious students who want all there is to get from an educational experience.

In the spring of 1904 Mr. Doughty and Mother built the house in the seven hundred block of East Fifth Street which was to be our home for the next twenty-five years or more. Perhaps I should have said it was to be the Doughty home rather than "our" home. I lived there only three and a half years, not count-ing summer vacations, and I never did get the feeling that it was an anchorage for me. It was, in 1904, an up-to-date house with most of the modern conveniences except central heating. There was still a large distrust of central heating on the ground that it was both inefficient and unduly expensive. The very latest in electric lighting was installed, and the reader will recognize how late that was by the fact that there were no wall switches or baseboard outlets, the two-bulb chandeliers were installed in the parlor and dining rooms and single drop lights in every other room. I was given a room of my own—the back bedroom, in fact— and I tried to fix it up to serve as a study as well as a bedroom. This worked pretty well in warm weather, but in wintertime it was cold as Greenland because there was no stove in my room. Aurel's room was equally cold for the same reason. So we two did most of our homework on the dining room table under the pallid illumination of the overhead chandelier. Since the dining room also served as a living room in cold weather, the parlor being curtained off, all of our study was done while the family chatter went on around us. This did not bother me much and perhaps helped me form the habit of not letting interruptions throw me off the track. In later life I seemed to have developed a multi-cylindered mind, which enabled me to deal with an interruption in one cylinder while the others went on with other things that I might be doing.

In the spring of 1905 my mother underwent surgery for a prolapsed uterus, a mechanical job which now is almost as routine as setting a broken bone. Perhaps the mechanics were as well understood then as now, but surgery of any kind then was attended with risks that are now scarcely imaginable. There was no hospital or other professionally equipped surgery in Ellensburg in 1905. Nor was there a specialized surgeon or an anesthetist of any kind. Mother's surgery was performed by our family physician, a general practitioner who had never performed such an operation before. The operation took place in our own home and our dining room table was used as the operating table. The anesthetic was administered by one of our neighbors who was a druggist and, therefore, presumed to know all about chloroform. The surgeon knew enough about asepsis to sterilize his instruments and wash his hands, but did not use rubber gloves or wear a face mask or hair cover. In fact, as I recall the detail, he wore a morning coat with striped trousers and a hardboiled shirt with detachable cuffs. Nevertheless, he did a good enough job, mechanically, so that Mother never again was bothered with any uterine prolapsus.

But something went wrong, and I don't pretend to know what it was. It could have been shock, aftermath of improper anesthesia, bedside infection, or a combination of these and other causes. What I do remember most unforgettably is that three serious complications set in. One was uremic poisoning, another was heart spasms, and the third was some kind of skin infection. As a result, Mother was deperately ill for several weeks, had to have nurses and doctors around the clock, and when she finally did pull through was left in a state of mind which caused her to be an invalid the rest of her life. From the time of her operation in 1905 until her death in 1953, Mother never knew a day in which she would admit that she felt well, and much of the time she was confined to her bed or was an ambulatory patient. I would not even try to guess the amount of time and money she spent in sanatoriums, hospitals, and nursing homes.

Mother's invalidism set the pattern of my home life until I finished high school and left home. She insisted on absolute quiet, could not be disturbed by company of any kind, and had to be waited on much of the time. That meant that Aurel and I could have no social life at home—could not even be boisterous and noisy between ourselves. The only real social life we had was away from home—at school, at church, or at the homes of kinfolk and friends. These circumstances should suffice to explain why the death of my sister in September, 1907, was almost more than I could take. There had alway been a close bond of affection and understanding between us, and Mother's invalidism had brought us even closer. Now she was in her second year in high school and I was beginning my fourth. We were looking forward to a wonderful year, because Mother was able to get along without special nurses, and we had a good housekeeper. Aurel seemed to be in excellent health, but was suddenly stricken with what was first diagnosed as typhoid fever but proved to be meningitis. She was ill about ten days and in a coma the last three or four, which made the situation ever harder to bear.

My final year in high school was darkened not only by Aurel's death but also by that of Tom Murray, one of my closest school friends. Tom was shot to death while in bed asleep, by a foster mother who was later adjudged insane. He was an end on the football team and I was the quarterback. We were roommates on trips, were in many of the same classes, and often attended the same school parties. Tom's funeral was the first at which I was asked to perform the sad and traditional function of pall-bearer. I have lost count of the number of times since then that I have served in that capacity. I went through all of the expected motions that year, did everything I was supposed to do, but paid the penalty in coming close to a physical collapse just before graduation. However, when summer came, and I started swinging a pick and shovel ten hours a day, my physique bounced back and my ailments promptly vanished.

Student Activities

When I entered the Ellensburg High School as a freshman, there was no program of student activities, athletic or otherwise. One reason we had no athletic teams was that the school had no athletic facilities—no gymnasium, no playing fields, no athletic equipment, and no athletic coaches. In my second year some of us thought we would like to have a football team, so we chipped in about five dollars apiece and bought a football and enough uniforms for each man. We were allowed to practise on the school grounds and dress and undress in the furnace room of the school building, but there were no showers, tubs, or other bathing facilities. We had no coach, but bought a rule book, elected a captain, and solved our problems by the symposium method. The only games we played were between two teams chosen among ourselves. Sometimes we did not have enough men for two teams, and then one or more men would do double duty, playing the same position for both sides.

In my junior year the school authorities rewarded our zeal by hiring an athletic coach. In the fall of 1906, Heber H. Ryan, a recent graduate of Whitman College, was employed by the Ellensburg High School to teach mathematics and German and coach athletics. A little money for equipment was provided and we arranged to practice on the town's baseball field. We fielded a football team that fall, and played games against teams representing the Normal School, the Yakima High School, the Sunnyside High School, and the Prosser High School. We did not try to field a basketball team, because we had no floor on which to play. In the spring of 1907, however, we went in for baseball in a big way and put out a crackerjack team. In those days, every boy, by the time he reached high school age, was a seasoned baseball player.

My athletic career was limited to football. I tried out for pitcher and first baseman on the baseball team, but was not good enough to make the grade. In football I held down the position of quarterback for two years. My chief value to the team was calling the signals and doing the short kicks, of which there were several at that time. I never was much of a ball carrier, but I did have a fairly well educated toe and could remember the signals better than any man on the squad. This was in the old, old days, before the forward pass, when we had three downs to make five yards and the onside kick and the drop kick were strong offensive weapons. I had fun playing football, got some good experience in the give-and-take of rough physical contact, and made a number of close friends, one of whom was the coach, Heber Ryan.

The high school faculty thought it desirable to foster student interest in dramatics and forensics, and a member of the faculty was assigned to supervise each of these activities. I found myself more gifted in these fields than in athletics. I had parts in several plays, and in two or three I had one of the "leads." None were plays that made great demands on one's histrionic potential, but all gave me some profitable experience in handling myself before an audience. It was in forensics (debate and oratory) that I had my greatest success. A statewide program of inter-scholastic debates had been inaugurated under the sponsorship of the state department of education, and the Ellensburg High School was invited to participate. Debate try-outs were conducted by members of the faculty and I landed a place on one of the teams, and after a round of elimination contests I wound up as leader of the first team. Oratorical and declamation contests for high schools were sponsored each year by the University of Washington, Washington State College, and Whitman College. Ellensburg was invited to send a representative to each of these. In my junior and senior high school years I was Ellensburg's representative in all three of these contests.

A statewide debating program was conducted by districts, on a round robin plan. In my junior year we debated the subject of capital punishment, and Ellensburg was eliminated by Yakima in the first go-round. In my senior year, on the question of the initiative and referendum, we defeated every school in Eastern Washington except Spokane, and we and Spokane fought it out in the semi-finals to determine which would oppose the winner on the west side of the state. Spokane had only one high school then, but it was about ten times larger than our tiny Ellensburg School, so we went into the contest feeling that it was a David and Goliath affair. But the judges did not seem to be impressed by this aspect of the debate. They decided that Goliath did the better job of arguing, so Ellensburg lost its shot at the state championship. But we had gone further than most Ellensburg people thought we could, so we were patted on the back by the local citizenry and praised for putting our town in the limelight. Regardless of the win-loss record, high school debating was a grand experience for me in several ways. Not only did I learn a great deal about forensic argumentation and get a great deal of beneficial experience in impromptu speaking, I got to travel a little and made friends in other towns than Ellensburg.

The oratorical contests in which I participated actually were declamation contests. Original orations were not permitted. Each competitor was required to memorize and recite a famous oration of the past. Patrick Henry's "Give Me Liberty or Give Me Death" was one of the favorites, though I personally never used it. I won first place in the tri-state declamation contest held under the sponsorship of Whitman College on May 2, 1907. My selection was part of an oration delivered in the English House of Commons by the great Irish orator, Henry Grattan, and my prize award was a gold medal, which I still have. In 1908, my senior high school year, I used Henry Ward Beecher's oration on the effect of the death of Lincoln, and participated in contests at Washington State and the University of Washington. I was an also-ran at the University of Washington, but at Washington State I won third place and a medal (bronze), which I also still possess.

Choosing a College

My football, my forensics, and my class ranking had results I did not foresee. In Ellensburg, naturally, I became a momentary hero, and had many nice things said about me and done for me. But I had not anticipated that these things would gain me any repute outside my home town. In fact I did not realize that anybody outside Ellensburg had an eye on me until I began to receive letters and then personal visits from college and university recruiting officers. This was flattering, but also confusing. My mind had long been made up on going to college. If I could possibly manage it, I was going. I knew I could manage two years in the Normal School, just as I had managed four in the high school, and several of the Normal School professors urged me to register there. As a last resort, I would have done so, because graduation from the Normal School would have insured me a teaching job by means of which I could have made the money to finish my education. But I preferred, if possible, to go to a four-year institution and thence on to a professional school, perhaps.

I just about decided that the University of Washington would be the right place for me. Several of my Ellensburg friends were already there and more were planning to go. Prospects of getting a job to help defray my expenses were excellent in Seattle, and I had met several members of the University faculty who assured me of their willingness to help me get established and make the right connections. It never occurred to me that Whitman College might have designs on me and would be ready to back those designs with money on the barrel head. The only Whitman graduate I knew was Heber Ryan, and I was tremendously fond of him. Heber talked Whitman to me, but did not try to exert any pressure. I had met President Penrose on one or two occasions and he had been very cordial. I had also met Professor Bratton when he served as judge for one of our regional debates, and Professor W. D. Lyman had called at my home on one occasion when he happened to be in Ellensburg. So I had a favorable impression of Whitman, just as I had of the University of Washington, but I thought my chances of making my own way would be better at the University. Then, one day in late May, 1908, I received a letter from Whitman College offering me a four-year full-tuition scholarship. I was flattered by this, but it was not enough to tip the scale in favor of Whitman; it merely put Whitman on a par with the University of Washington. At both places, in order to defray my living expenses, I would need part-time employment. So my reply to Whitman was a sincere thank-you for the honor scholarship award and an expression of regret that it would not be enough to enable me to attend Whitman unless I could find sufficiently remunerative employment. Almost immediately I had a letter back from Whitman offering me a job on the campus in the employ of the College itself. Since I had not yet found a job at the University, this offer put Whitman ahead in the bidding. Recalling the addage that the bird in hand is better than two in the bush, and having a genuine liking for the Whitman campus and the Whitman people I had met, I replied accepting the Whitman offer. Thus I came to choose Whitman as my alma mater, perhaps the most important decision of my life.

For more than two years I had been saving money for college expenses and had about $200 in gold stashed away. In 1908 that was no petty sum of cash. Yet it was far from enough to see me through four years of college. Even by supplementing my savings with good summer earnings, it looked as though I would have to earn upwards of fifteen dollars a month to break even. The Whitman campus job assured me of that for one year. Economic conditions were precarious in 1908, and everybody was wondering what next. In the fall and winter of 1907 there had been a sharp and severe depression accompanied by a banking fiasco which resulted in panic. Money disappeared from circulation, and there were prolonged periods when our only currency was depreciated bank scrip. My hoard was in gold coins—half-eagles ($5.), eagles ($10.), and double eagles ($20.). This I had secreted in a money belt which I wore on my person or hid away in my room. If I spent any of my gold, I would have to take depreciated scrip in exchange. So I held on to my gold and got through the year on credit, spending no cash until specie payments were resumed.

The foregoing may hint that I was a pretty hardfisted operator, and I suppose I was. But I had come by my money the hard way, and I did not propose to let it slip through my fingers carelessly or be cheated out of it. From the time I was fourteen I had worked every summer for top wages, namely, fifteen to twenty-five cents an hour for a ten-hour day, and I had saved much of what I made. Two summers I worked in the hay harvest; one summer I worked as an airbrake repair man at the Northern Pacific roundhouse and one summer I did pick and shovel work for a local cement contractor. I did not pay for board and room at home, but neither was I compensated for helping out on Saturdays in Mr. Doughty's business, bucking all the coal and wood necessary to stoke the insatiable stoves in our home, and running all the errands my mother had to ask me to do. Out of my own funds I bought all of my own clothing, all of my own school books and supplies, paid for all the newspapers and magazines that came into the house, and made all the contributions that the Doughty household made to the church and other charities. So I thought the score was about even.

The Chester Maxey who left Ellensburg in mid-September, 1908, to enroll in Whitman College was, I think, fairly well prepared, for he had all the credits required and several to spare.

He had learned how to study, and he had learned how to use the English language in both spoken and written discourse. Nor was he poorly prepared psychologically for the adjustments he would have to make in the course of his college years. He had learned, in his first eighteen years, a great deal about life and death, for he had a considerable variety of direct contacts with both. Though not a physical giant, he had been toughened by athletic activity and a large and consistent amount of hard manual labor every day of his life. He was seldom ill and seemed to have a high resistance to all kinds of infections. And he was filled with ambition to succeed. He was not yet clear as to what kind of success he wanted most, but he had a positive aversion to failure.

PART II

WHITMAN COLLEGE, 1908-1912

VI. FRESHMAN

Making a Start

To travel from Ellensburg to Walla Walla in 1908, one had to take the main line of the Northern Pacific to Pasco and there transfer to the branch line which ran from Pasco to Walla Walla. To make this connection, it was necessary to leave Ellensburg about 1 A.M. It was about a six-hour ride to Pasco and another two from there to Walla Walla. Having made this trip at least twice before, I knew what to expect.

During the summer I provided myself with a trunk large enough to contain the major articles I would need for the year. In addition, I bought two cardboard suitcases for hand luggage. On September 15, I had my trunk hauled to the depot and checked through to Walla Walla. I was too excited to sleep, so I sat up until train time. About a half hour before the train was due, I awakened my mother and stepfather, bade them goodbye, grabbed a suitcase in each hand, and hiked to the Northern Pacific depot, a distance of more than a mile. Why not a taxi? There were no such things in Ellensburg as yet. Why not a rig from the livery stable? There was no way to get it back to the stable after the train pulled out, unless someone went with me to the station, and there was no one I could conveniently call upon. Why not one of the Doughty rigs? I was feeling my independence very strongly just then and was not calling on my stepfather for any favors. Furthermore, why shouldn't I walk? I wasn't afraid of the dark, did not expect to encounter any thugs, and was perfectly able to lug two suitcases a mile, and more if need be, without taking a deep breath. I had been working for a cement contractor all summer, and lifting hundred-pound sacks of cement and pushing wheelbarrow loads of gravel had left me tough as a Chinese coolie.

I piled my luggage on the train and sat up in the day coach all the way to Walla Walla. There was a sleeping car in which I

105

could have had a berth, but I was not about to indulge in any such luxuries as that. By advance correspondence I had reserved a room at Billings Hall, then the brand new dormitory for men. Also, through previous correspondence with Otto Johnson, student chairman of the Y.M.C.A. welcoming committee, I knew I would be met at the station. Anxious to make a sharp impression and show that an Ellensburg boy knew what was what, I had arrayed myself in the most fashionable garb I possessed—an ensemble consisting of a derby hat, a wasp-waisted jacket, a white vest, peg-top trousers, a fried shirt, a wing collar, an ascot tie, and patent leather shoes. Thus exhibiting myself as a mould of form and glass of fashion, I descended from the train at the old Northern Pacific depot at the corner of Palouse and Main in Walla Walla. I was met by Otto and a delegation of Whitman greeters, and, after the customary amenities had been observed, I was told how to get to Billings Hall, which I already knew. Then the Ellensburg dude latched on to his suitcases and hied his way east on Boyer Avenue to the campus and Billings Hall.

Upon arriving at Billings, I discovered that I had been assigned to a room with Loren Dumas, a third year student in Pearsons Academy. This, I was informed, was but a temporary arrangement, as it was not the College policy for students of collegiate grade to room with Academy students. At the depot I had given my trunk check to a transfer man who was to deliver it at Billings later in the day. Pending the arrival of my trunk, there was little I could do to get settled, so I went over to the Whitman Memorial Building to see if I could do anything about getting registered and find out something about the job which the College had assigned to me.

Professor Bratton was in charge of registration, and he was no stranger. I had met him in Ellensburg the year before. This made the registration process easy. I doubt if Professor Bratton and I spent ten minutes lining up my courses for the year. There was nothing much to discuss. I took the prescribed courses, and that was that. These included a fifth year of Latin, a third year of German, one year of college mathematics, a year of English composition, and a year of Bible. I was also required to take two years of physical education. As an elective I chose Greek, because I wanted to know more than one ancient language. I did not object to the mandatory character of the curriculum. It had been that way all through high school, and seemed to me quite normal.

Then I found out about my job. Professor Bratton explained that I was to serve as fireman at Prentiss Hall (predecessor of the present building of that name), and that I was expected to begin work at once. Old Prentiss Hall occupied the site of the present Conservatory of Music. It was a rambling two-story frame structure which had been born of a *mésalliance* of the original Whitman Seminary Building and the original Ladies Hall. By a none too graceful job of carpentry, these two had been joined together to form an enlarged dormitory for women. In the fall of 1908 it housed some thirty girls. Since there was no central heating, each room was equipped with a wood-burning heating stove. Hot water was supplied to a bathroom on each floor from a basement tank heated by coils installed in a small coal-burning furnace. The College supplied all the fuel, and my job was to stoke the hot-water furnace and see that the woodboxes on each floor were kept supplied with enough wood and kindling to keep some fifteen stoves going around the clock.

The coal gave me less trouble than the wood. My chief task was to feed it into the furnace and carry out the ashes, but I had not been on the job long before I began to wonder if all the fires of hell would be enough to keep those dames in hot water. It seemed that no matter how much or how often I stoked the heater, they were always yelling for more hot water. But the wood and kindling really gave me a tussle. The stove fuel was slab wood sawed to fourteen-inch lengths. I had to split it to stove size and carry it from the basement to the ever-hungry woodboxes on the first and second floors. In addition, I had to cut and carry up enough kindling wood to supply the daily needs of each stove. One of the most consistent habits of the Prentiss Hall gals was to let their fire die down again and again throughout the day, and then toss in a batch of kindling to get them started again. I could never make the supply meet the demand.

The kind and quantity of the labor required of me at Prentiss Hall did not worry me a bit. Ever since I could remember, I had been doing that kind of work. As a hewer and carrier of stove wood and kindling, I was sure I could hold my own in any company. Where I grossly miscalculated, and the College did as well, was in figuring the amount of time that would be required to handle that job properly. It was supposed to be a part-time job, for which I was to receive the then handsome emolument of $15 a month, credited against my board and room bills at Billings Hall. And the emolument would have been handsome if the job had been really part-time. The College estimated that I ought to be able to do the work in about three hours a day, which, at the going rate of 20¢ an hour for student labor would come to about $15 a month. I may have been a slow worker, but I don't believe a much faster worker than I could have kept thirty girls and fifteen stoves fully supplied with hot water and fuel in less than six to eight hours a day, depending on the weather. There is no faster burning solid fuel than slab wood. No matter how much I bucked upstairs during the day, it was seldom enough to carry through the night, and it would have taken a 200-gallon instead of a 40-gallon tank to keep those girls from exhausting the hot water supply several times a day.

But none of this was apparent to me on that 16th day of September, 1908, when I was getting registered and settled for my first year at Whitman. After getting lined up for my job, I returned to Billings, got acquainted with Loren Dumas, and we both went to work unpacking and putting things in order in our room. Even though we both knew we would not be left together very long, we had to go through the motions of settling down for keeps. It might be several days, even weeks, before the authorities got the rooms and roommates sorted out as they desired. Since Loren's being an Academy student was the reason we could not be permanent roommates, this seems as good a place as any to say a word about Pearsons Academy. It was the successor of the Whitman Academy, which was the lineal descendant of the original Whitman Seminary. The Seminary was raised to collegiate status by the amended charter of 1883, but at that time and for many years thereafter there were so few four-year high schools in the Pacific Northwest that it was necessary for the newly born college to maintain a preparatory department. Shortly before I entered Whitman, this preparatory school had been rechristened Pearsons Academy in honor of Dr. D. K. Pearsons of Chicago a generous benefactor of the College. One of my duties as a scholarship student was to act as a study hall proctor in Pearsons Academy. In my freshman year the Pearsons study hall was located on the top floor of the Whitman Memorial Building in the room later used for mechanical drawing and after that, for several years, for the Museum of Northwest History. By my time, however, four-year high schools were multiplying so rapidly that Pearsons was soon to run out of enrollment. For that reason, it was discontinued in 1912.

After a week or less with Loren, I was assigned to a room with Paul Brainard, a senior in the College. I am sure that this change of roommates was an important factor in my freshman adjustment at Whitman. My orientation to the Whitman campus never could have been the same had Loren rather than Paul been my roommate through my first year in College. Not only was Paul a senior; he was a big wheel on the campus (football, glee club, debate) ; he knew everybody, had strong opinions about everything, and liked me well enough to take me under his wing as a protege. Inevitably, his friends became my friends, his associations my associations, and his views my views. Paul and I remained good friends for life.

I was taxed almost to the limit in my freshman year by the combined load of job and studies. The studies were not so terribly difficult, but the job took so much time that I had to slight some of the studies. I had to be up every morning at five o'clock and put in two or more hours at Prentiss Hall; then I often had to slip over there at the noon hour and take care of emergencies; and finally from three to six in the afternoon I had to try to get things wrapped up for the night. This was my regular schedule, but I was on call at all hours and had to put in a good deal of extra time. Since I had little time for study in the daytime, I had to count on 8 P.M. to midnight as my regular study hours, and this did not leave much time for sleep. It was not that the studies were so hard to get, but there was so much translating, theme-writing, and problem solving (in mathematics) that I could not keep up without cheating the job in some of the courses. I chose to do this in Greek and Bible, which I found I could neglect without being caught. Often I would let the work in these courses slip for weeks at a time, and then try to catch up by intensive cramming before tests.

The Spartan regime of job and studies left me no time for student activities, which was a great disappointment. I wanted to turn out for football, try for the glee club, and take a whirl at forensic competition, but there weren't enough hours in the day. Perhaps I should have quit the job, for I did not need the money as much as I thought, but I felt that would be an admission that I was too lazy or too feeble to do the work. So I stuck it out. For a time in the early spring I was afraid I was going to have to toss in the towel. I had caught some kind of infection which made me thoroughly miserable, but I kept on, and finally the sudden arrival of warm weather saved the day for me. The job tapered off to almost nothing.

My Studies

My manual labors as well as my mental endeavors might have been easier to bear if I had been entirely happy about my courses of study. Actually, it was the teachers rather than the courses which disappointed me. In Latin I had Professor E. E. Ruby, who was not an exciting teacher and, compared with my high school teacher of Latin, not a linguist at all. Of course I did not know then that Ed Ruby never should have been teaching Latin. French had been his major in college and graduate school, and how he came to be shifted to Latin at Whitman I never knew. In later years, when I became a member of the

110

Whitman faculty, I quickly discovered that Ruby was far more interested in administration, and much better at it, than in classroom teaching. My German instructor was Miss Rachel Hamilton, Whitman '10—in other words, a college junior at the time, and just about as competent as one would expect an inexperienced and little-trained undergraduate to be. She might have done fairly well with beginners, but never should have been allowed to teach a third-year course in German or any other language. It was more than she could do to keep up with the better students in the class.

In English I had H. G. Merriam, then in his first year of college teaching and still a tyro at the job. Merriam later made a distinguished career as a professor of English at the University of Montana, but he had not reached such a high level of proficiency when I had him at Whitman in 1908-09. In Greek I had Louis F. Anderson, a grand gentleman whom I was destined soon to know as a fraternity brother and warm personal friend. Greek was a new subject to me, so I could not compare "Prof. Louis" with anyone else. I liked him and liked Greek. The Bible course was given by Mrs. Gertrude Wylie, a considerably shopworn ex-missionary. I already knew the Bible well enough to pass her course with scarcely a peek at the Holy Word, and I did. The best teacher I had in my freshman year, and one of the best I ever had in any subject, was Professor W. A. Bratton. Under him I had trigonometry and analytic geometry, and if I had not been predisposed in other directions, I might have chosen mathematics as my major.

The Class of 1912

The Class of 1912 numbered 93 in its freshman year, and was the largest entering class in the history of Whitman up to that time. The total collegiate enrollment was less than 200, and there were about 175 non-collegiate students, 100 in Pearsons Academy and 75 in the Conservatory. Whitman had such a high rate of attrition that the freshman class usually made up about half of the collegiate enrollment. The Class of 1912 began with 93 and finished with 30. That was about par for the four-year course. Financial hardship was one of the causes of the large dropout, but not the principal one. The chief reason was the prevalent belief, almost universal in that era, that a college education was more a luxury than a necessity, and by no means essential to success. In 1908 nobody thought a college education had much value for a career in business, and multitudes, like my stepfather, thought the same about high school education. A college education, even two years of college, was not prerequisite for admission to law schools, medical schools dental schools, or even engineering schools. A college freshman who was not to a large degree motivated by sheer love of learning did not have much incentive to spend four years getting the degree of bachelor of arts. The only practical value it had was to enable the recipient to teach in high school.

Composing more than half of the collegiate student body, the Class of 1912 did not have to endure much in the way of hazing. We could not be forced to wear green "dinks" or any other badge of freshman inferiority. Occasionally a gang of sophomores might waylay an unwary freshman and heave him into Lakum Duckum, then newly constructed. Once they made bold to raid the commissary of a freshman party. Occasionally a freshman returning to his quarters would find his room "stacked' to the ceiling by sophomore prowlers. After a few weeks of this, we freshman decided to put an end to these hit-and-run forays. It was not hard to do. We got ourselves well organized, and one morning cut all classes, grabbed every sophomore we could lay hands on, tied him hand and foot, and, as a grand finale, loaded all of them into wagons we had hired for that purpose, dressed them in night clothes, exhibited our captives all over the campus and the main streets down town, then hauled them back to the campus and threw them all into Lakum Duckum. Since we outnumbered the sophs about five to one, and could repeat this stunt any time we chose, the hazing of the Class of 1912 came to a sudden and permanent halt. I have often wondered why the College authorities kept hands off and let us settle things in our own way. Perhaps they thought the results might be better that way.

There was very little strictly freshman social life. During the first week of the semester (the first semester, that is) there was a get-together party for freshmen and faculty members, but I do not remember another purely freshman party during the entire year. Most student parties were held in the social parlors of Reynolds Hall, then the principal dormitory for women. By custom, each year there was a junior-freshman party, a sophomore-senior party, and one or more parties given by each Christian association, each literary society, and usually by each of the regional clubs. Also by custom, these parties invariably featured such parlor games as charades, pinning the tail on the donkey, and clap in and clap out. Sometimes more elaborate stunts were staged and sometimes we were permitted to dance the Virginia reel. There were only two ballroom-type dances per year—the Varsity Ball, just before the Christmas holidays, and the Junior Prom, just before final examinations in the second semester. Being a lead-footed Methodist, I did not attend these dances in my freshman year. Learning to dance was to be a part of my college education, but not in my freshman year. It was all I could do to master the Virginia reel that year.

One social function in which I indulged to the full as a freshman was the so-called Sunday afternoon sing. All students were invited to these Sabbath eve trystings. Beginning at 5 P.M. every Sunday afternoon, the boys and girls would gather in the parlors of Reynolds Hall and spend an hour and a half singing hymns, consuming refreshments, and making dates for the evening church services. A boy could always be sure of a date for church, because that was the only sign-out permission a girl could have on Sunday evening. Asuming that only the pure in heart would want to go to church, the authorities not only gave their blessing to this dating bureau, but felt sure they were doing a fine service for the churches of the community. There was no way of making sure that a couple signed-out for church would actually get there, but the odds were in favor of church attendance because there was nowhere else to go—no movies or shows of any kind, no radio or TV, no night clubs or other hot

113

spots open on Sunday evenings. Moreover, a couple could hold hands and whisper sweet nothings more comfortably in church than anywhere else.

I was a faithful attendant at the Sunday afternoon sings, but my dating was much on the meager side. One reason was my job, which often called me to Prentiss Hall for an hour or two just around church time. Another reason was that I did not happen to know any Methodist girls on the Whitman campus, and, as a matter of fact, there were not more than two or three. I was a very uncompromising sectarian in my freshman year. I had transferred my membership from Ellensburg to the Wilbur Memorial Methodist Church of Walla Walla, and deemed it my duty to attend there. I did not propose to be seduced into Presbyterianism, Congregationalism, or some other denominational "ism" because some campus Delilah insisted that I take her to her own church. Although I could not have been lured away from my own church by a non-Methodist Helen of Troy, I really never did get into the swing of things in the Wilbur Church.

Religion at Whitman

Whitman College, in my freshman year, was in the early stages of a complete sectarian re-orientation. In connection with the Greater Whitman Program (of which more later) it had severed its official connections with the Congregational church, declared itself non-sectarian, and was doing its darndest to make capital, both pecuniary and otherwise, through a non-sectarian appeal. The Board of Overseers had just been created, and special care had been taken to see that it was not Congregationalist in affiliation or interest. Although I know nothing of the spiritual temperature of Whitman College prior to my freshman year, I can testify from personal observation that as the Greater Whitman Campaign went forward there was a perceptible decline of pietism and a corresponding growth of intellectualism in the religious life of the campus. This was manifested in various ways. The Young Men's Christian Association, of which I was an active member in my freshman year, discontinued its prayer meetings, forgot its missionary zeal, and became a sort of ethical

114

culture society. Before I graduated, it had virtually ceased to function at all. Unorthodoxy raised its head high in the faculty, and most of the admired members of the faculty were religious mavericks, as, indeed, was President Penrose himself. This I know because I took his course in philosophy and religion.

But in his freshman year Chester C. Maxey, '12, was neither confirmed in his Methodism nor proselyted to anything else. Though not unaware of the changing religious climate at Whitman, he was not much affected by it. He was a Methodist and a member of the Wilbur M. E. congregation. He did not feel quite at ease there, but not primarily for religious reasons. Aside from three or four Whitman boys who attended there, he had no close friends in that congregation and had very few casual acquaintances. This was not the fault of the Wilbur congregation or the fault of Chester Maxey, who was a stranger in the bosom of Wilbur Methodism not because he wanted to be or they desired it that way, but simply because there were no means by which a college student who was pinned down on the Whitman campus nine-tenths of his time could become well acquainted with the people of the Wilbur congregation. My ties with Methodism, naturally, had been a hometown affair. I grew up in that church and knew everybody in it. I did not expect to transfer that intimacy to Walla Walla, but neither did I expect to be on the outer edge of the circle.

Student Activities

Student organizations and student activities flourished on the Whitman campus in my undergraduate years, but in many ways were unlike their modern counterparts. All were voluntary and none were subject to faculty regulation to any great extent. This was conspicuously true of the Associated Students. I did not join the Associated Students in my freshman year. Membership was optional; a student joined, paid his dues, and took part in the business of the association or he did not, just as he saw fit. In my freshman year I did not see fit, because I was so busy with my job that I thought I could not spare the time for the

A.S.W.C. Compulsory membership, enforced by the College, addition of student dues to tuition charges, and submission to faculty oversight and control would have caused a student rebellion in those days. We thought student affairs were our business alone.

Every year the treasurer of the Associated Students put on a drive for memberships and had helpers canvass the students individually and ask them to join and pay up. Whether a student joined or not was pretty much a matter of personal loyalty; the only benefit of membership was a season ticket to all intercollegiate athletic contests. But if you did not want to attend all of them, you could save money by paying single admissions for the games attended. Everybody thought that was right and proper. The four intercollegiate sports—football, baseball, basketball, and track—received subsidies from the Associated Students. All other activities were supposed to pay their own way, and after a fashion, they did. The *Pioneer,* then as now the student newspaper, was financed by subscriptions and advertising revenues; the Junior yearbook (then as now named *Waiilatpu*) was financed by sales and advertising revenues; the Debate Council, which managed all forensics, was financed by contributions and admissions charges; the two glee clubs were financed entirely by concert receipts; all dramatic performances were financed by ticket sales and the literary societies, classes, and regional clubs were financed by dues and money-raising social events. In every one of these organizations the students were completely free to choose their own officers, manage their own activities, and spend their money to suit themselves. No financial report or accounting was rendered to any officer of the College, and, truth to tell, very little accounting was ever rendered to the members themselves.

Forensics, as I have said, were in the hands of a board known as the Debate Council. This board was composed of three undergraduates who had won their letters in debate or oratory and were chosen by the members of the Associated Students at the annual election in May. These three in turn chose two non-student members, who might be alumni, faculty members, or officers of administration. The five members thus selected then chose the president and the secretary-manager of the Debate Council, and these were the officers who, for all practical purposes, ran the whole forensic program. There was no coach and no faculty member who had anything to say about forensics unless he happened to be elected one of the non-student members. All debates and oratorical contests were arranged by the officers under the authority of the Debate Council; the selection of speakers and teams was in the hands of the Debate Council; all preparation was in the hands of the students alone. Under the authorization of the Debate Council, the manager set the admission charges for each contest, promoted the sale of tickets, and collected and disbursed all of the receipts. And, in surprising contrast to the present time, the audience and the gate receipts were almost always large enough to defray all expenses. I know this to be true, because, later in my college career, I served one term as secretary-manager and one term as president of the Debate Council.

There were two glee clubs, one for women and one for men. There was also a chapel choir, but it was a faculty-controlled activity for which academic credit was granted. But the glee clubs were simon-pure student activities. Each club elected its own officers, chose its own musical director, planned its own program, arranged its own tours, and managed its own finances. Glee Club expenses were supposed to be met by concert earnings, and sometimes they were. The usual thing was a deficit on the road trips offset by the fat profits of the home concerts. Since the admission charge was modest and the program entertaining, a large home audience was always assured. All the manager had to do was beat the bushes hard enough to sell the tickets.

Dramatic productions were monopolized by the sophomore and senior classes. There was no dramatics department in the College, no teacher of dramatics, and no course offering in dramatics. The one big dramatics production of the year was the sophomore play, the purpose of which was more monetary than artistic. The sophomore class had some time in the past acquired the privilege of putting on this play for the purpose of making money to help finance the publication of the *Waiilatpu* in its junior year. Therefore the sophomore play was just as completely a sophomore enterprise as the annual was a junior enterprise. The casting of the play was all from the sophomore class, the staging was by a director elected by the sophomore class, and the business management was in the hands of a sophomore student chosen by the class to be manager of the play. Some years there was a senior play and some years not, depending on how much initiative the seniors could generate in their final semester at Whitman. Since there were no comprehensive examinations and no senior theses, seniors could usually find time to do anything they wanted, and the senior play was almost always a feature of the commencement week-end. As in the case of the sophomore play, the senior play was exclusively a senior class affair.

The four literary societies were survivals of a past that was rapidly receding from view. There were two literary societies for men (Athenaeum and Phrenokosmian) and two for women (Libethrean and Philolithian). These societies made up a curious quadrilateral. The two men's societies were traditional rivals and so were the two women's societies, but there was a sort of brother-sister tie between Athenaeum and Libethrean on the one hand and Phrenokosmian and Philolithian on the other. Every student in college was eligible to join a literary society, but not all did. The joiners were usually those who anticipated cultural and social benefits from society membership, and the non-joiners were those who were little interested in such things. I joined Athenaeum because my roomate, Paul Brainard, was a member of that society and urged me to join it.

In former years the literary societies may have been primarily cultural in purpose, but by the time I arrived on the Whitman scene the culture had been somewhat de-emphasized. The men's societies were chiefly interested in debating and the women's societies in social life. Each year there was an Athenaeum-Phrenokosmian debate, which stirred up a storm of verbal strife both before and after its occurrence. The rivalry involved

118

not only the annual inter-society debate but also how many men each society could place on the varsity debating teams. The women's societies also engaged in debates, but without the heat displayed by the men.

Each year there was an Athenaeum-Libethrean banquet and a Phrenokosmian-Philolithian banquet, and these ranked with the Varsity Ball and the Junior Prom as the outstanding social events of the year. Each banquet was a dress-up affair. The members of both sexes gussied themselves out in their very best, made dates for the occasion just as for a dance, gathered around the festive board and ate themselves sodden. Then, when every one had reached a state of overstuffed euphoria, came the "toasts"—a long program of speeches in course of which the two sexes tossed verbal bouquets at each other and drank deep toasts in *aqua pura,* that being the only libation then permissable at Whitman. To be chosen to offer a toast at one of these banquets was a great distinction—like earning a letter in athletics or forensics. The best of the toasts were always published in the *Waiilatpu,* so as to preserve them for posterity.

The regional clubs were another feature of Whitman campus life that was headed for oblivion very soon, though nobody seemed aware of that in 1908. Initially these regional clubs had been established to serve as booster clubs, and they still went through the motions of aiding the College in promotional work, especially in recruiting new students. But their main interests, as I saw them in 1908, were social affairs and campus politics. I am not sure how many of these clubs there were, but I remember a Spokane Club, an Idaho Club, a Puget Sound Club, an Oregon Club, a Whitman County Club, and a Walla Walla Club. There were not enough Whitman students from my neck of the woods to form a regional club, so I was out in the cold so far as participation in any such activities was concerned. I enjoyed my exclusion by believing and saying the worst I could imagine about all of them, and there was plenty of suspicion to talk about. It had been the practice for each of these clubs to have one or more social parties each year, and they also had fallen into the habit of pulling wires and putting up nominees in class

119

and student body elections. Since I was on the outside with no chance to get in, my conscience prompted me to denounce these manipulations as utterly nefarious.

In the fall of 1908 we also had on the Whitman campus Republican and Democratic clubs, since this was an election year. William J. Bryan, running against William H. Taft, was making his third and final bid for the presidency. As a matter of course, I joined the Republican club, although I was rather lukewarm about Taft. I no longer detested Bryan, as I had been taught to do in early childhood, but I had begun to feel, as had multitudes of other Americans, that his day was done. My political idols at this particular time were Theodore Roosevelt and Robert M. La Follette (the Elder), and, since neither one was a candidate in 1908, I found the campaign rather dull. The Whitman student body was overwhelmingly Republican, but one or two of my friends were active in the Democratic club, and we managed to lock horns a few times in partisan arguments.

My freshman activities were restricted to the Y.M.C.A., the Athenaeum Society, and the Republican club. I had made a few solid friends among the men of the College, but among the fair sex I had only acquaintainces. I was not girl-shy but simply did not have any time for romantic dalliance. I was toiling so many hours a day that I hardly had time for a second look at any of the campus queens. Nor did I succeed in my freshman year in finding a guiding mentor on the faculty. Professors Bratton, Ruby, and Anderson were the faculty members I knew best, but I had no inclination to major in their subject fields and, therefore, no special reason for counseling with them. Since Whitman did not have a formal counseling program, I never was called in for a talk with any member of the faculty.

A Look at Whitman in 1908

The physical plant of Whitman College in 1908 was partly old and partly new. There were four spanking new buildings, all erected since 1900—Whitman Memorial Building, Billings Hall, Reynolds Hall, and the Hendrick Gymnasium. All stood on what was known as the new campus—all north of Boyer Avenue. There were none newer or better on any college or university campus in the Pacific Northwest. South of Boyer Avenue was the old campus where the original seminary and college buildings stood. These were all of frame contruction, destined eventually to be torn down. The names of these old buildings, as current in 1908, were Prentiss Hall, College Hall, and Association Hall. As I have already explained, Prentiss Hall stood on the site of the present Conservatory of Music and was used as a dormitory for women. College Hall stood approximately on the site of the present Prentiss Hall, and was being used in 1908 by the Conservatory, though it was destined the next year to be turned over to Pearson's Academy. Between 1882 and 1900, College Hall had been the main building of Whitman College. Association Hall had been crowded into a small space just east of College Hall and looked as though it might some day tumble into Professor Anderson's back yard. It was a square box of a building, originally constructed to serve as a men's dormitory, but now called Association Hall because it was the meeting place of the two Christian associations and other campus groups.

On the new campus, facing west on what is now Penrose Avenue but then was called College Avenue, was a row of frame dwelling houses which the College had acquired when it purchased the new campus. First to the north of Whitman Memorial, almost exactly where the Penrose Library now stands, was a large mansion which served as the president's house. Formerly it had been the D. S. Baker home. Northward of this was a small cottage which the College rented to members of its faculty and staff. On the corner of what is now the Penrose and Isaacs intersection stood Green Cottage, so named because it had so long been the home of the Green family. In 1908 it was being used as a dormitory for women. I cannot recall how many times in its checkered history Green Cottage was used as a dormitory; also it was used on two different occasions as a residence for President Penrose and finally as an infirmary. Just south of Reynolds Hall were the tennis courts—for women only—and adjacent to these was a huge root cellar half above and half below the surface of the ground. This testified to the fact that refrigeration was but an embryonic science in 1908.

My freshman existence centered in Memorial Hall where all classes were held, Billings Hall where I lived, and Prentiss Hall where I slaved. Three times a week I had to show up at the Gymnasium for physical education, though I was getting more exercise every day than any two members of the football squad. Maybe, if I had begged hard enough, I might have been excused from P.E., but I doubt it. Very few excuses were regarded as acceptable in those days. I had no counselor or adviser of any kind to tell me how to go about getting excused from anything, so I did not try.

Billings Hall, where I ate, slept, and studied, was advertised as one of the newest and finest men's dormitories in the country. By 1908 standards that claim probably was not an exaggeration, but by present-day standards Billings was a fire trap, a health hazard, and a den of iniquity. The facilities that Paul Brainard and I shared were typical. We had one room (dimensions 12 feet by 15, including a built-in 3 by 3 clothes closet) furnished with two cots, two upright chairs, two small study tables, and a tiny book rack. Paul and I furnished our own rugs, drapes, towels, bedding and embellishments such as pictures or pennants. Suitcases stored under our cots served the purpose of a bureau. Mirrors, if any, we had to furnish for ourselves. Down the hall a few paces from our "digs" was a combination bath and toilet room, shared in common with the twenty other men on our floor. This room was equipped with one four-legged bath tub (no showers), two toilet stools, two washbowls, and one large mirror. At certain hours, such as 7:30 a.m., there was always a terrific traffic jam in this room and a battle for the use of all of the facilities save the bath tub. The daily bath habit had not yet become a semi-religious rite in American life, so the competition for the bath tub usually occurred on Saturday evening. Discovering that I could have the bath tub almost any time on any other day than Saturday, I broke myself of the Saturday night bath habit. But I did not acquire the daily bath habit until long after my freshman year.

In the fall of 1908 the College had installed as a housemother in Billings an ancient maiden lady whose name was Miss Hatch, a dear New England soul who was some connection of either the Penroses or the Shipmans. She lasted less than one semester. The Billings roughnecks quickly discovered that she was terrified lest she encounter indecent exposure in the hallways, and they promptly gave her imagination so much to feed upon that she must have developed a rape complex. Anyhow, around Thanksgiving time as I remember, she departed in haste, and Professor Norman F. Coleman and his wife took her place. The Colemans were able to maintain a semblance of order in the dining room and on the first floor, where they lived, but advisedly they did not venture into the wilds above. Paul and I lived on the third floor, which, being farthest removed from the seat of government, was an untamed frontier. Some of the things that went on there simply beggar description.

To boys used to farm-type home cooking, the meals at Billings not only were vile but famishing. The College washed its hands of this, as the food service was handled by an independent contractor. Naturally, therefore, the Billings boys thought it no sin to raid the food pantries at every opportunity and to use unpalatable food as missles in dining hall riots. All Billings residents were responsible for cleaning their own rooms, but there never was any inspection or other effort to enforce the rule. If one wanted to live in a pig-sty, that was his privilege as far as the College was concerned. Other discipline was similarly lax. The day-to-day maintenance of law and order was supposedly in the hands of a student committee, elected by the Billings boys for a semester at a time. The Colemans were merely supposed to exert a moral influence and report observed misdoings to the student committee. Penalties were assessed and imposed by the student committee, and all too often were mere slaps on the wrist.

The College maintained no health service, no infirmary, did not even have an officer whose duty it was to advise and assist students who fell ill. In Billings Hall, if one of us was too sick to go to meals or classes, his roommate carried food up to him and waited on him. If he did not get well in two or three days, the roommate would call a doctor. What happened from there on was up to the doctor and his patient. Unless the doctor chose to report it, the College authorities might never know anything about the circumstances of the case. Should the disease prove to be quarantinable, the doctor would move the patient out of the dormitory at once and report the matter to the county health officer. Once or twice health officers threatened to quarantine Billings Hall, but never did. Perhaps they feared they might have to call out the militia to make it stick. However, if the ailment were one of those things, like influenza, that we were accustomed to living with, the doctor generally prescribed his standard potions and left the patient to the haphazard ministration of Billings Hall. I don't know why we and our parents did not raise hob about this indifference to student health, but nobody did. Living in an era of laissez faire, it did not occur to one that the College should have any responsibility for student health.

The Whitman Memorial Building housed the library, the laboratories, and all of the classrooms. There were no faculty offices or other offices except those of the president, the bursar, and the registrar. Professors were not supposed to have any need for offices; the only place they were supposed to meet their students was in the classroom. If a student wanted to consult a member of the faculty, it was necessary either to go to his home or catch him on the wing between classes. The former was not encouraged and the latter was chancy. In my freshman year I made no effort to have a conference with any faculty member on any matter, and no faculty member made a point of advising me. Nearly every one took it for granted that there was a natural and well-nigh unbridgable gulf between students and faculty. A few faculty members tried to overcome this aloofness by inviting students to their homes for dinner or other social occasions. In my freshman year I had such invitations from the Brattons and the Penroses, and was deeply gratified. I must confess, however, that in both homes I was ill at ease because of an unfamiliar code of table manners. I had never seen a meal served by a maid shuttling back and forth between the host at the head and the hostess at the foot of the table, and I had not the faintest idea what to do with so many knives, forks, and spoons. But I kept my eyes open and tried to imitate the host and hostess, thus getting my first lessons in the table etiquette of polite society.

Elsewhere in this narrative I shall comment at some length on the Greater Whitman Campaign, which was launched in 1908 and blew sky-high in 1912. The class of 1912 had the unusual experience of seeing this rocket through every stage of its trajectory. It soared high in my freshman year, and I did not have the slightest doubt that I would see the fulfillment of the whole grandiose plan before my graduation from Whitman. If any one had tried to convince me that it would be my job forty years later to liquidate the last vestiges of that fantastic excursion in the jungles of deficit financing, I would have thought him insane. The reason I was so deeply impressed with the Greater Whitman in my freshman year is easy now for me to understand. It was my first contact with high-powered "promotionism." The walls and bulletin boards of Memorial were fully bedecked with elaborately colored scale-drawings of the proposed new campus and buildings. Lavishly illustrated pamphlets were freely distributed among the students. Again and again at the chapel assemblies the students were assured that the Greater Whitman was in the bag. President Penrose even wrote an article specially for the 1909 issue of the *Waiilatpu* in which he predicted an enrollment of 1,500 for Whitman—which would make it the largest institution of higher education in the Pacific Northwest—and went on to specify that Whitman would have a school of technology, a school of forestry and irrigation, a school of commerce and banking, and a school of fine arts in addition to its already fine college of liberal arts. Capping the climax, however, was the nationally publicized educational congress held in Walla Walla on November 17 and 18, 1908, for the express purpose of launching the Greater Whitman drive. This meeting brought to the Whitman campus such eminent personages as President Northrop of the Univer-

125

sity of Minnesota, Dean Burton of the Massachusetts Institute of Technology, Anson Phelps Stokes, Secretary of Yale University, and Dr. D. K. Pearsons of Chicago, the College's chief financial angel. All of these gentlemen spoke not only at the meetings of the educational congress, but addressed the students in chapel. I listened with rapt attention, and if I understood their language, they said the Greater Whitman was far more than an idle dream. I thought they said it was soon due to be a reality. This had much to do with my decision to return to Whitman for my sophomore year.

In Sum

In several respects, some of which I have already mentioned, my freshman year had been disappointing. Although I had come through with good enough grades to retain my four-year scholarship, I had not been entirely happy about most of my courses. Although I had stuck it out to the end, I had been thoroughly unhappy about my Prentiss Hall job and had decided not to take it again. Indeed, I had resolved that if I could not do better than that at Whitman, I would try my luck elsewhere. But the Greater Whitman was truly something to look forward to. Should that become a reality, Whitman might very well be the best possible place for me to continue my education. For some time I wavered, but finally decided to give Whitman a second try.

In one respect my freshman year had been wholly good. I had come through the year in the black financially, rather handsomely so. My job had made it unnecessary for me to dip into my savings to any great extent, and with this backlog plus my summer earnings I was sure that I could easily manage a second year in college. I might even skin through without too much work on the side. So I went home for the summer and immediately got a job with a sewer contractor. The job? Digging ditches six feet deep and more for the expanded sewer system of the city of Ellensburg. On this job I did pick and shovel work ten hours a day for $2.50 per day and thought I was sitting on top of the world. By the end of the summer I had more than $150 saved up, was hard as nails, and was eager to get back to Whitman.

About two weeks before my return to Whitman my Grandfather Maxey passed away, and when his will was probated I discovered that I was to receive one-fifth of his estate. Though not a large sum, this would be sufficient to underwrite the rest of my college education, possibly a bit more. Grandfather had never told me that he had this in mind, but I understood his feelings about me and his ambitions for me well enough to realize that he had included me in the will to make sure that I would not be too handicapped in my efforts to get a higher education.

VII. SOPHOMORE
Friends and Fraternity Brothers

My mental attitude in the fall of 1909 was about 180 degrees removed from the depression I had struggled against the year before. Not only did I know my way around Whitman College; I was beset with no financial worries, had no millstones to carry. Otto Johnson, Bill Howard, and I had arranged for a two-room suite at Billings, one room for a study and the other for a bedroom. We thought this would save us money and at the same time provide a little more living space for each man. For about six weeks we were happy with the comforts of this arrangement. Then, almost on impulse, we moved out and rented a second floor apartment in a house on Boyer Avenue some two blocks west of the campus. Here we had much more room—a sleeping porch, a parlor, and a study with a large fireplace. We stayed in this apartment until the end of the first semester, when we moved again. Otto went to live at the Delta Phi Delta House and Bill and I returned to Billings. These peregrinations were typical of what was going on at Whitman that year, and symbolical of the unrest incidental to the second year of the Greater Whitman Campaign.

With its president and dean away most of the time and no one on the spot with authority to keep things running right, the College lapsed into demoralization. There never had been a compulsory residence rule for men, and there was no one to take the lead in getting one enacted now. Men were perfectly free to move in and out of Billings as the spirit moved them; also to board there or not, as they chose. Otto, Bill, and I were merely three of many who abused this freedom. There was a great deal of discontent at Billings—discontent with food, discontent with the rooms, and discontent with nothing in particular and everything in general. Whenever any individual or group thought the grass looked greener on the outside, out they went without so much as notice or by-your-leave. And if the outside pastures proved less verdant than expected, back they came to Billings just as unceremoniously as they had left. There was no one to lift a finger in opposition. The faculty was not sure of its authority, and the administrative subordinates who were keeping store while the president and dean were away knew they did not have authority to do anything.

Another factor in the exodus from Billings was the establishment of two local fraternities—the Illahee Club and the Delta Phi Delta Society. Whitman at that time had no rule either for or against fraternities; apparently the question had never before arisen. My guess is that the majority of the faculty would have voted to ban fraternities, but with the president and dean away, nobody wanted to stick his neck out. President Penrose finally was prevailed upon to take notice of the *fait accompli,* and his position was that, without the sanction of the Boards of Trustees and Overseers, the faculty had no legal right to rule one way or another on fraternities. In my opinion, he was technically correct in this conclusion, but, correct or not, it muddied rather than clarified the waters. It meant that the two *de facto* fraternities would acquire something akin to squatter's rights during the months (it actually took three years) the two boards would need to arrive at a well informed judgment on the fraternity question.

President Penrose was himself a fraternity man, and I am sure that he thought it would be good for Whitman to have the fraternity system. I am positive, however, that he had nothing to do with, and did not in any way anticipate, the formation of the two local fraternities in 1909. He was not close enough to what was going on at Whitman that year to have even a premonition of what was going to happen in student affairs. However, as an ever loyal D.K.E. from Williams College, he could not have been displeased and probably thought it offered a timely opportunity to find out whether national fraternities could be induced to take an interest in Whitman.

The Illahee Club was organized in the spring of 1909 with the expressed purpose of being a social club for men and getting a house for its members to occupy for the year 1909-10. During the summer the Illahees secured a large house (now the Brae Burn Apartments) on Clinton Street, three or four blocks from the campus, and when school opened they were running full blast in the style of a college fraternity, though for reasons of expediency they disavowed that nomenclature. They thought, and rightly, that the College might look upon them more benignly if they appeared to be just a casual group of boys who had found it convenient to take lodgings together for the year 1909-10. Also, as a hostage to fortune, they took in as an apparent faculty mentor and advisor one J. Merrill Blanchard, at that time athletic coach and professor of physical education, who incidentally was a member of Beta Theta Pi from Bowdoin College. If the Illahees and Blanchard did not have one great idea in common, namely, a chapter of Beta Theta Pi at Whitman, my inside information was all wrong.

In September, 1909, two members of the Class of 1910 James Alger Fee and John Barron Washburn, were rooming in a private home on the corner of Boyer and Penrose directly opposite the Conservatory of Music. It was then known as the Dr. Cropp residence, and is now the site of Cordiner Hall. Washburn was a transfer student from Westminster College, Missouri, and had become a member of Beta Theta Pi while attending there. Washburn, like Blanchard, thought it would be grand to have a Beta chapter at Whitman, but he had not been invited to become a member of the Illahee Club. Neither had Fee, but he was much interested in Beta Theta Pi owing to the fact that several of his hometown (Pendleton) friends were Betas at the University of Oregon. Washburn and Fee began to toy with the idea of starting a local fraternity which would definitely announce itself as such and at the same time announce that it would seek a chapter of Beta Theta Pi. They drew into their discussions a third senior—John Howard Shubert. Around Thanksgiving these three decided to give the idea a tryout, and began to solicit other students to join with them. The result was the Delta Phi Delta Society, a local Greek-letter fraternity which, in February, 1910, leased the Roxie Delaney house at East Rose Street and began its campaign for a charter from Beta Theta Pi.

There was a lot of speculation as to what would happen if both groups petitioned Beta Theta Pi, but all this was put to rest by the failure of J. Merrill Blanchard, owing to circumstances beyond his control, to return to Whitman in the academic year 1910-11. For good and sufficient reasons, he was fired. The Illahees then chose as their faculty member a man who was not only a member of Phi Delta Theta but one of its national officers, none other than Professor E. E. Ruby. After that there was no doubt about the intentions of the Illahees. They were going to be a fraternity and they were going to try for a chapter of Phi Delta Theta. The Delta Phi Deltas then decided that they too ought to have a prestigious faculty member and chose Professor Louis F. Anderson, who was not a fraternity man, but he was heartily for everything that had a tinge of Greek in it.

While all these developments were taking place, Chester Maxey was sitting on the fence looking both ways and, to some extent, being pulled both ways. He was not sure, in fact, that he wanted to join either group. He knew so little about college fraternities that he could not make up his mind on the basis of facts, pro or con. However, most of his closer friends were in Delta Phi Delta, and in May, 1910, he succumbed to the pressure and joined that group.

Such, in thumbnail summary, was the way fraternities got started at Whitman and the way I became a member of Delta Phi Delta and later of Beta Theta Pi. As I proceed with this narrative, I will relate other significant events in the development of the fraternity system at Whitman.

Sophs Elect a Frosh President

The opening week of the first semester, 1909-10, witnessed the most violent outbreak of freshman-sophomore warfare in the history of Whitman. It was so furious, and so disturbing to the College routine, that the faculty finally took a hand and enacted a body of regulations which not only forbade hazing and outlawed class fights, but placed all freshman-sophomore contests under the control of a faculty committee. This marked the beginning of a new era in undergraduate life at Whitman.

The cause of this historic eruption of inter-class mayhem was a sophomore prank which was a screamingly funny joke to everybody—except, of course, the poor humiliated freshmen. By perfectly executing a well-hatched plot, the sophomores (my class) succeeded in electing one of their own members president of the freshman class. Never did a long-chance frame-up work out more beautifully. Two transfer students, George Cole and Artis Chitty, entered that year with sophomore standing, but, being new to Whitman, were able to attend the first meeting of the freshman class undetected. Pretending to be freshmen, they took part in the meeting without arousing any suspicions. When nominations for president were in order, Cole took the floor and made an eloquent speech placing Chitty's name in nomination. Two or three other nominations were made, and then each nominee was called upon to introduce himself and make a little speech explaining who he was, where he came from, and so on. Chitty was a smooth talker, and managed to give the impression, though he did not say it in so many words, that he had been a hotshot in a well-known eastern preparatory school. When the votes were counted, Chitty won by a mile. The schemers managed to keep the thing secret until the next day, but the news gradually leaked out and finally was published in one of the Walla Walla papers. The original intention of the plotters had been to keep it quiet as long as possible, hoping that the explosion, when it came, would be that much greater.

As soon as the truth got out, the roof fell in on every male member of the sophomore class. The freshmen were so furious that they decided to clear the campus of sophomores and keep it cleared until we begged for mercy. This was not hard for them to do because they had us so vastly outnumbered. We had to go into hiding and stay there, or else exist on the receiving end of repeated kidnappings, paddlings, duckings, and other forms of corporal punishment. Soon, however, our absences from class rose to a number that stirred up the faculty and resulted in the intervention and regulatory action which I have already mentioned.

I am now going to make a disavowal. It was charged, and grew into one of those rumors that are handed down as part of the traditional lore, that I engineered the Cole-Chitty *demarche*. I plead not guilty, but I know who the culprit was. He was not a sophomore, but a senior, then as all through life one of my closest friends—none other than James Alger "Beany" Fee, a man not uncelebrated in Whitman history.

Better Jobs and Better Courses

One of the first things I did after the din of battle subsided was to look for a job, and soon I had just what I wanted. The Walla Walla Paper and Stationery Company took me on as a part-time clerk. This firm dealt in everything that could come under the heading of paper and stationery, including textbooks, office supplies, confectionery, and all sorts of gimcracks. I worked only in the textbook and educational supplies department, the idea being that a college boy behind the counter would pull in the college trade. The store occupied the first floor of the Ransom Building, Walla Walla's first "skyscraper." This building was destined to be converted into the Grand Hotel and finally to be razed in order to make way for a modern savings and loan building. My working hours were from 3 to 6 P.M., and I was paid at the rate of thirty-five cents an hour, which was quite something in those days. I had never had any experience in salesmanship or merchandising, but my commodities virtually sold themselves. By trial and error, I learned a good deal about retailing and store management, and have been grateful ever since that I had this opportunity.

I held this job until the middle of the second semester, by which time the textbook trade had fallen off to a small dribble and I was no longer needed. Meanwhile I had managed to persuade two city newspapers—the Spokane *Chronicle* and the Portland *Journal*—to take me on as a Whitman campus correspondent. Since neither paper had a regular correspondent in Walla Walla and this was the era in which Whitman was in the same athletic conference with all of the state institutions of Oregon, Washington, and Idaho, both were glad to get timely items from the Whitman campus. I was paid at space rates, and although the papers never used more than half of the stuff I sent in, my monthly check was enough to supply ample pocket money.

My courses of study as a sophomore were much more satisfactory than my freshman courses. I took Astronomy I under Professor Bratton, and this was not merely an eye-opener but a special thrill because 1909-1910 was the year of Halley's comet, which we followed intently in its dramatic tour through the Milky Way. I had two English courses with Professor Norman F. Coleman, whom I liked so well that I decided to major in English. Undoubtedly—I have not changed my mind in all these years—Professor Coleman was one of the greatest teachers I ever had at any time in any institution. I was fortunate indeed to have the opportunity to do a major under him. He left Whitman in 1912, and his distinguished career as a teacher and college president in other institutions often enabled me to point with pride that I had been one of his students at Whitman. Another course I thoroughly enjoyed was Modern European History under Professor W. D. Lyman, also an excellent teacher. In economics I was disappointed, not in the subject but the teacher. William Worthington never should have tried to teach economics; he was not trained for it and knew little about the subject. He was a theological school graduate, a Congregational minister, principal of Pearson's Academy, and no doubt was drafted to teach a course in princi-

133

ples of economics because there was no one else at hand who was better qualified. I was fascinated with the subject matter of economics, mastered the textbook, and saturated myself with all of the relevant supplementary literature I could lay my hands on. Possibly I learned as much as I would have under a better teacher, but I did not enjoy the class sessions at all. I was registered in one or two other courses which made little impression on me and had to take a second year of physical education. This year I did not object to the physical education, because I was leading a sedentary life and needed the exercise.

Student Activities

Having more free time and not being worn to a frazzle physically every day, I was able in my sophomore year to take quite a plunge in student activities. I tried out for the sophomore play and landed one of the leading parts, which happened to be the role of a ne'er-do-well who did not get the girl. This role seemed suited to my talents, and the whole thing was fun. I also tried out for the glee club and the chapel choir, and made both—though certainly not because of my musical attainments. In those days I could sing a deep *basso profundo* and hold the pitch fairly well. Since low bassos were in as scant supply as high tenors, I did not have much competition to beat. Both the glee club and the choir experiences were highly beneficial to me. I did not, of course, become a musician or even a proficient vocalist, but I learned something about vocalization and vocal music which I would not otherwise have learned. In addition, I learned a little something of how one should deport himself in the public presentation of a musical program.

As a glee club member, for the first time in my life, I donned a white-tie-and-tails outfit and caught on to some of the tricks of appearing at ease in a full-dress suit. Another thing I learned, because it was one of the glee club chores assigned to me, was how to walk out on the stage and make an announcement without behaving like a sagebrush yokel. The club itinerary that year took us to Seattle, Tacoma, Bellingham, Ellensburg,

134

and Yakima, and this trip brought me many new experiences. For instance, going from Seattle to Bellingham and back to Tacoma, we traveled by Puget Sound steamer, then a popular mode of transportation. It was the first time in all my twenty years that I had ever set foot in a boat of any kind, including a lowly rowboat or canoe. In Ellensburg I sipped the wine of self-importance with much gusto, since I was accorded special recognition in my hometown.

Other activities that occupied my sophomore year were the Athenaeum-Phrenokosmian debate, serving as treasurer of Athenaeum, being sports writer on the staff of the *Pioneer*, and making one of the speeches at the Athenaeum-Libethrean banquet. Because it was a great honor to be invited to offer a toast at this banquet, I took special pains with that little speech. It was well received at the banquet and was chosen for publication in that year's *Waiilatpu*, where, supposedly, it would be on exhibit forever as a Whitman classic. As I re-read it after the passing of more than fifty years, it strikes me as thoroughly sophomoric except for a somewhat better than average sophomore felicity in the use of English. Writing sports stories for the *Pioneer* was easy and also fun. Much of the time I merely expanded and adapted for campus consumption the stories I had already filed with the Spokane and Portland papers. The inter-society debate was much more exciting than a varsity debate would have been, and I went in for that rather than try out for a varsity team.

The coming of local fraternities did not perceptibly change the pattern of Whitman social life in 1909-10. Neither fraternity gave any parties that year, fearing that such things would be frowned upon as efforts to show off and prove itself *haut ton*. I went to many parties that year and dated several girls—the same kind of parties I had by-passed as a freshman and girls I had overlooked. In the second semester of my sophomore year I began keeping company somewhat regularly with a girl whose name in this narrative shall be Jenny. I sort of drifted into this relationship, and I believe Jenny did, too. Mutual friends got us started going to parties together, we liked each other without being much impassioned about it, and had loads of fun. As so often happens on co-educational campuses, we were soon paired off, in other peoples' eyes, as a "couple" and gradually came to behave as though we were. I was fonder of Jenny than any other girl I knew and I think she fully reciprocated that sentiment. For somewhat more than a year, we kept company almost as steadily as though we were engaged, and many people assumed that we were. Actually, we never did become engaged and so never became disengaged, though we did finally cease going together.

Metamorphosis

In my sophomore year I began slowly to drift away from Methodism. At first this was mainly subconscious. Whenever I went back to Ellensburg, I was a good Methodist, but in Walla Walla I was not. The Wilbur Church just did not have what I wanted, and I did not know what I wanted. I could not feel at ease in that congregation and yet could not explain why. Looking backward, I am sure that part of my dissatisfaction was the result of intellectual experiences that were shaking me loose from traditional moorings. One of the most influential of these undoubtedly was my course in astronomy. The cosmology I learned in that course was so wholly at odds with what I had been taught in the Methodist church that I began to grope for reconciliations that quite eluded me. The Wilbur Church was no help; on the contrary, it added to my confoundment. The church authorities decided that it would be a fine thing to have a special Sunday school class for Whitman men. To make it doubly appealing, they induced George B. Marquis, then assistant treasurer of the College, to teach it. Along with Otto Johnson, Bill Howard, Fred Clemens, and a few other Whitman lads of Methodist inclinations, I joined this class. George Marquis was a remarkably fine teacher, but he was not teaching the "old time" religion. All members of the class were taking or had taken college courses incompatible with the orthodox views, and it was inevitable that many of the points of conflict would come up for discussion in our Sunday morning sessions. George Marquis encouraged this, and before the end of the year most

136

of us had as many doubts as beliefs. My personal doubts were not too troubling at first, but grew stronger as I came to identify myself more fully with the intellectual outlook that generally prevailed on the faculty. If there were any old-fashioned believers among them, I failed to recognize them. All of the faculty members I studied under were evolutionists and rejected the Bible as the literal word of God, and there were several militant agnostics. Gradually it dawned on me that there were respectable Christian sects and many Christian ministers who did not hold with Methodist orthodoxy. Even more gradually, I discovered here and there evidences that a liberal minority was beginning to emerge in the Methodist Church itself. I was not enough de-Methodized in my sophomore year to take any drastic steps. I continued my membership and my attendance, but suffered a considerable decline of zeal.

Near the end of the academic year 1909-10 our class had a meeting to elect the editor and business manager of *Waiilatpu,* which was to be our major project for the ensuing year. Neta Lohnes was elected editor and I was elected business manager. Neta immediately appointed me to serve also as an associate editor, which meant a dual responsibility. About the same time I joined Delta Phi Delta and was elected to the office of vice president. As I have said earlier, I was undecided on the fraternity question for quite a while, and I might never have joined if it had not been for the persuasiveness of Otto Johnson. I had no closer friend at Whitman than Otto, and he had just been elected president of Delta Phi Delta for 1910-11. Otto very much wanted me to join, but he was much too smart to try to convince me that the fraternity would be a good thing for me. Instead, he bore down on the point that I would be good for the fraternity and through it might accomplish more for Whitman than I could as a "loner." That shot hit me squarely in the solar plexus of self-esteem, and I capitulated at once. Little did I realize that this was one of the fateful decisions of my life. For better or for worse, I say not which, my entire subsequent life would have been different if I had decided against being a fraternity man.

My sophomore year erased all doubts about continuing at Whitman. I had made a high academic record, had taken part in several student activities, had a growing number of close buddies, had acquired a steady girl friend, and had put all financial worries behind me. I decided to spend the summer of 1910 learning how to type instead of knocking myself out with manual labor. There was no place in Ellensburg where I could get instruction in typing, but I borrowed a machine and spent the summer teaching myself. I had no manual of instructions, but I could see that ten fingers were better than one or two. So I studied the keyboard carefully, started practising with the thumbs and fingers of both hands getting into the act. By the end of the summer I had developed enough speed to fool some people into thinking I had learned the touch system. Maybe I had, but it was a touch system of my own invention. Learning to type with rapidity and reasonable accuracy was one of the most profitable investments of time and effort I ever made. It was to be my destiny to turn out thousands of pages of manuscript, which would have been impossible in longhand and could not have been done with equal facility by dictation.

VIII. JUNIOR

Big Wheel

The first thing I had to do when I got back to Whitman in September, 1910, was to help Otto Johnson apply the pulmotor to Delta Phi Delta. Those grim reapers, Graduation and Dropout, had absolutely decimated our ranks. Of the sixteen who were on the campus in June only seven were back in September. These were Otto Johnson and Clarence Sappington, seniors; Rolla Hill, Albert Greenwell, and Chester Maxey, juniors; George McCoy and Ernest Wiley, sophomores. The lease on the Rose Street house had expired and could not be renewed. It looked like we might have to shut up shop. How could seven boys operate a fraternity house? Actually there would not be seven in the house, because Sappinton and McCoy were Walla

Walla boys who had to live at home and I, on account of my *Waiilatpu* responsibilities, had to live in Billings where my room could serve as a central office for the business staff.

New members, who could live in the house, were an immediate and urgent necessity, so we seven survivors took on that problem first. In about ten days we had pledged seven men who were agreeable to living in the house, provided we could find one. Otto and I took on the job of finding a suitable house. It would have to be a relatively small house at a low rental to be within our reach, and it would also have to be furnished, because we did not own a stick of furniture and had no means to buy any. After an intensive search, we found a little house on Cherry Street about seven blocks from the campus which could be had for a rental that eleven men could manage. There were not enough members, however, to support a dining department, so each man got his meals where he wished. For convenience, I boarded at Billings, but many of our members preferred downtown restaurants or boarding houses which were within easy walking distance. Before the year 1910-11 closed we took in enough more members to bring our total to twenty-five. From that year forward the active on-campus membership of Delta Phi Delta never fell below the safety point.

I am inclined to the belief that if Delta Phi Delta had winked out that year it would have meant the beginning of the end for the fraternity system at Whitman College. The Illahees were not doing much better than we. Like us, they had been forced into reduced quarters by shriveling membership and were having all they could do to hang on. Had we failed to survive, the Illahees would have been left in so vulnerable a position that they, too, probably would have folded soon after we did.

Academically, my junior year was everything I wanted it to be. Every one of my courses was interesting and profitable. My major courses in English were taught by Professor Coleman and Dr. Mabel Buland, a recent Ph.D from Yale. All were solid courses and superbly taught. I had logic and psychology from Dr. Penrose, whom I shall always regard as one of the ablest teachers I have ever known. And there was a new faculty member that year—Professor Charles G. Haines, just out of Columbia University with a doctor's degree—who was destined to point me in an entirely new direction. Dr. Haines was brought to Whitman in the fall of 1910 as part of the Greater Whitman expansion and for the express purpose of establishing a department of political science. This was one of several new departments which were added that year in order to assure the students and the general public that the Greater Whitman wagon was really rolling.

Political science was a subject I knew little about, but the study of government and public affairs had always interested me, and for that reason I enrolled in one of Dr. Haines's courses. Immediately I knew that this was something I had been inarticulately wanting all my life. Dr. Haines was a great teacher, as his nationally distinguished career after leaving Whitman was to demonstrate to the whole country. I had not been in his classes very long before I knew I wanted to major in political science if I could. Dr. Haines thought it might be possible, but advised that I continue with my English major and petition the faculty to graduate with a double major. This request was granted, and I thus became the first Whitman student to graduate with a true double major. There had been combination or allied majors (mathematics-physics, for example) before, but no one had ever done full-scale major work in two unrelated fields. Another course which brightened my junior year was Professor Lyman's American Constitutional History, which perfectly supplemented my political science.

As well as being a superfine academic year, 1910-11 proved to be my busiest student activity year. Except for athletics, I dabbled in almost everything, and greatly admired myself as a big wheel on the campus. The most demanding student activity proved to be the yearbook. As business manager, I had the chief financial responsibility; as an associate editor, I was assigned the job of putting the book through the print shop and bindery.

My principal job as business manager was to sell enough copies of the book and enough advertising space in its back pages to defray the costs of publication. To start with, I had a nest-egg of some two hundred dollars which had been earned by the previous year's sophomore play. This was quickly eaten up by the initial editorial costs, and then I had to stall off the creditors until our hoped-for income from sales and advertising was realized. The sale of advertising proved to be relatively easy. It was principally a matter of persistence in soliciting the business and professional people of Walla Walla. However, when it came to selling the book itself, I fell flat on my face. I was optimistic enough to believe that *Waiilatpu '12* would sell like hot cakes, but I was cautious enough, also, to try to promote the rush of buyers to the hot-cake stand by an advance sales campaign among the students, faculty, alumni, and even townspeople, and I was successful in getting a large number of signers on my subscription lists. But I did not take any down-payments or require anything more than a signature on a long list of names. My imagination could not conceive any possible slip between cup and lip. It never occured to me that scores who signed up would never bother to pick up their copy of the book, let alone pay for it. Nor did it occur to me that many who did take their *Waiilatpu* would ask for a few days of credit and then never manage to find the money to pay up. To my consternation, I suddenly had to face the fact that there was no way I could force the "welchers" to live up to their promises and no way I could collect from the deadbeats. So I came face to face with the biggest financial crisis of my young life. If the class would not get behind me, there was a good chance that the creditors might hold me personally liable for their money.

A meeting of the Class of 1912 was called to consider the problem, and the final decision was to levy an assessment of ten dollars each on the members of the class in return for which each would be given ten copies of the book which he might sell, if he could, and thus reimburse himself. I was darned lucky to get off that easily, and I learned a lesson I never forgot. Never again did I enter into any deal calling for the future payment of money without being sure where the money was coming from and making certain that it would be available when needed. In later life it fell to me to be responsible for the financing of enterprises of great magnitude, but I never again let wishful thinking delude me into supposing that the necessary money would come rolling in just because of my own enthusiasm for the project.

Since my duties as business manager of the annual took me down town nearly every day, Neta delegated to me most of the editorial chores which necessitated visiting the print shop. It was necessary for her to turn most of this liaison work over to me or some other male because, in those gone-forever days of the *entente cordiale* between the print shop and the nearest saloon, ladies were not supposed to venture into such alien territory, not if they wanted to preserve ladylike reputations. Our book was composed, printed, and bound in the plant of the Washington Printing and Book Manufacturing Company on East Alder Street. This company was also the publisher of the Walla Walla *Morning Union,* then the city's leading newspaper. So I had a wonderful opportunity to gain a liberal education on the inside operations of both a printing plant and a newspaper. I could not have had better training for my future work as a writer of books and magazines articles. Our yearbook staff held regular meetings on the campus at which we would make plans, assign work projects, edit manuscript copy, assemble text and photographs, and set up a dummy of the section of the book then being developed. It would then be my job to take this to the print shop, see that everything was set as we wanted, and have proof sheets struck off for the next meeting of the editorial staff. I liked this much better than what I had to do as business manager.

Forensics and Music

I should have been content with my managerial and editorial duties, but I was too self-important to settle for just two activities. I wanted to have a finger in every pie, if I could. I tried out for glee club again and easily made the grade. Our trip that year included concerts at Dayton, Colfax, Thornton, Ritzville, Spokane, Colville, and Nelson, B.C. I am sure I was not the only member of the club who could cite that tour as the occasion of his first experience with customs and immigration officers on both sides of an international boundary line. Financially, this tour was a complete bust, and this circumstance, in my senior year, would teach me another valuable lesson.

Varsity debate was another activity of my junior year. Otto Johnson, Don Campbell, and I met and defeated a team from the State College of Washington on the question: "Resolved, that the best interests of American Colleges justify the abolition of intercollegiate athletics." We had the affirmative, and thought we had the unpopular side of the question. But we succeeded in convincing the judges in our favor by a majority of two to one, for which feat we gave ourselves many hearty pats on the back. Having seen all aspects and depths of intercollegiate athletics in the fifty plus years since that debate, I am sure that our case was weak as compared with what might be built up today.

My arguments against intercollegiate athletics, on the debate team, did not impair my zeal as a reporter of athletic events for the Whitman *Pioneer* and the two newspapers for which I was still the campus correspondent. I continued on the staff of the *Pioneer* all through my junior year, and in the second semester was elected to the position of editor-in-chief. I served in that capacity for several weeks, but eventually had to give it up because the time demands of the annual were too peremptory.

Other positions I held in my junior year were president of Athenaeum, vice president of Delta Phi Delta, and chairman of the Billings Hall student government committee. The first named called for little time or effort, as literary societies were on their last legs. Delta Phi Delta took a good deal of time, because of my office and the social activities the fraternity drew me into. The chairmanship of the Billings student government committee was a troubleshooting job, which sometimes resulted in long and heated sessions in which we tried to decide the penalties to be meted out for various infractions of the rules.

In the second semester I was one of three persons nominated

143

for the office of president of the Associated Students of Whitman College. The other two were Jack Stone and Don Campbell. We had a lively campaign. Jack won the election, I was second, and Don was third. The election might be called the climax of my career as a campus politician. I was elected president of Delta Phi Delta about the same time, but that was not a campus-wide contest.

Society and Romance

Compared with the first two, my junior year was a gay social whirl. I learned to play cards, learned to dance, became an inveterate party-goer, and made a study of social *politesse*. In respect to the last mentioned, I had a good deal of catching up to do, because the etiquette of polite society was not a Maxey birthright. Not only was I a greenhorn in the proper techniques of manipulating table tools, I was quite innocent of the niceties of squiring a lady to the theater, to dinner, or even to church. I knew nothing about squiring—period. I was just as likely to put the left foot forward as the right. Had I not joined Delta Phi Delta my instruction in the social proprieties might have been long postponed.

Maybe it was because most of us were so far from being socialites that we Delta Phi Deltas so keenly felt the need of something to give us broader social opportunities. Social life on the Whitman campus offered little except soggy divertissements such as the Reynolds Hall "sings," the class parties, and the two dances a year. We felt the need for variety and liveliness, and we decided to do something about it. The first thing, we thought, was to make ourselves more eligible socially, so we made it a matter of fraternity policy to see that all of our members went through a polishing process. We held sessions in which instructions were given and criticisms dished out, and we made it obligatory for every member to learn how to play cards, dance, go down a receiving line, escort a lady, and so forth and so on.

The next thing we did was to ask the College authorities for permission to have a Five Hundred party at our fraternity house. Five Hundred was the card craze of that era, and progressive Five Hundred parties were all the rage in fashionable circles. It was an interesting game, not too difficult, and was adaptable to constant social chatter. Expecting our request to be turned down, we were almost bowled over with surprise when it was promptly granted. Apparently the powers that ran the institution welcomed an innovation in the social regime. Probably they were as bored as the students were with the stuffy old social pattern which had come down from the A. J. Anderson administration. Perhaps they wanted to give the Delta Phi Deltas a little encouragement, hoping they might break some ice that had been far too long unthawed. We did not have that in mind so much as doing something that would be the talk of the campus and give us a basis for putting on airs. So we put on a party the like of which had never before been seen at Whitman. With faculty patrons given due attention, we gave a Five Hundred party with refreshments, ragtime music, and other entertainment features that the whole campus gabbled about for days.

Emboldened by this taste of success, we next asked permission to sponsor and pick up the tab for an all-campus dance, to be staged as a "matinee hop" on the afternoon that College adjourned for the Christmas vacation. We pointed out to the authorities that, while classes ended at 4 P.M., none of the departing trains left until 9 P.M. or later. This left the whole student body with four or five hours of nothing to do but wait. If the College would let us use the gymnasium, we would hire an orchestra, provide refreshments, and invite every student on the campus to be our guest. Again the authorities granted our request. Our first "matinee hop" proved to be exactly what was needed to brighten up the dismal pre-train period. So we could strut around with another feather to display.

The Delta Phi Delta example was bound to be contagious, and it was not long before a great thaw set in. All social groups were permitted to give card parties, dinner parties, dances, masquerades, and so on. Whitman boys and girls, for the first time, could undisguisedly enjoy each others company as healthy, normal beings rather than as pseudo-Puritans pretending to be interested only in eternal salvation. There would come a time when I would feel that Whitman students could do with somewhat less in the way of social diversion, but when I hark back to the dark ages prior to 1910, I am sure that the evils of too much are no greater than those of too little. As far as I personally was concerned, the great thaw at Whitman came at precisely the right time—just when I was at the most receptive age and most able to profit by social emancipation and enrichment. I have always been glad that I was a student at Whitman during the transition from the puritanical to the liberal kind of social life.

Meanwhile, in the romance department, I was inadvertently drifting into a situation I had not anticipated or intended. The truth is that I had no intentions at all. Going with Jenny had been sheer delight and I was truly fond of her, but I did not entertain serious matrimonial intentions about her or any one else. Not that I was against marriage, but I was making some long-range plans which did not include marriage. If I had been less wrapped up in myself and my plans, I would have perceived that Jenny's ideas about love and marriage were more short-range than long-range, and hence were incompatible with mine. When I finally tumbled to the truth and saw that I could not continue going with her without building up presumptive obligations I had no intention to assume, I decided to make a break and did. It was not an entirely painless break, but we had no quarrel and parted friends.

After all this had happened, which was near the end of my junior year, I gradually became aware of the existence of a girl named Elnora Campbell. Where I first saw or met her I cannot remember. Very likely it was at a rehearsal of the chapel choir, for that was about the only place our paths could have crossed. She was a third year student in Pearsons Academy and a voice major in the Conservatory of Music. We were not taking any of the same courses, had no friends in common, and did not attend any of the same social events. So there was little chance that we could have met anywhere but at chapel choir rehearsals.

She was a soloist with the chapel choir and also in the choir of the Presbyterian Church, which I studiously avoided just as I was now beginning to avoid the Wilbur M. E. Church. Indeed, I had come to be much under the spell of Dr. Raymond C. Brooks, minister of the Congregational Church, and was not only attending services there but singing in the choir. Most of the church-going I did that year was to hear Dr. Brooks, who was a liberal, brilliant, and scholarly preacher. Perhaps, if Dr. Brooks had made the effort, he could have proselyted me for Congregationalism, but he was not that sort of person. I can remember spending hours talking religion and other subjects with him, but he never tried to exert the slightest pressure on me.

Since I was de-emphasizing women at this particular juncture in my life, my increasing awareness of Elnora did not lead to much. Two or three times I asked her to go some place with me, but she had conflicting engagements. She recalls my telling her that the next time she turned me down would be the last—I would not ask her again. I don't remember that, but it is typical of the mood I was in at that time. During the commencement week-end we did manage a date—the graduation exercises of the Conservatory of Music. After that, according to her recollection, I ignored her—did not even write to her all summer. I am sure her memory is correct on that point.

IX. SENIOR

Important Decisions

In my senior year at Whitman (1911-12) I began to establish definite directions which I would follow more or less faithfully for the remainder of my life. First of all, I decided that I wanted to be a political scientist. I had long thought I would take up the study of law after graduation from college, and did not altogether abandon this idea; but in my senior year I made up my mind that I would first try for a graduate degree in political science and then, hopefully, for a law degree later. The second most important decision I made that year was that

I wanted to do my postgraduate study in political science at Columbia University. Of course, these decisions were made under the guidance of Professor Charles G. Haines, whose ardent disciple I had become. I was the first major student whom he had guided toward postgraduate study, and for that reason he took special interest in helping me.

From Professor Haines I learned about possibilities in the field of political science which sounded highly attractive to me. These included not alone college teaching, but important jobs in governmental research, public administration, and civic promotion. At that stage of my thinking I do not believe I would have substituted college teaching for law as a future career, but the non-teaching possibilities of political science appealed to me just as strongly as law. Gradually I came to realize that I never had been attracted to the practice of law but rather to law as a study and as the doorway to a career in public affairs. The further I went in the study of political science, the more I became aware of the growing importance of public as compared with private law, and the more I relished the opportunity, through graduate study in political science, to become a specialist in public law. However, I did not reject private law, and, as I will later elaborate, carried the study of private law to the point where I was prepared to be examined for admission to the bar.

Professor Haines was confident that I might be able to qualify for some sort of financial aid at Columbia University—a scholarship or fellowship, perhaps—but pointed out that this would depend on my making a high scholastic average at Whitman and demonstrating an aptitude for research. I had a B-plus average on my first three years at Whitman and decided to shoot for a straight-A record in my senior year. I had the good fortune to come very close to the target I had set. In order to try my hand at research, I enrolled in a thesis course under Professor Haines and chose a subject which required me to dig deeply into the government documents available in the Whitman Library. Most of these were stashed away in remote and dark corners of the basement of the Whitman Memorial Building, and the library staff (then consisting of one fulltime and one part-time employee) had not been able to catalog and classify them. They did not know what they had, and were not anxious to have me meddling around in their unexplored territory. However, I managed to wheedle permission to see what I could find. The finding was not easy, because there were no indexes for me to use, and I was obliged to resort to needle-in-haystack methods. Tedious and time-consuming as this was, it taught me things about government documents that I might not have learned in any other way.

In the end I produced a thesis on pork-barrel legislation in Congress, which served me well in many ways. First, I got Whitman credits with an A grade for this paper; second, I submitted it along with my application to Columbia, as evidence of my talent for research; third, I warmed it over and enlarged it for my master's thesis at the University of Wisconsin; and fourth, I polished and condensed it into a magazine article which, under the title of "A Little History of Pork," was published in the *National Municipal Review* for December, 1919. Of course, I could not foresee all this mileage when I was poring through the documents in the musty basement of Memorial in 1911-12.

The courses I took in my senior year were chiefly major courses in English and in political science, and I do not hesitate to say that in those two fields I was getting as good teaching as could have been had in any of the topflight institutions of the country. Retrospectively, any one who was doing major work simultaneously under Norman F. Coleman and Charles G. Haines, can justly boast that there were few as good and none better, as their post-Whitman records so amply attest. In addition to major courses, I elected in my senior year a course in biology under Professor Brode, one in French under Professor Cooper, and one in philosophy under President Penrose. All were two-semester courses. The biology was taken to satisfy the laboratory science requirement for graduation. I would have preferred chemistry, but schedule conflicts made that impossible. It was a good thing, however, that I was forced into biology.

Professor Brode at that time was bearing down hard to make sure that his students were thoroughly instructed in the Darwinian theory of evolution. For a would-be political scientist it was more important to be well grounded in Darwinian theory than in the atomic tables. I elected the French because I had a liking for languages and thought it might be useful in graduate study, which it certainly proved to be. With my background of Latin, German, and a modicum of Greek, French was a breeze. My one year of French at Whitman sufficed to get me through half of my doctoral language requirement at Columbia and enabled me to read French political classics with ease. The philosophy was a combination of theism and comparative religions— provocative and absorbing courses, which completely diluted my religious fundamentalism. I have already paid tribute to President Penrose as a teacher, and he was at his best in this course.

Fraternity President

I gave more time to studies than to student activities in my senior year, but still found time to be fairly busy about the campus. In the fall semester I turned out for football, a thing I had been longing to do ever since I landed on the campus as a freshman. I had enjoyed high school football and thought I would enjoy the college game even more. However, it did not take many sessions on Ankeny Field to convince me that I was entirely out of my elment. The coach intimated that I would be doing the squad a service by absenting myself from the practice periods, and that I could write much better football than I could play. So I decided to stick to my last and do the things I was best fitted for. These, in my senior year, included the offices of president of the Debate Council, manager of the glee club, and, most difficult of the three, president of Delta Phi Delta.

Delta Phi Delta had closed the year 1910-11 in good shape both as to money and members, but there was one high hurdle to get over before a good start could be made on the next year. We had lost the house on Cherry Street and had been unable during the summer vacation to find a replacement. Bill Howard had been elected treasurer and house manager at the same time that I was elected president, and we two had agreed to return to the campus early enough in September to find a house before the rest of our members got back. This we did, and scoured the town fore and aft without finding a furnished house. The best we could do was an unfurnished house on the western corner of Fulton and Isaacs, but how could we use an unfurnished house? Bill and I decided to see what we could do in the way of installment buying. Both of us had done fairly well on summer earnings and had some spare cash. If both would pay a year's room rent in advance, it might be enough for a down payment. At least it was worth a try.

We knew how many men we could count on for the year and, therefore, about how much money we could promise to pay by the end of the year. Our chief headache was beds. Owing to the smallness of the bedrooms, we had to have double-deckers, and these could not be bought readymade in Walla Walla. So we took our problem to the Whitehouse-Crawford Lumber Company, hoping they might be able and willing to make doubledeckers for us before college opened. We were able to offer a small down payment with the balance to follow in regular monthly installments. Either we were very persuasive or they took pity on us, for they agreed to take the job on the installment basis, as we had proposed, and to deliver the manufactured doubledeckers to us within two weeks, which they did.

Next we went to Davis-Kaser Company, furniture dealers, and made a similar time-payment proposal on bedsprings, mattresses, dressers, tables, chairs, rugs, and the like. They, too, seemed glad to have our business and never questioned our ability to pay. As a result of these two deals, Bill and I had a house ready for occupancy by the time College opened. It was rather sparsely furnished, but livable nevertheless, and every stick of furniture was our own, or would be when we paid up. One priceless windfall came from Dean A. W. Hendrick, who, owing to the flop of the Greater Whitman, had resigned and was leaving Whitman. In various ways he and I had come to be fairly well acquainted, and one day he stopped me on the path in front of Memorial and asked if the Delta Phi Delta house could use any pictures. He said he had a number he did not want to ship and we were welcome to come to his house and pick them up. Bill and I borrowed a hand cart and wheeled them from his place on Otis Street to our house on the corner of Fulton and Isaacs. Twenty years later some of these pictures were still adorning the walls of the Beta house. We also, by reason of having more men in the house than had been estimated, had enough surplus income to pick up a few extra items of furniture throughout the year. However, we were not yet flush enough to establish a dining department. We boarded around wherever we chose just as had been done the year before. To make this story complete, I should add that Bill was a good collector and never failed to have money to meet the monthly payments due the two firms that had trusted us. By the end of the year Delta Phi Delta was out of debt.

I quickly found out that as a fraternity president I had much more to do than preside at chapter meetings and represent the group on social occasions. In addition to my formal duties, I had to be the chief law enforcement officer. We had drawn up a code of house regulations covering such matters as study hours, cleaning the house and sleeping rooms, taking turns firing the furnace, card games, having liquor in the house, and rough-housing. If there was ever a day, usually a night, without argument over a violation or alleged violation of one of these rules, it has slipped my memory. My job was to arbitrate if I could, issue orders if I had to, get them enforced if I was able, and bring charges against the violators at the next chapter meeting. I am sure that I learned more about how *not* to handle people in that one short year as Delta Phi Delta president than in all the previous years of my life. The fraternity had unanimously elected me as its president and it was unanimously behind me in the enforcement of the rules, but, with characteristic American independence, each member tacitly reserved the right to dissent and "tell me off" if he thought I was not doing my job right. Never before had I been in a spot where I had to have public opinion solidly behind me. It opened my eyes to certain of life's realities that I might have been a long time learning.

It also turned out that in 1911-12 my job as fraternity president involved important dealings with the faculty and a committee of the Overseers and Trustees. The question of whether Whitman would allow national fraternities was up for decision that year. A special committee of Overseers and Trustees had been created to study the problem and render a report with final recommendations at the annual meeting of the Board of Overseers in June, 1912. As a part of its work the committee undertook a critical examination of the four locals then existing at Whitman and asked the faculty for assistance in making this investigation. There were two men's groups (Illahee and Delta Phi Delta) and two women's groups (Gamma Kappa and Beta Sigma). The president of each group was on call at all times to answer questions and produce information. Wishing to make the best possible impression and not contradict one another, the four presidents fell into the habit of getting together semi-occasionally in order to take common counsel and reach common understandings.

We must have comported ourselves acceptably, for at commencement, 1912, the committee recommended and the Trustees and Overseers voted that national fraternities be admitted at Whitman. Dr. Raymond C. Brooks had been chairman of the special committee and probably had more to do with the favorable recommendation than any other person. Thereafter, the major problem of each Whitman local was to promote a successful petition to a national fraternity. Since I graduated in 1912, I took only a minor part in the petitioning process. Delta Phi Delta was granted a charter by Beta Theta Pi in the summer of 1915, and thus became the Gamma Zeta Chapter of the great national fraternity. In connection with the granting of the charter the first sixteen places on the chapter roll of Gamma Zeta were allocated to alumni and faculty members of Delta Phi Delta. I was Number Nine on that list, and this became my official seniority rating in the Gamma Zeta Chapter, but I was formally initiated by the Gamma Rho Chapter at the University of Oregon on June 9, 1916, a few weeks after Gamma Zeta was formally installed at Whitman. As I type these lines in Stepember, 1963, I note that only two of the sixteen Delta Phi Deltas who were taken into Beta Theta Pi are now alive, and that as Number Nine I now hold the highest seniority among the living members of the Gamma Zeta Chapter.

Glee Club Manager

Being president of the Debate Council was no great tax on my time in 1911-12, because I did not try out for any of the forensic activities and merely presided at meetings of the Council. But serving as manager of glee club as well as singing in both the chorus and the quartet took all the time I could spare. There was a rehearsal of one group or the other nearly every afternoon, and in addition I had to handle all the business transactions connected with both. In some ways the quartet kept me much busier than the chorus, for it operated both as a part of the glee club and as an independent organization. In two respects the quartet was entirely on its own. One was musical direction and the other was engagements other than glee club concerts. We had a good quartet, if I do immodestly say so. It consisted of Henry Filer, first tenor; Roy Knight, second tenor; Virgil Bennington, first bass; and Chester Maxey, second bass. The voices blended well and the ensemble was well balanced.

In the regular glee club concerts the quartet usually sang two groups of popular numbers, and this actually did not take much doing. But we soon found ourselves in demand for all sorts of occasions—banquets, club meetings, political rallies, funerals, and anything else that happened to come along—so we had to enlarge our repertoire far beyond the glee club's requirements. Most of the time we were paid for our services on off-campus occasions, but we always donated our services to Whitman affairs. It was through such donations that I first became fully aware how awfully sour the Greater Whitman effort had gone. President Penrose asked the quartet, as a service to the College, to sing at several fund-raising meetings in Walla Walla and near-by cities, and of course we complied. At these meetings we heard President Penrose and other speakers tell of the desperate plight into which the College had fallen, how it might not be able to open its doors in the fall unless some $200,000 could be raised before that time, and how a group of leading citizens of Spokane had indicated a readiness to pay off the Whitman indebtedness if the College would move to that city.

As business manager of the glee club I found an acute problem of retrenchment on my hands. The tour of the previous year had been a ball in all respects but cash receivable. In that department there had been a whopping deficit. The manager had booked the concerts on a percentage rather than a flat guarantee basis, which meant that the local promoters had little incentive to push the sale of tickets very aggressively. So the season closed with the club deeply in debt, and this debt was mine to liquidate, *or else*. The "or else" meant that if I failed, the College authorities might step in and put the glee club in leading strings, which all of us thought would be a disgrace and a disaster. I tried to work out an itinerary on the flat guarantee basis, but found only two sponsors willing to sign up on that basis and they did not want to pay fees that would be high enough to pay our expenses. Hence, I decided to shoot for the sure money. The home concert was always good for sure money, even big money because expenses were nil. The same was true of concerts in near-by places such as Waitsburg, Dayton, and Milton, where there would be no hotel or meal bills to pay. So I booked my season that way, made a wad of money, and was the most unpopular manager (with the members) that the club ever had. Such was my first battle with deficit financing. It would not be my last.

In my senior year the Methodist church seceded from me. That sounds silly, but let me explain. A long-growing rift in the congregation of the Wilbur M. E. Church finally culminated in a ruction which resulted in the withdrawal of more than half of the members, who then went over to the newly founded, rigidly fundamentalist Church of the Nazarene. Not having been a faithful attendant at the Wilbur Church for a year or so, I was not involved in this hassle between the conservatives and

155

liberals of Methodism. My sympathies were with the liberals, and I was glad they were left in possession of the church property. However, the presiding bishop stepped into the situation and closed the Wilbur Church on the ground that the surviving congregation was too small to maintain itself and meet its obligations. Thereupon all of the non-seceding Wilburites, including myself, were notified that we might obtain credential letters which would admit us to any other Methodist congregation. I never asked for such a letter of honorable dismissal. There were several reasons for this negligence. One was that I had no definite plans for the use of such a document if I took it. I knew I was going to be headed for graduate school in the fall, and might not be permanently located for several years, which proved to be a fact. Another reason was that I was not sure I wanted to join another Methodist congregation anywhere, and wanted time to shop around before making a decision either way. In addition to the desire to wait and see, I had a fear that if I should ask for the letter, I would be subjected to pressure by certain Methodist clergymen and laymen who were good friends of mine, who would try to persuade me to cling to my Methodist heritage. At that particular time I did not want to face up to any such pressure situation. So, by doing nothing, I became a sort of Methodist without portfolio. I never took a positive step, and have not to this hour, to leave the Methodist church. Perhaps it is not accurate to say that the church seceded from me, but I am sure that the church wrote me off, as it properly should have done, because I was a member of a defunct congregation and had not established a connection with any other.

Finale

Around the middle of the second semester word came through from Columbia University that I had been awarded a graduate scholarship in political science. This seemed to settle my plans for the ensuing year. The scholarship would take care of my tuition, and I had enough laid by to cover the remainder of my expenses. I looked forward to at least one year of postgraduate work at Columbia and hoped, really believed, that I would be able to manage to go straight through to a doctorate. On June 19, 1912, I received the degree of bachelor of arts, *cum laude,* from Whitman College, immediately packed up my possessions, said farewell to my friends, and left Walla Walla with the assumption that my direct associations with Whitman College were forever at an end.

Early in January, 1912, Elnora Campbell and I became engaged, and when I left Walla Walla, I took her with me to meet my parents, who had not attended the graduation exercises. We had begun going together some time around Hallowe'en in 1911, and by New Year's she had me fully roped and tied. However, we had an understanding that there was to be no marriage until I had my graduate work behind me. We did not literally live up to that understanding, but we did wait three years and a half, by which time I was well established professionally.

PART III
UP TO THIRTY-FIVE

X. OFF AGAIN, ON AGAIN

To Columbia

The beginning and the end of the summer of 1912 stand out clearly in my memory because of their association with my fiancée. Elnora went to Ellensburg with me after the Whitman Commencement exercises and visited among the Maxey clan for a few days. Near the end of the summer I went to Spokane for a visit with her before taking off for New York and Columbia University. Apart from these red-letter occurrences, my recollections of the summer of 1912 have to do mostly with the hay harvest on the Doughty farm some two miles south of town. There was always one crop of timothy and two or more of alfalfa to cut, cure, and put away for the winter. Each crop required from ten days to two weeks to complete. My principal jobs in the harvest were to operate a rake, "go-devil" (or lift-rake), stacker, and Jackson fork. On these machines I was considered a pretty able performer. Over the years I had become quite adept at that kind of work.

The dimness of most of my memories of the summer of 1912 could be due to the fact that most of the time my mind was wandering between Elnora Campbell and Columbia University. It having been prearranged that I would spend a few days in Spokane before going on to New York, I was eager for September to arrive. Another prearrangement had taken place between my good friend Alger Fee and me. This was to the effect that we would travel together all or part of the way to New York. We had set up this arrangement by correspondence. Alger was returning to Columbia for his second year in the law school, and we two, being fraternity brothers, fellow Whitmanites, and soon to be fellow Columbians, were almost simultaneously inspired with the idea that it would be fun to make the eastern jaunt together. "Beany" Fee agreed to meet me in Spokane on a stated day, and from there we were to travel by way of the Spokane and International Railroad to a junction point with the

161

Canadian Pacific on which both of us had booked passage eastward.

This was going the long way around to get to New York, but neither of us had ever made that trip before, and that was all the reason we needed for giving it a try. This fraternal trek to the great metropolis was not the beginning of the friendship between Alger and me, but it was our first jaunt together as a twosome. In a sense it was the beginning of a dual alliance that lasted until Alger's death in August, 1959. We knew, when we set off together in September, 1912 that we were good friends, but neither of us had or could have been expected to have the faintest idea how often and how closely our future careers would be linked together. For each of us, at several crucial turning points, the other was Johnny-on-the-spot with timely and useful assistance. While it could not be said, for example, that I made him first a United States district judge and finally a United States circuit judge, I did have a finger in both pies. Nor could it be truthfully said that he made me president of Whitman College, but he was chairman of the special committee which made the nomination.

But this is getting too far ahead of my story. In September, 1912, I was more concerned with my visit at Elnora's home than anything else. Since it was my first time there, I was acutely aware of being on exhibit before all of her kinfolks and family friends. I knew something of my capacity for unwittingly "spilling the beans," and hence was not too sure of myself. But I was made to feel much at ease, and after she and I had completed the expected round of calls, dinners, and entertainments, I began to get my sights pretty well levelled. During that visit Elnora and I discovered that we were cut from very similar bolts of cloth. She had a Southern Methodist background and was just as uneasy with it as I with my Northern Methodist background. As far as social status was concerned, we stood on the same footing. Her family moved in white-collar social circles and mine in blue-collar mostly, but mine had been more successful financially. We had similiar likes and dislikes, and best of all had closely kindred senses of humor. This common sense of humor was to be the life-saver of our long engagement and much longer marriage.

When the day of departure came, Alger and I set forth on the itinerary outlined above and traveled together as far as Winnipeg. In that city we both had to change trains, he to go to Chicago and thence to New York, while I had to get a boat train for Port Arthur, Ontario, where I was to take passage on a lake steamer across Lake Superior, through the Soo Canal, and across Lake Huron and its Georgian Bay to Toronto. After a day in Toronto, I was to go on to New York by rail. I had arranged this grand tour out of sheer curiosity. I wanted to see more of the north country and especially wanted to sail across the Great Lakes. I could have gone straight to New York in three or four days less time, but I preferred the wild-goose chase. I have never regretted this, because it enabled me to see enough of Canada to have a much clearer conception of the immensity and magnificance of the great Dominion to our north.

On shipboard, crossing the Great Lakes, I became friendly with a lovely French-Canadian family—father, mother, and eighteen-year-old daughter—who were fluent in both French and English. This afforded a chance for me to try out my schoolboy French, and my friends were delighted that I wanted to try speaking French with them. I was delighted, too, both because of the pleasure it gave and because it was a wonderful rehearsal for the language examinations that I expected to have to take at Columbia. Before we debarked at Owen Sound, Ontario, I learned that the father was minister of national parks in the Canadian federal government and was then on the home stretch of a long inspection tour. This also was rare good fortune for me, an embryonic political scientist. It was my first opportunity to talk with a high official of a foreign government and get information, as it were, from the horse's mouth.

The train trip to Toronto had been scheduled to put me into that city about noon, and I will never forget my first impression of Canada's second city. I thought I had arrived in a city of the dead. Then some fellow traveler reminded me that it was Sunday and that no wheel turned in "Toronto the Good" on the

163

Lord's Day. My train for New York did not leave until about 8 P.M., so I had lots of time to get around Toronto and see the sights. But I did not get far. There was nary a streetcar or a cab to be had. I walked the streets until I was footsore, then returned to the railway station and sat around until train time.

It was some time after noon the next day when I landed in Grand Central Station, New York. I had been told about Grand Central and had read about its immensity, but was totally unprepared for the labyrinth I now had to thread. I knew that there was a subway station at Grand Central and that by taking the right subway train I could get to Columbia University and eventually to Alger's nearby rooming house. But I did not have the faintest idea how to shuttle from Grand Central to Times Square and there catch the uptown Seventh Avenue train which would land me at Columbia. There would come a day when I could almost do that in my sleep, but on this September day in 1912 I was a hick from the hinterlands. There I was, encumbered with hand luggage, topcoat, umbrella, and various other impedimenta, as completely lost as though I were in an Amazon jungle.

Somehow I managed to solve this problem in personal logistics, though I don't remember how. The thing I most vividly remember is that I almost failed for the want of spendable cash. The only cash I had on my person was a few dollars in Canadian silver and three or four American ten-dollar gold pieces. The subway cashier turned up his nose at the Canadian coin, as it was not then being accepted at par in New York. When I proffered a gold piece, he looked at me as though I had just robbed a bank. I had not remembered that gold, even then, circulated only in the West and that my "tenner" probably was the first gold piece the subway cashier ever had seen. He picked it up, turned it over and over, seeming afraid to take it and afraid not to. I believe that he finally decided in my favor because he thought I was too much of a rube to be dishonest. Anyhow, after due deliberation and some questioning, he pushed a ticket through the wicket and gave me my change.

Alger had offered to share his room with me until I could find one of my own. Hence, upon landing at 116th and Broadway (Columbia station) I queried my way to his lodgings on one of the side streets east of Amsterdam Avenue. I had to wait around a while before Alger showed up, and the landlady was not sure whether to let me stay or send me on my way. I suppose that, like the subway cashier, she finally concluded that I had too much hay in my hair to be a crook. Anyhow, she did let me hang around, and in an hour or so Alger made his appearance and took me in.

The next morning I set out to do two things: (1) get registered at Columbia and (2) find a room. Before going through the registration mill, I wanted to have a talk with Professor Charles A. Beard. Professor Haines had advised me to do this. He knew Beard very well and thought him the man for me to tie to at Columbia. I was glad to accept this advice, because Beard was about the only Columbia political scientist I knew anything about. We had used his textbooks at Whitman and Dr. Haines had told me a good deal about him. Early in the morning, therefore, I made my way to Hamilton Hall, where Beard's office was located, and sought an appointment. To my utter dumbfoundment, I was informed that Beard was on leave of absence for the ensuing academic year. This was bad news (to me) and just about knocked the props from under me. I did not even start looking for a room and made no appointment for pre-registration counseling. Instead, I got hold of Alger as soon as I could find him and asked his advice. We chewed the problem over at length, and I took his advice to make haste slowly.

For two or three days I scouted around the Columbia campus to learn what I could about the political science program for 1912-13, and what I learned did not please me very much. Gradually I argued myself into the belief that if I had known Beard was to be away, I would not have come to Columbia this year. This was not true, but I convinced myself that it was. If I had known in advance that Beard was to be away, I probably would have asked Dr. Haines to suggest some other member of the graduate faculty as an adviser. But in my disappointment about Beard, I reacted with the feeling that I wanted no other adviser and would not want to do work under the men who were substituting for him that year. Then I hammered down in my mind the clincher, which was that I would be a fool to stick around Columbia and put out my hard-earned money for courses I cared so little about. Thus I made up my mind to get up and get out.

What to do and where to go? Suddenly I remembered that the University of Illinois was located at Urbana, that Grandma Collins and Aunt Anna still lived there, and that by paying them a visit I could incidentally discover what the University of Illinois might have to offer in the way of graduate courses in political science. After Alger and I had hashed this over for a day or two, I packed my bags and lit out for Urbana. The University was already in session when I got there, and this made it easy for me to get the information I sought. No purely graduate courses in political science were being offered that year. At Illinois, as at most American universities then, graduate students and upper-division undergraduates were thrown together in the same courses, the chief differentiation being that graduate students, if the professors rode herd on them efficiently, were supposed to do more and better work. Columbia was one of a tiny minority of American universities in which graduate instruction was entirely segregated. I much preferred this type of graduate instruction.

After a few days in Urbana, I decided that the University of Illinois was not for me. However, I was having an enjoyable time and was in no hurry to move on. Everything was pleasantly different from what I remembered of Urbana from our brief residence there nine years before. Aunt Anna seemed pleased to have a grown nephew to squire her around, and I was equally pleased to be her escort to concerts, shows, and football games. Nevertheless, I realized that I could not loiter there indefinitely, and began to figure the angles on getting a job to help replenish my now somewhat depleted savings. From every angle the most sensible thing, it seemed, would be to get back to the Pacific Northwest where I knew my way around. Accordingly, I bought a ticket for Walla Walla. Since I had many friends there, I thought I might have a better chance there than elsewhere to land a suitable job.

Whitman Interlude

It was Columbus Day, 1912, when I landed in Walla Walla. This I clearly remember, because I took the streetcar from the Union Pacific Depot up Main Street. This would take me straight to the Delta Phi Delta House, where I knew I could put up as long as I liked. As we passed the county courthouse I saw a huge crowd assembled on the lawn, and a fellow passenger told me that the occasion was a dedication ceremony for a statue of Columbus, October 12 having been chosen as the most appropriate time. That statute still stands on the courthouse lawn and bears an inscription to the effect that it was dedicated on Ocober 12, 1912.

Naturally, one of the first things I did after reaching Walla Walla was to have a talk with Professor Haines. I could see that he was disappointed in me, but he was kind and understanding just the same. Best of all, he had a job for me right away. A few weeks earlier he had been instrumental in promoting an organization called the League of Pacific Northwest Municipalities and had been made its executive secretary. Office detail had piled up on him to such an extent that he was up to his ears in paper work and needed immediate help. Would I take the post of assistant secretary, at a modest honorarium and help him get caught up? Since Haines did not type and I had considerable facility on the rattle-bang machines of that day, he thought I was just the man to give him the needed lift. I gladly accepted his offer. Another job that quickly came my way was that of singing bass in a mixed quartet at the Congregational Church. Dr. Brooks did that for me. The church job and the secretarial job together paid enough to keep a roof over my head and keep me in meat and potatoes until I could find something better.

Shortly after Christmas, the "something better" dropped out of a clear sky, not in Walla Walla, but in my home town. Mr. E. J. Klemme, former principal of the Walla Walla High School, had become superintendent of schools in Ellensburg. He and I had become good friends in the Wilbur M. E. Church, but how he learned that I was in Walla Walla and might be open for a teaching offer, I do not know. However that may be, one wintry morning I received a telegram from Mr. Klemme saying that there was an unexpected vacancy in the Ellensburg High School faculty, and would I consider taking the job for the second semester? The salary would be eighty dollars a month, and I would be required to teach alegbra, geometry, and English (one course in composition and one course in literature).

If I had not been getting short of funds I might have declined, for I was not keen to leave Walla Walla. Furthermore, if the requirements for high school teaching had been what they are now, I would have been oliged to decline. I could not have satisfied a single one of the present-day requirements for teaching certification. I had taken no education courses, had read no teaching manuals, and had no practice teaching. All I knew about teaching was what I had seen in action in the Ellensurg school system and in Whitman College. But I had some good models to follow, and was not at all worried about my ability to handle the job. I was not specially interested in teaching as a career; in fact, at this juncture was actually disinterested. But the Ellensburg job did not look like the prelude to a teaching career. It was for one semester only, and would ease my financial situation enough to enable me to continue with my original plans. I took the problem to Dr. Haines, and he advised me to accept Mr. Klemme's offer. He was not sure how much longer the League of Pacific Northwest Municipalities could afford me and thought a semester of teaching would be good for me. That settled it. I sent a telegram of acceptance to Mr. Klemme right away.

High School Teacher

In more ways than one taking the Ellensburg job was a fateful decision for me. If I had not taken that job I might have been financially unable to get back to graduate school as soon as I did. And if I had not taken that job I might never have discovered that I had both an aptitude and liking for classroom teaching. As a substitute teacher in the Ellensburg High School I found out for the first time that teaching could be fun. I had always thought of teaching as a dull, tread-mill type profession, but the moment I walked into my first class I found that I had a battle of wits on my hands. This was exciting, the kind of excitement I had always loved. I was a substitute teacher, green as a cucumber, tossed into the lions' den in the middle of the year. My predecessor had been a favorite, and so the students expected me to be a washout. They had nothing against me except that they did not want me. Some of them may have felt sorry for me, but none of them showed it.

There was one thing these Ellensburg youngsters did not know, and neither did I until the heat was on. That was how fast I could work under pressure. The English courses gave me little concern or trouble. I was assigned a sophomore course in composition and a senior course in Shakespeare (*Julius Caesar* and *The Merchant of Venice*). I was well prepared in these courses and articulate enough to hold the reins in any classroom go-round. But I was very rusty in algebra and geometry, and therefore had to do a double job in those subjects—keep up with the daily lessons and also brush up on the previous semester's work. This meant reviewing almost all of my high school and college mathematics fast enough and thoroughly enough so that the little devils could not catch me with a problem I did not know how to work. To succeed in this, I had to do a lot of intensive cramming, mostly at night. Many a night I saw the dawn come before I was sure of my "math" work for the next day.

I could boast that hard work won the day for me, and it is true that I could not have done it without hard work. But I believe that the thing which contributed most to my success as a teacher was a skill which I had been developing since I was a small boy and in which I was now highly proficient, namely, public speaking. Anything my mind absorbed I could stand on my feet and tell to other people in language they could understand. I had been working at that ever since the first grade.

Not only had I learned how to put words together; I had also learned how to get and hold the attention of an audience. A few things about public speaking can be learned from books, but the difference between boresome and enjoyable public speaking has to be learned by countless years of trial and error. By the time I stood before my classes in the Ellensburg High School, I had experienced seventeen years of real trial and error in public speaking.

An audience of high school kids is basically no different from any other, except that it is likely to be more homogeneous and therefore easier to handle. I knew that if I could get the kids to pay attention, it would not be hard to convey my thought to them, whether in English or in mathematics. In getting and holding attention a speaker often has to use tricks, and there were few of those tricks I did not use. Shamelessly, I took advantage of their natural curiosity by tricks of gesture, diction, intonation, and dramatic suspense which were tied in with earthy concerns always uppermost in the teen-age mind. Before long I had them in the mood to listen attentively because they were afraid they would miss something if they did not. By the end of the semester I had established myself as a good enough teacher to be rehired. Mr. Klemme offered me a promotion in rank and a substantial increase in salary if I would sign a renewal contract, but I declined. I had made up my mind to get back on the graduate school assembly line as soon as possible, and I thought I could see my way clear to do that in the fall of 1913.

Though still intending to try for a doctorate at Columbia, I had become interested in some of the exceptional things that were being done in political science at the University of Wisconsin. At that time the legislative reference and bill drafting bureaus of the University of Wisconsin were being widely featured in newspaper and magazine articles. Why not, I asked myself, take a year or so at Wisconsin and possibly a master's degree before trying Columbia again? It was an appealing idea, and I acted upon it by applying for a graduate scholarship at the University of Wisconsin. With this application I submitted much the same supporting material that I had used at Columbia the year before. My application was successful, and for the year 1913-14 I was awarded a university scholarship which covered tuition, fees and a small cash honorarium in return for which I was obligated to grade papers and conduct quiz sections for members of the department of political science. I did not object to this requirement, because I thought it might give me a bit of college teaching experience to trade on in the future. I was now back on the main line again, headed for my chosen destination. This time I was determined not to be sidetracked.

XI. UNIVERSITY OF WISCONSIN, 1913-14

Graduate Student

I spent the Christmas vacation of 1912-13 in Spokane with Elnora, and at that time we made plans to go to Walla Walla for the Whitman commencement in June, 1913, after which she would accompany me back to Ellensburg for another visit with my folks. These plans were duly carried out, and in mid-September I was in Spokane again to spend a few days with my fiancée before setting out for Madison, Wisconsin. Again I was to enjoy the company of a fraternity brother on the eastward trip. This time it was Arthur W. ("Shelley") Blomquist of the class of 1913. "Shelley" (nicknamed after his home town in Southern Idaho), was a political science major at Whitman. He and I had lived together in the Delta Phi Delta House; he was vice president while I was president of the fraternity; we had double-dated on fraternity parties; and we had sat side by side in many of Dr. Haines' classes. Together we had developed an interest in postgraduate study, and if I had stayed at Columbia, he probably would have come there to be with me. We had that sort of feeling toward one another.

When I suggested the University of Wisconsin for 1913-14, Art was enthusiastic about the idea, and we accordingly made plans not only to travel together but to room together in Madison. As previously arranged by correspondence, Art met me in

Spokane, and we took the Milwaukee Railroad from there to Madison. It was the first time over this road for both of us and this made it doubly interesting. In Madison we had no trouble finding a two-room suite in a rooming house at 631 Langdon Street, within easy walking distance of the University.

Arthur Blomquist and I did not register for identical programs of graduate study at the University of Wisconsin. I leaned more to the legal and he more to the historical aspects of political science. My principal courses that year were constitutional law, administrative law, international law, labor legislation, statute lawmaking, federal administration, and railway regulation. In addition I audited courses in sociology and economics. As a scholarship student, I was required to conduct quiz sections and grade papers in the course in federal administration. This brought me into close and friendly association with Blaine F. Moore, professor of political science at the University of Kansas, who was serving as an interim professor at Wisconsin that year. Moore gave the lectures in federal administration and I (for undergraduates only) read all of the examination papers and conducted two quiz sections. I was mighty glad for my previous classroom experience in the Ellensburg High School.

In administrative law I had Arnold B. Hall, a brilliant teacher who later became president of the University of Oregon. He and I became good friends, and he later made an effort to get me on the faculty of the University of Wisconsin. After he became president at Oregon I met him at various places in the Northwest and once had the pleasure of introducing him as a speaker at Whitman College and at the Walla Walla Chamber of Commerce. In international law I had Stanley K. Hornbeck, who later achieved international distinction as Director of the Office of Far Eastern Affairs in the Department of State and climaxed his public career as United States ambassador to the Netherlands. It was widely said by those in a position to look behind the scenes that the Far Eastern policy of the United States between 1920 and 1944 was more shaped by the hand of Stanley Hornbeck than any other person. A few times during those years I had opportunity to meet and talk with him.

In labor legislation I had John R. Commons, the nation's leading authority in that field and one of the great pioneers in the study of the labor movement. Commons was an unforgettable teacher, not because he was a spellbinder in the lecture room, but because he had the rare gift of perspicuity and fully illuminated every topic he touched upon. My course in statute lawmaking was conducted by two professors, Chester Lloyd Jones, author of the leading textbook on that subject, and Charles McCarthy, director of the legislative reference bureau of the state of Wisconsin. Part of the work was done on the University campus and part at the state capitol building a mile across town. In this course I gained a great deal more than a knowledge of legislative organization, procedure, and drafting; the most important thing I learned was how to use English as a precision instrument in stating legal rules. Although my training in English was much better than average, I had not been forced in any previous work to discipline myself to exactitude in the use of language. If Chester Lloyd Jones and Charles McCarthy did nothing else for me, they made me understand that there is no excuse for obfuscation in legal language or any other kind.

In addition to the foregoing credit courses, I audited a course in general sociology under the famed Edward A. Ross, whose books were then on the bestseller lists, and one in principles of economics under Richard T. Ely, then regarded as America's most original economic thinker. I have often thought I went to the University of Wisconsin at just the right time. I could not have had a better choice of courses or greater teachers anywhere in America, possibly not anywhere in the world. Under the leadership of one of its greatest presidents, Charles R. Van Hise, the University of Wisconsin had surged to the front in nearly every field of study. In the social sciences it was easily the peer of such institutions as Harvard, Columbia, and Johns Hopkins.

Arthur Blomquist and I had a good year together in Madison. We were good friends and congenial companions. We worked like beavers, but we also took time to play a little. There were

173

many interesting things going on—departmental smokers, lectures, concerts, athletic events, picture shows, outings on the lakes, and now and then a specially interesting church service. It was really something to be in Madison in the heyday of the La Follette era. Old Bob was then at the crest of his senatorial career and Young Bob was a freshman in the University, just initiated into Beta Theta Pi. Madison was awash with politics and politicians, and it seemed to me that there were nights when every meeting place in town was boiling with debates, resolves, protests and proposals. Art and I took in many of these affairs.

One thing, however, we did not do; we did not date any girls, which was quite a privation for both of us. We were both engaged to Whitman girls and played square with them. My engagement "took," but his just barely survived that year in Madison. Though I am not sure about his situation, there was one additional reason why I had no dates with girls that year. My funds were getting so low that I could not afford it. Toward the end of the year I was so hard up that the only way I could get by was to cut down on my eating. From the first of April to the middle of June I lived on two meals a day at two-bits a meal. I did not starve, probably was not much malnourished, but if I had needed to lose twenty-five pounds, which I did not, I could not have chosen a surer way. I had miscalculated the cost of a year at Wisconsin. I had not been able to save much from my one semester salary at Ellensburg and actually had borrowed about $300 from a money lender there, but even with my scholarship stipend, I had barely enough to skin through. I was doubly glad, therefore, when on the 17th of June, 1914, I marched to the platform in the University gymnasium and received the diploma which awarded me the degree of Master of Arts.

West Again

Wisconsin had not disappointed me in any way. Quite the contrary. It had given me a wonderful year academically, had given me invaluable personal experiences, and had brought me into friendly association with some of the leading members of the University faculty. More than that, Wisconsin started me off as a college professor. Around the middle of the second semester Chester Lloyd Jones called me to his office and showed me a letter from U. G. Dubach of the Oregon Agricultural College asking Lloyd Jones to recommend a man for an instructorship in political science in that institution. L. J. said that if I would apply for the job, he would write a supporting letter for me, and suggested that I get other members of the department to do the same. In my financial condition, I would have applied for a job in Patagonia, if there had been a prospective one there. The prospect of going to O.A.C. seemed too good to be real. I followed Lloyd Jones' suggestions to the letter, and in the course of a month or so the job was mine, at the munificent salary of $1,300 for two semesters with extra pay for summer school, should it be held. Aside from the fact that this job took me right back to the Pacific Northwest, where I most wanted to be, I really thought I was being handsomely paid. It was nearly $600 a year more than I had been paid as a high school teacher in Ellensburg, and considering that the going salary for a full professor was around $2,000 a year, I thought I was making a fine start. I had only a vague idea of what I would be required to teach at O.A.C., and I knew nothing about Ulysses Grant Dubach except that he had received his doctorate at Wisconsin a year or two before and was highly regarded there. But I was in a hurry to get going and regretted the intervening summer vacation.

On my way back west I stopped off at Spokane for a visit with Elnora, and quite naturally we discussed our marriage plans. If I had not been so nearly broke, we doubtless would have been married that summer. But I was in debt to the tune of $300, and had barely enough cash to get me to Corvallis, Oregon. Elnora would have taken me debts and all, but I did not want it that way. I held the now archaic idea that a bride is entitled to an unmortgaged husband, and I still think I was right. Our marriage could have gone on the rocks the first year, as myriads of others have done, mainly because of the difficulty of making personal adjustments and pinching pennies at the same time. If Elnora had been with me that first year in Corvallis, not only

175

would she have had to endure financial privation but would have been deprived of my company most of the time.

It was after the Fourth of July when I got to Ellensburg, and I planned to go on to Corvallis in the latter part of August. There was not much summer work to be had around Ellensburg that year, so, except for a few days in the hay harvest, I put in most of my time boning up on some of the courses I thought I might be teaching, come September. I knew I would be teaching American Government, and I was well prepared on that. I had been told that I might be asked to take a section of beginning economics, and I had done enough brush-up work under Ely at Wisconsin to be confident I could handle that. But there were several unknowns in the equation, and I worried a little about them, but not nearly as much as I would have if I could have foreseen what lay ahead.

One specially vivid memory of the summer of 1914 is the outbreak of World War I, or, as we then styled it the Great European War. No one dreamed at that time that the United States would be drawn into that war. News did not travel as rapidly then as now, since there was no radio or television. All of our knowledge of the war came from newspapers, and Ellensburg had no paper capable of handling a great volume of war news. We had to depend on the Seattle papers and their special editions, which nearly always reached us a day late. But it was still fresh news for Ellensburg, and newsboys peddled the latest edition of the Seattle papers all over town. Ellensburg had never known anything of this kind before, and great excitement resulted.

I would not have said in 1914 that the war news was slanted, though now I know it was. I did notice, even then, that what I read in the Seattle papers was far from being pro-German. This troubled me a little. I had studied German for three years and was fairly well informed on European history. I thought the American government was right in following a policy of neutrality, but I had a slight suspicion that the news purveyed by the Seattle press was not in line with that policy.

XII. OREGON AGRICULTURAL COLLEGE, 1914-17

Corvallis

The institution now known as Oregon State University was originally the Oregon Agricultural College. In 1914 it had an enrollment of about a thousand students and hence was rated as a big institution, which, for those days, it truly was. As I recall, it was the second largest institution of higher learning in the Pacific Northwest, being exceeded only by the University of Washington. In addition to its flourishing school of agriculture, it boasted a school of forestry, a school of engineering, a school of pharmacy, a school of education, a school of home economics, and a school of commerce. Not only was there no school of liberal arts; O. A. C. was forbidden by law to teach liberal arts as such. English, foreign languages, history, and such like could be taught only as auxiliary or service subjects in connection with the offerings of one of the technical schools. The departments offering service subjects were independent, floating portfolios attached to none of the organized schools.

My appointment was in the school of commerce, which was composed of departments of accounting, business administration, economics, political science, and sociology. Every department in the school of commerce offered courses which were required for the degree of bachelor of science in commerce, and in addition each offered one or more service courses for other schools. As an instructor in political science, I gave American government courses which were set up by sections, *e.g.*, one for commerce students, one for agricultural students, one for engineering students, etc. The same thing was done with other political science courses, and also with other economics courses, accounting courses, and the like. Great care had to be used in determining and describing the content of every course we offered, lest it infringe the law enacted by the state legislature which required all purely liberal arts courses to be given at the University of Oregon in Eugene.

I was blissfully unaware of such academic complications when I rolled into the small city of Corvallis in September, 1914. I came on the Oregon Electric Railroad, not by automobile. At that stage of my life I had not thought of ever owning an automobile. Very few people owned horseless carriages then, and even fewer used them for long trips. I did not own a car, did not expect to, had never driven one, and had enjoyed only one or two brief rides in cars owned by others. It was my opinion that the automobile was still pretty much a toy and would never replace Old Dobbin as a common carrier.

By correspondence in advance I had arranged to take a room with a Mrs. Pinkerton and to board with a Mrs. Russell. My first steps in Corvallis were to get settled in these arrangements, call on Dr. Dubach, and then finagle a loan at the bank to cover the cost of my first months board and lodging. I had landed in Corvallis with about five bucks in my jeans, and that was not enough to carry me to my first pay check. The bank loan was not hard to negotiate. Once I established the fact that I was a member of the O.A.C. faculty, my credit was good. The College was not merely the principal industry of the town; it was just about the sole industry. Most of the bank's business came directly or indirectly out of the College. Corvallis was then a town of three to four thousand, not counting students, and was a completely collegiate community.

My quarters in the Pinkerton residence were a bit Spartan by modern standards, but were exactly suited to my requirements. For all practical purposes the whole second floor was mine—a combination study, bedroom, and bath, entirely independent of the rest of the house. This little apartment was heated by a very good woodburning stove, and I knew from long experience how to get the most and best out of that kind of heating equipment. There were times when I had to fetch my own fuel from the basement, though the son of the family, a high school boy, was supposed to take care of this chore. Having been a wood toter most of my days, I did not mind his lapses too much. It was a great advantage to have my own heating and hot water system, because I could then keep any hours that suited me.

My accomodations with the Pinkerson family were entirely typical of the time and locale. As was then true of all Willamette Valley communities, Corvallis was exclusively a wood-fueled town. Gas was unavailable; electric heating had not yet been developed; and coal was prohibitively expensive. But, if there was one thing Western Oregon possessed in greater abundance than anything else, it was wood. Every fall, in every town and even in the metropolitan city of Portland, tall ricks of cordwood filled every parking strip and many of the sidewalks. From September to late spring the whine of the woodsaw mangled the air, and shirtsleeved householders could be seen bucking the stove-sized chunks of fir, pine, or post oak into basements and woodsheds. The nabobs as well as the nobodies had to do this all through the heating season, and every one took it in stride.

The Russell boarding house proved to be a joy beyond words. The cuisine was impeccable and the associations were exciting. The clientele was limited to O.A.C. faculty members. A few married couples occasionally dined there, but most of the regulars were unmarried members of the faculty who were mostly of junior rank. Although the men outnumbered the women, there were a few wonderful gals from the home economics and physical education departments to keep us on our toes. Since the boarders came from all schools and departments, Russell's came as close to being a faculty club as anything then existing at O.A.C. It was a perfect crossection of the junior faculty personnel of the institution, meeting around a truly festive board three times a day. At formal faculty meetings, we juniors were expected to be seen more than heard; but at Russell's we had a forum thrice daily. We had prodigious arguments, discussed everything discussable, exchanged gossip unblushingly, concocted fantastic schemes, planned and put on various social events and public performances, and naturally, formed firm and lasting friendships. In a week's time at Russell's I had a lowdown on the whole institution.

There had been several exchanges of letters between Dr.

Dubach and me, and he had made the tentative arrangements for me at both Pinkerton's and Russell's. I was eager to meet him, and was not disappointed. From the moment we first clasped hands, I was sure I was facing an extraordinary man who would become a warm and durable friend. Dubach proved to be all I could have hoped. I could not have broken into college teaching under better chaperonage than he gave me. Dubach was a sound and superb teacher, a thorough student, and able administrator, and the very epitome of common sense. Although only in his second year at O.A.C. he was already recognized as a "comer." His subsequent career as dean of the college there and, after retirement, as a distinguished teacher at Lewis and Clark College in Portland, amply fulfilled his early promise.

I doubt if he relished it, but one of Dubach's first acts after meeting me was to hand me a bundle of bad news. This had to do with my teaching load for the first semester—the whole year, in fact. I was to have three sections of American government, two sections of principles of economics, three sections of business law, and one section of sociology. This totalled twenty-seven classroom hours per week, with four subjects to prepare. Dubach did not intimate that this was excessive, and I did not protest. The truth is that I had no idea how heavy a load it would be, and I doubt if Dubach did, either. O.A.C. registration was growing by leaps and bounds, and the kids had to be taught. Heavy teaching loads were the rule rather than the exception in all institutions of higher education in those days. O.A.C. may have been a bit worse than some, but not much. To the taxpaying public, twenty-seven hours a week looked like a lazy man's job. That a teacher might have to put in three or four times as many hours outside as inside the classroom was incomprehensible to the general mass of farmers, lumbermen, and small-town business people whom the institution must look to for support.

Young Instructor

I really had a wonderful time that first year at O.A.C., yet I doubt if I ever put in longer working hours or applied myself more intensively. The chief cause of my time-eating labors was the three sections of business law. For all my other courses I had a pretty fair background of undergraduate and graduate courses, but in business law I had nothing. The public law courses I had taken at Wisconsin supplied no preparation whatever for such subjects as contracts, agency, negotiable instruments, bailments, sales, partnerships, corporations, insurance, and real and personal property. Dubach had set up the business law course to run through the entire year at three hours per week. Spencer's *Manual of Commercial Law* and Bays's *Cases on Commercial Law* were the required textbooks, and both assumed a teacher well enough trained in law to cope with the technicalities of the subjects enumerated above. I had to give one section for commerce students, one for agriculture and forestry students, and one for engineering students, and was supposed to be able to adapt the material to their varying degrees of preparation and the special needs of their respective professions. I should have been scared to death, but I was too ignorant for that. I thought I could swing it, and accepted the assignment without a murmur.

My only hope of success lay in learning law fast enough to keep ahead of my classes, and that is what I set out to do. This meant assimilating the two textbooks and delving deeply enough into collateral reference material to be sure I knew what I was doing and saying, and the only way of doing this was an intensive cram schedule. My daytime hours were devoted to meeting classes, conferring with students, and preparing for all subjects other than law. My nights were exclusively reserved for law. Immediately after dinner I would take a short nap and then hit the law books until 3 A.M. Then I would go to bed and sleep until seven, when my alarm clock would pull me out. A hasty toilet, a race to Russell's for breakfast, and then a sprint for an eight o'clock class was the way I greeted every day but Sunday.

It was a brutal grind, but I did learn law. Chief Justice Marshall is said to have studied law no more than three months before qualifying for admission to the bar. I was not that good a sponge, but I did develop an absorptive capacity I did not know I had. I had never realized that one's ability to learn could be so tremendously cranked up. I taught business law for three years and constantly reworked the course material. By the end of the third year I believe I could have made a good stab at the bar examinations anywhere in the country. For several years I actively nursed such an ambition. I registered with the board of bar examiners in Oregon, but moved out of the state before achieving residence eligibility to take the bar examinations. I took pre-examination steps also in New York and Ohio, but changes of residence spoiled those plans also. Finally I came to the conclusion that if I never entered the practice of law, and I had little intention of that, the advantages of admission to the bar would be too slight to justify the effort. There was only one reason why I ever regretted that decision. Admission to the bar would have qualified me for membership in the local, state, and national bar associations, which would have a unique distinction for a professor of political science and might have been helpful to me professionally.

Some time in the spring of 1915, April as I remember it, President Hendrick of the University of Nevada visited O.A.C. He was the same Archer W. Hendrick to whom I had said farewell at Whitman some three years before—the man who had been dean of the college during my four years at Whitman. His business at O.A.C. did not involve me particularly (so I thought), but for old times sake we had lunch together. Our conversation touched upon a wide variety of topics, mostly reminiscences, but he seemed to be much interested in what I was doing at O.A.C. and how I liked it. Finally, he asked me if I would accept a position at the University of Nevada. I said I would, provided we could agree on satisfactory terms as to salary, rank, and subjects to be taught. He thought there would be no difficulty about that, but said the matter would have to be taken to the board of regents before an offer could be made. He promised to write as soon as this was done. However, before Hendrick got my appointment through the board of regents, he had a falling out with the board over another matter and was summarily dismissed. I have often wondered what would have happened if Hendrick had remained at Nevada and I had gone there to be associated with him.

Marriage

At exactly noon, June 17, 1915, Elnora Campbell and I were married. The wedding took place at her home in Spokane, and we honeymooned for a week or so at the summer place (Kamel Kamp) of her cousin, Johnston B. Campbell. This was snugly tucked away on the south shore of Liberty Lake, some seventeen miles from Spokane. The rest of that summer we spent in leisurely visiting around with kinfolk in Spokane and Ellensburg. Around the middle of August we moved into our first home at 427 North Fifth Street in Corvallis. I had rented this little furnished house before leaving Corvallis in June, and it was supposedly ready for occupancy when we arrived. For the most part it was. The owners were an elderly couple named Schaffer, who wanted to leave most of their household things there while they spent a year or two traveling.

Elnora and I did not own a thing except what we brought in our bags and trunks, and counted ourselves lucky to get the Schaeffer house. Not only did it save us the expense of buying furniture but also china and kitchen utensils. It was a five-room house of fairly recent construction, and quite modern according to the notions of the time. There were a living room, dining room, kitchen, bathroom, two bedrooms, and a roomy basement for wood storage. There was a woodburning range which supplied heat and hot water for both kitchen and bathroom, and there was a woodburning heater midway between the dining room and parlor. All the rest of the house was heated, presumptively, by circulation from these two stoves. If all doors were left open, that presumption was approximated, save in extra cold weather. Once again I had a wood bucking job on my hands. Our fuel, slab wood for the range and post oak for the heater, was delivered at the curb on Fifth Street. I had to employ a sawyer to cut it to stove size, and then I lugged it to the basement and stacked for the winter. Every morning, regardless of the season, I had to build a fire in the range and in cool weather also in the heater. The noise I made shaking down the ashes and starting the fires served as Elnora's alarm clock.

We lived in the Schaeffer house for two years and enjoyed every moment of it. It was convenient in walking distance both to the business section of town and the campus. And we walked wherever we went. We preferred walking to bicycling, which was the only other mode of transportation possible for us. Never having enjoyed central heating, electrical appliances, or soft living of any kind, we were not troubled about the limitations of the Schaeffer house. We were not troubled about owning nothing more than the clothes on our backs. We were making plans for a future that involved far away things and places.

Marriage opened up a new kind of life for me. Elnora and I were immediately drawn into the social whirl of the O.A.C. faculty and the town of Corvallis. We were on the go most of the time, it seemed. There were dinner parties, dances, shows, lectures, concerts, receptions, and everything else characteristic of a college town. We found ourselves in demand as chaperones for student dinners and dances, and also soon found ourselves in demand as entertainers. With her lovely voice and musical ability, Elnora soon became leading soloist, choir director, and voice teacher of the town. She could also do a creditable job on the piano and organ. Given easy music of the Harry Lauder type, I could grind out a passable bass or baritone, as the music might require. With Elnora as accompanist, I fooled the public well enough to be invited again and again to do a solo at some public function. She and I also worked up a few duets which proved highly popular. Altogether, we had all the going and all the performing we could find time and energy for.

In my second year at O.A.C. I was promoted to the rank of assistant professor and given a salary increase. Also I began to be tapped for faculty committee service and was called upon to make speeches and deliver lectures in Corvallis and various other cities under the auspices of the extension division of the institution. Somehow I got the job done, and well enough apparently to be invited again and again. What the audiences got out of my performances I hate to imagine, but I got enormous benefit from them. Most of all I got growth—growth of mind, growth of personality, and growth of skill. In my third year I received an additional salary increase and was told I could look forward to something better in the future. But Elnora and I had decided that as soon as we were financially able I would ask for a leave of absence. I wanted to go to Columbia to finish my work on the doctorate and she wanted to study in the Institute of Musical Art (forerunner of Juilliard). Our hoard grew large enough, finally, to enable us to finance the year 1917-18 in New York. I requested leave for that year, and my request was granted.

Leave of Absence

The war in Europe seemed far away and likely to be of brief duration when I joined the O.A.C. faculty in 1914, but as our country became increasingly entangled, virulent controversies broke out, even on our remote and rural campus. Though a Republican in antecedents, I had been for Woodrow Wilson in 1912, but in 1916 I was all for Hughes. I did not like the way Wilson had handled the issue of freedom of the seas. I thought he was letting the British get away with murder, and also the Germans. I wanted him to crack down hard on both and equally on both. It infuriated me just as much to have the British violate American rights as the Germans. In short, I was aggressively neutral. Faculty sentiment at O.A.C. tended to be anti-German, and there were several Anglophile and Francophile professors who thought the United States should immediately leap into the fray on the side of the Allies. I thought the United States should go about its own business, and not try to pull any one's chestnuts out of the fire. Expression of this conviction got me labeled in some quarters as pro-German. Some of the pro-Ally professors got their heads together and concocted a resolution addressed to President Wilson and to Congress urging an immediate declaration of war on Germany.

185

They presented this at an O.A.C. faculty meeting and moved its adoption.

This triggered a nasty intramural war of words. Some (of whom I was one) thought it improper for the faculty as an official body to speak its opinion in questions of foreign policy. Some argued that the faculty had the constitutional right of freedom of speech and should exercise it as the majority saw fit. Some thought that if the president and administration of the college did not gag the faculty, the legislature eventually would. I was against gag rule either by the college administration or the state legislature. I felt sure that a majority would vote against the resolution once it came to a vote, but also thought it might do great harm to allow it to come to a vote. There did not seem to be any way a majority could prevent that. By discreet inquiries, however, President Kerr discovered that once the motion was made, a majority would readily vote for a motion to refer it to a select committee for special study as to its form and phrasing. This motion was duly made and passed, and the resolution went to the special committee. Before the committee got around to report it back to the faculty, the United States had entered the war.

By April, 1917, Elnora and I had perfected our plans for a year in New York and I had been granted a leave of absence for the ensuing academic year. We could not tell whether the war would interfere with these plans. There was no reason why I should rush forward and volunteer for military service. Congress had passed a selective service act under which all males of military age had to register for compulsory military service. If your number was drawn, you went; if not, you waited. I registered and waited. My number never was drawn, although that could have happened any time before the armistice on November 11, 1918. Elnora and I decided that a draft call would be no more of a gamble in New York than in Corvallis, as my number was determined by my registration in Corvallis. We had money enough for one year in New York. If the selective service took me before the end of the year, that was that. By the same token, it would have lifted me out of the faculty at O.A.C. If I should be taken while in New York, Elnora could go on with her musical studies, which would be preferable to being a war widow in Corvallis. So we decided to take the chance.

We spent most of the summer of 1917 visiting in Ellensburg and Spokane, and set out for New York early in September. The admissions office at Columbia had informed me that I must pass the foreign language examinations before I would be allowed to matriculate for the Ph.D. I had elected to be examined in French and German, and the examinations were set for the last week of September. It had been three or four years since I had done any work in those languages, so I felt the need of a brush-up before the examinations. That was the reason for our going to New York so long before the opening of the semester. I knew I could work in the Columbia library and would find there all the review materials I might need.

XIII. COLUMBIA UNIVERSITY, 1917-18
Foreign Language Cram

Elnora and I arrived at Grand Central Station about midmorning. This time I knew my way around well enough to put on a sophistication act for her benefit. As though I had done it for years, I steered her through the crowds and out to the taxi line on Vanderbilt Avenue where we took a cab for the Hotel Irving, which was located on the south side of Gramercy Park not far from Madison Square. I had made reservations at the Irving on the recommendation of Dr. Mahan, our family physician in Ellensburg. I have always been glad I followed his suggestion, for the Hotel Irving, like its contemporary, the Brevoort, was one of the last survivors of the Little Old New York of Washington Irving's day. Its Old Knickerbocker decor and accommodations together with its setting on quaint old Gramercy Park are remembrances we have always cherished. We intended to stay at the Irving only two or three days, but were actually there nearly three weeks.

The reason it took so long for us to get settled in an apartment of our own was that I immediately became so totally immersed in French and German review work that I felt I could not take time out to hunt for an apartment. I taught Elnora what I knew about the subway, elevated and trolley car lines, took her out to the Columbia University district for a look around, and then left the apartment hunting to her. It happened to be a year in which the housing situation was tight and we were determined to find what we wanted within walking distance of the University. That took a longer time than we had anticipated.

I regularly started my cram sessions in the Columbia library about nine in the morning and did not knock off until 5 P.M. or later. On this schedule I soon began to make real headway. I had been informed that the language examinations would emphasize reading ability and that the material I would be required to read with professional proficiency would be taken from French and German treatises and journals in the field of political science. This simplified my task a great deal. The two most important things were to refresh my memory on the grammar and acquire the necessary technical vocabulary in each language. All I required to do this was enough time to backtrack through my textbooks and actually read enough of the professional literature of each language to be able to translate without the aid of a dictionary. In three weeks I had it done, and passed without trouble in both French and German.

I would not have been obliged to go through this preliminary ordeal merely to register as a graduate student at Columbia, but there was an inflexible rule that no one could matriculate for the Ph.D. until *after* he had passed his language examinations. I have always been glad that Columbia enforced this requirement to the letter. It gave me a bad time for my first three weeks, but later on it greatly speeded up my progress toward the Big Degree. If I had been allowed to postpone the language examinations and had become involved in the great quagmire of courses, seminars, special reports, theses, and other moils and toils of graduate study, I might never have been ready for the language examinations. I certainly could not have finished my graduate programs in record time, faster, as it turned out, than any of my contemporaries at Columbia.

While I was reviewing languages, Elnora was learning the ropes at the Institute of Musical Art and becoming a warm friend of Ruth Moell, nee Brown, a pretended cousin of mine. Ruth was the daughter of a Nebraska sister of my Uncle George Hogue (Aunt Sina's husband). Ruth had often visited in Ellensburg and had actually attended school there part of one year. During this time Ruth and my sister Aurel became buddy-buddy friends, and Ruth and I had agreed that though we were not related by blood we would consider ourselves cousins just the same. Since I had last seen Ruth, she had married a young physician in Lincoln, Nebraska, whose name was J. F. Moell. The Moells had come to New York for the year 1917-18 so he could do special study and research in certain New York hospitals and clinics. Neither the Moells nor the Maxeys had children then, and this made it easy for them to see the town together. Elnora and Ruth became especially cordial friends and bummed around together like two co-eds come to the big city for a lark. It was good for both.

Ph.D. Candidate

Soon after I passed my language examinations Elnora and I left the Hotel Irving and moved out to Morningside Heights, where we rented half of an apartment in a building named the Poinciana. The address was 434 West 120th Street, and the building occupied the southeast corner of 120th Street and Amsterdam Avenue. It was a convenient location for both of us, about four blocks from Kent Hall on the Columbia campus, where my activities were centered, and about the same distance from the Institute of Musical Art. I wonder sometimes what we would have said to one another on the day we took residence in the Poinciana if we could have foreseen that twenty-eight years later both of our daughters and their husbands would be attending Columbia University and living in the Poinciana just as we had.

189

Part of our first year in the Poinciana we shared the apartment with a Miss Eleanor Lally and her mother. Miss Lally was a normal school teacher from somewhere in Kansas who was taking advanced work in the Teachers' College at Columbia. The latter part of the same year we shared the apartment with Mr. and Mrs. Elmer D. Graper, and this was a much more congenial arrangement than the first half year had been. Graper was a doctoral candidate in the Columbia Faculty of Political Science the same as I; we attended many of the same courses and had much in common. Being about the same age and having similar tastes and interests, the Grapers and the Maxeys enjoyed each other's society and often went out together to shows, night clubs, and Sunday outings in the vicinity of New York. After completing his doctorate at Columbia, Graper became a faculty member at the University of Pittsburgh, where he had a long and distinquished career as a teacher and writer. Many times over the years he and I met at various professional gatherings and renewed our oldtime friendship.

Registration at Columbia in the autumn of 1917 was a perfunctory matter of signing up for the requisite number of hours (they were called points at Columbia) and paying the tuition fees. But matriculating for the doctorate was something else. I have already explained the pre-matriculation language tests which I had to take. The next step was an interview with the Dean of the Graduate Faculty of Public Law and Political Science, who at that time was Dr. F. J. E. Woodbridge. If the dean approved the applicant, the next step was a preliminary oral examination by a faculty committee appointed by him. My interview with Dean Woodbridge was thoroughly delightful. It was his job to size me up both as a potential political scientist and as a person. He carried me through an hour's conversation in which I enjoyed hearing myself talk while he, I am sure, made a careful inventory of the qualifications I seemed to display. When I left his office, I did not know whether I had passed or failed, but in a few days I received written notice to present myself, at a stated time and place, for a pre-doctoral examination by a committee of the graduate faculty.

Never having taken such an examination, I had visions of mumbling, stumbling, and foundering. I knew I was going to be questioned by five of the best minds in the political science profession and I also knew their principal purpose would be to ascertain whether I was far enough advanced in this field of study to be admitted to candidacy for the doctorate. I was sure I would be closely questioned on my work at the University of Wisconsin and possibly on my undergraduate major at Whitman. The committee members were extremely courteous, but pulled no punches. I was given a thorough going over and made to prove that I knew what I should have known, with the many hours of political science already on my record. Finally the commitee sent me out of the room and asked me to wait a half an hour or so for a decision. When called back, I was told that the committee would recommend my admission to candidacy and was generously congratulated on my performance. It would have been a much poorer performance if it had not been for my three years of college teaching at O.A.C. I am sure of that.

Dean Woodbridge and other faculty members told me that although a doctoral candidate was required to register in specific courses, that was chiefly for the purpose of reckoning tuition charges. The faculty would not hold me for either attendance or examinations in those or any other specific courses. My job as a doctoral candidate was to get myself ready for examinations which would span the whole field of political science, and that I would also be expected to show some glimmerings of intelligence in related fields such as history, philosophy, jurisprudence, and sociology. It was the privilege of a doctoral candidate to attend any lectures and seminars he might think helpful to him, and it would be up to me to make the best possible use of that privilege. Doctoral candidates, they said, were accorded special facilities in the library, and by wise use of this opportunity I might do myself as much good as by attending formal class sessions. In short, I deduced that I was being tossed into the deep, deep sea to make my way to shore as best I could.

I registered for four courses in public law—constitutional law, international law, conflict of laws, and municipal corporations. Although the first two were repetitious of the work I had done at Wisconsin, I knew that the doctoral examinations would bear down heavily on them and I wanted to take the courses given by men who would be sitting on my examining committee. I registered for two or three courses I never attended, but spent a great deal of time visiting the courses given by such distinguished scholars as John Dewey, James Harvey Robinson, Franklin K. Giddings, William A. Dunning, and E. R. A. Seligman. The professors whose courses I attended most consistently were John Bassett Moore in international law, Thomas Reed Powell in constitutional law and conflict of laws, and Charles A. Beard in American political ideas.

The Beard Resignation

I did not have Beard long, however. Shortly after Thanksgiving he resigned from the Columbia faculty in vociferous protest over the action taken by the University trustees in dismissing two faculty members (H. W. L. Dana of the English department and J. McKeen Cattell of the psychology department) on the charge that they were pro-German and disloyal to the government of the United States. One whose memory does not embrace World War I simply cannot imagine the state of hysteria which gripped the minds of the American people after our declaration of war against Germany on April 6, 1917. Even in snug and secure Corvallis, where we were living at the time, the local magistrates immediately organized a home guard and posted sentries to guard the waterworks and other public utilities night and day. We had visions of German saboteurs around every corner and goosestepping German legions being landed on the nearest seaboard. Anglo-French propaganda in the past three years had done its intended work so well that millions of Americans seemed to be scared of their own shadows.

In New York City there was a German or German-derived population numbering hundreds of thousands, and the feeling between the pro-German and the pro-Ally partisans was so constantly bitter that riot calls were an almost daily feature of police duty in certain precincts. I never knew for certain whether Dana and Cattell really were pro-German, but I think not. I think they were merely loudmouthed pacifists. But in the winter of 1917 being a pacifist was the equivalent, in pro-Ally quarters, of being pro-German. From what Charles A. Beard told me months afterwards, I deduced that he himself did not know or care whether Dana and Cattell were pro-German. They had been summarily booted out of the University with no hearing, no notice, and no consultation with the faculty or even with the officers of the faculty. In Beard's opinion they had been denied their rights in the academic community, and therefore the paramount issue was not pro-Germanism but academic tenure and academic freedom. He hoped that his resignation would precipitate that issue and force the Columbia trustees to recognize faculty rights. I am not sure that it had any such effect. I am not sure, indeed, that any of Beard's faculty colleagues at Columbia were behind him on this issue. He had not consulted in advance with any of them or told them of his intention to resign. He explained it to me thus, "I was so damned furious that I did not want to risk being talked out of resigning. So I went up to my country place in Connecticut, wrote out my resignation, mailed it to President Butler, and stayed there until the story exploded in the papers."

Beard's resignation caused a ten-day sensation on the Columbia campus, and that was about all. Everything went on as before except Beard's courses. Special arrangements were made for substitutes to take over his work. In the American political theory course Francis W. Coker (then of Ohio State University but soon to go to Yale) finished the year. Coker and I became good and lifelong friends. He was a grand person and a sound scholar, but, of course, he was only a temporary replacement and he was not Charles A. Beard. The students who suffered most from Beard's resignation were those who were doing doctoral theses under his guidance. Most of those had to choose between giving up the ghost or finding a new adviser and a new thesis subject. Several whom I knew chose the former course and never finished their doctoral work at Columbia.

Fortunately, I had not yet settled on a thesis, and was not greatly discommoded. Even if I had been I think I would have stuck it out at Columbia. I was five years older and considerably more mature than when I stalked off the Columbia campus in 1912, in high dudgeon because of the absence of Charles A. Beard. In those intervening years I had learned a few things about the inner operations of large institutions of higher education.

Boning for Doctoral Examinations

One result of Beard's resignation, which proved advantageous to me was the formation of a little study group of which Elmer Graper was the pivotal member. As a friend of Elmer I had the good fortune to be included. Elmer had been named as Beard's graduate assistant for the year 1917-18, and as such had the use of Beard's office in Hamilton Hall. In this office Beard kept a large part of his private library, particularly books and documents related to the courses he was currently teaching. For some reason neither Beard nor the Columbia authorities thought his resignation called for any change in this arrangement, and as a result Elmer was left in sole and undisturbed possession to the end of the academic year. In addition to me, he invited Harry J. Carman (later to achieve national repute as dean of Columbia College) and Alfred B. Butts (later to attain high distinction as chancellor of the University of Mississippi) to share Beard's office with him and make it our headquarters for our cram sessions.

We four were the regulars who met four or five nights a week and "examined" each other on subjects we expected to face in our doctoral examinations. Three or four others joined us semi-occasionally. Our sessions generally ran from 8 to 11 P.M., whereupon we would adjourn to a near-by saloon for a snack and a beaker of beer. Thus refreshed, we would return to the firing line for a second session, which seldom broke up before 1 A.M. It was grueling work but pleasant, none the less, because of the good fellowship which accompanied it.

During one of these cram sessions a half dozen of us made

plans to attend the annual meetings of the American Political Science Association and the American Historical Association, to be held that year at Philadelphia during the Christmas holidays. Accordingly we reserved two connecting suites at the Bellevue-Stratford Hotel, which would enable us to operate a bachelor club during the conventions. No wives were to go along with us. For me, this was the first political science professional meeting, and I think the same was true of all the others.

An additional incentive for our attendance as a group was the fact that Monroe Smith, professor of Roman Law at Columbia and a gentleman whom we all respected and liked, was president of the American Political Science Association that year. We were sure his presidential address would be something special. Throughout the three days of the two conventions we listened to dozens of papers, panel discussions, and after-luncheon and after-dinner speeches. We attended I know not how many smokers and cocktail hours and took part in countless gabfests in hotel lobbies and corridors. Incidentally (and not so incidentally, either, because it was an object we all had in view), we met and made the acquaintance of scores of political scientists from all parts of the country. It was a great experience for me, and one which had much to do with future events in my life.

An Offer from Wisconsin

Previous to the Philadelphia meeting I had received a letter from Arnold B. Hall of the University of Wisconsin saying he was going to attend that convention and would hope to see me there. I replied informing him that I was planning to attend and would be sure to look him up. I had no idea that he had anything more than social amenities in mind, but as soon as we got together he told me he had been authorized to offer me a second semester appointment as instructor in political science at the University of Wisconsin. "A.B." said the department at Wisconsin now regretted that it had not kept me there instead of letting me go to O.A.C. and now they wanted me back. Would I accept an instructorship at $1,800 a year, effective the second semester, which was now about five weeks away? The salary was excellent for that time. Hall assured me that I would have a teaching schedule light enough to enable me to do graduate work on the side and thus complete my doctorate at Wisconsin in three or four years.

This offer would not have been much of a temptation if I had not been so fond of Wisconsin and all of the political science personnel there. I asked A. B. Hall to give me a few days to talk things over with my wife and consult my advisors at Columbia, and he agreed to that. The more I weighed and considered, and the more I talked it over with Elnora and my Columbia friends and counselors, the more certain I became that the Wisconsin offer should be declined. Already I had passed my languages at Columbia, also my pre-matriculation examinations, and was definitely scheduled for final examination in subject fields in May, 1918. All this progress would be lost if I returned to Wisconsin. Furthermore, Elnora was just getting a good start at the Institute of Musical Art, and would lose most of what she had gained if she did not complete at least one year there. It simply did not make sense to let sentiment prevail over practicality, so I regretfully wrote my good friend Hall a deeply appreciative note of thanks and refusal.

Was this decision a mistake or not? Who can say? It was passing up a relatively sure thing to take a big leap in the dark. At Wisconsin I could readily have gone up the ladder to a full professorship; that was virtually assured me in advance. A professorship at the University of Wisconsin offered about as much in prestige and professional opportunity as one could aspire to. What sort of career I might have made there is anybody's guess. The only thing of which I am positive is that if I had accepted that offer, I certainly would be writing a very different sort of autobiographical narrative than this one has to be.

Having cast my lot, for better or worse, with Columbia, I settled down to the night-owl sessions in Beard's office, and with the rest of our gang, plodded ahead with the business of getting ready for the May examinations. Our labors paid good dividends. When the time came, every one of our group sailed through with flying colors. The men who composed my examining committee included such renowned scholars as Howard Lee McBain, Thomas Reed Powell, John Bassett Moore, William A. Dunning, James Harvey Robinson, and Edwin R. A. Seligman —all lustrous names in the annals of Columbia. Every member of the committee took a turn sampling my wares, and when they were through I knew I had been thoroughly examined. But I was also much elated, because the only thing that stood between me and the Ph.D was the doctoral dissertation.

XIV. NEW YORK BUREAU OF MUNICIPAL RESEARCH,

1918-20

Interne and Staff Member

Shortly after resigning from Columbia, Charles A. Beard was appointed director of the New York Bureau of Municipal Research, a world renowned research organization which then had offices at 261 Broadway, directly across the street from the City Hall. This organization was founded in 1906, as I remember, by a group of independent citizens who intended it to serve as a watchdog over the government of the city of New York. Beard thought he saw an opportunity to make the Bureau a good deal more than that, and one of his ideas was to develop in connection with that organization a practical training school for public service. He thought there was great need for a school which would afford doctor and near-doctors in political science an opportunity for the clinical study of public administration. This was welcome news to the little group of political science pals to which I belonged. At Beard's invitation several of us subwayed down to 261 Broadway to talk with him about it. We were made warmly welcome and told to keep on coming.

Part of Beard's training school concept was a program of internship under which young political scientists such as I would go on the staff of the Bureau as internes and be paid a small monthly stipend for our work. If he could persuade the trustees of the Bureau to provide the money, he proposed to establish two or three such internships immediately. It did not take long for him to put this scheme into effect, and I was one of those who was offered an internship in public administration. This offer came just after I had passed my subject examinations at Columbia. Should I accept or not? I was due to return to O.A.C. in September, where I could expect both a salary increase and a promotion in rank. But I still had a dissertation to do for my doctor's degree and hoped I could stay in New York or somewhere not far distant until that task was completed.

However, living in New York was not cheap, and the stipend for the internship at the Bureau of Municipal Research was only $75 per month. We could not live on that. Fortunately, just at the time this decision had to be made, Elnora got a job as a part-time desk clerk in the Mott Haven branch of the New York Public Library, and that would add another $75 month a month to our income. With this in addition to the Bureau's stipend, we could make ends meet. Both of us wanted to stay in New York if possible, and we felt sure we could make it for a few months on $150 a month. So we decided to gamble, and I wrote Dr. Dubach tendering my resignation from the faculty of the Oregon Agricultural College. For both Elnora and me it turned out to be the right decision.

One thing that had been a major influence in our decision to remain in New York, if at all possible, was an offer by Dr. Beard to help me get ahead with the dissertation business at Columbia. He told me that if I could get the Columbia people to approve a dissertation subject in the area of public finance or public administration, and if the final dissertation proved to be suitable for publication by the Bureau of Municipal Research, he would have the Bureau assume the cost of publication. This looked like a golden opportunity to me, because the Columbia rule was that a doctoral dissertation had to be published at the author's expense, and furthermore that a stipulated number of free copies must be deposited in the Columbia University library before the author could come up for examination on his dissertation. If I could satisfy both Columbia and Beard, I would save myself a thousand dollars or more.

Naturally, I proceeded immediately to make inquiries at Columbia. The only Columbia political science professor whose subject field could possibly yield a dissertation suitable for publication by the New York Bureau of Municipal Research was the Eaton Professor of Municipal Administration, Howard Lee McBain. I knew McBain pretty well, had been in one of his classes and had done a research job or two for him. So I went directly to him. He was very friendly, but not particularly enthusiastic about my dissertation hopes. He said he was skeptical about my being able to do anything of Columbia dissertation stature in connection with my work at the New York Bureau. However, in view of the money I might save, he suggested two or three possible dissertation subjects and advised me to investigate them, talk them over at the Bureau, and then report back to him. All this I did, and the only subject on which I could get both McBain and Beard to agree was "School Finance in American Cities of 100,000 and More." McBain accepted this reluctantly, and Beard thought I could have done better. I agreed with both of them, after a fashion. But I had to get something going, and I thought we had a three-way understanding that I would go ahead with the ctiy school thing. Beard as well as I understood it that way, and he allowed me to draw my stipend for some three months of researching on that subject alone. Then came the Delaware Survey and with it a total change of plans for me.

One day in the early part of September, 1918, Dr. Beard called me into his office and told me that the New York Bureau of Municipal Research had been engaged to do an exhaustive survey of state, county, and city government in the state of Delaware, and that, if I were willing, he would like to put me in charge of the county portion of that study. I could hardly say yes fast enough, and Beard forthwith appointed me a full-time member of the staff with a starting salary of $200 a month, which was big money in my eyes then. And it actually was better than I could have done as a college professor, except in a few leading institutions. It was several hundred dollars a year more than I had been offered at the University of Wisconsin the year before.

Since I was going to make a field study of county government, Dr. Beard suggested that I might be able to develop a better doctoral dissertation from that study than from the city school subject on which I was then working. I heartily agreed, and hotfooted it up to Columbia for a conference with McBain. He agreed that something in county government might be preferable to the school study but doubted whether I could get dissertation material out of a field study of that sort. I put up as strong an argument as I could for making a stab at it, and he finally said to go ahead and see what I could turn up.

A Look at the B.M.R.

Although I have explained how I came to be a member of the staff of the New York Bureau of Municipal Research, I have said little about the Bureau itself. At the time I joined the staff the Bureau occupied the entire ninth floor of the building at 261 Broadway. As I have already said, it was founded in 1906 as an outgrowth of civic movements designed to keep watch over the government of New York City and keep the search light of publicity turned on the machinations of Tammany Hall. In order to do this sleuthing job most effectively, the Bureau had built up a staff of experts in such phases of municipal administration as finance, accounting, public safety, public works, public health, public education, and city planning. In short, the organization of the Bureau on a small scale parallelled that of the city government. In its first decade or so the government of New York City had been the main, if not the sole, concern of the Bureau of Municipal Research, and its work was so well done that it was given large credit for the set-backs suffered by Tammany under Mayors McClellan, Gaynor, and Mitchel. Under Mayor Mitchel, a Fusionist and anti-Tammany, the Bureau of Municipal Research became almost an annex of the city hall and was constantly on call for investigatory services.

200

Which explains why the Tammanyites called it the "Bureau of Municipal Besmirch."

Even if it had wanted to stick to its New York City knitting to the exclusion of all else, the Bureau probably would have been unable to do so. Its reputation went far and wide, and requests for its services poured in from all quarters of the compass. It was the first organization in the United States to devote itself exclusively to the advancement of integrity and efficiency in municipal government by means of scientific research. Its success was so dramatic and its repute so high that it was flooded with pleas for help. Civic leaders, even public officials, in cities all over the country begged it to lend them a helping hand. It was asked to conduct surveys, lend-lease its staff members, draft municipal charters, and recommend appropriate reforms for local government agencies all over the United States and Canada.

The bureau found it increasingly hard to turn down these requests. Not ony did they represent an opportunity to do a nationwide service, but they also offered an escape from complete submergence in New York City affairs. And after Tammany got back into power through the defeat of Mayor Mitchel in 1917, the Bureau was *persona non grata* at the city hall. If it had not been for the huge and constant volume of work that it was called upon to do for chambers of commerce, taxpayers' associations, voters' leagues, and city and county governments throughout the country, the Bureau might have had to go out of business. But it turned out that the Bureau had more business than it could handle, most of it outside of New York. The fees it charged for its services were sufficient to defray all costs and provide a modest surplus for promotion. At the time I became a member, the New York Bureau was engaged in or had recently done general surveys of city government in such widely scattered municipalities as San Francisco, Indianapolis, Norfolk, Rochester, Denver, and Toronto. In addition, it had done scores of special problem studies and had published an extensive series of documents reporting and explaining its work.

The foregoing will suffice as a preface to my account of the Delaware Survey, which, as I have said, was my first major assignment with the New York Bureau of Municipal Research. This statewide survey was made for the Delaware State Council of Defense, an official body created during World War I to coordinate the defense activities of the state government. But the financial underwriting of the survey came not from the state government, but from certain members of the du Pont clan. Pierre was the one we had most often to deal with, and it may have been exclusively one of his charity projects. I never knew.

As the end of World War I approached, there was a vast amount of desultory public chatter throughout the country about the supposed problem of post-war reconstruction. There were visionaries who thought the time was ripe for the inauguration of a new heaven and a new earth. Also there were serious students of public affairs who thought the war had so greatly overtaxed the economy and the machinery of government that sweeping readjustments were inevitable at all levels of government. And, of course, there were shrewd opportunists who thought they saw conditions favorable for the attainment of certain specific goals. The Delaware Survey had its feet in both the second and the third of the foregoing categories.

The State Council of Defense sponsored it, probably at the instigation of the du Ponts, and the du Ponts picked up the tab for all of the costs. For a century or more there had been no overhaul of the political machinery of the little old Blue Hen state, and certain civic leaders thought that the current interest in post-war reconstruction might afford a chance to mobilize public opinion in favor of some much-needed changes. Pierre du Pont was one of the leaders of this group of Delaware citizens. It may have been he or it may have been someone else (I am not sure) who conceived the idea that a comprehensive survey by the New York Bureau of Municipal Research would be just the ticket for getting the reform movement off to a good start. Despite the fact that the du Ponts paid the freight, the survey was a semi-official affair, done under the auspices of the State Council of Defense. I will further say that the New York Bureau was given an entirely free hand. Neither the State Council of Defense nor any of the du Ponts attempted to exert any pressure on us.

It chanced to be my great good fortune to be a student interne in the New York Bureau when the contract for the Delaware Survey was made. Since it required an immediate enlargement of the staff, and I had been around long enough to know everybody and acquire a working knowledge of New York Bureau routines and methods, I was tapped not only for the Delaware job but for a permanent full-time position on the staff. Just why Dr. Beard picked me to do the county government portion of the survey was a bit puzzling. I was no expert in county government and told him so. None of my post-graduate work had been in the field of local government as such. Beard's answer was that I was as much an expert on county government as anybody else, because there just weren't any such "critters" around. Further, he said for me to get busy and bone up on county government and in a short time I would be qualified to handle anything that would come up in the state of Delaware.

I was to discover that there was more to county government than either Beard or I imagined, but, after a few days of concentrated cramming, I had to admit that he was right about there being no recognized experts on county government. Nobody had ever taken the pains to pay much attention to it. The entire literature of the subject was so sparse that I was able to absorb most of it in less than a week's time. By the time I took the field in Delaware, I could honestly represent myself as highly knowledgeable in the field of county government. I had read and digested everything there was in print on that subject.

At the same time that he picked me for the county job Beard chose a fellow interne, Arthur Eugene Buck, to do the field work in state government. Buck and I together were to do the survey of city government. The plan was that Buck and I would go to Delaware, survey by personal visitation all of the state, county, and city offices, accumulate notes, documents, and other data which we would bring back to New York for the Bureau staff to whip into shape for the reports and recommendations. This plan was carried out, and Buck and I did all of the on-the-spot interviews, inquiries, and examinations. In addition, we collected all of the papers and documents we thought relevant to the findings resulting from our personal visits to the various offices. Knowing that I would be on the grill both in Delaware and New York, I kept a journal day-by-day, recording where I had been, whom I had seen, what was said, and what had been done. Thanks to this diary, I am able forty-five years later to present a fairly lucid account of what I did in connection with the Delaware Survey.

Gene Buck and I started our field work in Delaware on September 10, 1918, and continued this work until October 12. Then we returned to New York and spent a month or so in staff conferences and report drafting. I did not expect to draw a final writing assignment. Although I had done all of the field work in county government, it would have been in full accord with Bureau usage for a senior member of the staff to be charged with writing the final report. This I expected, but one day Beard asked me to do a first draft of the county section of the report and submit it to him. This I did, and after a few days he called me to his office to go over the first draft with him. He picked it up, riffled through the pages, and then said, "Maxey, do you know you can write?" I replied that I hoped this was true, but it was the first time anyone had ever told me so. Then Beard said, "You have style, and style is something that cannot be taught. You have it or you don't." This prompted me to ask, "What is style?" I have never forgotten Beard's reply. "Style," he said, tapping his desk as he uttered each word, "is rhythm, and rhythm is as necessary to prose as to poetry."

Because Beard thought my writing had style, he had me do the final report on county government in Delaware, but this did not spare me the agony of running the gauntlet of staff criticism and mandatory rewriting. In the New York Bureau at that time every report or publication, before final issue, was gone over by the whole staff and mercilessly picked to pieces, edited, and rewritten until everybody was satisfied. This was good medicine for me, especially after Beard's compliments on my writing. I needed to be deflated right away, and I was. One thing I learned as a result of the gorings I took from the staff members was that a smooth literary style is no substitute for taking pains.

After we had our reports all approved in the tentative draft stage, Buck and I made a second excursion to Delaware and went over all of the reports with the officials concerned. Taking note of their criticisms, objections, and comments, we returned to New York for another ordeal of staff rehashing. Then we whipped out the final report. Dr. Beard made an appointment to deliver the required dozen copies of the final report to Governor Townsend and the members of the State Council of Defense at the Hotel du Pont in Wilmington one evening in the last week of December. Thinking he might need some factual prompters to answer questions for him, he took Buck and me with him. As a reward for the beatings we had taken and also because national prohibition was taking effect on January 1, 1919, Dr. Beard treated us to a champagne dinner with all customary appurtenances. This I vividly remember, because it was my first feast *avec le vin bon*.

I seem to have put the cart before the horse in the matter of time sequence. To do justice to the Delaware Survey, I should have told something about the field studies before describing the staff work. The field studies were long and tedious, and the best thing I can do to convey this to the reader is perhaps to quote briefly from my Delaware diary. Buck and I made our headquarters in Dover, the state capital, as quaint and lovely a colonial town as I have ever seen. We were welcomed by the director of the State Council of Defense who was also the secretary of state. There was no office space for us in the capitol building, but the senate chamber was turned over to us for that purpose. The senate not being in session, we could spread out all over the chamber, use as many desks as we liked, and leave our papers unfiled as long as we wished. Buck spent nearly all of his time in Dover, but I had to travel over the whole state so as to get a first-hand look at the three county governments and the several cities. The following excerpts from my diary will give a good idea of what I was doing:

September 12. Drafted form letter to be prepared for Mr. Johnson's approval. Conference with Mr. Johnson. Problem: To translate our program into what Mr. Johnson terms the Delaware dialect.

[The Mr. Johnson referred to in the preceding diary entry was the Director of the State Council of Defense.]

September 14. In the afternoon visited the office of the Clerk of the Peace. Talked with the deputy-clerk three-quarters of an hour. Arranged for a visit at a later time to examine his records. Found that the Clerk of the Peace is seldom in his office. Deputy assured me there was not enough work for two men, so Clerk of the Peace works his farm and comes in only when there is extra work at court time.

September 17. Went to Georgetown to meet Governor Townsend. Was introduced to Sussex County officials by the Governor. Had a brief conference with members of the Sussex County Board of Assessment. Returned to Dover about 6 P.M.

September 23. Took train to Georgetown at 9:00 A.M. Arrived in Georgetown at 10.30. Spent afternoon calling on county officials, as follows: Comptroller, Clerk of the Peace, Clerk of the Orphans' Court, Register in Chancery, Sheriff, Recorder of Deeds, Prothonotary, Register of Wills.

September 24. Attended session of Levy Court. Observed method of allowing bills. Discussed use of triplicate requisition form for purchase of supplies. Discussed consolidation of offices. Board of Poor Trustees, consisting of farmers, want to put money in a barn at expense of inmates. Moral conditions bad. One white woman had given birth to two Negro children since she has been in the almshouse.

September 27. Worked on survey of state department of agriculture; also worked over details of some county offices.

October 1. Spent some of forenoon attending session of Kent County Levy Court. Much tobacco smoke; little business.

October 2. Worked in Kent County offices and on county budget problem.

October 4. Trip from Dover to Wilmington. Arrived about 10.30 A.M. and registered at Hotel du Pont. Called on Clerk of Peace, Mr. Wright. Presented letter from Governor Townsend.

October 10. Visited office of Recorder of Deeds. Found longhand method of recording in vogue. Recorder said law required it. He is doubtful of permanency of typewriter ink.

October 11. Traveled from Wilmington to Georgetown. Took Cartwright through Sussex offices. Back to Dover. In evening, conferences with Buck, Watson, and Cartwright.

The Watson mentioned above was William Watson, the Bureau's specialist in governmental accounting, and the Cartwright was Otho G. Cartwright, a New York financier who had achieved some repute as an authority on county finances as a result of his work on the New York Constitutional Convention Commission of 1915. Dr. Beard had told Buck and me that if we ran into problems calling for technical knowledge we did not possess, just let him know and he would send down properly qualified experts to give us a lift. Cartwright and Watson were two of these. We had several others down on engineering problems, health matters, and other areas calling for scientific training.

Watson worked with both Buck and me, but Cartwright worked exclusively with me. I took him through every county office in the state, went over all of my field notes with him, and had him examine all of my collected papers and documents. In my diary I find such notations as: "Spent major part of afternoon in Comptroller's office, Mr. Cartwright analyzing accounts and I picking up miscellaneous information." "In afternoon put Mr. Cartwright in Treasurer's office while I worked on J. P.'s and Coroner." "Worked through Kent County offices with Mr.

Cartwright. Prepared memoradum for Governor Townsend *in re* Farmers' Bank."

Author

Those few and rather scattered quotations from my daily journal indicate the kind of work I was doing. Actually, I visited every county office in the state two or three times, examined their accounts and records, studied their operating methods and procedures, and talked with all of the official heads of offices as well as many of the deputies and subordinates. I took copious notes and collected countless forms, reports and statistical items. Dr. Beard said, and later put it into print that mine was the first comprehensive and thorough survey of county government ever made in the United States. Indeed, he thought so highly of it that he made arrangements to have it published. For some time he had been negotiating with the Macmillan Company, one of the major publishing firms of Great Britain and the United States, to put out a series of public administration studies. He completed this deal just about the time I put the finishing touches on my Delaware county report and was struck with the idea that my Delaware report would be ideal for the initial volume of this series. He told me this and asked me to proceed at once to get the manuscript ready for submission to the editorial board of the Macmillan Company at 60 Fifth Avenue.

I was instantly transported to Cloud Nine. For a long time I had been hoping somehow to break into print in an impressive way, and had made a few stabs at it. In the March-April issue of the *American Law Review* for 1918 I had managed to get the tip of my nose in the tent in the form of an article entitled "Is Government Merchandising Constitutional?" I had written this is connection with my constitutional law course at Columbia and sent it to the *American Law Review* on the chance that it might be accepted. Owing to the unprecedented expansion of governmental powers incidental to World War I, there was much current interest in governmental invasion of various spheres of business. The *American Law Review* snapped up my article and gave me enough reprints to supply a bar association. I fattened my ego by handing out reprints to various student and faculty friends at Columbia. One day Professor Monroe Smith very kindly let the wind out of my pretensions by remarking that any man who wanted to gain recognition as a substantial writer must get his stuff between hard covers.

That was exactly what Dr. Beard was doing for me—a thing I would have had a hard time doing for myself. Not only was he putting me between hard covers as the author of an important book on a neglected subject, but, since my book was to be the first of a series of public administration studies under Beard's editorship, he decided to write an introduction for it. What better send-off could a budding author have?

Doctor of Philosophy

When it was settled that Macmillan would publish my book, Dr. Beard suggested that I get approval to use this for my doctoral thesis at Columbia. If this could be done, it would be possible at small expense to have the required number of library copies struck off with special paper cover and fly-leaf to conform with Columbia specifications. Not only would this save me a tidy sum of money; it might enable me to get my doctor's degree at the opening of the fall semester, 1919. I hastened to get in touch with Professor McBain and sent him proofs of the forthcoming book. He took all summer with these, and early in September informed me that the book was not up to doctoral standards. His chief objection was that the documentation was inadequate and that was evidence that I had done no scholarly research. McBain had no patience with my argument that I had done more real research than most doctoral candidates ever had a chance to do. I had to admit that most of my data came not only from unpublished material but even from unprinted material. Most of it came from direct personal observations and direct conversations with public officials. Why, I asked, should such data be less scientific or less scholarly than data grubbed from the musty tomes of a library? All I got for an answer to this question was thumbs turned straight down. This roiled me enough to vow to myself and to my wife that I would not give up without a fight.

In this mood I took my case to Dean Woodbridge, who heard me out with great patience and understanding. He asked if I thought any other member of the Faculty of Political Science would sponsor my Delaware book as a doctoral dissertation. I did not know, but suggested Thomas Reed Powell as a possibility. I had taken more courses with Powell than any other member of the faculty and knew him better socially. Dean Woodbridge said he would speak to Powell and let me know the outcome. In about ten days I was officially notified to deposit three hundred copies of my dissertation in the Columbia library and notified to appear for examination on this volume at a specified time and place about a month hence. I complied with the deposit requirement and duly appeared before the examining committee, which consisted of Thomas Reed Powell, chairman, Edward M. Sait, Monroe Smith, Franklin K. Giddings, William A. Dunning, and John Bassett Moore.

To my amazement, I suddenly found myself defending, not my dissertation but Charles A. Beard. I had forgotten to have Beard's introduction omitted from the dissertation copies, and some members of the committee, having read this, were offended, or so pretended, by some of Beard's remarks. In the introduction Beard had said that the New York Bureau of Municipal Research was "the first institution in the United States, or for that matter in the world, to introduce into the study of government (at least on any considerable scale) the methods of natural science, namely, first-hand observation of the primary material of government, disregard for the traditional habits of inquiry, generalization from original data, experimentation with actual installations. Moreover, the Bureau first pointed out, in a detailed way, the analogies between private corporate organization and management and public organization and management, bringing to the consideration of the latter the results of tested experiences in the former field." Did I believe that? Could I prove Beard was right? The committee badgered me with questions of that kind for some two hours, then excused me from the room and took another half hour to decide my fate. When they finally called me back and congratulated me on an

210

able defense of my thesis, I thought I could detect a gleam of humor in the eyes of several of them. I did not begrudge their having a bit of fun at my expense. One of them told me later that they did not know enough about county government to ask me any penetrating questions and so decided to put me on a hot spot respecting Beard's introduction.

My diploma for the degree of doctor of philosophy was issued on October 29, 1919. At long last I had it made. That was the way I felt at the moment, but in later years, when comparing my experience with that of other doctoral candidates at Columbia and elsewhere, I became aware that in reality I had won the degree in record time. One year of residence work at Wisconsin, one year of residence work at Columbia, and one year on the thesis—that was somewhat under par for the course.

The Macmillan Company had published my book, *County Administration*, in August, 1919. It was neatly bound in blue cloth with gold lettering, and was the book I looked at most often and most fondly for several weeks. I could not help being a bit swelled up about it, because it got good notices and had a respectable sale. However, it was the only book I ever wrote on which I did not make one thin dime. All of the royalties were assigned to the New York Bureau of Municipal Research in payment for the thesis copies supplied to me for deposit at Columbia. The Bureau, at Beard's instruction, had advanced the money to the Macmillan Company and the royalties were supposed to reimburse the Bureau. Perhaps they did; I never knew. In coin other than cash *County Administration* rewarded me handsomely. It made me nationally known as a political scientist, not because it was such a good book but because it was the first of its kind. In so far as uniqueness brings eminence, I had achieved more through the authorship of this book than I could have by many years of classroom drudgery. And I was not yet thirty years of age.

Supervisor of Training School for Public Service

In the fall of 1919 I thought I was set for life. I fully expected to spend the rest of my days on the staff of the New York Bureau of Municipal Research. Following the completion of the Delaware Survey, Dr. Beard gave me a promotion and a generous salary increase. In fact, he boosted me to $3,000 a year, which does not look like much now but was real "gravy" then. It was more than full professors in most colleges and universities were getting, and the new title and job which came along with the salary increase carried equivalent prestige. In fact, a new job was created for me, namely, Supervisor of the Training School for Public Service. I have already mentioned Beard's great dream of a supergraduate school of public administration incorporated with the New York Bureau of Municipal Research. He was now ready to launch this school and wanted an executive at the head of it who could handle all of the routine and detail of its day-to-day operation, leaving him free for the overall direction of both the Bureau and the Training School. That was my new job, and I was tremendously enthusiastic about it. It was not a full-time job but did require me to reduce my regular staff work by half. This meant I could no longer give as much time to field work as I had before.

We all had some rather grandiose dreams about the future of the Training School for Public Service. We even talked of obtaining a charter from the State of New York and awarding a degree in public administration. But there was an obstacle to that, which we were never able to surmount. Under New York law a degree-granting institution had to have an endowment of at least $500,000. We had no endowment, no stable income of any kind, and little immediate prospect of either. Still, it did not seem unrealistic then to believe that both were well within reach. We could dream, couldn't we?

Instruction in the Training School was carried on chiefly by conferences, seminars, and directly supervised work projects. We intended to keep it that way, but to systematize the program enough to assure each student of as broad and thorough training as the resources and facilities of the Bureau could afford. It was my job to develop and carry on such a program, and I was fascinated with my work. We had room for not more than a dozen students at a time and required that all of these be graduate students, preferably doctors or doctoral candidates. We had no rigamarole of terms, semesters, or quarters; no credit-bearing courses; no examinations or tests of any sort. Each student was individually guided in a scheme of studies, research assignments, and workshop conferences which brought him into contact with all members of our staff and gave him an opportunity to participate in every phase of the work of the Bureau. He might be with us six months, a year, or even longer. Under my general supervision, each student worked on until there was a consensus among the members of the Bureau staff that he had absorbed all we could teach him. I would have been happy to spend the rest of my life at this job. In some ways it was the most stimulating and satisfying work I have ever done. From my standpoint, it was professional education at its best.

Field Studies

Although my time for field studies was curtailed by the Training School for Public Service, I was able to take part in such of these as I could do on a part-time basis, provided they did not require me to be away from New York more than two or three days at a time. For example, I did the entire personnel survey and helped out in the budgetary survey of the city of Newark, New Jersey. This was possible because I could get to and from Newark in a matter of minutes via the Hudson Tubes. I was also sent to Boston as a member of a team of three which was asked to do a study of the problem of unifying the government of the metropolitan area. It fell to me to write the final report and submit it to Mayor Peters of Boston. Three years later I condensed and rewrote this report and offered it to the editor of the *National Municipal Review*. It was accepted and published in August, 1922, as a supplement of that month's issue of the *Review*. Being the first general article ever published on the subject of metropolitan government, my little essay received wide attention. Finally it won the cachet of inclusion in hard covers by being published as Chapter XXII of Joseph Wright's, *Selected Readings in Municipal Government,* Ginn and Company, 1925.

I was sent in January, 1919, to represent the Bureau at a national conference held in Washington, D.C. under the auspices of the National Popular Government League. It was a conference on governmental reforms and I was assigned the topic "Changes in Framework Necessary to Make Government Equal to Democracy's New Tasks." My speech on this topic was published in pamphlet form by the *League,* and this led to my being invited to contribute a chapter in a book entitled *Democracy in Reconstruction,* published by the Houghton Mifflin Company. The book was edited by Frederick A. Cleveland, former chairman of President Taft's Commission on Efficiency and Economy, and Joseph Schafer, vice chairman of the National Board for Historical Service. My chapter was entitled "The Rights and Duties of Minorities." I felt that I was in good company, for the other contributors included such celebrities in the social sciences as Charles A. Beard, W. W. Willoughby, W. F. Willoughby, Harold G. Moulton, William F. Ogburn, Samuel P. Capen, Carl Kelsey and Samuel McCune Lindsay. The New York Bureau was moving me up the ladder of professional recognition at a rapid rate.

If I had searched the world for the best opportunity to do post-doctoral study and launch a career in my chosen field, I could have found nothing superior to the advantages provided by the New York Bureau of Municipal Research. Our own staff was as good as could be found anywhere. In any roster of nationally recognized experts in their respective fields, such men as our William A. Bassett (public works), Carl E. McCombs, M.D. (public health), Bruce Smith (public safety), E. P. Goodrich (city planning), William Watson (accounting), Philip H. Cornick (taxation), Luther H. Gulick (municipal administration), and A. E. Buck (budgetary procedure) would have held high rankings. In addition to its own staff of specialists, the New York Bureau had close interties with the professional personnel of the National Municipal League, the National Short Ballot Organization, the American Proportional Representation Society, the National Popular Government League, and the International City Managers' Association. Thus we were in close touch with about all that was going on in the world of governmental reform and the people who were pulling most of the wires. It was through these organizational interties that I had opportunity to learn directly from the "horse's mouth" just exactly how the crusade for the city manager plan of government was propelled from its launching pad. Some ten years later, in a book entitled *Urban Democracy,* I put into print the first authentic account of that series of events.

At Whitman I had had a solid undergraduate major in political science. At Wisconsin and Columbia I had received a thorough exposure to the best graduate work in political science that America had to offer at that time. In the New York Bureau I received an intensive and extensive exposure to office-holders, politicians, business men, labor leaders, newspaper men, and professional reformers. Academically, I was qualified for teaching, research, and writing. Extra-academically, I was qualified for public administration, public finance, civic promotion, and practical politics. I could spin out a political theory with professional virtuosity, but I could also make a budget, analyze accounts, decode a tax levy, direct a survey, and do scores of pragmatic things that professors seldom learned.

New Yorker

Believing that our future would be in New York, and also having achieved a comfortable income, Elnora and I decided to find a more desirable apartment than was to be had in The Poinciana and to acquire some furniture of our own. After some weeks of hunting, we found exactly what we wanted at 362 Wadsworth Avenue in the Washington Heights district. We moved there October 1, 1919. We could not have found a more conveniently located place or a more pleasant one. It was only a block and a half from the 191st Street station of the Seventh Avenue subway line. I could climb aboard there and ride clear down to the Park Place station in lower Manhattan without changing trains. Both stations being at the extremities of Manhattan Island, I could always be sure of a seat and put in the forty-five-minute ride profitably reading newspapers, browsing through books, or checking notes and documents connected with my daily work.

Our apartment was on the western side of the building and afforded one of the most spectacular views of all of Greater New York. Since our apartment building stood on the western rim of Washington Heights, we could look down from our living room a hundred feet or more to the floor of the valley which was threaded by St. Nicholas Avenue, upper Broadway, and Fort Washington Avenue. On the heights across the valley we could see the Billings Estate with its crenelated hilltop castle and beyond that the famous Palisades of the Hudson River. From sunrise to sunset and all through the night this magnificent panorama presented an ever-changing scene of beauty and unceasing human activity. The sunsets were unbelievably gorgeous. We thought we would never want to move from that apartment.

In the last week of December, 1919, the American Political Science Association and the National Municipal League held their annual meetings in Cleveland, Ohio, both in the Hotel Statler. There were several joint programs, mostly having to do with a project in which both associations were much concerned. This was the so-called Model State Constitution. The National Municipal League was actively sponsoring and financing this, while the American Political Science Association was a deeply interested collaborator. At the New York Bureau we had been helping the League with some phases of this project, and I had been assigned to draft the county government sections of the proposed model constitution. Dr. Beard decided that he himself would attend these joint meetings and would take with him the staff members who were helping with the drafting work. Each of us was supposed to take part in the debates and discussions having to do with the sections of the draft on which he had worked. As I now recall it, I was on my feet in two or three of of the joint sessions, and was more than a little elated because it was my first appearance as a speaker before the august learned societies in my own professional field. Of course I also enjoyed the receptions, smokers, luncheons, and dinners which made the social life of the annual meetings such gay affairs. But I did not have the faintest idea that fate was at work during these splendid meetings, dealing me a new hand.

XV. WESTERN RESERVE UNIVERSITY, 1920-25

Beard Leaves Bureau

It was some time in February, 1920, that Dr. Beard broke the news that he was resigning as director of the Bureau of Municipal Research. In common with all of the other members of the staff, I was thunderstruck by the announcement. Perhaps I should not have been. Anyone who had worked as closely with Charles A. Beard as I had might have seen it coming. There was growing evidence that he was losing interest in the Bureau and the Training School, but there are none so blind as those who will not see. We all wanted Beard to be director of the Bureau as long as we were associated with it, and so we overlooked his four-day week-ends, his growing distinterest in new projects, and other evidences that he was bored with the Bureau.

Beard was a man of independent wealth (mostly inherited) and in addition he had a handsome income from his books and other writings. Of administrative temperament he had little and of administrative ability not much more. The nine to five daily routine of the Bureau drove him to distraction. He simply could not put his heart into it. Another thing that cooled Beard's interest in the Bureau was an approaching financial crisis. Although I was not aware of this at the time, I should have guessed it. Since the Bureau had no endowment or other source of stable income, it was entirely dependent on annual contributions and earnings. The major contributions had always come from a small group of wealthy New Yorkers who were primarily interested in New York City politics and government. The Bureau for some years, and especially since Beard had been its director, had been increasingly occupied with projects and activities outside of New York City. Consequently the old backers began to lose interest and cut or withdrew their annual subscriptions. The Bureau had been able most of the

217

time to offset these losses with equal or greater earnings from the fees charged for its outside work, but this was a hand-to-mouth existence. Some years were fat and others lean. To enlarge and stabilize its income, and thus continue its nationally slanted program, the Bureau needed thorough refinancing through a sound plan of long-range fund-raising. Charles A. Beard had no taste for money-raising and did not propose to cultivate one. So he got out.

Beard's going left the New York Bureau suspended in mid-flight. There was no one to replace him for the moment and no assurance that any successor would be able to keep the Bureau out of a tailspin. One thing was clear, however, beyond a reasonable doubt. Immediate curtailment of the Bureau staff was imperative unless there could be a quick and substantial increase of income. Beard saw the handwriting on the wall and advised those of us who could get other positions to do so. For the older members of the staff this would obviously be more difficult than for the younger ones. In respect to obtaining other employment I was somewhat better circumstanced than most of the others. I already had my doctorate; I had the prestige, for what it might be worth, of published books and articles; and I held what some would view as a distinctive title and position in the Bureau organization. Though I preferred to remain in New York and hoped to find another position there, I had no family ties or material possessions to make it difficult to go elsewhere. So I volunteered to lay my head on the block. I told Dr. Beard my feelings about the matter and said that as soon as I could land another position I would resign.

A week or ten days later Beard rang me up on the interoffice telephone and asked if I could step into his office for a moment; there was someone there who wanted to see me. When I got there who should be waiting but A. R. Hatton, professor of political science at Western Reserve University, Cleveland, Ohio. An introduction was unnecessary, because Hatton and I had become acquainted at the association meetings at Cleveland the previous December. After some preliminary chit-chat, Hatton asked if I would be interested in a position at Western Reserve.

I did not know, but said I would consider it, and if the salary was right, I might be interested.

Offer from Western Reserve

Since joining the staff of the New York Bureau I had gone on the assumption that I would never return to college teaching. The combination of research and education that I enjoyed at the Bureau suited me so perfectly that I did not want another job of any kind anywhere. Vaguely I had supposed that if I ever left the New York Bureau, it would be to take a similar position with a municipal research bureau in some other city. Such organizations were springing up like early dandelions all over the country, and all of us New York men were prime material to head them. Furthermore, I was deeply interested in governmental research and in the embryo science of public administration, and feared that a return to the academic world would cut me off from these special interests.

In my conversation with Hatton I had expressed some of these thoughts, and he hastened to assure me that Western Reserve University particularly wanted me because my special training and experience might enable the University to develop its own program of governmental research and public administration. He said Cleveland was a city which offered rare opportunities to combine a university teaching career with government research. He thought, and very correctly it turned out, that Cleveland at this time was the likliest city in the country for sweeping municipal reforms, and the man who was in charge of things at Western Reserve University would have an unparalleled opportunity to combine the theoretical with the practical.

Hatton at this time was on leave of absence from Western Reserve, doing field work for the National Municipal League. He kept an office at the University, participated in faculty deliberations, but drew no salary and did no teaching. If I went there, he thought there would be some rare opportunities for him and me to team up together on a number of extramural projects. Hatton was a very persuasive person, and I was

219

in a mood to be persuaded. Finally he asked me if I would consent to go to Cleveland at the expense of the University and talk things over with the president, the dean, and the faculty committee in charge of this matter. To this I consented, and made the trip to Cleveland around the middle of March, 1920. I spent a whole day on the campus, talked with all of the University "brass," and returned to New York with the idea that going back to college teaching might not be so bad after all. A week or ten days later I received a telegram offering me a three-year appointment as associate professor and acting head of the department of political science. The salary was $4,000 a year without summer school, and I could expect an additional $800 if I were to teach in the summer school. This was $1,000 to $1,800 a year more than I was getting at the Bureau and was far above the national average even for full professors. It was also more than most Western Reserve professors were getting, but I did not know this at the time. I thought I was being offered a position in a very rich institution.

Elnora and I took two or three days to mull the thing over and I also discussed it with Dr. Beard and several of my closest colleagues at the Bureau. The consensus was that I ought to snap up this offer before it could get away, and I did, thus sending my wheel of fortune on another spin.

I left the New York Bureau before Beard's resignation took effect, and also left New York, so that ended my close association with Charles A. Beard. In later life I met him a few times at political science association meetings, and we remained good friends. In a way I regret my last visit with him, because he was then a prematurely old man, with impaired health and badly impaired hearing, but I shall never forget the Charles A. Beard I knew so well in his prime—the flaming red hair slightly flecked with gray, the steely blue eyes, the Roman visage, the erect figure with the athlete's stride, the sense of humor, the roar of laughter, the hatred of sham, the intellectual stimulus that radiated from him, the eloquence not only of his speeches but of his daily conversations, and most of all the warmth of his friendship. It was a rare privilege to be one of his "boys."

Seattle Interlude

Since my duties at Western Reserve did not begin until mid-September, there was a question of what to do in the meantime. I could have stayed on at the Bureau all summer and then made the move to Cleveland, and if Elnora and I had been as "commonsensical" then as we now think we are, that is what we would have done. She was then in the sixth month of her first pregnancy; we had a lovely and comfortable apartment; and she was under the best of medical care. The birth was due in late June or early July, which would have left ample time for her to recover her strength before going on to Cleveland. However, it had been three years since we had seen our parents, and they, of course, were much excited over the prospective arrival of the first grandchild. They begged us to come west for a visit before settling down in Cleveland, and we liked the idea as much as they. The only hitch was that I did not want to spend the summer twiddling my thumbs with no pay checks coming in. So I said we would come, provided I could find some sort of remunerative employment in the Pacific Northwest for the summer.

I could think of nothing I would rather do than teach in the summer school of the University of Washington. Accordingly, I dashed off a letter to Professor J. Allen Smith, head of the political science department there, and told him I would be available. It was so late in the season that I really did not expect a favorable reply. But luck was with me. My letter brought an immediate reply offering me $600 to do three five-hour courses in the summer session of 1920. This was enough to pay the freight, so I promptly wired my acceptance and made my resignation from the Bureau effective on May 1. After selling off all possessions we could not pack in trunks or boxes, Elnora and I headed for Spokane via the New York Central and Northern Pacific. My work at the University was to begin about June 15, so, after two or three weeks in Spokane, I went on to Seattle. Elnora remained in Spokane, and our Marilyn was born there on June 24, 1920.

221

Aside from the fact that I had to live the life of a lorn bachelor for twelve weeks, the summer session at the University of Washington was a delightful experience. I had comfortable quarters with Professor and Mrs. Leslie Ayer. He was a prominent member of the University faculty, and the Ayers made me so heartily welcome that I felt quite at home. Of course I had numerous friends in Seattle—old Ellensburg friends, Whitman friends, and professional friends—so I did not lack for places to go and things to do. I was a guest at week-end beach parties, went to numerous picture shows and vaudeville performances, called on friends, and made use of the Beta Theta Pi house as off-campus social headquarters. Herbert Ringhoffer was living at the University of Washington Beta house that summer, being registered in the law school where he was doing brush-up work in preparation for the fall bar examinations. I had become acquainted with Herbert in the fall of 1912, when he was a freshman at Whitman and a new initiate of Delta Phi Delta. Since Herb was then unmarried and I was going through a temporary interlude of bachelorhood, we found it agreeable to "do" Seattle together on many occasions. This was the beginning of a cordial friendship which spanned all the years until Herbert's death in 1962.

During that summer I made several week-end trips to Ellensburg, and on one of these occasions Elnora came over from Spokane and brought Marilyn with her. I had not seen my bouncy and squalling daughter before, and neither had any of her Ellensburg kinfolk. Marilyn was having a battle with colic at that time, and she proceeded to make everybody aware in her loudest tones that a bellyache was no fun. As Elnora and I sized up the problem of getting settled in Cleveland, we concluded that she and the baby should remain in Spokane while I went on to Cleveland and found a place to live. I had not tried very hard by correspondence to rent an apartment or house in Cleveland, because I had no good leads or connections. Moreover, I was sure that in a day or two on the ground I would have no difficulty finding satisfactory quarters in Cleveland. It actually took me more than three months.

Cleveland in 1920

Cleveland, when I arrived in early September, 1920, was in the throes of a housing shortage the like of which I had never seen before. I thought I knew a little about the post-war housing problem. It was bad enough in New York, but there and elsewhere that I had observed the situation, you could always get something if you were willing to pay the price. In the fall of 1920 in Cleveland, there was nothing to be had for love or money. I scoured the city again and again with no results. In order to be near the Western Reserve campus, I took a room in the Hotel Regent, then situated at 106th and Euclid, thinking I would be there only a week or two at the most. I remained there, at hotel rates, until the middle of December. After a long search, I located an apartment building then under construction at 11483 Hessler Road, about three blocks from the University campus. From the blue prints I rented an apartment in this building to be finished. For this three-room unfurnished apartment I paid $85 a month—in 1920!

The year 1920 was a presidential election year, and one of the least exciting in American history. By moving from New York to Ohio, I lost my vote that year but tried none the less to work up some interest in the presidential campaign. It was not easy. Woodrow Wilson had made it impossible for the Democrats to win, and they knew it. Both presidential nominees were from Ohio, but neither did much campaigning in their home state. Harding conducted a psuedo-McKinley front-porch campaign and seldom left the bounds of his home city, Marion. Cox did most of his campaigning in other states, and the only Democrat of national stature to campaign in Cleveland was Franklin D. Roosevelt. We had him at the University for a speech and reception. I heard and met him there, and was favorably impressed. As always, though technically a Republican, I was about as much interested in what was going on in other parties as in my own. It was my opinion that Roosevelt would have been a more popular presidential nominee than Cox, but nobody could have turned the Republican tide that year.

The thing I most clearly remember about the Republican campaign in 1920 was the effort made, mostly in Ohio, to squelch the rumor that Harding was of Negro descent. Just how this got into circulation, I do not know; but it was spread abroad by gossipmongers of all hues and affiliations. Russell Weisman of the Western Reserve economics department was also a member of the editorial staff of the Cleveland *Plain Dealer*. He told me the *Plain Dealer* had documentary proof that one of Harding's grandparents was a mulatto. It could have been true. All I know is that the *Plain Dealer* never published these documents nor announced that it had them. Harding ignored the whole hullabaloo about his ancestry, neither affirming nor denying, and probably gained votes by so doing. But other leading Republicans went to bat for him and declared the whole thing was a campaign smear. If there was any proof, somebody did a good job of getting it suppressed.

Elnora, with her mother and Marilyn, arrived in Cleveland on December 18. Mrs. Campbell came not only to help Elnora on the train but also to assist her in getting settled in Cleveland. I had been living in the Hessler Road apartment a week or so with no furniture except an in-a-door bed, so our first problem was furniture. By dint of extra effort and quite a little luck, we managed to get the apartment comfortably furnished before Christmas, and we celebrated the holiday with a fine dinner, beautiful Christmas tree, and the usual gala spirit.

We came to be very fond of our little Hessler Road apartment. It was on the second floor of a cozy and unpretentious building tucked away in the last block of a dead-end street. There were only twelve apartments in the building, and most of the tenants were young business and professional people, approximately our own age and just getting well launched in life. Two besides ourselves were Western Reserve faculty families. In a short time a real community spirit developed and the residents of our apartment house were neighboring back and forth all over the building like small town folks. Marilyn was the only infant in the building, and was given more attention that she deserved. Any time Elnora wanted to get away she could find some friend in the building who was delighted to have Marilyn for an hour or two. We did not appreciate this free baby-sitting as much as we should have. But we did appreciate the fact that we were close to the University, close to good neighborhood shopping centers, and close to the Euclid Avenue street car line which would take us to the downtown business district in fifteen minutes.

Troika at Western Reserve

I thought I had learned much about Western Reserve University during my visit there in the previous March, but I was due for a number of surprises. The first surprise was to discover that I was a member not of one faculty but three. The second was to find out that I was expected to teach, keep office hours, and attend faculty meetings on three separate campuses. The third was to discover that Western Reserve University was almost as headless as though it had no president and no governing board. If I was told anything about the troika in which I would have to operate, I had failed, on my March visit, to grasp the true significance of it. My conception of university organization had been formed at the Oregon Agricultural College, the University of Wisconsin, and Columbia University, and I had taken it for granted that Western Reserve would be very similar to these. I could not have been more mistaken.

Western Reserve University had grown like Topsy through the casual affiliation of independently established institutions whose principal bond in common was that they were located in Cleveland. They had a common president, but no common campus, no common board of trustees, no common faculties, and no common student bodies. There was an undergraduate college for men named Adelbert, an undergraduate college for women soon to be named Flora Mather, a partially graduate school of law, a partially graduate school of dentistry, a wholly graduate medical school, a wholly graduate library school, and a wholly graduate school of applied social sciences. I was a member of the faculty of Adelbert College, Flora Mather College, and the School of Applied Social Sciences. Each had its separate campus and buildings, fortunately within easy walking distance of one another. I had an office on each campus, taught classes on each, and otherwise functioned as a three-ring performer. My salary was paid from the income of the M.A. Hanna Foundation, which was part of the endowment of Adelbert College, and there was a sort of international settlement arrangement between Adelbert and the other two schools, by which Adelbert was reimbursed for their respective shares of my services.

The president of the University was a nominal chief executive, who actually had very few administrative duties and no administrative powers. Like the monarch in England, he reigned but did not rule. Each separate school or college ran its own affairs just about as it chose, and in each the faculty rode high in the saddle. Each chose its own dean and determined just how much authority he should have, which usually was very little. Each had its own separate financing. Some were fairly well endowed and others were entirely dependent on tuition fees and annual gifts. So far as I could ascertain there was no such thing as a university-wide budget or any university-wide financial leadership or responsibilities.

Adelbert College was fairly typical of all. It was run by a group of full professors officialy designated as the Permanent Officers, but unofficially called the P.O.'s. These men had permanent tenure and were the only members of the Adelbert faculty who did. They formed a closed corporation, and filled all vacancies occurring in their own ranks. This little oligarchy, about a fourth of the faculty, hired and fired all faculty members, chose the dean, made the annual budget, set salaries, granted or withheld promotions, and otherwise managed the affairs of Adelbert College. Educational policy and the approval of all courses of instruction were supposedly prerogatives of the whole faculty, but the P.O.'s could usually get their way in a showdown, because they had full control of money and personnel. Nobody could have permanent tenure unless he were a full professor, and all promotions to that rank had to be voted by the P.O.'s.

In my faculty troika the School of Applied Social Sciences was the most democratic, and that influenced me to spend more time on that campus than any other. I was in my office there every day, but in my other offices usually only three times a week immediately before or after classes. It took me a good while to form a judgment on the Western Reserve pattern of university organization. It was so different from anything I had ever known that it intrigued me at first, but eventually I came to the conclusion it was the chief cause of Western Reserve's failure to measure up to its magnificent opportunity to become one of America's leading universities. In the years I served there Western Reserve had two good but undistinguished undergraduate colleges and five good and correspondingly undistinguished professional schools. Western Reserve could and should have been comparable with Columbia, the University of Chicago, the University of Pennsylvania, Harvard, and other great metropolitan universities. Instead, it was, and has continued to be, a solid, respectable, and persistently provincial institution, little known outside the state of Ohio. There was no place in Western Reserve University for great leadership to function.

Curricular and Extra-Curricular Activities

A. R. (Augustus Raymond) Hatton was, as I have said, on leave from his professorship in Adelbert College, but he retained his office there, was active as a Permanent Officer, and used the University as a headquarters from which to carry on his work for the National Municipal League and his political activities in Cleveland. Pending his return to active duty, I was acting head of the political science department, did all of the administrative work and student counseling, and carried a twelve-hour per week teaching load. Associated with me in the capacity of instructor or assistant professor were Raymond C. Atkinson (1920-21), Martin L. Faust (1921-22), and Earl L. Shoup (1922-25). I was also allowed funds for three student assistants.

In Adelbert College the political science enrollment was

always heavy. My freshman-sophomore course in American government always had an enrollment of three to four hundred, and my upper division courses usually ran in the neighborhood of forty to fifty. At the Fem Sem (campus nickname for the college for women) the freshman-sophomore enrollment averaged around fifty and the upper division courses in the tens and twenties. Students in the School of Applied Social Sciences could register in my upper division courses in either Adelbert or Flora Mather, but had to do extra work under my direction for graduate credit. My show-window specialty was supposed to be the advanced course in municipal government and administration, a full year course for three hours per week. With the background of the New York Bureau, I was expected to be a star in this subject, and I tried not to disappoint. Fairly soon I was able to tie the course in with what was going on in the city government of Cleveland day by day, and this served to make it a feature course in the curriculum of the University.

Hatton had not exaggerated when he told me that Cleveland would offer unlimited opportunity for off-campus activity. Before I fully realized what was happening I was up to my ears in outside activities that involved many different aspects of the civic and political life of the city. I made innumerable speeches, conducted lecture series, carried on researches, served on boards and committees, worked as a technical advisor, wrote reports, and got myself into so many different jobs that there were times when the University saw very little of me. I managed to get my teaching schedule arranged to allow me four afternoons a week for downtown activities. On the days of these afternoons my regular routine was teaching in the forenoon, then down town for lunch either at the City Club or at a committee meeting held at a hotel or restaurant, and spending the rest of the day at the headquarters of the Chamber of Commerce, the Citizens' League, the Cleveland Foundation, or whatever other organization I might be currently working with. In the summer time I could put in even more time down town, because, even though I always taught in the summer school, all of my afternoons were free. I might add that I did not do all of this extra-curricular work out of the goodness of my heart. For most of it I was paid—very well paid, in truth. There were years when my outside income was larger than my University salary. For the 1920's this was big money.

My nights were just as busy as my days, for most of my evenings from seven to midnight were devoted to writing. One of the major publishing houses (then bearing the name of Doubleday, Page, and Company) had signed me to a contract to do two books—one a textbook on municipal government and the other a book of selected readings on the same subject. Only at night could I find uninterrupted time to work on these books. I finished this project in late 1923 and the two books were published early in 1924. The textbook was entitled *An Outline of Municipal Government* and its companion was called *Readings in Municipal Government*. The publishers tried to give these books a good send-off, and as a result I was able to collect a goodly number of reviews. Some of these came from quite unexpected sources. In addition to the conventional reviews in the professional and trade journals, my two books received wide notice in newspapers and popular periodicals. The following are typical examples of such notices:

The *Rotarian* said, "Every man who is really interested in his city will find some new incentive in *An Outline of Municipal Government*. This study is comprehensive but compact."

The Chicago *Evening Post* said, "The clear, logical style of the author, his compact method of presenting his subject, make the two volumes very valuable additions to the college or normal school, while the intelligent citizen seeking information as to the means and methods of successfully running modern municipal machinery will find much suggestive thought for the accomplishment of his desired goal."

The Detroit *News* said, "If you seek information on municipal government which is readable as well as instructive, you need look no further than these books."

The *Independent,* a weekly news magazine, said, "We must make ourselves familiar with the administrative problems of our cities by reading such books as Professor Maxey's, in order to understand the importance of practical foresight in city planning, and to appreciate the various elements of public safety, not only in their relation to public health and security of property, but equally in relation to moral and intellectual welfare."

Writing in the Baltimore *Sun,* a noted English critic, Herbert W. Horwill, said, "If municipal government in America still falls short of the Utopian ideal, it is certainly not for the lack of exhaustive discussion of its problems. Here we have two more books on the subject, compiled with a scholarly thoroughness that leaves nothing to be desired."

My personal opinion always has been that the *Outline* was unduly praised and the *Readings* never genuinely appreciated. The former I knew to be little more than an expanded and smoothly written syllabus, whereas the latter was a compendium of invaluable source materials never before available to the reading public. In compiling the *Readings* I drew heavily on survey reports of the New York Bureau of Municipal Research and on little-known official documents. By editing this material and getting it published in convenient form in hard cover, I made it available to multitudes of readers who never would have had access to the originals. Among its contents are some things that I would still rank as classics of political literature.

I had just turned thirty years of age when I went to Western Reserve, and as I now look back over the intervening forty-three and more years, it is difficult for me to understand how I found the time and energy to grind out books while spinning around so dizzily on the whirligig of academic and civic activity. As for the time, Elnora says she knows where I found it; I stole it from her and the children. She is no doubt right as to that. Most of my writing, as I have said, had to be done at night. In our tiny Hessler Road apartment there was no room for me to have a study or even a desk or typewriter table. But on the University campus three blocks away I had three offices in which I could spread out as I pleased. During the three years we lived on Hessler Road most of my nights were spent in one of these offices, usually the one in the social science building. As for the energy, that must have been an inborn endowment. I did get terribly tired sometimes, but I always bounced back quickly and completely.

On April 24, 1923, we were blessed by the arrival of a second darling daughter whom we named Aurel. Although she did not take up a great amount of space at first, it was enough more than we had to force us to seek roomier quarters. That summer we moved to 3420 De Soto Avenue in Cleveland Heights, some two miles from the University. There we rented the second story of a newly built duplex, some six rooms in all. I fitted up a makeshift study in the attic and did most of my writing there. Now I was at home in the evenings, but my being incommunicado in the attic did not much improve the situation from Elnora's standpoint. One thing, however, is less vivid in her memory than in mine. That is the long stretches of time when I held forth in Cleveland alone. She was in Spokane from May to September in 1922, from February to June in 1924, and again in 1925 from May to August when I joined her. These were long and lonely months for me, and it was good that I had lots of work to absorb my time and energy.

In the summer of 1921, after taking a thorough course of training in a driving school, I bought our first automobile—a second-hand Oakland, this make being the predecessor of the present Pontiac. This vehicle we kept and used all that summer, but I sold it in the fall because we did not need it for transportation and had no place to keep it except at a public garage. We did not get another car until the summer of 1923 when we moved to Cleveland Heights. There it was a necessity for transportation to and from my work. Since that time we have never been without one or more of those gas-guzzling monsters.

"In Dutch" with the P.O.'S

The Cleveland merry-go-round kept me so preoccupied with divers doings that I scarcely gave a passing thought to the Permanent Officers of Adelbert College. Through part of 1923 and all of 1924, in addition to the things mentioned above, I took one or two courses a semester in the law school of the

University, for I still had not given up the idea of seeking admission to the bar. I was so infernally busy that faculty politics scarcely entered my mind. I knew the score as far as permanent tenure was concerned, but did not give it a second thought. As a matter of fact I was not thinking in terms of long tenure at Western Reserve. Like my two immediate predecessors at Western Reserve (Raymond Moley and Harold W. Dodds), I expected to move on. For Moley, Western Reserve had been a stepping stone to the Cleveland Foundation and then to Columbia University; for Dodds, it had led to the secretaryship of the National Municipal League and thence to the presidency of Princeton University. I thought something like that might be in the offing for me. Indeed, I was not yet fully convinced that I wanted to remain in college teaching. If a good offer in the governmental research field had come along, I would have been strongly tempted to snap it up.

However, even if I had been concerned about getting permanent tenure at Western Reserve, I probably would not have conducted myself very differently. I certainly would not have paid court to the Permanent Officers of Adelbert College, because I was totally unskilled in that art and had little taste for it. Nor would I have suspected that A. R. Hatton was doing all he could to get me "in Dutch" with the P.O.'S. I did not realize that he was developing a deep feeling against me on account of some of my speeches and writings on the new city charter in Cleveland. One reason my first year at Western Reserve had been so absorbing was the adoption in November, 1921, of an amendment to the Cleveland city charter by virtue of which the manager plan with proportional representation would replace the old mayor-council form of government. Having enjoyed a ringside seat, I had learned a great deal about how this sweeping and sensational reform in city government had been brought about. The Cleveland charter amendment attracted nationwide attention, and the editors of the *World's Work*, one of the leading monthly magazines of the time, asked me to do an article on it. This article was featured in the issue of the *World's Work* for April, 1922. I now quote one paragraph of that article:

The manager amendment was presented on an initiative petition of a body of citizens known as the Committee of One Hundred, representing a wide variety of organizations and interests. The chief of staff of this committee (although he held the title of vice chairman) was Dr. A. R. Hatton, who is a unique figure in the public life of Cleveland. Coming to the city some years ago to accept a professorship of political science in Western Reserve University, he quickly became an active leader in public affairs. In 1912 he was a candidate for Congress on the Progressive ticket; in 1913 he was a member of the charter commission which prepared the existing Cleveland charter; in 1915 he was a Progressive candidate for mayor, but withdrew before the election. For a number of years he has been in the service of the National Municipal League as field representative and charter consultant, and probably has had a more extensive and varied experience in municipal politics than any other individual in the country. Familiar with all the cross-currents of Cleveland politics, a formidable debater, an expert draftsman, an effective writer, and fortified with the wide information of a scholar, Dr. Hatton was supremely qualified for leadership in this campaign. No small part of the success of the manager campaign must be credited to his indefatigable labors and sound political judgement.

I would not change a single word of that if I were rewriting it today. Nor would I change a single word of what I said in the same article about the proportional representation feature of the Cleveland charter amendment. This I boiled down to one paragraph which read as follows:

To appreciate the revolutionary character of the new system, one must compare it with traditional American ideas of government. For so long that there is scarcely any precedent to the contrary the American people have believed that their representatives in legislative bodies should be elected on a territorial basis; and the only issue has been the size of the territorial unit and the number of representatives to be chosen by each. Under the new Cleveland plan of government members of the Council are chosen by the Hare system of proportional representation, which aims to give representation to "interests" rather than areas. What realignment of political forces will result from this altered basis of representation can better be imagined than described. Government will be conducted by the representatives of articulate and cohesive groups of voters, regardless of place of residence, and while this does not foreshadow class war or social upheaval, it does mean something entirely foreign to American experience.

Hatton thought this was unduly skeptical, especially since I had always seemed to be strongly in favor of proportional representation. During the time that he was drafting the charter amendment and leading the campaign for its adoption, he and I had occupied adjoining offices at Adelbert College. Knowing that I had been trained in legislative drafting and knowing also of my municipal research experience, Hatton often used me as a guinea pig on points both of principle and phrasing. I think we talked over everything in the proposed amendment at one time or another. I was just as much in favor of incorporating proportional representation as he was, but I did not have the same emotional feeling about P. R. Hatton was convinced, both intellectually and emotionally, that proportional representation was indispensable to the success of city manager government, while on this point I had no real convictions pro or con. All I had was curiosity. I wanted to see P. R. tried out on a large scale, and Cleveland offered the first opportunity for this. So I was just as eager as Hatton to have P. R. adopted, but I did not have unshakeable faith in the outcome. Hatton took this to mean that I did not have true faith in him.

The Cleveland charter amendment was approved by the voters on November 8, 1921, with a proviso that it should take effect

234

on January 1, 1924. This meant that the first election under proportional representation would have to be held on November 6, 1923. In the intervening two years the county board of elections would have to set up the machinery and determine the procedure for casting and counting by the Hare system some 130,000 ballots. This not only was a task of first magnitude but one for which the election board was not technically qualified. The board felt the need of advisers who knew something about the Hare system, and asked me to be one of them. I was delighted to accept this appointment, because it would give me an inside view of every step of the first largescale P. R. election in American history, but Hatton did not want me to take it. He felt that if I worked with the election board I would be fraternizing with the enemy.

Of course I did not know that Hatton was planning to run for the city council in 1923, and that the enemy he had in mind was Maurice Maschke, the Republican boss of Cuyahoga County. He figured that Maschke would be in control of the election board and would be trying to use me and other technical advisors as stalking horses to distract public attention from the trickery by which P. R. would be undone. I could see how Hatton might fear such a thing, but I thought it a groundless fear. I thought I could see through the trickery as well as he, and would be in a far better position than he to disclose it to the public. So I went along with the board of elections, watched everything, studied every step of the procedure, was given access to anything I wanted, and had the free run of back-rooms of the municipal auditorium where the big count was conducted. I came out with the conclusion that the election was fairly and honestly conducted. Hatton himself was one of those elected, as he no doubt would have been under any other system of representation.

During the two years that Cleveland was making ready for its first P. R. election there was a tremendous effusion of public chatter on that subject. The newspapers were full of it, and I think every organized group of people in the city listened to one or more speeches about it. I made my share of those speeches, and so did Hatton. The general theme of my speeches was "Wait and see." I thought there were too many imponderables in the equation to be as cocksure of the answers as Hatton was. I did not criticise him personally, but press accounts of some of my speeches gave the impression that I was predicting failure for P. R. I did not predict failure for it, even after going through all of the involutions and convolutions of the 1923 election. I now wish I had, because I could now pat myself on the back as a prophet vindicated. There is no deader fish in the murky waters of political reform than proportional representation is today.

What I did attempt to do after the election was an objective analysis of the results. I had personally watched every phase and step of the election procedure, and by courtesy of the board of elections I had collected all of the relevant documentary and statistical data that were available. After spending eight months studying these I wrote an article summing up my findings. This was published in the Western Reserve University *Bulletin* for July, 1924. Walter Graham, editor of the *Bulletin,* was a member of the English Department and a good friend. Many times at the faculty luncheon table Walter and I had discussed proportional representation. He knew what I had been doing with the board of elections and that I was writing the article. He insisted that I let him publish it in the *Bulletin* because it was, he said, exactly the sort of thing the *Bulletin* ought to specialize in publishing.

My article was an attempt to evaluate the first P. R. election in terms of the claims made for P. R. by the Committee of One Hundred in the 1921 campaign. The Committee in that campaign had put out a pamphlet, which Hatton had written, in which it was flatly declared that proportional representation would (1) insure that a majority of the voters would elect a majority of the Council, (2) prevent the control of the Council by political bosses, (3) provide the best safeguard against racial and religious prejudices, (4) guarantee the election of candidates who would in some measure express the true will of the voters, (5) provide fair representation for women, (6) put a premium on political independence, and (7) be simple for the voters to operate. In my article I turned the magnifying glass of statistical analysis on these seven advance claims, to ascertain what substantiation, if any, could be found in the factual data of the first election. I found so little substantiation that I wound up with the legendary Scotch verdict of "not proved." In the final paragraph of the article I said:

It is not easy to summarize the foregoing observations. If they establish anything, it is that proportional representation is not a panacea, but a most valuable and promising experiment, which, though it has not measured up to all of the predictions made with regard to it, certainly has not failed. It has not miraculously emancipated the electorate; nor has it destroyed partisanship and boss rule. It is no guarantee of good government, and not necessarily of representative government. But it has given the voters a means of self-emancipation and an opportunity to strike down boss rule, if they care to do so. And it does make good government and representative government easier to attain, because it removes the most serious obstacles to independent political action and free expression of public opinion.

I thought this was a fairly temperate summary, but Hatton construed it as an attempt to show him up. I had made the mistake of not consulting him in advance about it or letting him know that it was going to appear in the Western Reserve University *Bulletin*. He might have been somewhat mollified if I had tried to smooth his feathers ahead of time, but I did not. Never even thought of it. So I probably earned his enmity and deserved to have him do all he could to see that I was separated from the Western Reserve faculty as soon as possible. If I had cared much about Western Reserve University, this would have been a blow. I liked Cleveland a great deal, but I never grew attached to the University or aspired to make a career there.

Sounding Off on Teapot Dome

Another thing that somewhat damaged my standing with the elder statesmen of Adelbert College was some loud sounding off that I did on the notorious Teapot Dome scandal. In the academic year 1923-24, the Womens' City Club of Cleveland paid me a handsome honorarium to do a series of lectures on current affairs. This series was in no way connected with the University. The lectures were delivered in the main auditorium of the Women's City Club's downtown headquarters, and were open only to members and their specially invited guests. But representatives of the press were always invited, and the good ladies wanted as much publicity as they could get, as that would be helpful in keeping their membership rolls filled to the brim. The United States Senate hearings on the leasing of the Teapot Dome, Elk Hills, and other naval oil reserves had begun somewhat obscurely in October, 1923, but it was not long before they were making national headlines. The lecture committee of the Women's City Club asked me if I would include the Teapot Dome hearings in my series and I agreed to do so. To that end I gathered as much documentary material as I could on the issues involved.

In the spring vacation of 1924 I went to Washington and attended the hearings myself. The opportunity was just too good to miss. Elnora and the babies were on a visit to Spokane; I had a new Buick; and I could see no reason for spending a lonely vacation in Cleveland. So I invited two bachelor friends, Walter Graham whom I have previously mentioned and Peter Reed who was my graduate assistant, to go along for the ride and share the fun. On the drive both ways we stopped wherever there was anything of interest, spending nearly a day on the Gettysburg battlefield and taking in all of the sights of the capital and vicinity. I personally spent enough time auditing the Teapot Dome hearings to get a clear idea of what was going on. Therefore, when I got back to Cleveland I could speak not only as a reader of reports but as an eye witness on the scene.

I put plenty of eyewitness color into the two Teapot Dome lectures I delivered at the Womens' City Club, and the reporters gobbled it up. I had come to the conclusion that the weight of the evidence was turning against Secretary of the Interior Fall and Secretary of the Navy Denby, and that the two oil magnates, Doheny and Sinclair, were as black as any villains could be. I pulled no punches in expressing my opinions. I wanted to make the headlines, and, boy, how I did! I also made the editorial pages in the Republican papers (owned by the Hanna family) and was given a good spanking for tossing a monkey wrench into the works of the chamber of commerce and other booster organizations which just at that time were trying to raise enough money to entice the Republican national convention to Cleveland in 1924. I was told in pontifical editorials to keep my big mouth shut. Most of the Adelbert P.O.s' heartily concurred. If I had known then how the Teapot Dome affair was going to end, I would have spouted more and louder than I did. Fall and Sinclair went to jail, Doheny barely escaped the same fate, and Denby retired under a cloud.

The Mock Election

The P.O.'s had further reason to doubt my prudence because of the outcome of a mock political convention that I sponsored on the University campus in May, 1924. Because the Republican convention had decided to come to Cleveland, there was a lively interest in convention organization and procedure. Several times the matter was brought up in my classes, and, on the theory that one of the best ways of learning was by doing, I suggested the mock convention and intimated that it would be more fun if it could be staged as a Republican convention. That was all the students needed; from there on they picked up the ball and ran with it. All I did was to get them organized according to Republican rules and get permission for them to use the University gymnasium to stage their show. Of course the news quickly spread all through the University, but it also aroused a great deal of interest throughout the city. So we decided that the best thing to do was to invite the public to sit in the galleries, and I personally invited all of the county officers and leaders of the Republican Party.

A few days before our convention, a group of boys came to me and asked if I had any objection to their trying to nominate a

239

"dark horse" candidate and stampede the convention for him. It was certain, they said and correctly, that Coolidge was going to be nominated by acclamation, but what was the fun of having a mock convention without any fireworks? I agreed and asked what kind of fireworks they had in mind. They replied that they wanted to try to swing the convention to La Follette. "Fighting Bob" was anything but a dark horse, but he was a chronic maverick, and right then he was spouting threats to start a third party if the Republicans nominated Coolidge. I thought that would start a real fight on the convention floor, and told the boys to try the stampede if they could. They did, and La Follette carried our mock Republican convention by a landslide. Result: I was spanked again by the Hanna newspapers, which took it for granted that I was the Ethiopian in the wood pile. In a way I was, for I could have stopped the La Follette boom, I suppose. But I saw no reason for trying to stop it. It did not occur to me that any one would view the La Follette nomination as a deliberately planned insult to Coolidge on the eve of the convention. Maurice Maschke, the Republican boss, who was my personal guest at the mock convention, did not see it that way, either. He soon sensed what was going on and enjoyed seeing the college boys let off steam. But some of the Adelbert P.O.'s were deeply shocked, so they said.

A New President

Probably my least pardonable offense, from the standpoint of the Adelbert P.O.'s, was to help draft a committee report which proposed to upset their sacred applecart. Charles F. Thwing, longtime president of Western Reserve University, retired in 1922. Dr. Thwing was a beloved and venerable personage who had been a great ornament to the University but had never exercised any real authority in its management. The Trustees decided to replace him with a dynamic young man, and chose as his successor Robert A. Vinson, then president of the University of Texas. Vinson had made a fine record at Texas and was still only in his forties. He looked like just the right man to get Western Reserve on the high road to greater things.

One of the first things President Vinson did was to appoint an all-university committee to study the existing organization and procedure of the institution and make proposals for needed changes. From Adelbert College he appointed one permanent officer and two of junior rank. I was one of the latter. Most of the Adelbert P.O.'s took offense at this, thinking the president should have given them at least a majority of the Adelbert representation. This despite the fact that they constituted about a fourth of the Adelbert College faculty.

The general committee was broken up into sub-committees, and I was assigned to the sub-committee on undergraduate education, which had the job of plotting a future for Adelbert College and Flora Mather College. There were many meetings with prolonged discussions, and I was one of those chosen to collaborate in drafting the final report. This favored a plan of reorganization which would give most of the precious managerial powers of the Permanent Officers to the President of the University. We thought the President would have to have such powers, not only for the undergraduate colleges, but for all other schools and divisions of the University. If not, there was little hope that he could launch and carry forward the unified program necessary for the proper development of the University.

I had been reappointed in 1923 for a two-year term, which, of course, was to expire in 1925. I was sure the Adelbert P.O.'s would not renew my appointment a second time, and it did not make much difference what Flora Mather and the School of Applied Social Sciences did, because they were contributing only small fractions of my salary. I decided to move on, but before announcing this decision I had a long talk with President Vinson. He wanted me to stay at Western Reserve and offered to do battle for me, but I said no. He was already in trouble with the several faculties because of the reorganization report, and I saw an intramural fight ahead of which I wanted no part. I was not sure Vinson could win, and as a matter of fact he did not. Two or three years after I made my exit from Western

241

Reserve he likewise departed, a victim of the intrenched faculty oligarchies.

No Regrets

I left Western Reserve with no regrets and no ill will. I had come to take such a dim view of the future of political science in that institution that I had no real desire to stay on there. In the course of my five years there I had discovered how unlikely it was that Western Reserve would ever be an auspicious place for an undergraduate major in political science. At Flora Mather there was little demand because so few of the girls were interested in political science as a major. At Adelbert most of the political science majors were drained off into the School of Law for the senior year and so never completed their undergraduate major. In the School of Applied Social Sciences there might have been a good opportunity for graduate instruction if there had been any money to underwrite such a program. There was not, and no plans were being made to improve the financial underwriting of the School. Western Reserve, in my time there, was predominantly an urban institution, and drew more than three-fourths of its students from the Cleveland metropolitan area. A large portion of its students attended Western Reserve because they could go cheaper there than elsewhere and large numbers transferred at the end of the first two years. Of those who remained, the great majority tried to get into one of the professional schools at the earliest opportunity. As a day school, a street-car university, Western Reserve was pretty good, but it had little prestige either at home or elsewhere. Throughout the United States it was scarcely known at all, and in its own bailiwick it was rated below Ohio State, Miami, Oberlin, Kenyon, the University of Cincinnati, and other better known institutions.

I cannot say, however, I did not regret leaving Cleveland. That great city had been good to me and for me. In the years that I lived and worked there it was politically one of the most exciting cities in the country, and I had a chance to be right up on the battle front all of the time. I got to know scores of wonderful people and took part in more things than I had ever dreamed would be possible for me. Also I made more money there than I had ever made before, or had ever expected to make. I thought I saw investment possibilities there which might have made a great deal more money for me. But, of course, I never had a chance to find out how right or wrong I was on that. Some of my investments there washed out during the depression, and this probably would have happened even if I had been living there and able to look after them.

A Crucial Decision

Elnora and I were in something of a quandary in deciding which way to leap after leaving Cleveland. Perhaps it would be truer to say that she had few doubts and I had many. I thought it might be better to try to get back to New York or somewhere on the Atlantic Coast, but Elnora was for the Pacific Northwest without any doubts or reservations. If it had not been for our parents, I don't believe I would have been satisfied without one more try at the New York region. Elnora's parents were getting along in years and would soon be dependent on us for support, she being the only child. She could not see how it would be possible to transfer them from Spokane to some unknown place on the Atlantic Coast or even to New York City. My mother was an invalid, bedridden much of the time, and seemed to have a brief life expectancy. I was her only living child. If possible, Elnora wanted—needed—to be near enough to Spokane to get there in a few hours, and I needed to be near enough Ellensburg to do the same. The place which would come closest to meeting both our needs was Whitman College and Walla Walla.

I had no idea whether there was or would be a position open at Whitman. So I decided to do a little scouting before making application. I wrote to Dorsey Hill, whom I had known since my student days at Whitman and who also was a brother Beta. Dorsey was then treasurer of Whitman, and I felt sure he could tip me off if there was a vacancy or any likelihood of there being one. Two or three weeks passed, and instead of a reply from Dorsey, I received a letter from President Penrose offering me the Miles C. Moore Professorship of Political Science at Whitman. Dorsey, as I learned later, had simply handed my letter to Dr. Penrose and he had decided to make a vacancy for me. I immediately accepted the offer, and thus my course was set for the rest of my days.

Elnora and the children set forth for Spokane early in June, but I had to stay at Western Reserve until the end of the summer school. The year before, by way of investment, we had acquired a twenty-acre farm in the Spokane Valley, and Elnora's parents had moved on to this place. She and the children were to spend the summer on the farm with them. During the summer Elnora went to Walla Walla and rented a house, which happened to be the old Kyger mansion at 430 Lincoln Street. I shipped our belongings by freight and kept bachelor quarters the rest of the summer with two of my colleagues on the Western Reserve faculty. As soon as the summer school ended, I headed west in our little old Buick Four. As a companion I took along Ernest J. Bohn, a Western Reserve graduate who had been a major student of mine and had become a very close friend. Though he came along mostly for the ride and to see the country, Ernie did as much of the driving as I. It was the first long motor trip for both of us. Driving across the United States on the dirt and gravel roads of 1925 was bound to bring adventures, and we had our share. We were arrested in Wisconsin for speeding at twenty-five miles an hour, had so many blowout and tire repairs that we lost count, broke a spring near Miles City, Montana, and had to make a replacement ourselves in an old-fashioned country blacksmith shop where the proprietor turned us loose because he did not want to bother with it.

Some time after I had been appointed at Whitman, I wrote to President Penrose and asked if there would be any objection on the part of the College if Elnora took a few private pupils in voice at our home. Our girls were getting old enough so that she could have a little free time, and she wanted to get her hand back into music on a small scale. Dr. Penrose immediately replied that they had no objection to her doing a little private teaching but they would much rather have her on full-time as a member of the faculty of the Conservatory of Music. This posed a problem. We did not see how she could swing a full-time job unless she could have a great deal of domestic help. We had not counted on anything of the sort and did not know whether adequate help could be found in Walla Walla. After some days of hesitation and discussion, Elnora made the decision. She would take a chance—try it for a year at least. That year stretched into nineteen. Elnora remained on the Conservatory faculty until 1944, and could have taught longer if she had wished.

PART IV

WHITMAN COLLEGE, 1925-1948

XVI. WHITMAN PROFESSOR

Impressions After Thirteen Years

In the thirteen years between 1912 ond 1925 I had little contact with Whitman College. After my departure for Ellensburg in December, 1912, I visited the campus only twice, and both of these visits were too brief and casual to enable me to learn anything significant even if I had tried, which I did not. When, in September, 1925, I came back as a faculty member, my remaining impressions of Whitman were a mixture of undergraduate memories and general ideas of education sharpened by experiences in other institutions of higher education. I thought I knew pretty well what I was coming back to, but I did not. I soon found that I had to get acquainted with Whitman all over again. I had to learn to see Whitman through the eyes of a contemporary faculty member and put aside all preconceived ideas. In connection with this shifting of mental gears I gained some impressions that were shocking enough to fasten themselves firmly in my memory.

One shocking impression had to do with the condition of the campus and physical plant. They looked seedy and run down. I did not remember them that way at all. The Whitman of my "old grad" memories had a just-built appearance, and in fact most of the principal buildings were of very recent construction when I came to Whitman in 1908. All of the buildings north of Boyer were so new that a freshman of 1908 could easily imagine that in some places the paint was hardly dry. Memorial and Billings were just eight years old, Reynolds five, the Gymnasium two, and the Conservatory was just going on the drawing boards. All of the furnishings and equipment were correspondingly new, and were said to be of the finest quality. A lovely lagoon (Lakum Duckum) had just been formed by damning up the little campus brook; young trees and freshly planted shrubbery gracefully bedecked the recently planted lawns; and the many winding footpaths about the campus were neatly trimmed and cindered.

Decrepitude would be the best word to picture my impression of the Whitman buildings and grounds in the fall of 1925. The roofs leaked, every one of them; the walls of every hall, class-room, and office were dingy and dirty; doors and window frames were worn and scarred; the wall plaster was riddled with cracks and in numerous places huge chunks of plaster had fallen out; tables, chairs, and desks were teetery, scratched, and begrimed; window shades were laced with rips and perforations; window panes looked like they had never seen soap and water; and evidence of fresh paint was nowhere to be seen. Entirely typical of the worst that greeted my astonished eyes was the unpainted, paper-roofed, weather-worn, library shack which had been hulk-ingly stuck on to the west end of Memorial to serve as a reading room. It would have been hard to find a barn in Walla Walla County more barnlike than this hideous and dilapidated library annex.

Another source of disenchantment was the faculty. It, too, looked seedy and run down. Only six of the faculty of my generation remained. These were Anderson (L.F.), Bratton, Brode, Brown, Penrose, and Ruby. Anderson was semi-retired; Bratton was a dean and not teaching a full schedule; Brode was going on as usual and so was Brown except that he had announced that he was in his last year of full-time teaching; Penrose, handicapped though he was by blindness, was trying to administer the office of president and at the same time teach a full schedule of courses in philosophy; Ruby was now full-time registrar and doing no teaching at all. All who had been added to the faculty since 1912 I regarded as newcomers, though most of them considered themselves veterans. After allowing for all prejudices inspired by undergraduate nostalgia, I had to admit to myself that most of the newcomers did not impress me as first-raters. Those in the social science field were good examples of mediocrity. I was sure of that, because I had a nationwide acquaintance with political scientists, economists, and sociologists. One characteristic was common, however, to both the older

250

and the newer faculty members. To a man they were discouraged, dispirited, and anxiety-ridden. Not only had they largely lost faith in the future of Whitman College; most of them were fearful of calamities to come. They worried constantly as to whether they would be able to meet next month's bills, whether they would be able to educate their children, whether they would be able to lay away savings against the day of retirement. The outlook was far from bright. In vain they had hoped and hoped for adequate salaries, for lighter teaching loads, for money to buy library books and laboratory equipment, and most of all for any dependable evidence that they could look forward to something better in their remaining years at Whitman. They would not have minded making bricks without straw if there had been some hope of a promised land ahead.

The commonest and most absorbing topic of conversation in faculty circles was if and when President Penrose would retire. Many rumors were afloat, but no one knew the truth. Every member of the faculty did know, however, that Whitman was desperately in need of dynamic executive leadership; everyone knew, regardless of what the outside world imagined, that Whitman was sailing without a pilot. There was surprisingly little animosity toward Dr. Penrose and many sincere expressions of personal affection for him, but there was not one single expression of confidence. To have expressed confidence would have been to fly into the face of incontrovertible evidence of gross incompetence. If I had been told in the fall of 1925 that the governing boards of the College would shrug their shoulders and allow this ruinous state of affairs to continue nine years longer, I would not have believed it. Only by living through it did I become convinced finally that Whitman was in the throes of an era of callous neglect.

Another first impression that still lingers in my memory was the difference in the composition of the student body "then" and "now." In my undergraduate years we had scarcely 200 students of collegiate grade, and in 1925 the freshman class was larger than that. The total enrollment of the College was more than three times larger than in my day. An overwhelming majority of the students in my time at Whitman were farm boys and girls or small-towners like me. We came from tiny, isolated high schools; none of us had ever been anywhere or seen anything; few of us had any money; most of us were as innocent of guile as the Knights of the Round Table; but practically all of us had been thoroughly drilled in foreign languages (especially Latin), English, mathematics, and basic science. In the Whitman student body of 1925 the city kids predominated. They were pretty smooth as compared with our generation, even sophisticated, I would say. But they were not nearly as well prepared for studies of collegiate grade as our generation had been. They did not seem to be as well prepared as my students at Western Reserve had been. In truth, I somehow got the impression that Whitman must have let down the bars since the time when I had to present my standard sixteen Carnegie units for admission. I found out before long this was true, and further, that it reflected the urgent financial necessity of getting enough students to assure a minimal tuition income. I began to have doubts as to whether I would like teaching at Whitman, but in the end it proved to be one of the satisfying and stimulating experiences of my life.

Classroom Teacher

Computations made from my class records, all of which I have kept, show that in twenty-three years as a full-time instructor at Whitman a total of approximately 5,700 students were enrolled in my classes. This would average out as about 248 a year and 124 a semester. For the subject of political science in a small college, this was a large enrollment, and it gave me a heavy working load. From 1925 to 1935 I was a one-man political science department, which means that I not only taught all of the courses offered in that subject but had to offer enough courses to provide a thirty-hour major concentration. This called for a good deal of spreading out, and I soon realized the value of my broad undergraduate, postgraduate, and professional training and experience. In case of need I had the background to teach nearly everything in the area of political science that needed to be taught. In 1935 President Clemen gave me a half-time instructor as an assistant, and in 1947 President Anderson gave me a full-time instructor, thus making political science a two-man department for the first time.

I can truthfully say that up to the time I became president of Whitman in 1948 I was a regular classroom teacher, and met two or more classes every day. I deemed that job to be my primary responsibility and tried to give it first priority on my time. I met every class promptly and regularly. I was seldom ill, and, when sent out of town on College business. I always endeavored to arrange to schedule my travel as much as possible to avoid missing classes. In part this was a matter of professional ethics with me, but it was just as much a matter of pedagogical theory. I believed that unbroken continuity was an important element in the process of instruction.

I also made it a rule never to enter a classroom without having made some sort of previous preparation for that particular class meeting, and I followed this rule no matter how many times I had taught the course or how well I knew the subject-matter. My theory was that a recap just prior to the class period would not only serve as a brush-up but would freshen my interest and suggest new ideas regarding old topics of instruction. This worked well for me, and I am sure that I did better teaching in many a class just because I had given myself an intellectual shot in the arm just before the class session.

Though I never had a stereotyped teaching method, I did try to have a definite plan of procedure for every class meeting. Before I started the session, I tried to formulate a clear conception of what I wanted to accomplish and how I would go about it. Sometimes I wrote out a lesson plan much as one would prepare agenda for a business meeting. After some years of this, I found myself increasingly able to extemporize lesson plans as I went along, thus synchronizing my system with events as they took place in the classroom. This gave me confidence and I think it gave the students a feeling that the class session was a spontaneous proceeding for both instructor and pupil.

Never having been the victim of any courses on how to teach, I was entirely on my own as to classroom techniques. All I knew about the psychology of the learning process I had picked up through personal observation and experience. In my utterly untutored philosophy of education, I believed that the great majority of college students want to learn and will readily respond to the right kind of learning stimulus. My most important job, as I saw it, was to discover and apply the stimuli which would do the job best. Accordingly, an essential part of my advance preparation for each class was to think up various tricks, stunts, or acts by means of which I could dramatize the instruction I was trying to drive home. In more ways than one I was a ham actor in the classroom, but there was always an instructional motivation behind the ham.

There are many ways of classifying collegiate courses of instruction. In this discussion I am classifying them according to the teaching problems they pose. In the field of political science, as I saw it and still see it, there are three kinds of basic teaching to accomplish, namely, the informative, the analytical, and the individualized. In every course a certain modicum of each is necessary, but most courses tend to be preponderantly in one of these three categories. In an informative course, such as comparative government, the major purpose is to convey information, and the methods of instruction must be adapted to this end. In an analytical course, such as American constitutional law, the major purpose is to give the student personal experience in critical analysis. In an individualized course the major purpose is to put each student on his own resources in the execution of some project (research, reading, reporting, writing, etc.) in which he will perform under observation and advice of the teacher. For informational courses I relied principally upon the lecture-discussion method; for analytical courses I used the Socratic or cross-examination method; and for individualized courses I employed as far as practicable the Oxford tutorial method.

As a lecturer I tried to be unmechanical and informal. I preferred the conversational to the oratorical type of discourse, though I could turn on the rhetoric when necessary. I invited interruptions, urged the students to break in at any time with questions and comments, and when they sat on their hands, I often pulled myself up short and tried to toss out a bone of contention. Such digressions and interruptions were no bother to me, because I had things well enough planned so that I could get back on the main line with little difficulty. In fact, these stops and starts furnished the best possible means of dramatizing the discourse. I would not have been half as effective without them.

In the analytical courses the main thing in applying the Socratic method was to frame questions in the best form and sequence to impel the students to think analytically and logically. I was never able to rely upon the inspiration of the moment to put such questions in my mouth. Usually I had to work over each case or problem in advance and formulate a series of questions to engender the kind of thinking I was using it to foster. This was far more exacting work than preparing a lecture and would have been a forbidding task had it not been for my past experience in the study and teaching of law.

My individualized courses were conducted almost entirely through separate personal conferences with each student. In such conference I endeavored to guide the student in a program of reading, research, documentation, and writing on a topic chosen to occupy a full semester or even a full year of intensive work. Sometimes I was not sure whether I was teaching political science or English composition. Neither in college nor in preparatory schools do college students get much training in expository writing. Often I had to bear down harder on matters of syntax, even spelling, than on form and methods of treatment. I was hardboiled in demanding effective English, because it was a favorite dogma of mine that a good command of English was indispensable to success in the study of political science, or any other subject for that matter.

My teaching load at Whitman usually varied between twelve and fifteen semester hours per week. This was rather more than I should have been doing, especially after I became a dean, but the work had to be done, and I did it alone until 1935. After receiving part-time help that year, I was generally able to hold my load to nine hours. Nearly every year I taught one or more sections of a course open to freshmen and sophomores, and the rest of my work was at the upper division level. I liked this distribution because it brought me into contact with a good cross-section of the entire student body. My Western Reserve specialty —municipal government and administration—had to be gradually de-emphasized on account of Whitman's rural locale, but I had been well enough trained in all areas of political science to shift easily to other fields of special interest. In the end my chief specialties were threefold—public law, political philosophies, and party government.

I trust that the foregoing summation will be sufficient to convey a fairly clear idea of how I functioned as a teacher from 1925 to 1948. The work was by no means as tedious and dreary as it may sound in the telling. I never was bored with my teaching duties. Very seldom was there a class session or a conference in which I was not rewarded by a stimulating experience of some kind. One thing I discovered is that intellectual stimulation is a two-way street. The more stimulation the teacher imparts to the student, the more he gets in return. I would have been happy to go on teaching through my years as president, and did try to, but extensive and unavoidable travel made it impossible to do justice to the course (Political Philosophies) that I tried to teach. I taught the course the first two and last two years I was president, but in the intervening seven years I had to give it up. At any rate I could say, and did say with sincere pride, that I closed my career as an educator just as I began it forty-seven years before—a classroom teacher.

Counselor

In some measure a college professor is always a student counselor. The students enrolled in his classes have the right always to rely upon him for advice. I had that duty at Whitman, of course. In addition, I was of necessity the major counselor of all students electing political science as a major study, and there were always from fifty to a hundred of these. After the 1934 reorganization, under which I became Dean of Social Sciences, it became my duty to serve as academic counselor for all freshmen registered in that division, and this gave me from seventy-five to a hundred additional counselees. Altogether, in one capacity or another, I did most of the counseling for two hundred or more students. This was always a time-consuming job and sometimes a very onerous one.

In order to be readily accessible to students wishing to consult with me, I kept stated office hours, and in those periods I sat in my office with the door wide open and everybody welcome to walk in. As much as possible I tried to avoid "booked'" appointments and never required an appointment in advance except in registration periods when it was necessary to meet nearly all of my counselees in the span of four or five days. In my twenty-three years of regular student counseling hundreds of boys and girls sat in my office and talked, not merely about academic matters, but of shoes and ships and sealing wax and everything else under the sun they wanted to talk about. Many of these became close personal friends and have remained so through the years. During World War II, I carried on a heavy correspondence with student counselees who were in the armed services in all parts of the world. Most of the letters I wrote to these service men had little to do with counseling; they were merely letters written to friends on every battle front, keeping them up to date on Whitman news and letting them know they were not forgotten.

The achievements of my major students has been a source of great pride to me. Not that I could claim huge credit for their successes, for most of them were the kind who would make good in life regardless of college counseling. I did, however, have the opportunity of advising them in their specially plastic years, and I liked to think my counsel had weight in some of their choices. Not many of the men who majored with me went into political science professionally, although the few who did have been highly successful. I am sure that more of my men went into law than any other profession, as political science was not only a natural but a strong pre-law major. Dozens of my pre-law majors are now leading members of the bar, several have become prominent judges, and some have achieved distinction in the teaching of law.

I would say that the second largest group of Maxey majors were those who took up business careers. Several of these have risen to high positions in great business corporations, especially banking, but even more have gone into business for themselves. Some have thought it strange that political science majors should choose business as a career, but there is enough government in business these days to make political science a valuable pre-business major. My third largest group of majors were those who made careers in government service. Political science was a natural major field for these students, and I am sure their number would have been much greater if government service could have offered a more attractive career. Fourth in size was the group of majors who went into educational work. Some of these became college professors and many others made careers in various branches of public school administration. In addition to the four groups just enumerated, I had major students who achieved success and eminence in such diverse careers as medicine, the ministry, military service, social work, journalism, and farming. All of which goes to prove nothing at all except that what a person does with his education is as important as what it does for him.

Committee Work

The most joyless work I did as a college professor was committee service, and at Whitman I had more than I wanted of this. Colleges and universities are as committee-prone as other American social institutions, but Whitman, I think, was less committee-ridden than most institutions of higher education. Except in the administration of President Winslow S. Anderson, Whitman has made little use of permanent faculty committees, but I cannot remember a year in which Whitman did not have in action one or more highly important *ad hoc* committees. It was my lot to serve on many of these and to be chairman of several of them.

In one respect the Whitman faculty during my period of service was typical of all faculties I have ever known anything about. Without half trying it could get itself into a furious uproar over controversies which were momentarily taken to be of earth-shaking importance. On such occasions passions would burn so fiercely that the quickest and easiest way to cool down the hotheads was reference of the matter to an *ad hoc* committee which would be empowered to study the issues and report back its conclusions. Even though the committee might find no solutions, the cooling-off period usually was long enough for at least a partial restoration of sanity. These special committees generally were named by the president, but there were times when the faculty itself would insist on making the choice. Having done duty on a goodly number of such committees, I have a keen memory of the interminable hours of gabble that went into the procreation of a committee report. Most of the special committees on which I served were purely faculty committees, but I did serve on three which were joint committees of the faculty and governing boards of the College.

The purely faculty committees which come most vividly to mind are seven in number: the committee on compulsory chapel; the committee on the one-degree plan; the committee on the three-term vs. the two-semester system; the committee on the foreign language requirement; the committee on faculty reorganization; and the committee on general education. I was chairman of five of these, which meant of course that I had to be the principal beast of burden. I could write a little essay on each of these committees, but that would give me little pleasure and the current reader even less. Suffice it to say that each of these had to deal with a burning issue. Whether any of these issues will ever burn again, I would hesitate to predict. Certain of them very well might, for in a college faculty few things are ever settled forever.

The three joint committees on which I served deserve more extended treatment, because each in its own way was a history-making committee. One was a faculty-trustee committee set up in 1932 for the mutual consideration of defaulted faculty salaries.

The second was a faculty-trustee-overseer committee established in 1933 for the purpose (1) of planning and executing a Whitman seventy-fifth anniversary program at commencement, 1934, and (2) to plan and carry out appropriate exercises in honor of President Penrose on the occasion of his retirement in June, 1934, after forty years as president. I was made chairman of this committee. The third joint committee was a faculty-trustee-overseer committee appointed at commencement, 1941, to search for a successor for President Walter A. Bratton. I was made secretary of this committee.

By 1932 Whitman had fallen so much in arrears in the payment of faculty salaries that it seemed impossible to go on. My own case was fairly typical. I was paid more than some members of the faculty and less than others. In 1930-31 the College withheld payment on about 25 per cent of my salary and in 1931-32 on about 20 per cent. With salaries as low as they were, any default was a blow, and a repeated default was a disaster. There was no way of telling how much would be defaulted or when, so it was impossible to look ahead and make plans. The faculty demanded, as it certainly had the right to do, that it be informed as to the outlook for the payment both of arrears and current salaries. President Penrose would give no definite answer to this question, so the faculty, after an informal caucus, asked that the Board of Trustees name a committee to meet with a committee named by the faculty and that the two committees meet and act jointly in exploring the salary problem. The Trustees designated Messrs. D. F. Baker and Allen H. Reynolds and the faculty chose Walter A. Bratton, Frank L. Haigh, and Chester C. Maxey.

Mr. Baker and Mr. Reynolds told us flatly that immediate payment of salaries in arrears was impossible and refused to make any commitment as to when it might be possible. As to the payment of current salaries, they said that if the faculty would agree to a salary cut of 20 per cent, it should be possible to pay all current salaries promptly and in full. We wanted a pledge in writing that this would be done, but they pleaded that they had no authority to make such a promise. As a sort of *quid quo pro,* we then asked that the College, through properly empowered officers, be required to give any faculty member requesting it a promissory note for all or any part of his unpaid salary. If this were done, we would recommend acceptance of the salary cut of 20 per cent. Mr. Baker and Mr. Reynolds agreed to recommend this to the Board of Trustees, and Bratton, Haigh, and Maxey then advised the faculty to agree to the salary reduction.

I have never been proud of my part in this affair. At the time it seemed to be the best deal that could be made in behalf of the faculty, but I later came to think that we should have made no concessions at all. I speak only for myself, but I have a strong feeling that Bratton and Haigh would agree that if we could have foreseen that the College would make no effort whatever to raise money for current salaries and would do everything it could to discourage the taking of notes for unpaid salaries, we would have been far more stubborn than we were. We could have forced an immediate showdown and possibly a liquidation of enough of the assets of the college to pay all the arrears. As events actually took place, the faculty had to wait two years before any effort was made to pay current salaries in full and five more years before there was any substantial payment on the arrears. As a matter of fact, the arrears were never paid in full. During the debt-raising campaign of 1936-39, every faculty member was asked to donate a part of his unpaid salary to help reduce the size of the amount to be raised. By this waiver route, I surrendered more than $500 of my unpaid salary. It is indicative of the spirit that then prevailed in the top management of Whitman College that we were told that if the faculty refused to cooperate through these sacrificial contributions to the debt-retiring fund, it would be impossible to get contributions in Walla Walla or elsewhere in sufficient amounts to do the College any good. I now know that was a totally false representation; they made no effort to get money on the outside until they had first bled the faculty for all they could. A somewhat more particularized account of this unhappy episode will be found in a subsequent section of this narrative.

In 1933, under circumstances to be related later, President Penrose tendered his resignation, to be effective June 18, 1934. Since 1934 was the seventy-fifth anniversary of the founding of the Whitman Seminary and the fortieth and final year of Dr. Penrose's tenure as president, it seemed a propitious time for a big academic clambake. With that in mind, the governing boards in joint session at commencement, 1933, chose a joint committee of board members and faculty members to plan and carry through an appropriate program of exercises for this historic occasion. For reasons still unknown to me, I was elected as one of the faculty members and was later designated chairman of the committee. It soon was clear to me that the whole job was being tossed into my lap. I was given authority to employ a secretary and authorized to proceed on the supposition that I would have some money to spend. Actually, though I was not told so at the time, no budget money had been earmarked for the 1934 celebration, and it did not appear that there was enough in the operating budget of the College to spare more than chicken-feed for anniversary purposes.

It was apparent that if I was going to have any money to spend for the 1934 blowout, I would have to raise it myself. Although I had never done any fund-raising, I decided to take a chance and see what I could do. So, in connection with the planning, programming, and working-out of the exercises, I also carried on a money soliciting campaign. Luck was with me. Enough money came in to defray all of the costs of the four-day celebration and leave a comfortable balance for the general expense fund of the College. From this first money-raising experience I learned that the best trade secret of the successful fund-raiser is unremitting toil.

The only help I had in carrying on my begging work was secretarial; all the rest I did myself. But in all the other responsibilities of the chairmanship I had all the helping hands one could wish. The Walla Walla Chamber of Commerce gave me invaluable help in sponsoring and promoting a great pioneer parade and in putting on a diamond anniversary dinner. Mrs. Edith M. Davis of the Whitman faculty was indispensable. She produced and directed three featured entertainment events of the week-end—a play, a pageant, and a campus revue. R. V. Borleske, Whitman athletic director, was similarly helpful in arranging several interesting athletic contests for the week-end. Howard E. Pratt, director of the Whitman Conservatory, helped arrange a concert and also provided musical numbers for all luncheons, dinners, and receptions. And scores of students and alumni unselfishly gave hours of time in preparation for the events in which they participated. My principal job during the four-day affair was to coordinate everything and see that things came off as planned.

The one part of the week-end that I handled alone was the special recognition program for Dr. Penrose. I sent invitations to a hundred or more institutions to send delegates, and most of them responded by sending presidents, deans or distinguished professors to pay tribute to President Penrose. I rented the Keylor Grand Theater for this program, and we had all of the delegates on stage in their academic regalia, with Dr. Penrose front and center in the position of highest honor. The program consisted of speeches interspersed with musical numbers. All of the speeches were salutes to Dr. Penrose, and representatives of all of the leading institutions in the West took part in this. The climax and finale of the four-day extravaganza was reached at 4:30 P.M. on June 18, when the class of 1934 was graduated, Dr. Penrose given a parting accolade, and the new president, Dr. Rudolf A. Clemen, inaugurated.

It was in connection with this 1934 celebration that I wrote a little brochure which brought me undeserved repute as a local historian. This little booklet was entitled *Historical Walla Walla Valley* and was published by the Inland Printing Company of Walla Walla. For many years the Walla Walla Chamber of Commerce had felt the need of a pocket-size history of this area which could be easily distributed as publicity material. Since the diamond anniversary of the City of Walla Walla and of Whitman College both came in 1934, that seemed an ideal year to put out such a historical booklet. Being the Whitman chairman, I was drawn into several conferences about this matter.

Finally an agreement was reached. The Chamber of Commerce would underwrite the printing and binding costs in return for a stipulated number of copies for its own use; the Inland Printing Company, as printer and publisher, was to have the right to sell as many copies as it could in retail channels; I, for a fee of fifty dollars, agreed to produce the manuscript.

In producing this manuscript I did no original research—did not have time. I simply turned to the well-known histories written by such authors as Lyman, Gilbert, Bancroft, Gray, Snowden, and Fuller, and without plagiarization, appropriated what I needed for an abridged and composite history of the Walla Walla country. The manuscript ran to about 8,000 words. The Inland Printing Company employed the late Ed Smith, then county engineer, to do marginal drawings to accompany the text of the pamphlet. Smith had a nice gift for pictographic sketching, and his drawings added immeasurably to the attractiveness of the brochure. In no time at all, it seemed to me, the supply was exhausted and in a year or two it became a collector's item. Reprinting was impossible because the Inland Printing Company had broken up the forms and thrown away all of the type and cuts. In 1953 there was a partial second printing in a booklet published by the Walla Walla Chamber of Commerce and entitled *The Walla Walla Story*. In addition to selections from my little booklet of 1934, the *Walla Walla Story* included much other material and was cast in an entirely different format.

The joint committee of 1941, which I mentioned previously was appointed by the chairman of the Board of Overseers and given the duty of seeking a successor to President Walter A. Bratton. How I came to be on this committee, was named to serve as its secretary, and other pertinent matters will be told at a chronologically more appropriate place in this biography.

Dean

In May, 1931, I was asked to do recruiting work for Whitman in the Yakima Valley. This involved visiting high schools and striving to create good will among city school superintendents, high school principals, class advisers, and high school seniors who might be interested in Whitman College. Those were the days of the "hard sell"' in luring students to college. The depression had decimated college enrollments and few prospective students had any money for expenses. Taking my own car, I started at Pasco and worked my way from town to town up the Yakima Valley as far as Cle-Elum. The trip took all of ten days, and needless to say accomplished little in the way of recruiting. On returning home I went to President Penrose to report the outcome of my trip, and, when we had finished talking about that, he informed me that in my absence I had been appointed Dean of the Academic Group.

I did not have to fake surprise about this, because I had not received the slightest hint in advance that I was even being considered for this deanship. Had I known about it ahead of time, I might have made an effort to prevent the appointment, for at that time I had no desire to be the dean of anything or to have anything more to do with the Administration of Whitman College than I already had. I tried to beg off, but Dr. Penrose would not take no for an answer. And Steve Penrose, as I perhaps can testify as well as any person living, was not an easy man to refuse. He insisted that I was the best man available for the position, that I had just the kind of qualities he wanted in that spot, and furthermore that I would not be overburdened with administrative routine. He was sure the deanship could not possibly take more than four or five hours a week, and in return for that he would add a hundred dollars a year to my salary. The salary part meant nothing, as far as I could see, because the College was then defaulting salaries and I did not really expect the extra hundred dollars ever to be paid.

Nevertheless, Dr. Penrose finally talked me into taking the deanship, but I did it with my eyes open and not for money. The chief reason I accepted the deanship of the Academic Group was that I wanted to get out of the External Relations Group, in which I was the Officer on Community Relations. I was completely fed up with this job, which was a terrific bore and had about as much to do with community relations as with mink farms in Missouri. The deanship of the Academic Group had become vacant the year before by reason of the resignation of Professor E. E. Ruby. Professor Frank L. Haigh had served as Acting Dean for one year but did not wish to continue, so Dr. Penrose said. I thought being Dean of the Academic Group might be far more interesting than bumbling around in the External Relations Group with my hands tied, even though it might mean much more work.

The Three-Group Organization

From approximately 1912 to 1934 the entire Whitman faculty was divided, for administrative purposes, into three groups named respectively the Academic Group, the Internal Life Group, and the External Relations Group. This organization was a pet brain child of Dr. Penrose and he set great store by it. I worked in it long enough to believe that in some respects it had great merit, but was not without serious shortcomings.

Each group met and acted, separately from the others, as a sort of subfaculty, taking actions within its assigned sphere which had later to be ratified by the whole faculty. Every member of the faculty was assigned to one of these groups, and in that group he acted as an administrative officer of the College in charge of a certain specified function or group of functions. Each group also was broken down into committees of three members each, and as a rule every faculty member in the group served on one of these committees. There were no general faculty committees except the *ad hoc* committees created from time to time as I have described above.

The dean was chairman of his group and the administrative supervisor of each of its officers. All of the group committees reported to him. The deans of the three groups plus the dean of women (there was no dean of men at this time) met once a week under the chairmanship of the president of the College. Thus assembled they functioned as a board of deans, in which capacity they served as the chief cog in the policy-making and administrative processes of the institution. Nearly all actions of the three faculty groups were reported to the Board of Deans

266

and thence to the general faculty. It was a moot question, and one which often generated heat, whether *all* actions of the Board of Deans had to be ratified by the general faculty. An even "mooter" question was whether the general faculty could reverse the Board of Deans. It seemingly had authority to do so, but never essayed to exercise that authority.

The Internal Life Group had general jurisdiction over student life in the dormitories, student discipline, and student-faculty relations. On these matters it made recommendations and reports to the Board of Deans. The External Relations Group had jurisdiction over alumni matters and all other public relations. The domain of the Academic Group included all legislation and all administrative actions having to do with scholastic requirements, requirements for graduation, the adoption of new courses of study, the discontinuance of old ones, the grading system, the keeping of academic records, and nearly all other matters growing out of or relating to the curriculum. For instance, if a student sought to be excused from an academic requirement or have it modified, he had to submit a petition to the Academic Group; if a faculty member wanted to introduce a new course or cancel an existing one, he must first make a request that the Academic Group so recommend to the general faculty; if the numbering of courses was to be changed or the registrar's records altered, approval by the Academic Group was the first step. Every meeting of the Academic Group was occupied with scores of items of business growing out of questions similar to the foregoing. In addition, the Academic Group had the responsibility, on its own initiative, of making class schedules and examination schedules, preparing the annual academic calendar, certifying the satisfaction of degree requirements, awarding scholarships and grants in aid, and making up the agenda for the so-called educational meetings of the faculty.

One of the great weaknesses of this three-group organization was imbalance. The Academic Group was overloaded with business; the External Relations Group was much underloaded; and the Internal Life Group operated on a feast-or-famine basis, being overworked on special occasions but grandly idle most of the time. The dean of the Academic Group was the only one of the three who had a genuinely administrative job. His group was obliged to hold regular weekly meetings and between meetings he had to see that numerous transactions were correctly carried out in detail. The two other groups found it unnecessary to have weekly meetings and sometimes did not meet oftener than once or twice a semester. Although I did not relish the administrative load my deanship involved, it proved to be a profitable experience for me. By this deanship I was forced to become thoroughly knowledgeable about the things which make the wheels go round properly or improperly in the business of translating catalog announcements and stated academic rules into everyday operation. This knowledge proved to be highly valuable in my later years as president of the College.

In 1934, after President Clemen took over, the administrative organization of the faculty was completely changed. President Clemen thought the three-group organization unrealistic and unwieldy. One of his first official acts was to appoint a committee on reorganization. He asked me to serve as chairman of this committee and I accepted the job, though I knew it would make the summer of 1934 one of the busiest of my life. President Clemen wanted the reorganization committee to report at the first faculty meeting in the fall, so that the new system, if approved, could be put into effect at the beginning of the first semester. In late June and early July the committee had several meetings with President Clemen and was given a complete rundown of his views on collegiate organization. I found myself in sympathy with most of these.

At the same time I was busy putting through the several stages of proofreading the first edition of my book, *The American Problem of Government*. Before I could dispose of this and also before I could whip out a committee report for President Clemen, I had to take off for Ann Arbor, Michigan, where I was to spend the remainder of the summer as a member of the Carnegie Endowment's workshop on international law. Therefore, the final stages of my committee job had to be done through correspondence carried on at the same time I was finishing work on the book and researching reports for the workshop in international law. By working early and late, I managed to get a tentative draft of the committee report to President Clemen before I returned to Walla Walla.

When I got back to the Whitman campus, around the first of September, I found that President Clemen was ready to go on the reorganization business. He had taken the tentative report, edited it a bit, and accepted its recommendations. This I reported to the committee, and we accordingly disbanded, assuming that our job was done. At the first meeting of the faculty Dr. Clemen called for a report from the committee on reorganization and I presented the one he had already approved. He called for discussion on this report, but nothing much was said. Then he asked if there was a motion, and I, as chairman of the committee, moved the adoption of the report as submitted. This motion was promptly seconded and when the question was put, the motion carried without a dissenting vote.

I have stated these details because of a story that was later put into circulation, charging President Clemen with putting over the 1934 reorganization by steamroller methods. It has always been my view that persons who stand mute when given an opportunity to vote should never complain of steamroller tactics. In this case, no doubt there were faculty members who would have voted no if they had not been afraid of getting in bad with the new president. But President Clemen said or did nothing to intimidate any one. He did heartily endorse the committee report and say he hoped it would be adopted. But that is common procedure and far from jamming a motion through in spite of opposition. As an interesting footnote I might add that no effort was ever made, after Dr. Clemen left Whitman, to repeal or even substantially modify the faculty organization adopted in 1934. No real change was made until I became president in 1948, and I initiated those changes myself.

The 1934 reorganization abolished the group system and established in its place a system of division faculties correlated with the natural breakdowns of the College curriculum. The previous group system had no relation to the content of the curriculum, but was supposed to reflect logical administrative functions. Under the new organization three divisional faculties were established—Social Sciences, Letters and Arts, and Basic Sciences. Since the Conservatory of Music did not readily fit into this scheme, it was left as a dangling appendage for several years. Each of the three divisions was made up of departments, each of which embraced a unified subject-matter field or area. I was made Dean of the Division of Social Sciences. This division included the departments of economics and business administration, education, history, philosophy, political science, psychology, and sociology. These represented organized major study fields, but were not separate administrative units. Department heads had no administrative powers or duties, but were major advisers and senior professors in their respective teaching fields. For administrative purposes, the division was the basic unit, and the divisional dean was its executive officer.

Each divisional dean was appointed by the president and was directly responsible to him. The three divisional deans together with the president, the dean of men, and the dean of women constituted the Board of Deans. This board inherited all of the general functions of the former board of deans and a good deal besides. The board was divided into two standing committees, one known as the academic committee and the other as the committee on student affairs. The academic committee took over most of the work of the former Academic Group and the committee on student affairs took over most of the duties of the former Internal Life Group. The functions of the former External Affairs Group were taken over by the office of the president and were exercised without consultation with the Board of Deans. This organization was obviously more streamlined and better articulated than its predecessor, and it was not long before most of the faculty were willing to concede that point.

As Dean of the Division of Social Sciences my duties were threefold in character. First, it was my duty to preside at all meetings of the divisional faculty, appoint all divisional committees and supervise their work, coordinate the work of the major advisers, and represent the president in such matters as faculty appointments, promotions and salaries in my division. Second, I was the academic counselor of all freshman students whose registration indicated a future major in the Division of Social Sciences. I saw these students through their first year in college and tried to get them satisfactorily assigned to major advisers for counseling after the freshman year. For all students majoring in my division, I was the official agent of the Board of Deans in disciplinary matters—not the agent for administering discipline, but for the pre-disciplinary investigation, if any. My third major responsibility was service on the academic committee, of which some of the time I was the chairman. In this capacity I was doing much the same sort of thing as I had done as Dean of the Academic Group.

From the foregoing summary it is clear that the 1934 reorganization considerably enlarged the role of a Whitman dean. It was almost as though he were the head of a separately organized school in a large university. The demands upon his time were so many and so constant that he could not be expected to carry a full teaching schedule, as I had done under the old organization. In 1935, by providing a man to teach half-time in history and half-time in political science, President Clemen enabled me to reduce my teaching load to nine contact hours a week, the lightest teaching load I had ever had at Whitman or elsewhere.

XVII. OFF-CAMPUS ACTIVITIES

Writer

I classify writing as an off-campus activity because most of my writing was done at home. When I was in my office on the campus, there were too many interruptions to do much writing. From 1918, when my first magazine article was published, there has never been a time when I did not have one or more writing projects in the works. These included books, articles, and book reviews, and I often found myself working on one or more of each type simultaneously. Teaching and writing were the kinds of work I liked best, and I was ambitious to be recognized as good at both. Writing in my professional field was highly satisfying both because of the recognition it brought and because it sometimes proved rewarding in cash. Perhaps I was somewhat actuated by a gambling instinct. There was always the possibility that some day I might hit the jackpot with a best-seller and make a mint of money. The chance of making big money is just as good in the textbook field as in fiction. A best-selling textbook can yield royalties fat enough to make any popular novelist envious. None of my books ever did that well. *Political Philosophies* was a best-seller in its field for twenty-five years or more, but the field was too small to produce huge royalties. It did, however, make a respectable sum of money both for me and the publisher. *The American Problem of Government* was one of the top five in its field for nearly twenty years and brought me some fairly substantial royalties. My other books were less successful than these, but all made something. Income from my writing has been sufficient to pay for our home and many of the other possessions we have acquired.

I have often been asked how I managed to get so many books published, and by such outstanding companies. There is no mystery about this. I had the good luck to get off on the right foot with my first book. In a previous chapter I have told how, through the good offices of Charles A. Beard, the Macmillan Company of New York published *County Administration,* my first book. To be a Macmillan author was as good a set of credentials in the publishing world as any new writer could have, for Macmillan was, and still is, one of the world's most famed and successful publishing firms. All publishers are looking for new writers—must have them if they are going to stay in business. Scouting for new writers is one of their constant activities, and one source they never fail to scout is the new book lists of rival publishers. This will explain why soon after *County Administration* came out, men from the Alfred A. Knopf Company, Doubleday, Page and Company, and other New York publishing houses began to find reasons for dropping in at the headquarters of the New York Bureau of Municpial

Research just to get acquainted with me. They were not there, it seemed, just exactly to talk turkey, but just incidentally they would like to know if I was tied by contract with Macmillan for future books, and if not, did I have anything I might submit for consideration by their firms now or in the future.

Before I moved to Cleveland I had tentative understandings with representatives of the Knopf and Doubleday firms, and these understandings soon matured into formal contracts. For the former I did a book entitled *The Problem of Government* and for the latter two books, *An Outline of Municipal Government* and *Readings in Municipal Government,* both of which I have told about in a previous chapter. As a result of these publications, I was well enough known that the publishing houses did not lose track of me when I transferred to Whitman. Traveling representatives of all of the leading textbook publishers visit every college campus once a year or oftener, and those who came to Whitman always had instructions to sound me out on possible manuscripts in preparation. Everything I said was reported back to the home office, even though it might be no more than an idea for a book which I might do in the future. If the editors were interested, they quickly got in touch with me. As a result, I could usually find an outlet for my writings. I don't mean to imply that I sold everything I wrote. No writer does that. But I never had the door slammed in my face, even when I "laid an egg."

My first published book after coming to Whitman was *The Problem of Government* (1925), written and put through the press while I was still in Cleveland but not issued until September of that year. My first book written at Whitman was *Urban Democracy,* published by D.C. Heath and Company of Boston in 1929. Though this book did not do too well in the marts of trade, thanks to the onset of the great depression, I have always regarded it as one of the best pieces of writing I ever did. I had much the same experience with my next book, *You and Your Government* (1931), also published D. C. Heath and Company. This book was my first and last venture in high school textbook writing. For undertaking this job I had no better motivation than to bag the fattest goose I could. It was one of those sad things which come under the heading of "might have been." The book won a generous mead of praise from the reviewers and critics, and started to pick up adoptions, but this did not last. In the terrible summer of 1931 hundreds of school boards could not scrape up enough cash to pay routine expenses, let alone buy new textbooks. By the time the depression had lifted enough for new textbooks to find a market, *You and Your Government* was no longer new. I did not lose any money on this book, in fact made a little, but the publishers lost so much that they did not want to risk a revised edition after the market picked up.

In 1934, while busy as a one-armed paperhanger, as I have already mentioned I managed to get *The American Problem of Government* through the press of F. S. Crofts and Company of New York. The Crofts firm had purchased the textbook department of Alfred A. Knopf, for whom I had written *The Problem of Government*. To boost sales, Crofts proposed putting out a revised edition of this book, and I countered with the proposal that I completely rewrite the book and give it a more specific title. Crofts went along with my suggestion, and I did such a thorough job of overhauling that *The American Problem of Government* was in fact a new and different book. In some ways this is the most successful book I have written. It has gone through six editions and has been a consistent and fairly substantial producer of royalties.

No writer is qualified to evaluate his own books, but I am going to take the liberty of saying that I think my best scholarship and some of my best writing went into *Political Philosophies,* published by the Macmillan Company in 1938, with a revised edition in 1948. It took me ten years, off and on, to do this job—including, of course, the time devoted to reading, research, and compilation of data as well as the actual writing. This book has been used as a textbook and work of reference not only throughout the United States but in foreign countries as well. In fact, at the time of this writing (October, 1963), the foreign sales exceed the domestic by a wide margin. I am unable to explain this, but I rather like it. I have received letters about the book from as far away as Ceylon. Such experiences warm the cockles of an author's heart. Sometimes I wonder if *Political Philosophies* has not done more to prolong my reputation as a political scientist than all of the other professional work I have done.

I have already hinted at books I wrote and failed to get published, books I partly wrote but never finished, and books I agreed to write but never started. In the first category was *A Preview of the Social Sciences*. I never doubted, when I finished this book, that any publisher who had a chance at it would immediately grab it. But I peddled that manuscript from one publishing firm to another without stirring a ripple of interest. I finally gave up in despair, and still don't know why it was such a "dog." When I took office as president of Whitman I had two book manuscripts spoken for by publishing firms and partially written. One of these dealt with international power politics and the other with party government in the United States. On account of the pressure of presidential duties, I was forced to put these manuscripts aside. The one on party government I finished after I retired as president, and it was accepted by the Caxton Printers Ltd. and published in February, 1965. Maybe I will be able to do the same for the one on international power politics, but that remains to be seen. Also at the time I took office as president, I had a third book in the incubation stage. It was to be called *Constitutional Government*. I had done a lot of reading and note-taking on this project, but had put nothing in writing. I don't believe that I shall ever return to this.

Though not a prolific writer of articles, I did contribute semi-occasionally to such journals as the *National Municipal Review,* the *Western Political Quarterly,* and *Northwest Science.* The *Whitman College Bulletin* also published articles written by me. In addition to articles, I also did occasional book reviews for the *Annals of the American Academy of Political and Social Science,* the *Journal of Social Forces* as well as the magazines named above. I continued to do book reviews after my retirement.

Public Speaker

A college professor with any ability as a public speaker is sure to be swamped with invitations to wag his jaw on all sorts of topics and on all sorts of occasions. I was no exception to this rule. I turned down more speaking engagements than I accepted, but still took on more than I should have. I spoke for service clubs, chambers of commerce, business and professional organizations, church brotherhoods, parent-teacher associations, farm organizations, labor unions, political conventions, and banquets without number. Once in a while I was paid, but most of my speeches were made gratis, as a service either to Whitman College or the group to which I was speaking. By no means all of this speaking was done in Walla Walla. As a matter of fact there are few cities of consequence in the Pacific Northwest in which I did not make one or more speaking appearances. In some of these places I gave a lecture series under the sponsorship of some local organization.

The kind of speeches I made could be roughly classified under four general headings: extemporaneous, memorized, recited from manuscript, and conversational from notes. I did not care for extemporaneous speaking but often had to do so. Fortunately, I was fluent enough to be an acceptable off-the-cuff speaker, but I always felt these were my poorest speeches. Once in a while I wrote a speech and committed it to memory, but I did this only when it was imperative to keep within a fixed time limit and also have an exact record of what I said. For longer speeches, when there was no time limit or a very liberal one, and yet it was necessary to have a manuscript in order to guard against misquotation, I wrote out the speech and then recited rather than read it. I use the word "recited" because it aptly describes my technique. Being a rapid reader, it was easy for me to run my eyes over the pages of a manuscript and take in whole sentences and paragraphs. These I could recite almost as though I was speaking impromptu, thus giving the impression that I was not tied to the manuscript at all.

My favorite mode of public speaking, the one I always employed in the classroom and elsewhere as far as possible was to talk from notes. This was a totally colloquial or conversational technique. First I would get up a set of notes in outline form, to serve as the skeleton of the discourse. On this framework I would fill out flesh and features as I talked. I did not have to keep my eyes glued to the notes; a glance now and then was sufficient to keep me from straying, and left me free to make use of inflection, diction, gesture, and the like just as though I might be chatting informally with each member of the audience as an individual. If necessary, I could throw in an oratorical flourish, but did so quite sparingly. I preferred this mode of speaking because of its easy adaptability to many different subjects and audiences. After I was on my feet I could shift gears, change tempo, and even modify the substance of the speech according to the audience reaction.

Most of my speeches, 90 per cent I would say, related to government and public affairs—my own professional field. Once in a while I yielded to the temptation to talk through my hat on subjects I knew little about. This was dangerous, but sometimes fun. I list hereafter the titles and occasions of a few of my speaking performances. These are typical of the hundreds of speeches I made during my thirty-four-year professional career at Whitman: "The Brain Trust of 1787" (Whitman Fall Convocation, 1937); "The Challenge of Bureaucracy" (Institute of Government, University of Washington, 1936); "What is Republicanism?" (Young Republican Club of Spokane, 1932); "The Commonwealth of Business" (Washington State Bankers Association, 1931); "Power-Politics in Anglo-American Relations" (Institute of International Relations, Eastern Washington College, 1944); "The Dangers of Doctrine" (Lewiston Normal School Commencement, 1936); "The Dilemma of the Independent Voter" (League of Women Voters, 1932); "The Welfare State" (Walla Walla Rotary Club, 1948).

Civic Activities

I was one college professor who could not find much time to

277

repose in the suppositious ivory tower. Many a time I would have loved such a hideout from reality, but none appeared on the pathway I had to follow. Mine was almost as much a civic as an academic career, for the pressure to take part in civic affairs was insistent and almost irresistible. It was not merely that I felt a duty to do what I could for the betterment of society, but also that I thought I would be a better political scientist by reason of participation in civic affairs. In Walla Walla many opportunities for such participation came my way. I had not been on the Whitman faculty a month when I was invited to join the Kiwanis Club. I was a member of this organization for several years, served on several of its committees, and in 1929 was elected president of the club. In that capacity I was sent as a delegate to the international convention of Kiwanis and took part in those deliberations. The leading service activity of the Walla Walla Kiwanis Club was the establishment and maintenance, on upper Mill Creek, of Camp Kiwanis, a facility designed primarily for such organizations as the Camp Fire Girls and the Girl Scouts. I did my share of work on that project.

I early joined the Walla Walla Chamber of Commerce and worked on a number of its committees. In 1931 I was the principal speaker at the annual dinner of the chamber of commerce. In keeping with the major concern of the time, my subject was "Fighting Depression." This was one of the few times that I ventured outside my own professional domain, and consequently I took special pains with that speech—wrote it out and memorized it. As I now re-read the manuscript, I find that I had much to say about the business cycle that I had learned at the feet of Ely and Commons at the University of Wisconsin back in 1913-14. This in particular: "If our economic experts were always as practical as they are profound, I think they would more often and more emphatically tell us that the most frequent cause of economic depression is uncurbed and indiscriminate prosperity; that in periods of prosperity we allow our appetite for profits to betray us into business practices which are so fundamentally unsound and unwise that their cumulative effect in the course of three or four years of zooming prosperity is to produce a sudden collapse of the health of our economic organism." Then I went on to argue that the best time to fight the "bust" is when the "boom" is on. That did not offer much comfort for those who were looking for a miracle to cure the hard times of 1931. But it did not keep me from being invited many times afterwards to speak at meetings of the Walla Walla Chamber of Commerce.

In that same dismal year of 1931, if my memory is correct, though it might have been a year or two earlier or later, I served as chairman of the community chest drive. We fell far below our goal, which is why I am sure it was one of the depression years. There just was no money to be had. We were lucky to scrape together enough to keep some soup kitchens and bread lines going through the worst of the winter. I took the job that year because nobody else would. In those days there was no money for a paid staff or even paid clerical help. Everything was done by volunteers, and my job was to enlist the volunteers and then plan and direct their work. I certainly did not distinguish myself in that capacity.

In 1934 I helped found the Walla Walla Community Concert Association, was elected its first president, and served in that capacity for four years. This job took a great deal of time and effort at first, because money was still tight and the idea of a package sale of a concert season to a group of voluntary subscribers was novel to Walla Walla. For at least one year, and possibly more, I served as president of the Walla Walla County Camp Fire Girls Association. I was much interested in this because both of our daughters were then active in Camp Fire. One year I conducted a downtown seminar once a week for the Walla Walla Credit Bureau. I had no particular qualifications for this except a willingness to stick my neck out, but I did manage to hold all of the credit managers together in a weekly meeting in which they had a useful exchange of views about credit problems.

I got myself deeply involved in Republican politics, became a member of the county committee, was chosen a delegate to the county and state conventions, and was a frequent speaker at Republican rallies. I also became a candidate for office, but that story will be the subject of a separate chapter later. I was inexorably drawn into the work of the Whitman College Alumni Association, served on many of its local and regional committees, spoke at alumni meetings in Walla Walla and elsewhere, and held several offices. All this was a labor of love. The same was true of my twenty-three years of service as adviser to the Gamma Zeta Chapter of Beta Theta Pi.

The foregoing are by no means all of the civic activities in which I engaged during my professorial years at Whitman, but they are a good sample. There never was a time when I was not involved in some public service activity. Regardless of the value of the services rendered, I enjoyed most of the activities, and they were good for me whether they helped anyone else or not. They made me many personal friends, they enriched my social experience, and they brought me into contact with many aspects of community life that I could not have experienced as a recluse on the Whitman campus.

Professional Associations

A college professor can, if he has the interest and the opportunity, make himself an interesting collateral career in service of the learned societies of his profession. Always there are several professional organizations for which he is eligible. I could have been a member and an active worker in a dozen such, but I joined only four—the National Municipal League, the American Political Science Association, the Northwest Political Science Association, and the American Society of International Law. I attended national and regional meetings of all, and occasionally served on committees. I served two three-year terms on the national executive committee of the American Political Science Association, and attended several of its pre-convention meetings. I was one of the founders of the Northwest Political Science Association, served on its executive committee, and was its president for one year.

Undoubtedly, if I had remained in the East or the Middle West, I would have been far more active in professional associations. After I came to Whitman in 1925, it was exceedingly difficult to attend the national meetings of the great professional associations. These meetings were seldom held on the Pacific Coast, and when they were held in such places as Chicago, New York, or Washington, time, distance, and the lack of money for travel made it impossible for me to attend very often.

XVIII. EUROPEAN JUNKET, 1926

The Invitation

In the spring of 1926 I received an invitation from the Carnegie Endowment for International Peace to be a member of a European Conference of American Professors of International Relations. Behind this imposing official name was a project sponsored and financed entirely by the Carnegie Endowment. Fifty American professors of international relations were invited to be the guests of the Endowment on a tour of the important European centers of international organization and activity. The Endowment would not only pay all travel expenses for its guests but would give each a liberal spending allowance. Never before had there been a privately financed European junket of such scope and magnitude, and I doubt if there has been one since.

As announced in the formal invitation, the objects of the forthcoming European Conference of American Professors were four in number:

1. To enable American teachers to be more conversant with the problems of international association and cooperation.

2. To enable American teachers to form direct contacts with some of the leading personalities engaged in the work of international cooperation.

3. To enable American teachers to investigate the sources of documentation relating to international association and cooperation.

4. To assist American teachers in their effort to keep

in touch with international cooperative movements for the purpose of making their writing and teaching more effective.

A fifth, but unannounced, object, as I was later to learn, was to influence American teachers away from isolationism in the hope that they would contribute to the formation of public opinion favorable to the League of Nations and the World Court.

Just as fast as I could get a letter in the mail, I accepted this invitation. Why I had been included among the favored fifty, I did not know, but I saw no sense in raising such questions. Technically, I was an American teacher of international relations. I had taught such courses at O.A.C., Western Reserve, and Whitman, but had not made a specialty of them and had no established professional reputation in international relations. But, for a free-loading junket to Europe and return, I could develop a fervent interest in international relations awfully fast. Not only did I let no grass grow under my feet in accepting the invitation; I proceeded immediately to follow all of the Endowment's instructions as to "shots," passports, visas, and the like.

Thereupon the roof suddenly started to fall on my head. I got an urgent call to go to Ellensburg at once, and when I got there I found that my step-father would have to undergo immediate surgery for stomach cancer. I stayed in Ellensburg until Mr. Doughty rallied from the operation and was pronounced out of immediate danger. I was fearful that my mother would collapse, and so made arrangements for her to be taken care of. Then I drove back to Walla Walla over those old-time, washboarded gravel roads at the reckless speed of forty-five miles an hour, finished the college year at Whitman, and did another rough and reckless journey in transporting the Maxey family to our farm in the Spokane Valley. Elnora's parents were then living on the farm, and she and our children would stay there for the summer.

Then other complications arose. At Ellensburg I had found financial trouble. Mother did not have enough cash in the bank to pay Mr. Doughty's surgical, hospital, and drug bills. Though his assets were ample for a large bank loan, Mother had never done that kind of business and could not be talked into it now. So I put up the money. When I got to the farm, I ran into other financial problems in the form of unpaid wages for hired help and lack of money to meet the costs of the forth-coming harvest. By this time I was too short of cash to put up the money myself, so I went to the old Farmers' State Bank on North Monroe in Spokane and talked them into lending me enough on my personal, but unsecured, note to tide things over until the end of the year.

The Carnegie tour would take me out of the country from the latter part of July to the latter part of September, and I was not sure that I should take the risk that my stepfather might die in that interval, and the further risk that things might go to pot on the farm. But Elnora, bless her, said for me to go on the Carnegie junket whether or no, and she would mind the store both in Ellensburg and Spokane while I was away, which she did magnificently well. Mr. Doughty lived about six months after the cancer operation, Mother did not collapse and Elnora found that she could market livestock and crops as well as any natural born farm gal.

Cleveland and New York Again

I left Spokane on July 16, 1926, via the Great Northern Railroad, and as soon as I was settled on the train I began a diary in which I made a record of the events of every day from then until September 20. Most of the ensuing comments on the European trip will be based on or quoted from this diary. Naturally I could not think of going through to New York without a stop at Cleveland. Throughout the past year I had been in correspondence with Peter Reed, Ernest Bohn, Jerome Curtis, and other former associates there, and here was an opportunity to see them all again. Ernie Bohn had bachelor quarters in an apartment house at 83rd and Euclid, and he invited me to be his house guest as long as I stayed in Cleveland. I reached Cleveland on the morning of July 19 and stayed until the morning of the 23rd. In those four days I visited all over the city, saw many former friends, and attended several parties. Meanwhile, Ernie had decided that he would like to go on to New York with me. He had never been there, had just acquired a new Buick, and since the summer before he and I had driven to the Pacific Coast in my car, he thought we should now drive to the Atlantic Coast in his. I thought the same, and cancelled my train reservations.

The first day out Ernie and I drove from Cleveland to Geneva, New York, in a leisurely fashion, stopping and gawking everywhere we saw anything interesting. I had been through this country many times by train, but this was the first time I had seen it close at hand. I had thought it lovely from the train window, but in a pokey drive in an open car it was twice as lovely. The same could be said for the country crossed on our second day—Geneva to Newburgh, New York. The third day we rolled down the Hudson to New York City, stopping on the way to take a look at West Point and other places of interest. In New York we registered at a then relatively new hotel named the Empire. I had three days to report to Carnegie Endowment headquarters, get my steamship ticket, and have my passport properly visaed and stamped by the consuls of the various countries through which we would travel. This did not take anything like three days, so Ernie and I had plenty of time to see as much as we wished of New York City. Having a car at our disposal, we could come and go as we pleased and New York traffic in 1926 was not dense enough to slow us down very much. During the day we drove around the metropolitan area and at night we went to shows. In those three days I think I saw more of New York than in the whole three years I had been a New York resident.

On the morning of July 28 I went over to Hoboken and boarded the S. S. President Harding, the ship on which the Endowment had booked passage for our party. We sailed about noon. For the next three days my diary deals chiefly with *mal de mer,* which kept me in my bunk most of the time. On the morning of August 4 we sighted the Irish coast and about 4 P.M.

that day we put into the harbor of Cobh (Queenstown in the old days), where both passengers and mail were discharged and taken on. We were within a stone's throw from shore, but only passengers debarking for the Ould Sod were allowed to leave the ship. So, technically, I could say that I had been in Ireland, though I did not set foot on Irish soil. About 5 A.M. the next morning we entered the port of Plymouth, England, and stood there for an hour or more, loading and unloading, but again none but debarking passengers were allowed to land. It was a transparently clear morning and the view from shipboard was lovely, but it was a bit disappointing to have to say of England, as of Ireland, that I had been there without getting off the ship.

Paris

From Plymouth we sailed directly across the English Channel to Cherbourg. Under the date of August 5, my diary said:

Landed at Cherbourg about 4 P.M. Quaint and beautiful French shipping town. Looked as though might have been lifted from a picture book of mediaeval France. Customs inspection—damn nuisance. Railway and dining car tickets to procure. Then an hour's delay before train for Paris. Fortunately there was a bar in the railway station. The beer was good. Also other concoctions. Felt better pronto. Got 320 francs for $10.00. French cigarettes good, though unusual flavor. Train departs. Countryside is lovely. Surely it is La Belle France! Apple orchards—hay fields—rolling hills— canals—poplars. Little wonder the French peasant loves the soil! How could he want to leave such a land? Called to dejeuner at 8 P.M. Table d' hote—soup, salad, roast, potatoes, legumes, ice cream, cheese, bread, and wine—for about 75¢ including tip. Uneventful journey to Paris. Arrived about 2 A.M. To bed at Hotel Lutetia at 3 A.M.

This was the beginning of six weeks of over-crowded days and nights. The Carnegie people had planned to give our party the maximum exposure to international organizations and personalities, and to that end had laid out a schedule which kept us hopping most of the time. Sundays, nominally, were "free" days, but we were always on call and often had Sunday appointments to keep. We began this schedule in Paris bright and early on the morning of Friday, August 6. After a general conference with the officers of the Endowment at our hotel, we went to the French Foreign Office and spent most of the morning there. We were shown through the building, saw the rooms in which many renowned international conclaves had been held, and were taken into the archives and shown the originals of several famous documents, among which I noted the Treaty of Versailles and the treaties of 1778 and 1783 between France and the United States.

On the afternoon of the same day we visited the International Commission of Aerial Navigation, Rue Kleber, and were thoroughly briefed on its functions and operations. In the evening we were guests at a banquet at Cercle Interallie, Rue du Faubourg Saint Honore, and were addressed by such eminent personages as Count Fleurny of the French Foreign Office, the great industrialist Louis Loucheur, and Colonel Phillipe Bunau-Varilla, negotiator in behalf of Panama of the Hay-Bunau-Varilla Treaty whereby the United States obtained the Canal Zone. After the banquet a small group of us slipped away to see some of the night life of Paris, and divided our time until nearly daybreak between the Cafe de la Paix and the Olympia (a famous dance hall).

All of our days in Paris followed much the same pattern. Our Carnegie appointments took us to the American Library of Paris, the International Reference Bureau, the Bibliotheque Nationale, the International Office of Hygiene, the Institute of Intellectual Cooperation, the International Bureau of Weights and Measures, the International Bureau of Bibliography, the War Museum, and the French Senate. Vaguely, I knew something about most of these organizations, but had never found it necessary to study up on them. In four days of direct visitation in Paris I gathered information about them which would have taken weeks of reading, assuming I had the documents at hand.

My diary also tells me that I was one of a group of four who used a little free time to spend half a day at the Louvre, half a day at the Hotel des Invalides, an afternoon at Vincennes, and an evening at dinner at the Cafe des Univers on the Boulevard de l' Opera.

The Hague

On August 10 we went by rail from Paris to The Hague. My diary notes that we passed through Noyon, Mons, Brussells, Malines, Dordrecht, and Rotterdam. It also notes that I was one of a group occupying a compartment with Manley O. Hudson, Professor of International Law, Harvard School of Law, and that we argued long and loud the question of whether international law should be taught at the undergraduate level. Hudson was as positively against it as I was positively for it, and we had a good jawing match, which I think we both enjoyed.

Our first Carnegie appointment in The Hague was with the Academy of International Law, a sort of super-graduate school for the special benefit of diplomats and other foreign service personnel from all countries of the world. Next we visited the World Court, and its registrar took time out to explain its methods and procedures. The Court was not then in session, which I regretted because my Columbia professor of international law, John Bassett Moore, was now one of the judges of the Court. Both the Academy and the Court were housed in the famous Peace Palace, built some two decades earlier with funds given by Andrew Carnegie. Next we went to a reception given in our honor by the municipality of The Hague. The reception was held in the Burgomaster's Palace, and was followed by a lavish banquet at the Hotel Tweestaaden, this posh tie and tails affair being given by the Carnegie Endowment in honor of certain distinguished citizens of the Netherlands. This was our first formal function, but others were to follow. We had all been instructed to bring dress clothes with us, and I have not forgotten how great a nuisance it was to lug a dress suit around with me and have it ready for use, with appropriate linen, on short notice.

My diary mentions among other events in The Hague certain

287

visits and meetings at the Permanent Court of International Arbitration, the library of the Peace Palace, and the Hall of Knights (meeting place of the Dutch parliament). It likewise records attendance at a series of lectures given by Dr. Loder, one of the judges of the World Court, and Dr. Duvel, director of the Institut Intermediare Internationale. From the same source I am reminded that on August 13 we went by bus first to Delft and then to Leyden. At Delft we visited the cathedral which houses the tomb of the famed Hugo Grotius, often called the Father of International Law. After a round of speechmaking, our party placed a wreath on the tomb of Grotius. Then we proceeded to the royal palace known as The House in the Woods. This was where the first Hague Peace Conference (1899) held its meetings. We were shown through the palace and gave special attention to the Orange Room in which most of the meetings took place. From there our bus took us to Leyden, where we were given a reception at the University of Leyden, founded by William the Silent in 1575. While in Leyden we paid a sort of ceremonial visit to the home and church of John Robinson, pastor of the Pilgrims before they migrated to America. This was followed by a huge meal at the famous Gilded Turk Cafe, whereupon we motored back to The Hague and there, about 4 P.M., entrained for Geneva, Switzerland.

The trip to Geneva took us down the valley of the Rhine through Essen, Dusseldorf, Cologne, Mannheim, Freiburg, Basel, and Bern. We reached Geneva about 2 P.M. on August 14 and registered at the Hotel Suisse, where I had the good fortune to draw a single room. For the first time on the trip I could stretch out a bit and have some privacy. This was very restful. We remained in Geneva, then headquarters of the League of Nations and many other international organizations, for three weeks.

Geneva

Because it would be unbearably tedious to recite in detail the events and experiences of our three weeks in Geneva, I am going to do a hop-skip-and-jump summary. In taking us to Geneva the Carnegie Endowment had three major purposes:

288

(1) to bring us into close contact with the daily operations, structural machinery, and working personnel of the League of Nations, the International Labor Organization, the International Postal Union, and several other important international agencies having headquarters in that city; (2) to expose us to the thinking of noted world leaders in international law and international politics; (3) to give us opportunities for friendly social contacts with the great and near-great figures in contemporary international affairs. All members of our party, without exception, were in full accord with those objectives. In addition, most of us entertained purely private objectives. Mine were: (1) to make as many lasting friendships as possible with fellow members of the Carnegie party; (2) to collect everything I could lay a hand upon, preferably documentary material, which might be helpful in future teaching and writing, and (3) to kick up my heels, with due respect to commitments and proprieties, and have a bit of fun. I believe I achieved success in all three of my private objectives.

In pursuance of the Endowment's first objective we were called upon to attend sessions of the Council and the Assembly of the League of Nations, visit the offices of the principal administrative sections of the Secretariat of the League of Nations, visit the offices of the League's Permanent Mandates Commission and its Commission on Intellectual Cooperation, and take part in lecture-conference sessions with high officials of the International Labor Organization, the Interparliamentary Union, the International Institute of Agriculture, and the International Postal Union. We went into all of these offices and agencies as serious students rather than casual tourists. We asked questions, took notes, examined books and papers and did our best to comprehend what we saw and heard.

In furtherance of its second object the Carnegie Endowment filled many of our afternoons and evenings with meetings addressed by big-name personages from many different countries. Many of these names have faded, but in 1926 there were none more lustrous. My diary takes special note of speeches by Dr. Arnold Wolfers, an eloquent Swiss then on the faculty of the

Hochschule für Politik in Berlin; Harold J. Laski of the London School of Economics, whom I was subsequently to hear more than once in the United States; William Rappard, rector of the University of Geneva; James Brown Scott, director of the legal section of the Carnegie Endowment; Dr. Christian Lange, secretary-general of the Interparliamentary Union; Salvador de Madariaga, a brilliant Spanish scholar and diplomat; Albert Thomas, French minister of munitions in World War I; Gustav Stresemann, German foreign minister; Aristide Briand, French foreign minister; Sir Arthur Salter, noted British economist; Alfred E. Zimmern, eminent British writer and publicist; Sir John Fischer Williams, leading member of the Reparations Commission; Ascher Hobson of the International Institute of Agriculture; and Paul Mantoux, a noted French publicist.

The third major objective of the Carnegie Endowment, comprehending its various social aims, was promoted by means of receptions, luncheons, teas, dinners, theater parties, and excursions. There were enough of these functions that if I were to tell something of each, the reader certainly would get the impression the Carnegie professors were wining and dining most of the time, which was far from the truth. A few of these social events still linger pleasantly in my memory. One was a reception, one lovely summer afternoon, at Nyon, several miles up the lake from Geneva. We made the trip both ways by steamship and found that the reception was really an outing on the sweeping lawns of an estate owned by Mrs. Stanley McCormick of Chicago, who was our hostess. This estate had once been occupied by Voltaire and later by Joseph Bonaparte, and almost reeked with history. Mrs. McCormick was one of the International Harvester McCormicks of Chicago, but her husband, for reasons of mental health (as I heard it), had been kept in Europe most of his life so that the rest of the clan might be spared the embarrassment of his presence in the United States. Other unforgettable social events were a tea dance at a chateau on the lake shore two miles northeast of Geneva, a sumptuous dinner-dress banquet at the Hotel des Berges in Geneva, a theater party at the University of Geneva, and an excursion to Mont Saleve.

My private objectives proved easy to realize. In such a party as ours, friends are easy to make. I had no difficulty in getting on easy and friendly terms with nearly every one of our group, but, as is always the case in a group of fifty or so, some became closer friends than others. By virtue of the kind of associations that are inevitable on shipboard and in rail travel, I became one of a group of eight or ten men who just seemed naturally to gravitate together in social situations. Several of that group became lifelong friends. The collection of teaching material also proved easy. Before I realized it I was so embarrassed with riches that I had to send many things home by mail, because I knew I would not have luggage space for them. As for kicking up my heels, I found several good friends with the same idea, and so I always had plenty of company. I think the best way to show what I was doing and thinking during these Geneva days and nights would be to introduce the following typical excerpts from my diary:

At afternoon reception at Nyon met President and Mrs. Hetzel of the University of New Hampshire. Had interesting chat with them. [This was a sort of reunion, as Ralph Hetzel had been director of extension at O.A.C. when I was there. I had done a good deal of work with him. Mrs. Hetzel was a good friend of Elnora's.]

At 8:30 P.M. a scintillating and provocative address by Harold J. Laski of the London School of Economics. Subject: "International Government and National Sovereignty." An extension of guild socialist doctrine to the realm of international affairs. His argument specious in many points, but was as brilliant as the attempted replies of Manley Hudson and Raymond Fosdick were stodgy and absurd. Laski has an irritating manner but a remarkably acute mind. Fosdick has a charming personality and a very ordinary mind. Hudson has a jarring personality and no mind at all.

Started after dinner with Baker and Patterson to discover some of the wicked places of the city. Gave up in despair at 10 P.M.

He [one of the speakers] felt that the success of the League in forcing small states to follow its dictates will build up a body of precedents which will make it easier in the future for the great powers to submit to the League. One wonders what would happen should Germany, Russia, and the United States be added to the membership of the League.

Unfortunately some of the questions revealed that some members of our party have not read the Treaty of Versailles, the Covenant of the League, the Dawes agreements, or the daily papers of their own country.

Dinner with Martin, Baker, Patterson, and Russell. Then to Cafe de la Poste where heard good music and imbibed good drinks. Then to La Mascotte (night club), having been joined by Stuart, Nixon, and Chubb. More drinks lots of dancing, and company of Za Za and Jeanette [night club entertainers].

After dinner started out to attend session of the Study Com mission of the Interparliamentary Union, but it began to rain, so stopped off at the Casino, where there was a musical comedy called "La Belle de New York." A very shabby and amateurish performance. The singing was poor, the dancing rotten, and the ensemble atrocious. Not even legs and breasts could excite interest. The girls were nearly all built on Clydesdale or Percheron proportions and about as coy as elephants. Did not stay to end of performance.

At 10 A.M. to meeting of World Court signatories . . . long debate in which it was obvious that the principal concern was to find a formula by which U. S. reservations could be accepted without seeming to give the U. S. a veto on the advisory opinions of the Court or in a position of special privilege. Some urged a counter-proposal asking the U. S. for an interpretation of the phrase "claims an interest," but others feared that this might cause the U. S. to withdraw altogether. It seemed to be the opinion that the paramount thing is to get the U. S. in. They would like to save their faces if they can, but will accept the Senate reservations at any cost.

A number of distinguished personages were present. Had quite a chat with Jane Addams of Hull House fame. Not many attractive dancing partners, but the liquor was wonderful, also the food.

The climax of the trip. Crashed the gate at the Salle de la Reformation at 10 A.M. and saw Germany admitted to the League of Nations. Had been told it would be impossible to obtain tickets, and it was. But took a chance and squeezed through with the crowd.

I was called upon for a few remarks and ventured an opinion that international relations in the Orient were being neglected by American internationalists. Proposed, somewhat facetiously, a Carnegie tour of American professors to the Orient. Hudson thought I was criticising the present junket and made a caustic rejoinder, to which I did not reply. Afterwards many members of group came to me and expressed indignation that Hudson should treat me so rudely. I was not peeved, as I thought Hudson was just showing off a bit, which was his privilege as one of the organizers of this tour.

Misadventure

The Carnegie party went from Geneva to Paris on September 10, from Paris to Le Havre on the morning of the 11th, and boarded the French liner *La Savoie*. About the subsequent adventures of this veteran *paquebot* of the Atlantic, I will let the diary do the talking:

September 11. Train took us to the dock. Thence through customs and immigration inspection to the ship. *La Savoie* looked interesting, though not a modern ship. Pulled out of harbor about 1 P.M., while we were at lunch. After we had been going along for some time we suddenly stopped. Great consternation. Investigation showed a man over-

293

board. It was a member of the crew—intoxicated it was said—who decided he wanted to go back home, so jumped overboard and started to swim for shore. He was fished out and returned to his duties. Breton sailors were heard to murmur that a man overboard before you get out of port means bad luck.

September 15. Sailing through fog most of the day. Siren blowing almost constantly. Just after dinner, while second sitting was being served, I was in salon conversing with Smith of New Hampshire University when a sudden wrench brought us to our feet. Looking out, we saw what appeared to be the prow of another ship driven into the side of our own vessel. Was it a collision? How bad? Rushed to the deck, as did everyone who could get there. Saw other ship pull away and disappear in the fog. Also noticed on our port side what appeared to be a big hole. Too dark to be certain of anything. Crew began to lower lifeboats, so of course we all thought it was serious. Could obtain no information, and not permitted to go near the damaged portion of our ship. A good many began to get panicky. Prospect of hours or days in lifeboats did not look good. I decided to stand by and wait for instructions. Finally, after an hour of suspense, we were notified that the damage was not serious and *La Savoie* would proceed on her course. Much sleeplessness on account of doubts of truth of information given us.

September 16. Not much to record. Everybody is discussing the accident. We have learned that we collided at a glancing angle with the British freighter *Melomsley*, or some name sounding like that and that no material damage was done to her, either. Our captain says it was a miraculous escape. Sea perfectly calm until dinner time; then a blow comes up. By bed time sea was so violent it was impossible to stay in my bunk. A regular Northeaster, so they say. Not much chance to sleep.

September 17. Storm worse than ever. Old travelers say it is the worst they ever saw. But they always say that. Captain and crew look a bit worried. Waves running over top of ship constantly. Wind blowing spray until it is as dense as fog. Ship tossing like a chip. Every door and window fastened tight. Passengers forbidden on decks. From one or two vantage points it is possible to see out. I never could have believed the ocean could be so agitated. Waves seem to be running a hundred feet high. Ship's bulletin at noon says we are in a hurricane. Many people badly scared and so am I. Fear we can never get through, as believe our ship badly weakened by the collision. I don't know. Impossible to do anything but hold on. I found a seat in smoking salon that was securely bolted down and stayed in it most of the day, subsisting on beer and champagne cocktails from bar about four feet distant. Storm subsided about 7 P.M. By midnight the worst was over.

September 18. Now we know what we have been through. By radio we got reports this morning of the Florida hurricane and the terrific damage done at Miami. Officers say wind was blowing at least 90 miles an hour at height of storm yesterday. Looked like 200 to me. No wonder it wrecked the Florida coast. We are all thrilled and thankful. It is something to have been through a storm that had the old salts worried.

September 20. We make New York about daylight, but lie in quarantine until 10 A.M. Then permitted to land. Good old terra firma! Good old New York!

What was supposed to have been a five and a half or six day crossing had stretched out into nine, and it would take me four days more to get to Walla Walla. Fortunately, I had not told Elnora exactly when we were due to arrive in New York, so she was not worried about our being nearly four days overdue. I telegraphed her as soon as I could after reaching New York, and she thought I was getting home right on schedule.

Evaluation

This Carnegie tour was one of the cardinal experiences of my life, not merely because of the European travel, but chiefly because it rewarded me with an abundance of direct information and insight relative to international affairs. It was equally rewarding in warm and enduring personal and professional friendships. Another consequence which I did not foresee at the time was that it put me on the eligible list for future clambakes underwritten by the Carnegie Endowment for International Peace. In 1928 the Endowment paid my expenses to Washington, D. C. and return, so that I might participate in a program jointly sponsored by it and the American Society of International Law, of which I was a member. In 1934, as I have incidentally mentioned above, the Carnegie Endowment paid my travel and living expenses to participate in a six-week workshop on international law at Ann Arbor, Michigan.

As might have been expected, I was home scarcely long enough to get my bags unpacked before I began to be flooded with speaking invitations. This continued for months, and I encouraged it because I thought I owed that to the Carnegie Endowment. The League of Nations was not yet a dead issue in American politics, and one question then at fever heat was whether, with reservations attached by the Senate, the United States should adhere to the statute establishing and regulating the World Court. I have no idea how many speeches I made on these and related topics. Finally, I wrote an essay of some 10,000 words which I called "Some Reflections on the League of Nations and the World Court." I used this paper for the Inquiry Club of Walla Walla, to which I belonged, and also allowed it to be published as a number of the Whitman *Aumnus*. In the closing paragraphs of this paper I stated some opinions which I thought were sound then and which I think still have a certain relevance to the posture of international affairs thirty-seven years later. I quote briefly as follows:

The negative answer to that question [should the United States have joined the League in 1919-20?] involves nothing that has not already been settled as far as time can settle anything, but the affirmative answer raises a few points of more than historic interest.

Passionate friends of the League in the United States are in the habit of insisting that what they denounce as the "desertion" of the United States has been chiefly responsible for the failure of the League to materialize the exalted and perfected "parliament of man and federation of the world" portrayed by Mr. Wilson in his most ecstatic periods. If such is the case, America certainly deserves the execration and obloquy of all mankind. But I doubt if facts can be adduced to prove that the defection of the United States— if, indeed, it was such—has been a material cause of the failure of the League of Nations to measure up to the expectations of its most extravagant protagonists.

If it be said that the influence of the United States would have directed the League along lines of moderation, reason, justice, and constructive progress, I reply that this is pure fancy. If the United States under the crusading leadership of Woodrow Wilson could not write justice and moderation into the peace treaties, is it not preposterous to suppose that the United States under Harding and Coolidge would have rescued the League from the infamies of *realpolitik*?

As I recall the history of the last eight years, the moral leadership of the United States has suffered an almost complete eclipse. No other country, so far as I can recall, has experienced greater extremes of social insanity and hysteria, and I know of no other country in which persons who dared to suggest moderation and justice with reference to Germany or Russia or Turkey or with reference to reparations were subjected to such virulent and venomous attacks as they were in the United States. It may be flattering for us to think of ourselves as the only rational people in an unhinged world, but the facts hardly bear out that assumption.

There is another reason why I do not regard the nonparticipation of the United States in the League of Nations as a dire calamity. The absence of the United States has removed all possibility of "passing the buck" to the United States, of using the United States for purposes of mediation between contending groups of powers, or of manipulation to swing America's weight from one to another. . . . The anti-American feeling which is sweeping over Europe was bound to come irrespective of American participation or non-participation in the League, and if we were in the League, it would necessarily share our present unpopularity, and European politicians would now be denouncing the League as an American scheme for obtaining priority in world affairs.

Writing in the 1960's, when another wave of anti-American feeling is sweeping over Europe, it cannot be said that the League's successor, the United Nations, has put the United States in such a good posture before mankind as to prove that it was a great mistake not to join the League of Nations.

XIX. A FLING AT POLITICS

My Party Affiliation

My participation in politics was governed by an elastic conception of the individual's role in party government. I believed in party government and thought the two-party system best for the United States. I also believed that a citizen could make his influence count more through being either a Democrat or a Republican than by being an independent. Since my party heritage was Republican and I had no overpowering reason to change, I cast my lot with the GOP. If and when the law required party registration, I enrolled as a Republican. I publicly accepted the Republican label, and tried to contribute what I could to the organizational strength of the Republican Party. Even when I disagreed with the policies and nominees of the Republican Party, I did not bolt the ticket and go over to the opposition. I merely held my peace and waited for the time when the Republican Party would swing my way again.

On the other hand, I believed that the suffrage was a sacred trust, and that it was the duty of every voter to take his conscience with him to the voting booth. I took the view that the ballot was given, not to the party, but to the individual. Hence, I thought it the duty of the individual to follow and express his best judgment as an individual when he came to mark his ballot. How he voted was his own private affair, and he was under no obligation to disclose this to any one. Consequently there were many times when I stuck with the Republican Party all through a campaign, but in the end did not vote Republican, or at least, not straight Republican.

This ambivalence may have deserved the name of hypocrisy, but I did not think so. I thought that being a staunch partisan and at the same time an unshackled individual voter were not incompatible. Indeed, I thought it to be one of the strong points of the American system of self-government that partisanship did not entail individual self-immolation. An American citizen could uphold his party and strive to make it a more effective instrument of government, but at the same time, if he chose, administer it a private rebuke. This, I thought was one of the main reasons why, here in the United States, we had enjoyed so many decades of stable and yet free government. We had been able, with amazing consistency, to keep the pendulum of power swinging back and forth between the two major parties, and even in the direct crises had never succumbed to dictatorship.

The foregoing profession of ambivalence may serve to clarify some things I shall have to say about my political activities. I took part in party politics in four states of the American Union —Oregon, New York, Ohio, and Washington. In all four I identified myself as a Republican and worked in and with the precinct, ward, county, state, and national party committees and other organizations. I was a member of Republican committees, attended countless Republican meetings, was a delegate to Republican conventions, made Republican speeches, and contributed to Republican funds. Except for the year 1932, I was just a rank-and-file Republican. But in that memorable year, I aspired to get out of the rank and file. I sought the Republican nomination for Congress in the fourth congressional district of Washington.

As soon as we moved to Walla Walla I became active in

Republican circles both official and unofficial. This was what I had done everywhere else we had lived, and I was not gunning for preferment of any sort—just following my longtime inclinations and convictions. In addition to a feeling of civic duty, I also had a feeling that I would be a better teacher of political science by gaining political experience right down at the grass roots. This had proven true in other places, and I was sure it would be the same in Walla Walla.

After the election of 1928 the Republican Party, both nationally and locally, began to have painful internal disturbances. Sooner or later this would have happened regardless of the stock market collapse of October, 1929, and the rapid onset of the severest economic depression in American history. But the depression hastened the crack-up of the Republican Party. Herbert Hoover proved to be all that a president should have been except a political magician. In the book of politics he missed few of the mistakes. Instead of supplying the masterly political leadership so desperately needed in this crisis, Mr. Hoover gave the impression of being unequal to the emergency. He was unable to hold his party together, and in the 1930 by-elections the Republicans lost control of Congress. By 1932, not only Mr. Hoover but nearly all Republican members of Congress, both senators and representatives, were faced with strong opposition in their own party.

The Issues of 1932

Representing the fourth district of Washington in the national House of Representatives was Dr. John Summers, a resident of Walla Walla. A onetime occulist who found politics more suited to his taste, if not his talents, Dr. Summers was finishing his seventh term as a member of the House of Representatives. First elected in 1918, he had been subsequently re-elected six times with practically no opposition. But after 1930, opposition to Summers began to grow among Republicans as well as Demo.-crats. I heard many Republicans say that they hoped some other Republican could take the nomination away from Summers, so the party would not be stuck with him in 1932. They felt sure that almost any Democrat could beat Summers in the next election, but thought a new name on the Republican ticket would have a good chance to carry the district for the GOP again. Several of my Republican friends and well-wishers started a little boom for me, but I held back. Quite frankly, I could not see much in 1930 to make an issue between Summers and any other Republican.

It was different by 1932. By that time there were several issues on which I could part company with Congressman Summers. In the economy of the country and in Republican politics as well everything had changed for the worse. Many fourth district Republicans were saying that rather than vote for Summers again they would vote Democratic in 1932. Talk about my running against Summers for the Republican nomination sprang up again, and this time I did not discourage it. It rapidly grew to such volume that the *Spokesman-Review* sent a reporter to interview me. On January 29, 1932, that newspaper published a story in which I was quoted as follows:

Naturally, I was interested to learn that I am being considered as a probable candidate for Congress. Not being an officeseeker and being occupied with a job that keeps me more than busy, I am in no position to evaluate political rumors.

My interest in the coming campaign is chiefly in the issues it may raise, and those issues are yet unborn. The timidity of the Democrats as to issues is matched only by the uncertainty of the Republicans. The only issue that looms at all at the present time is Mr. Hoover.

If the Democrats can make no better issue than that and the Republicans are satisfied to do no more than defend Mr. Hoover, the campaign will indeed be a sorry spectacle. I should not care to have anything to do with such a ruckus.

But if the campaign should take another turn, one involving fundamental and constructive issues, my attitude might be different.

To an extent this was temporizing, but it was six months

prior to filing time; neither party had held its national convention; there had as yet been no county or state conventions in Washington; and no one could foretell what Congress might do before election time. In January I could truthfully say that my mind was not made up. I knew what I thought the campaign issues ought to be, but it would be mid-summer before there could be enough clarification for me to decide whether I should try to take the Republican nomination away from Dr. Summers. Since the primary election did not occur until September 13, there would be plenty of time to wage a vigorous campaign, even though I should wait until the first of July to announce my candidacy. Most of my boosters agreed on the wisdom of waiting.

The Primary Campaign

By the first of July I had definitely decided to toss my hat into the ring and take a fling at running for office. There was nothing to lose and possibly much to gain. With the indispensable help of a small group of active supporters (chief among them were E. L. Casey, Herbert Ringhoffer, Carl Roe, Lowden Jones, and Leslie Hoagland), plans were made for launching my campaign. It was decided to kick things off with two public meetings, which we chose to call mass meetings, as they were supposed to demonstrate that I was responding to a call from the grass roots. The second of the two meetings really was a mass meeting, but the first was a handpicked crowd of two or three dozen men who were the only ones invited, who knew in advance why they were invited and what they were to do. The only business transacted at the first meeting was the adoption of a resolution asking me to run and appointing a committee to give me formal notification to that effect.

The second meeting was the notification meeting. It was held in the chamber of commerce auditorium (now the city council chamber) in the city hall on the evening of July 20. All possible publicity had been given to the resolution adopted at the first meeting and the whole community was invited to attend the meeting on July 20 when I would respond to that resolution. There was standing room only at this meeting. In saying yes to the request that I run, I delivered a prepared speech in which I defined and discussed the issues as I saw them.

The first and foremost issue, I said, was the Hawley-Smoot Tariff Act, which had been enacted by Congress on June 17, 1930. Of this measure I said, "I was opposed to the Hawley-Smoot tariff at the time of its adoption, and I still am. It is not a protective tariff but a destructive tariff. Every fruit and vegetable grower in the Walla Walla and Yakima Valleys will bear witness to the truth of this assertion. It is not a Republican tariff; it flies in the face of the best tariff traditions of the Republican Party. It is a lobby-made tariff: unbalanced, uneconomic, the fruit of an unholy alliance of political pressure groups." Summers had voted for the Hawley-Smoot bill, and I took pains to point this out.

My second major issue was the Farm Board, which had been created by the Agricultural Marketing Act of 1929. This board had been established primarily to make loans to farm organizations for the purpose of facilitating the storage, processing, and marketing of farm products. For purely political reasons, I thought, the Board had far exceeded its legal authority and embarked upon a program of price stabilization in course of which it had lost several million dollars in marketing operations. In denouncing this, I said: "The Farm Board, I think, has long outlived its usefulness and should be abolished. Its continued existence after having lost the confidence of the American people in general, and the American farmer in particular, is a depressive influence both at home and abroad. It darkens the prospect for sound agrarian legislation, and creates uncertainty and hesitation in foreign markets where the American farm surplus must find its outlet."

The third of my paramount issues was that of taxation and retrenchment. On this I said: "The revenue measure adopted to balance the budget is in my judgment an inexcusable makeshift. I think every man who voted for it should be retired to private life. In a panic of fear they defeated the sales tax because a few noisy demagogues said it would throw the burden on the little man, and then they turned around and passed a measure as unjust to the little man as the sales tax possibly could have been, and without any of the virtues the sales tax is known to possess. . . . It is doubtful if this new revenue law will balance the budget. . . . The government prognosticators were about a billion wide of the mark last year and may be again. . . . Everybody agrees that the budget must be balanced, but there is no justification for increased taxation until the cost of government has been cut to the bone. This has not been done, nor has there been any honest effort to do so."

Lastly, though I would have gladly passed it by, I had to face up to the question of prohibition. My private opinion, sometimes publicly expressed, was that prohibition was a red herring that would divert attention from more basic issues. I was for the repeal of the Eighteenth Amendment. The Republican Party had not gone that far, but had declared itself in favor of resubmitting the prohibition question to popular vote. On account of this, many of the irreconcilable Drys were threatening to bolt the Republican ticket, and no doubt would have done so if the Democrats had not been wetter than the Republicans. Apropos of all this, I said: "Extreme Prohibitionists have harshly criticized the Republican Party for proposing even to reconsider the question, but they are tragically mistaken. They forget that the Eighteenth Amendment, though a part of the Constitution, is in essence a sumptuary law, and the experience of mankind proves that sumptuary legislation cannot be enforced without the sanction of an overwhelming body of public opinion. If we have reached the point where popular approval of the Eighteenth Amendment is so dubious that we dare not submit it to a referendum, how in the name of reason can we hope to enforce it? It is far better to meet the issue squarely and let the people have their way."

These were issues on which I could clearly differentiate myself from Dr. Summers. Not only had he voted for the Hawley-Smoot bill; he had publicly and repeatedly defended it, insisting that Congress had been forced to retaliate against Canadian duties imposed on American farm products under the government of Premier Bennett. It was easy to refute him on this, because there was readily available documentary proof that Congress had enacted the Hawley-Smoot tariff more than a month prior to Premier Bennet's election in Canada. Summers had not been keeping abreast of Canadian news. As to the Farm Board, Summers had done a good deal of talking out of both sides of his mouth. As a member of the House of Representatives, he had voted for it; later he changed front and attacked it; then he reversed himself again and gave it a second blessing. This inconsistency made him an easy target. Summers was also vulnerable on the revenue bill of 1932 and the budget increases made in the face of the great economic collapse. Being a member of the House appropriations committee, he could not disavow responsibility for the unbalanced budget. On the prohibition question he was also an easy mark, because he had voted against the resubmission of the 18th Amendment, which was squarely contrary to the Republican platform.

Campaign Activities

My major campaign problem was to get around over the twelve counties of the fourth district and force Summers to face the music. This required organization and money, and I had little of both at the start. My Walla Walla supporters set up a Maxey-for-Congress committee, established headquarters on the second floor of the Baker and Baker Building, corner of Second and Alder, and started a drive for funds as well as votes. Leslie Hoagland, one of my original boosters and a prominent Walla Walla business man, was appointed to act as my manager. He and I together had most of the responsibility for planning and conducting the campaign.

I have no idea how much money altogether was raised and spent in my behalf, but I do know how much cleared through our headquarters. It was exactly $1,114.81, and this came in as the result of contributions from more than a hundred individuals and firms. Indirectly, I heard that certain firms of grain dealers, acting independently of our committee, spent a great deal more money to promote my candidacy. This could have been true, for the grain dealers, on account of my stand against the Farm

Board, were solidly behind me. As to the expenditures made through our office, I kept an accurate record of where every penny went. More than 90 per cent of our outlay was for newspaper advertising. There were thirty-three newspapers in the fourth district, and we took space in all of them. The rest of our money went for stenographic help, office supplies, printing, postage, and radio time. There was no commercial radio in the fourth district anywhere but Yakima, and all of our radio money went there. Neither Leslie Hoagland nor I drew any expense money. We both paid our own traveling expenses, and I footed the bill for the filing fee of one hundred dollars and various other personal costs.

As I have said, our campaign had to be spread over twelve counties. We tried to concentrate on the three most populous counties, which, in 1932, were Walla Walla, Yakima, and Whitman. But we could not afford to by-pass the other nine counties entirely, so we took time to canvass each of them at least once. There was no television then and radio was of consequence only in Yakima County, so we had to rely mainly on the time-honored and traditional methods of getting to the voters. We probably made more use of the person-to-person, door-to-door technique than any other. In every town we would go up and down the principal business streets greeting people, passing out cards and pamphlets to all who would take them, and striking up as many informal conversations as we could. We tried to enter every important business establishment in town and get acquainted, not only with the boss, but with the employees as well. When time permitted, we tried to do the same sort of personal canvassing in the residential districts.

As for public speaking, I did all kinds. As I have already said, the only radio talk I made was in Yakima. Elsewhere I tried to wangle invitations to speak at service clubs, chambers of commerce, farm organizations, labor unions, and even county fairs. I was not often refused a chance to speak. Sometimes we hired a hall and tried to drum up attendance at a public meeting; on several occasions I got permission to speak on the courthouse lawn; and in one county seat we hired a truck, borrowed a cowbell, and drove from one corner to the next ringing the bell to draw a crowd. From the tailgate I would make my little pitch, and then we would move off to the next corner. I expected every moment that the police would haul us in, but they must have liked our show or else decided that we were just a couple of harmless lunatics.

It was hard to tell how great an impact our campaign was making. My backers were overly enthusiastic, I thought; so I tried to be realistic. I knew that Summers had some built-in advantages. In the first place, he had two opponents instead of one. A Sunnyside lawyer named Oscar Boose had also filed for the Republican nomination from the fourth district, and this meant that the opposition to Summers was divided. In the second place, Summers had going for him an organization he had been fourteen years building—jobholders he had placed in soft positions, individuals for whom he had done favors, chambers of commerce, veterans' groups and many other organizations for whom he had done errands in Washington. Most of these could be expected to stand by him in this campaign. Boose and I had to go for the unattached voters, and they were hard to reach.

So the primary campaign jogged on to its end on the 13th of September. The final results of the balloting on that day were: Summers 17,176, Maxey 8,078, Boose 4,936. Obviously I could not have won even in a two-way race, but I might have made it a good deal closer than it was. If the present blanket primary system had been in effect instead of the closed party primaries we had in 1932, my chances of beating Summers would have been better, because I might have drawn both independent and Democratic votes. Summers was defeated in the general election in November, 1932 by the Democratic nominee, Knute Hill, who undoubtedly received much help from the disaffected Republicans who had voted for Boose and me in the primaries.

Although I lost the primary election, I did well enough to be regarded as a "comer" in Republican politics. Many of my backers wanted me to announce right away that I would run again in 1934. This I declined to do. Not that I did not want to keep a finger in the Republican pie, but I was not sure I wanted to commit myself to a political career. For one thing, I had books to write that could not be finished if I went into politics again. Furthermore, the affairs of Whitman College were approaching a grave crisis, and I wanted to be free to take a hand in the working out of a solution for that. I was basically more interested in trying to get Whitman College out of the woods than in getting myself elected to Congress. I had enjoyed the campaign, and would have enjoyed another, but I was very doubtful if I would ever enjoy serving in the House of Representatives, even if I should succeed in being elected.

I have never regretted this fling at electioneering. It cost me more money than I could well afford at the time, but I regarded that as tuition well spent in learning about politics in the school of experience. It was not a bitter campaign, and in the long run it made me more friends than enemies. I am sure that it enriched my teaching and also helped with some aspects of my writing. Finally, I feel that it taught me things about the so-called art of public relations which were to prove immensely valuable in my later career.

XX. UNDER FOUR PRESIDENTS

Before Penrose

Up to now Whitman College has had eight presidents, of whom I was the seventh. It was my lot to serve as a professor and dean under the four presidents immediately preceding me. In these capacities as well as in my later capacity as president, it was my lot to be obliged to inform myself as extensively as possible about many of the details of Whitman College history. Thus I came to know a great deal about the regimes of Alexander Jay Anderson and James F. Eaton, the two presidents immediately preceding Stephen B. L. Penrose, under whom I began my service on the Whitman faculty. By reason of this knowledge added to that acquired during my thirty-four years as professor, dean, and president, the time was bound to come, if I lived long enough, when I would know more about the inside history of

Whitman College than any living person. That time seems now to have arrived.

This biological and chronological fact does not of necessity impose upon me an obligation to "tell all," and I have no intention of attempting any such thing. All that is inconsequential I shall ignore, no matter how much human interest it might hold. There are, however, certain rectifications that I think should be made, certain misconceptions that should be dispelled, and certain records that should be made known. This I am going to undertake to do as objectively and dispassionately as I can. I cannot pretend to divest myself of all emotion in recounting some of these events, but I can truthfully say that the passing of the years has greatly cooled some emotions I formerly felt.

My service at Whitman College began, as I have said, under its third president, Stephen B. L. Penrose. History has treated Whitman's first president, Alexander J. Anderson, very kindly, and its second president, James F. Eaton, very shabbily. Anderson served for nine years (1882-1891), and there is no doubt that he was more instrumental than any other person in transforming the defunct Whitman Seminary into an institution of collegiate grade, getting it on a sound academic footing, and building up its financial strength. Eaton served only three years (1891-94), and was summarily dismissed with a stab in the back. The poor fellow was in the East manfully trying to raise money for the College when the Board of Trustees notified him that he was through and need not return. My information about the "railroading" of Eaton came from the man who put up the cash to pay the arrears of Eaton's salary so he could be fired without notice. I knew this gentleman well in his older years, and he confided many things to me.

My opinion is that the firing of Eaton was the outcome of circumstances not entirely of his own making. My informant told me that he turned against Eaton because Eaton double-crossed him in regard to the selection of a proposed new and enlarged campus for Whitman College. Three sites were under consideration, and my friend had a large personal stake in one of them. He thought he had Eaton's promise to support this one, but when the showdown came, Eaton backed away from all three and began to dally with an alleged offer from Olympia, whereby the College, by moving over there, would be given a tract of land big enough and valuable enough to insure its future. It has never been proved, or disproved, either, that Eaton really had such an offer from Olympia. But there is plenty of proof that he would have been condemned to walk on live coals if he had come out in favor of any one of the three Walla Walla proposals. It is conceivable that he might have been trying to use the threat of removal to Olympia as a means of pressuring the three Walla Walla factions into some sort of mutual compromise. If so his tight-wire balancing act failed to come off.

I have made a careful study of the available records of the Eaton years and have found certain facts quite visible to the naked eye. From the moment he stepped on the Whitman campus, Eaton was an avowed and energetic expansionist. Almost immediately he announced that it was his purpose to build Whitman into a university comparable with Harvard and Yale. In the first catalog of the College published after he took office, Eaton expanded on the theme that Whitman, then the only four-year college north of California between the Cascades and the Rocky Mountains, could look forward to an incomparable future. Why should it not, like the recently founded Stanford University of California, expect to become the one great private institution of this imperial domain? Eaton was very successful in firing the imaginations of his board members, of the Congregational clergy throughout the Northwest, and of scores of leading citizens of Walla Walla with this grandiose dream. Students, faculty, trustees, townspeople, and even the national College and Education Society of the Congregational Church rallied behind him with great enthusiasm. Eaton knew that he would have to raise large sums of money to realize his grand design, and he set out with great energy and dedication to do just that. Should he succeed, and he had no doubt that he would, the tiny six-acre campus Whitman then possessed would be entirely inadequate. I think he was so certain of success that he betrayed himself into the fatal mistake of getting the cart before the horse. He started action to acquire the new campus before he had gathered in enough money to enable him to control the situation.

Eaton was no fool. He had the very best connections in the East, where most of the money would have to be raised, and he had no doubts as to his own ability to do the job. And he just might have succeeded—IF. If he had not collided head on with a financial hurricane (the great panic and depression of 1892-93), he might have garnered enough Eastern money to give him the whip hand in Walla Walla. But as things turned out, he had trouble getting pennies. He could not even raise enough money to pay the running expenses of the College, and, as so often happens, when he ran into financial trouble, he found himself beset with many other troubles. He was no longer a hero, and some began to call him a rascal.

His finesse as to the three proposed campus sites in Walla Walla failed to work, and a faction of the Board of Trustees turned against him. Then he ran into faculty trouble. A prominent faculty member, in later years revered as an elder statesman, had aspired to succeed A. J. Anderson and thought he had been promised the job. As soon as Eaton's popularity declined, this worthy professor conceived the notion that Eaton was an arbitrary tyrant and should be opposed. He took the lead in organizing anti-Eaton activities among both students and faculty. Eaton then tried to get the Board of Trustees to declare his position vacant, but the Board refused to do this and tried to effect a reconciliation between Eaton and the rebellious professor. To accomplish this, both were brought before the Board and told to get down on their knees and pray for mutual forgiveness. My informant, who was present and saw and heard everything, told me that no good was accomplished by recourse to prayer. The very next day, he said, Eaton and his faculty foeman were clawing away at each other as usual.

Eaton may have been the cause of much of his own bad luck, but I deem it only fair to say that he seems to have had more bad luck than ordinarily falls to the lot of a college president. If he could have had more time, if the depression had not undercut him before he got fairly started, and if he had been as Machiaevellian as he was charged with being, he might have made a great success. It is not generally remembered that Dr. D. K. Pearsons, who was to become Whitman's first large benefactor, became interested in Whitman through the efforts of President Eaton. It was President Eaton also who won for the College the strong financial support of the College and Education Society of the Congregational Church. I have gone through the annual reports of this society for the years from 1882 to 1896. The Society began giving small sums to Whitman under the administration of A. J. Anderson; under Eaton these annual gifts were sharply and substantially increased; under Penrose they were abruptly stopped. Why the stoppage? I can only suggest that perhaps this was the Society's way of protesting the firing of President Eaton.

Stephen B. L. Penrose

In picking Stephen B. L. Penrose to follow Eaton, the Board of Trustees made one of their own number president of Whitman College. At that time Dr. Penrose was minister of the Congregational Church in the neighboring city of Dayton, Washington. A Presbyterian turned Congregationalist only a short time before, he was not quite thirty years of age and was in the fourth year of his pastorate at Dayton. He was elected a member of the Board of Trustees of Whitman College at commencement, 1893, and was made secretary of the Board at the same time. The big crisis for Eaton was just beginning to build up at this time, and there is no doubt that Dr. Penrose became thoroughly familiar with the ins and outs of all of Eaton's trouble with the Board, with the faculty, and with the students. No doubt this was one of the reasons the Board wanted him for president, and it is significant that on becoming president he did not relinquish his place on the Board of Trustees. But there were additional and even better reasons for believing that Dr. Penrose would be an excellent man to succeed Eaton. Already he had displayed those qualities of personality and mentality which made him stand forth in all company as an exceptional man. I knew Steve Penrose for more than forty years, and I never ceased to admire his outstanding abilities.

Stephen B. L. Penrose was president of Whitman College from 1894 to 1934. No man can be the executive head of any organization, educational or otherwise, that many years without leaving behind him a vast accumulation of legend which may largely conceal both the real man and the real president. On the occasion of the inauguration of Dr. Louis B. Perry as its eighth president, Whitman College was editorially congratulated by the *Spokesman-Review,* which said that the alumni and friends of the College had every reason to be gratified as Dr. Perry assumed "the leadership made vacant by the resignation of Dr. Chester C. Maxey and made famous by the late great Dr. Stephen B. L. Penrose." The Seattle *Post-Intelligencer* also offered Whitman editorial congratulations but was a wee bit more flattering to Maxey. It gave him credit for building a bridge between the golden age of Penrose and the glorious era soon to come. The writers of those editorials were industriously perpetuating a myth that has no foundation in fact.

There was a span of twenty-five years between the retirement of Penrose and that of Maxey, and in that quarter-century, not Maxey alone, but also presidents named Clemen, Bratton, and Anderson (W. S.), toiled and strained not to build a bridge between Penrose and Perry but just to pick up the pieces and re-lay the foundations of an institution that Penrose had left almost in ruins. This is a hard thing to say and especially hard for me, an affectionate admirer of Stephen B. L. Penrose. But it is the truth, and in justice not to me alone but to all other successors of Dr. Penrose that truth should be told.

It was my privilege and pleasure to know Stephen B. L. Penrose very well in several different relationships. As an undergraduate student I took four courses in philosophy under him, was an occasional guest in his home, and had dealings with him in connection with various student activities. As a Whitman faculty member, I was not only one of his deans, but was his neighbor, was a frequent walking companion, lent him books, borrowed books from him, talked books with him many times, worked with him on many Whitman projects, and was a fellow-member of the Inquiry Club, a very close-knit organization. After his retirement from the presidency in 1934, he continued on the faculty as professor of philosophy, and that subject was in the division of which I was dean and I had many transactions with him in that connection. On some occasions he and I arranged to have his class in the history of philosophy and mine in political philosophy meet together and we jointly lectured and conducted the combined sessions. Under Presidents Clemen, Bratton, and Anderson I continued to serve as a professor and dean. Through this experience I gained an abundance of direct knowledge about most of the post-Penrose problems. After I myself became president in 1948, it was necessary for me often to check back through the files and other records left by my predecessors, and thus I amplified and further verified my factual knowledge of what had taken place in the past, and why. I mention all these things not to boast, but to qualify the witness.

In retrospect, my thinking now divides the Penrose administration into four distinct decades. The first (1894-1904) was magnificent; the second (1904-1914) was pivotal; the third (1914-1924) was critical and also pathetic; the fourth (1924-1934) was an utter debacle. I shall give a brief resume of each of these.

Taking over in 1894 a bankrupt and struggling little freshwater college, President Penrose seemed a miracle-maker. Everything he did seemed to succeed in a big way. By 1904 the material resources of the institution had been multiplied a hundredfold; its faculty had been more than doubled; and its enrollment had risen by more than 300 per cent. The curriculum had been widely diversified and enriched, and the reputation of Whitman College had spread all over the United States. Stanford and Whitman were often paired together as the two first-rated institutions of higher learning west of the Mississippi.

The second Penrose decade did not go so well. In 1908, as I have related in an earlier chapter, an ambitious expansion program called the Greater Whitman was launched. Some of Eaton's expansionism may have rubbed off on Penrose, although

314

I can testify from long first-hand association that Dr. Penrose was a thoroughly capable visionary in his own right. He had no need to borrow grand ideas from any one. The grand idea at the heart of the Greater Whitman project was to convert Whitman into a multiple-school university. The original Whitman was to continue as a school of liberal arts, and to be associated with this in a university organization were a school of music, a school of engineering (all branches), a school of forestry and irrigation, a school of commerce, and a school of art. The enrollment (around 200 in 1908) was to be lifted to 1,500, and a fund of $2,000,000 was to be raised for the construction of new buildings and making provision for additional endowment. By way of comparison, be it noted that the enrollment of Stanford at this time was 1,400, that of the University of Washington 792, that of the University of Oregon 508, that of the University of Idaho 420, that of Pomona College 291, and that of the University of California only 4,476. Obviously, the Greater Whitman was designed to be one of the big ones as well as one of the best.

I entered Whitman as a freshman in the fall of 1908 and saw the Greater Whitman rocket lift off, make a sudden rise, just as suddenly fail to orbit, and then crash back to earth with an awful thud. By 1912, my graduation year, it was all over. It was hard to believe—especially hard when I recalled the many times during my four years as a Whitman student that I had heard President Penrose, Dean Hendrick, and various others make speeches in which they positively declared that Whitman was surely on its way to become "the Yale of the West," that $600,000 had been pledged the very first year, that the Conservatory building (erected in 1909) was the first of the Greater Whitman buildings. I could not help remembering how lavishly the halls of Memorial had been adorned with architect's drawings of the new buildings and enlarged campus and how I and other Whitman boys took it all so seriously that we even picked our rooms in the proposed new dormitory for men. We were sure we would be living there as seniors, if not as juniors. Nor could I fail to recall the three faculty members specially added to the staff in 1908 to inaugurate the curriculum of the school of engineering. They actually set up and offered two years of engineering work, and a number of my close friends enrolled in those courses.

Just when it occurred I never learned, but slowly I and other students became aware that there had been a switch of plans. The fund-raising campaign was suspended; the development of the existing campus was halted; and every energy was focused on a political maneuver to induce the United States Government to give Whitman the land and buildings of Fort Walla Walla (now the Veterans' Hospital). It had been known for some time that the fort was going to be discontinued as a military reservation, but who conceived the idea that it might be transformed into a multi-million-dollar windfall for Whitman College I do not know. I believe, however, that the responsibility for making the switch could be narrowed down to three men—Stephen B. L. Penrose, Archer W. Hendrick, the dean of the College, and George Turner, then chairman of the Board of Overseers and a former United States senator and federal judge. These three were the prime leaders in the Greater Whitman movement, and I think they determined most matters of policy. The Fort Walla Walla idea looked like a short cut to success. With the hundreds of acres of land it could make available to Whitman, enough could easily be sold at residential lot prices to realize the financial goal of the campaign and still leave the College ample acreage for a campus.

For two years President Penrose, Dean Hendrick, and the other promoters of the Greater Whitman spent much of their time in Washington, D.C., trying to lobby through a bill giving Fort Walla Walla to Whitman College. From all we students could hear, everyone was sanguine of success. It was, therefore, both a surprise and something of a shock to learn in the spring of 1912 that the Whitman Bill had been defeated. Dean Hendrick immediately left the service of the College to take a business position in Portland. Then we heard more shocking news. A group of leading members of the Board of Overseers issued a signed statement saying that if some $200,000 could not be immediately raised to pay off the accumulated debts of the College, Whitman would be unable to open its doors in the fall. At the same time a not wholly unfounded story was put into circulation to the effect that a group of Spokane business leaders had offered to raise the money to liquidate the Whitman indebtedness, provided the College would move to that city. That there was some fire behind that smoke, I happen to know was true. Just a year or two later the same group of Spokane men did put up the money to move Whitworth College from Tacoma to Spokane.

Immediately the Greater Whitman project was laid to its final rest, and a high-pressure, almost hysterical, debt-raising campaign was launched in Walla Walla and vicinity. As a member of the varsity male quartet, as related in a previous chapter, I had a small part in this. Our quartet supplied the musical entertainment for several of the public meetings that were held to promote the debt-raising campaign. After hearing the sad plight of the College described and explained several times, I was able to gain a fairly clear idea of what had happened. Very few of the Greater Whitman pledges had been paid, for the reason, principally, that they were long-term pledges payable in moderate annual installments *after* the total goal had been reached. Therefore, the Greater Whitman campaign had been run on borrowed money—partly borrowed from local banks and partly from the current operating income of the College. In other words, a very considerable amount of endowment income, tuition fees, and even board and room charges had been diverted to the underwriting of the Greater Whitman campaign.

The blame for the Greater Whitman fiasco should not rest on President Penrose alone, for a good many others were involved. But he was the man at the head of the movement, and it was probably just that he should shoulder more of the responsibility than any other individual. This he did not do. Eventually he developed such a feeling of guilt about the Greater Whitman failure that in his book, *Whitman, An Unfinished Story,* he tried to shift the blame to Dean Hendrick, and offered a rather lame apology for yielding so easily to the suasions of his dean. But that book was written twenty-four years later, when Penrose was old, infirm, and blind. As one who knew both men well between 1908 and 1912, and admired both, I am obliged to say that I did not have the impression that Archer W. Hendrick was a wily knave and Stephen B. L. Penrose an easy dupe.

I think, after evaluating the whole business retrospectively, that the Greater Whitman was doomed the moment the direct money-raising was suspended in favor of the effort to get Fort Walla Walla. All the men who went to Washington to lobby for the Whitman bill were babes in the woods as respected political machinations. They thought all their cards were aces, and they did not anticipate any real opposition. But real opposition did develop, some of it from War Department sources and a great deal of it from Roman Catholic sources. Both should have been foreseen. Bureaucratic opposition almost invariably arises whenever there is an attempt to transfer large tracts of government land to private hands, whether for a price or for free. In the latter case the opposition is bound to hold a lot of honor cards. As for the Catholic opposition, that was a natural reaction to the bitterly anti-Catholic attitude of all of American Board missionaries, and particularly men like H. H. Spalding and Cushing Eells who had much to do with the founding and promotion of Whitman College as a memorial to the Whitmans. In retelling the Whitman story, these brethren repeatedly charged certain Catholic priests with inciting the Whitman Massacre. The charge was totally without foundation. Dr. Penrose himself did not believe it and never repeated it. But the harm had been done long before his time.

It is easy to leap to the conclusion that the Greater Whitman affair was a wild goose chase. But as I weigh the facts with the benefit of hindsight, I must conclude that it had real possibilities. I think it was within the bounds of the attainable and probably would have succeeded if its leaders had not decided to gamble on a short-cut. If they had not deceived themselves as to the chances of getting Fort Walla Walla, if they had rejected this temptation and followed through with the original fund-raising campaign, I believe they could have put it over the top. In this case Whitman might indeed have grown to become a "Yale of the West."

The $200,000 that the Overseers said must be obtained to keep Whitman from folding in the fall of 1912 was not all raised in that year, but enough came in to stave off imminent disaster and keep the College in Walla Walla. Two years later the debt-lifting campaign was successfully concluded, and this enabled President Penrose to enter upon his third decade with a clean financial slate. He was then forty-nine years of age, still in his prime, and presumably ready to make an effort to recover lost ground and still go forward to expansionistic goals. But he did just the opposite. The Penrose of 1914 was not the Penrose of '94, '04, or even '08. Somehow he seemed to have lost the will to win. Instead of a forward march, he did an about face, turned his back on everything he had championed in the Greater Whitman campaign. He announced that the future enrollment of Whitman College would be limited to 500 (300 men and 200 women.) "Quality, not quantity" was the new Whitman slogan, and the curriculum was to be limited to pure liberal arts. After taking this defeatist position, Dr. Penrose made little systematic effort to raise money, and allowed the College to slide ever more deeply into the morass of indebtedness.

In his third decade (1914-24) President Penrose and other officers of the College became involved in some rather tortuous transactions affecting the invested funds of the College. Witness, for example, the following item from the minutes of the Finance Committee for May 16, 1919: "It was moved and carried that S.B.L. Penrose be granted a loan of $28,000 on N½ of Sec. 16, Tp. 8, NR31,EWM at 6% for five years." And then this item from the minutes of the Board of Trustees for January 6, 1922: "It was moved and carried that the Board accept a deed from Mr. Penrose to N½ of Sec. 16, Tp. 8N, R31 in lieu of a note and mortgage of $28,500. It was moved and carried that the Treasurer be instructed to charge off from the College books the note of Mr. Penrose amounting to $21,500." What these quotations testify is that the president of the College, himself a member of the Board of Trustees and of the Finance Committee, borrowed money from the endowed funds of the institution to engage in a speculative investment—a very dubious and poorly engineered irrigation project. When, through poor management the land included in this project became worthless, the Board of Trustees voted to take the land and discharge the debt. President Penrose was not the only one. Other members of the Board of Trustees, various administrative officers, and one or two faculty members were allowed to do the same thing. They did not invest in the same things as Mr. Penrose, but all borrowed from the College on security the banks would not touch. The minute books record the fact that the meetings at which these loans were granted were all opened with prayer. Whitman College surely was standing in the need of prayer.

But prayers did not help. No miracles came to the rescue of poor old Whitman. Feeling some slight qualms of conscience about writing off President Penrose's $21,500, the Board of Trustees, with him fully participating in the transaction, decided to square the account for the benefit of the College. This was done by taking that amount from the Clement Biddle Penrose Professorship of Latin and transferring it to the unrestricted endowment funds. It is typical of what was being done in the third Penrose decade, with his personal approval and the willing collaboration of the Board, that all professed to believe that taking money from one college fund and putting it in the other accomplished a rightful restoration of the money that had been written off.

As might have been expected, the third Penrose decade ended with the College facing another desperate financial crisis. To get out of this jam, President Penrose, in 1924, launched a campaign to raise $1,500,000. In the hope of insuring success, he employed the New York money-raising firm of Tamblyn and Brown, by reputation one of the best in the business. The amount actually raised in this campaign was $308,291, of which $75,324 was used to pay off old debts. Subtracting this and the amount taken by Tamblyn and Brown as a service fee, the net return to the College was less than $200,000. Meanwhile, the College had saddled itself with a bond issue of $495,000 for the construction of the heating plant, Lyman House, and Prentiss Hall. If all of the $200,000 realized in the 1924 campaign had been applied against the bond issue (none of it was), Whitman College still would have ended the third Penrose decade with a debt encumbrance of $295,000. Starting with a clean slate in 1914, the College closed the year 1924 with depleted resources and a heavy burden of bonded indebtedness.

Such was the prelude to the fourth and final Penrose decade. In 1925 Dr. Penrose became totally blind. Three or four years earlier he had lost the sight of one eye through detachment of the retina. Unfortunately the surgical techniques of the time were not good enough to save either eye. In the initial shock of his blindness Dr. Penrose offered to resign, but the Board of Trustees urged him to continue in office. The Board should have known better than to do this, and Dr. Penrose should have known better than to be so easily persuaded that he could carry on as usual. To me and others who had to watch what followed, the ensuing ten years were both tragic and pathetic. In a very short time Dr. Penrose had persuaded himself that he was doing his job as well as ever. He said to me and I am sure he said to others that he saw no reason why he could not continue as president another fifteen or twenty years.

The ghastly truth, of course, was that he was not doing half as well as he thought. He could sit in his office every day and dictate to his secretary, which he did. He could attend meetings, and did, but could not preside effectively and finally ceased to try. As the senior dean, Walter Bratton presided at all faculty and deans' meetings. Dr. Penrose could have conferences with individuals, and did have many, but if they were not persons he had known for many years, he was never sure enough of the voice to be certain he was actually talking with the person he was supposed to be. He could not read back his own dictation or sign his name to letters, and hence never was sure of what went out over his name. He was entirely dependent on hired readers and was limited by their speed. Consequently he could

321

not begin to keep abreast of the memoranda, reports, and other papers which must be read every day if he was to keep up with what was going on. He tried to travel on College business, and I went with him on two or three trips. It was heart-rending to see him try to transact business in a hotel, not realizing that even with such assistance as I was able to give he really was not transacting business at all—just going through empty motions.

From 1924 onward the financial condition of Whitman College grew worse every day. Even in the hectic prosperity which lasted until October, 1929, Whitman College went down the skids instead of up. It was reeling when the depression struck and by 1933 it was flat on its back. It owed its faculty $74,611 in past due salaries; it owed local banks and mercantile establishments $157,942; and it was obligated in the amount of $60,000 a year for the amortization of building bonds. It forced its faculty, as I have explained above, to take a salary cut of 20 per cent and then went on defaulting on the reduced salaries. At this point the downtrodden worm rose up and demanded action. In short, the faculty rebelled. One spring afternoon in 1933 a meeting was held at the home of Professor Walter A. Bratton. The three deans (Bratton, Haigh, and Maxey) had taken the initiative in calling this meeting. Bratton was elected chairman of the meeting and I was made secretary. Having an inkling of what was in the wind, I took my portable typewriter along.

After much talk, it was unanimously decided to submit to the Board of Trustees a statement, signed by all present, saying in effect that we would not continue in the service of the College if President Penrose's retirement were not forthcoming in the near future. I typed out this statement, everybody signed, and Walter Bratton then transmitted it to Mr. Allen H. Reynolds, who was the president of the Board of Trustees. At commencement, 1933, it was announced that Dr. Penrose had decided to retire at the end of the academic year 1933-34, his fortieth as president of Whitman. At the same time the Board of Trustees appointed a committee to plan and direct the diamond jubilee of Whitman College and provide appropriate appreciation exercises for Dr. Penrose in June, 1934. I have already told how

322

I came to be made chairman of that committee and described the program that was put on. I tried to give Dr. Penrose the finest send-off I could, and, as I have already explained, I personally raised the money to do it.

I cannot conclude my remarks about the Penrose regime without a few words of epilogue. Although I realize that any comment in terms of pluses and minuses is bound to be inadequate to describe so complex a character as Stephen B. L. Penrose, I have already said so much that I feel I owe the reader something of a summary. I can say without reservation that I have never known a man of more imposing physical presence or greater personal charm than Stephen B. L. Penrose. I have never heard a better public speaker or a more scintillating conversationalist. I have already acknowledged and gladly acknowledge again that he was one of the best teachers I ever had. In my career I have worked under seven college or university presidents, and not one in my judgment was the intellectual peer of Dr. Penrose. I have never known a president who set higher standards for his faculty, who defended their freedom more valiantly, and who appreciated their scholarly and other professional attainments more genuinely. On the other hand, I have never known a president who had less concern for the material welfare of his faculty, who had less ability as an executive, and who had less aptitude for the management of money; yes, also less sensitivity to the principle of trusteeship in the handling of college funds. I owe Stephen B. L. Penrose a great deal more than I can say, but I was also one of those who suffered much through his shortcomings, and the latter were as much the result of his intrinsic qualities as the former.

Rudolf A. Clemen

The name of Rudolf A. Clemen, like that of James F. Eaton, bears no luster in Whitman history. Clemen was president less than two years—twenty-one months, to be exact. But in those twenty-one months tremendous things happened at Whitman, and it is my opinion that Dr. Clemen deserves more credit for some of these accomplishments than he has ever received.

It could be that I am the only person now living who knows how Rudolf A. Clemen happened to be chosen as Dr. Penrose's successor. His name was first suggested to the Board of Trustees by Hugh Elmer Brown '04, then minister of the leading Congregational Church in Evanston, Illinois, and also an overseer of Whitman College. After I became president of Whitman I had occasion more than once to have long visits with Brown, and in the course of one of our conversations he told me of his part in the choice of Dr. Clemen. Brown insisted that he *did not ever* recommend Clemen to the Board of Trustees or anyone else. He said he did not know Clemen well enough to recommend him for anything—in fact, had never met him. But he did, he said, know about Clemen through other persons, and thought Clemen might be worth investigating. That, said Brown, was the sum and substance of what he wrote to the Board of Trustees, and he was as much surprised as anyone when he heard that Clemen had been appointed.

I had no reason to doubt that "Hez" Brown was telling the plain, unvarnished truth. He had no reason to do otherwise. Why, then, did the Board of Trustees elect Dr. Clemen without even taking a look at any other presidential possibility? I think I know the answer to that question. The members of the Board were in close consultation with Dr. Penrose, and were inclined to let him pick his own successor. I know that to be a fact and I know the kind of successor Dr. Penrose wanted. He did not care too much about the particular man, provided he were a Congregational minister and also had some stature as a scholar. Clemen seemed to meet these requirements perfectly. He was a doctor of philosophy in economics from Harvard University, a bachelor of divinity from the University of Chicago, had recently been ordained a Congregational minister, and was temporarily serving a pastorate in the Chicago area. Following Dr. Brown's suggestion, the Board of Trustees got in touch with Clemen and found that he was actively interested in becoming a college president.

In January, 1934, Dr. Clemen, on invitation of the Board of Trustees, visited the Whitman campus and spent two or three days getting acquainted. I remember having two or three pleasant chats with him, and I am sure he had similiar talks with nearly every member of the faculty. Most of his time, however, was spent with President Penrose and one or two local members of the Board of Trustees. President Penrose quickly succumbed to his personality, and so did the Board members. On this visit to Whitman, Clemen handled himself well—I would even say cleverly. Without exactly saying so, he managed to drop a hint that other colleges were interested in him, that he was a man of wealth, and that he was in touch with large monied interests both in the Middle West and the East. Dr. Penrose was anxious to continue at Whitman as professor of philosophy, to live in Green Cottage on the north side of the campus, and play the role of elder statesman. Clemen readily agreed to this. He told me so himself—later.

Is it any wonder that Dr. Penrose and the Board members made up their minds in a hurry? Had not the Lord seen their need and sent them a man who met all of their specifications? Did he not also have the stamp of approval of the much respected and fully trusted Hugh Elmer Brown, D. D.? My guess is that they never had read Brown's letter carefully and did not bother to re-read it. They were in a hurry to get the thing settled and half fearful that some other college would get Clemen before they could close with him. Surely, in their wishful thinking, they had no reason to suppose that Brown would recommend a man he did not personally know, so why not close the deal as soon as possible?

They did, and they got a president who was as great a paradox as I ever knew. I served as a dean and professor under Rudolf A. Clemen, chairmanned important committees by his appointment, traveled with him, belonged to the same clubs and social organizations, and was often a guest in his home and he in mine. There were times when I thought I understood him and other times when he completely baffled me. One of the first things I learned was that he was not going to take much advice from any source, and from Stephen B. L. Penrose none at all. A strongly opinionated man, he made it evident from the first that he was inordinately ambitious and was not averse to Machiavellian means of realizing his ambitions. Although he was an ordained minister with a degree in theology, his religion did not exclude profane swearing and ribald remarks. Laughingly, he once told me that he took theology and was ordained because he thought that might be the quickest way to land a college presidency. He was equally candid in saying that he looked upon Whitman as merely a stepping-stone to the presidency of a large university, preferably in the Ivy League. He boasted to me, and I am sure to others, that he was wealthier than any man in Walla Walla. Actually, he did not have a dime of his own, but his wife really was an heiress. Her father had been one of the big men in the Marshall Field Company in Chicago.

The Board of Trustees and Dr. Penrose thought they had picked another Penrose, and what they got was a bull in the china shop. Having said that I must also hasten to add that Rudolf Clemen was not all wild man and down underneath was by no means as silly as he sometimes sounded. From the very outset he had a pretty clear idea of what needed to be done to get Whitman back on its feet, and he immediately set about doing that job—with all the finesse of a man putting out a fire. He should not be too much blamed for that, because he did have something close to a conflagration on his hands. And in spite of his fire-brigade methods, he did get some badly needed things done. If he had been a smoother politican and had not been in such a tearing hurry, he might have accomplished a great deal more.

One of the first, and best, things President Clemen did was to force the Trustees and Overseers to cease defaulting faculty salaries and to start making payments on arrears. The governing boards, in order to avoid defaulting payments of principal and interest on the building bonds, had elected to default faculty salaries. Dr. Clemen denounced this as shameful, and insisted that the Boards default the bonds and work out a refinancing agreement with the bondholders. Another thing on which he demanded and got immediate action was the expenditure of $25,000 for the upkeep and improvement of buildings and grounds. He raved in public about the "Roman ruins" that had been allowed to develop on the Whitman campus, and he was so close to the truth that they had to let him have his way. But feelings were hurt just the same, especially among those who had been most responsible for the "Roman ruins."

Perhaps the most durable Clemen accomplishment was the Russell Report. Measured by long-range results, this report marks the beginning of a new era at Whitman. Unfortunately it is an extremely elusive document. There were an original typescript and four carbon copies. Enough additional copies to supply the members of both boards were made by mimeograph. Most of these have long since disappeared. By happenstance I came into possession of one of the carbon copies and one of the mimeographed copies. On learning that the Whitman College Library had never received a copy of the Russell Report, I gave the Library my carbon copy. Lying around in old files, or perhaps stashed away in trunks or attics, there may still be a few copies of this report in existence, but most of them, I suspect, have long since gone to feed the flames in city dumps.

One of President Clemen's first acts after taking office was to urge that a competent outside expert be employed to make a careful and impartial survey of the existing condition of Whitman College and accompany this with recommendations for the the correction of anything found to be undesirable. He first presented this matter to the Board of Deans and was given a hearty endorsement. Then he took it to the Board of Trustees, which also concurred. One member of the Board of Trustees, the late Reginald Parsons of Seattle, offered to pay the cost of the survey, whereupon the Board gave Dr. Clemen the green light. He immediately arranged for Dr. John Dale Russell of the University of Chicago to conduct the survey. Dr. Russell was a specialist in higher education and had made a nationwide reputation by conducting just such surveys as that proposed for Whitman.

Dr. Russell came to Walla Walla in early September, 1934,

just about the time of the opening of the fall semester. I remember having several conversations with him and I know that he interviewed many other members of the faculty. He also spent a great deal of time getting facts from the bursar and the treasurer, examined all of the current financial records, and some going back into the past. I am sure that he also talked with all of the Walla Walla members of the two governing boards of the College. He must have remained in Walla Walla a week or ten days. My memory is not precise on that. Returning to Chicago, Dr. Russell prepared a preliminary report, a copy of which he forwarded to Dr. Clemen for review and criticism. Dr. Clemen asked me to do a check-reading job on this preliminary report, and I think he asked several others to do the same. Then the preliminary report went back to Russell, who proceeded at once with the writing of the final report.

I clearly recall the arrival of the final report, because Dr. Clemen telephoned and asked me to come to his house that evening, saying he wanted me to go over the Russell Report with him. That evening we sat down in his study and went over the report page by page. When we had finished, Dr. Clemen asked my opinion, and my comment was, "It's loaded with dynamite." He said that was exactly what he wanted and that he was going to detonate some of that dynamite. And he did—right away. Maybe it would have been better if he had had the report printed and given it wide circulation before he began touching off his bombs. He might have generated some favorable opinion that way, but Clemen chose to keep the report under wraps. He gave out press releases and made speeches about it, but only the Trustees and Overseers saw copies of it. None were made available to members of the faculty. I think probably Walter Bratton and I were the only faculty members who ever got a look at it. I don't believe Clemen was trying to be secretive or that he had any hesitation about making the report public. Rather, I think he was trying to dramatize the thing and arouse public curiosity with the intention of releasing the report when he thought the build-up had reached maximum effectiveness.

If I am correct in that surmise, Clemen's build-up backfired before he was fully prepared to use it. I think he was surprised by the reaction that came from certain eminent personages who claimed that the Russell Report libeled them. None of them had read it, but they had heard gossip about its contents and took the gossip to be true. Actually, there was nothing libelous in the Russell Report; it did not even hurl epithets. For the most part, it was factual, low-keyed, and prosaic; but that made it all the more damning. It paraded the simple facts so clearly and effectively that its pages shouted to the world that Whitman College had been grossly mismanaged. Without mentioning specific names, it pointed an unerring finger at the persons most responsible for this mismanagement. Following its indictment were sixty-six definite recommendations. Dr. Clemen demanded that they all be adopted, but none were. However, after he left the College, fifty-seven of them were quietly adopted and put into effect—not all at one time, of course, but year by year as circumstances became favorable.

In view of the almost complete acceptance, in the end, of the Russell recommendations, it is difficult for one who was not in the midst of the fray to understand why there was such a furore. There was nothing in the substance of the report or its sixty-six recommendations to have caused such an uproar if it had not been for the reckless way Dr. Clemen tried to use them. I will give one example of this. The report had said "In the opinion of the writer the best interests of the institution demand a somewhat wider geographical representation on the Board of Trustees. It is therefore recommended that a definite limitation be placed upon the number of board members from the local community. This regulation, if adopted, should not operate to disturb the tenure of competent members of the present Board; the policy should be introduced gradually and should take effect principally as replacements are necessary in the Board membership." There was no good reason why the Walla Walla members of the Board of Trustees should have taken offense at this, but they did. Seven of the nine members of the Board of Trustees were then residents of Walla Walla, and this was not good for a college which claimed the whole Pacific Northwest as its constituency. Not only was there too much provincialism in the Whitman Board of Trustees, there was far too little breadth of outlook and experience. All seven Walla Walla trustees were good men, but not all by any means were informed and able men. It was obvious to Dr. Russell, and would have been equally obvious to any outsider, whether an expert or not, that the critical plight of Whitman College was basically due to the fact that the Walla Walla members of the Board of Trustees had displayed gross incompetence.

The Russell report recommended that this be corrected by a limitation on local membership, to be put into effect in gradual stages. But Rudolf A. Clemen was no gradualist. He was in a hurry about everything, and seemed to be in more of a hurry about this particular Russell recommendation than any of the others. I think he felt that his chances of having a free hand in running the College depended on replacing most of the Walla Walla trustees as soon as possible. His first play was to try to get a Seattle member elected president of the Board in place of a Walla Walla member. This failed. Then he tried to get the Board to adopt a limitation as suggested by the Russell report. This, too, failed. Next he tried to draw the Board of Overseers more largely into the management of the College, as three-fourths or more of the members of that board were not Walla Walla residents. But this was not easy, because the Board of Overseers had only one regular meeting a year. Finally Dr. Clemen decided to try a squeeze play. He addressed a letter to the Board of Trustees in which he made a number of specific demands and said that he would resign if these demands were not met. He was dumbfounded when the Board, instead of complying with his demands, voted to accept his resignation. He had not expected his squeeze play to boomerang, and apparently had been bluffing all the time. When his bluff was called, he fell back on the technical defense that he had not actually resigned and consequently that the Board's action was invalid. When the Board of Trustees stood its ground, Clemen engineered a special meeting of the Board of Overseers, hoping that the Overseers would overrule the Trustees. After a day-long debate

330

the Board of Overseers did not overrule the Trustees, but passed a rather equivocal resolution to the effect that President Clemen ought to be allowed to recall his resignation, referred this to the Board of Trustees, and then adjourned and went home.

That really blew things apart. Some members of the Board of Trustees thought the Overseers' resolution ought to be followed and others said they would resign if it were. As a result, the Board of Trustees did nothing but mark time. Meanwhile, on the campus there was a sorry state of confusion and uncertainty. We of the faculty did not know whether we had a president or not, and had no assurance that any effort ever would be made to settle that question one way or the other. One thing was clear, however: whatever the outcome, the faculty would be hurt most of all. A few of us talked the situation over and decided to call a meeting of heads of departments to see if we could get together on some sort of action for the protection of the faculty. This meeting was held at my house, and it was unanimously decided that we should go on record demanding that the Board of Trustees stand firm on its action accepting President Clemen's resignation. It was not so much that we had grievances against Clemen and wanted to get rid of him as that we felt sure, if he were restored to office, the fight would go on, maybe for years, and we would be its helpless victims. We appointed a committee, of which I was one to go to the president of the Board and ask him to call a special meeting which we might attend. This was done, and the meeting was held in Jim Crawford's office. Our committee went over the whole situation with the Trustees and explained why we thought President Clemen should not be re-instated.

A majority of the Board then voted to notify Dr. Clemen that the Board would not reconsider his resignation. The Board also voted to set a terminal date about two weeks hence for the end of his tenure as president. Walter A. Bratton was made acting president, effective as of the same date. One member of the Board of Trustees and three members of the Board of Overseers immediately resigned in protest against this action. This surprised me a great deal, as I had taken it for granted that Clemen had

331

a much greater following than that. As a means of informing the public, and especially the alumni of Whitman College, of the reason for Dr. Clemen's sudden separation from the College, a joint committee of board members, faculty members, and alumni officers was established. I was made a member of that committee and got the duty of writing the first draft of a statement which was given to the press and sent as a letter to all persons on the mailing list of Whitman College.

Walter A. Bratton

In selecting Walter A. Bratton as acting president, the Board of Trustees showed a good understanding of the needs of the situation. As a pacificator and harmonizer, he was an ideal choice. He had been a member of the Whitman faculty forty-one years. He had rendered brilliant service as professor of mathematics, and under President Penrose he had served as Dean of the External Relations Group and under President Clemen as Dean of the College. After two years as acting president, the Board gave him a much deserved vote of confidence by making him president.

Dr. Bratton's principal task, in addition to the restoration of confidence and good will, was carrying through to a successful conclusion two undertakings which President Clemen had begun: (1) the refinancing of the building bonds and (2) the liquidation of the more than $230,000 of floating debt which had been accumulating since 1924. In both of these undertakings Dr. Bratton was eminently successful, and the only criticism of his work that I ever heard was voiced by faculty members who thought he should not have put the bite on them to donate a substantial part of their unpaid salaries to the debt-lifting fund. In this I think Bratton was overeager to please certain Walla Walla trustees and overseers who were primarily concerned in not having the bite fall very heavily on them. I think the idea of levying on the faculty originated with them and not with Walter Bratton.

If President Bratton had continued in good health, I am sure he would have been able to accomplish much more than he did.

Unfortunately, in his third year in office, he was stricken with a serious illness which greatly curtailed his activities and led to his death a short time after his retirement in 1942. Unavoidably, therefore, the last three years of the Bratton administration were standstill years. The president lacked the vigor and vitality to furnish the necessary leadership. Always in college administration, when the president slows down, the whole institution slows down.

The announcement at commencement, 1941, that President Bratton would retire one year hence, naturally gave rise to a flurry of speculations and chatter as to his successor. My name was among those mentioned, and I was officially asked if I would allow my name to be considered. I replied that I would not. The same thing had happened at the time of President Penrose's retirement, and my reasons for refusal were the same in 1941 as in 1934. I simply did not aspire to be the president of Whitman or any other college. This was not a matter of humility or want of ambition. My tastes and interests just did not lie in that direction. Although I had discovered early in life that I could, if necessary, mobilize a goodly amount of executive talent, I had no liking at all for that kind of work. At various times it had been temporarily thrust upon me, and those experiences had strongly confirmed my prejudice against it. In respect to fund-raising I had had similar experiences, and with even stronger adverse reactions. The most boring kind of work I could imagine was raising money, and the next most boring was administering the routine of a college. Teaching, writing, and dabbling in politics were what I enjoyed most of all, and I wanted to be free to spend the rest of my days that way.

At the annual meeting of the Trustees and Overseers in 1941 the chairman of the Board of Overseers, Judge James Alger Fee, was authorized to appoint a committee of five—two trustees, two overseers, and one faculty member—to conduct a search and submit recommendations for a successor to President Bratton. From the Overseers Judge Fee appointed Stanly A. Easton and Russell Miller, from the Trustees D. F. Baker and Harper Joy, and from the faculty me. Mr. Easton was appointed chairman of the committee and I was made secretary. Although I did not want to be considered for president, I was glad to serve on this committee and to be its secretary. Because I positively did not want to be the next president, and did not intend to be, it was specially gratifying to me to have something to say about who would be the choice. One thing above all else I hoped to prevent, and that was the choice of another Clemen.

Winslow S. Anderson

As secretary of the presidential search committee, it fell to me to carry on the correspondence, compile the data, keep the records, and handle most of the other details of getting our job done. My records show that the committee made some controlling decisions at its first meeting. One was that we definitely would not seek a clergyman—Congregationalist or any other species. In making this decision the committee followed the advice of one of the most distinguished clergymen on the Board of Overseers, who simply said that his long experience led him to doubt whether the kind of president Whitman needed could be found in the ranks of the clergy. A second controlling decision was that the committee would prefer a man whose undergraduate education had been obtained in a small liberal arts college similar to Whitman. And the third controlling decision was that the committee would not limit its search to the Pacific Northwest or any other special section of the country, but would canvass the entire nation.

At its first meeting the committee decided on the procedure it would follow in the transaction of its business. It was agreed that each member individually would make inquiries through all channels available to him and report all suggested names to the secretary. It would be the secretary's job to try to assemble adequate biographical information with regard to each name thus sent to him. It was also agreed that the secretary should have the responsibility of canvassing the professional associations and learned societies, such for instance as the Association of American Colleges and the United Chapters of Phi Beta Kappa. I spent most of the summer of 1941 carrying forward these tasks.

Altogether I assembled data on some forty men, and reported to the committee members what I had done. Near the end of September the committee met in Walla Walla to go through the material I had gathered and decide what next to do. After an all-day session at the Marcus Whitman Hotel, the committee reached agreement on five men who were deemed to be the cream of the crop, and it was decided to ask each of these five to come to Whitman for a personal interview. The next question, of course, was which should be invited to come first. Somebody said why not take them in alphabetical order, and everybody thought that was as good a way as any. Thus it came to pass that Winslow S. Anderson, Dean of Rollins College, Winter Park, Florida, was the first of the five to be invited for an interview. It was the luck of the "draw" and nothing more.

As soon as the committee had agreed that Dean Anderson should be asked to come first, Mr. Easton turned to me and said, "Why not get Dean Anderson on the phone right now and make arrangements for his visit? Then we will all know before we adjourn what our next step will be." Everybody said yea to that idea, and I picked up the telephone and immediately put through a call to Winter Park, Florida. In less than half an hour I had Dean Anderson on the line and completed arrangements in the hearing of the entire committee whereby he would come to Walla Walla, at our expense, on October 15, would spend three days at Whitman, and then go on to Spokane where there would be a meeting of our whole committee.

This schedule was carried out to the letter. Frank Baker and I, the only Walla Walla members of the committee, met Dr. Anderson at Pendleton and drove him to Walla Walla. We had already set up a program of dinners, luncheons and receptions intended to bring Dean Anderson into contact with all of the local trustees and overseers as well as most of the members of the faculty. At the end of his three-day stay in Walla Walla, Frank Baker and I drove Dr. Anderson to Spokane where Stanly Easton and Harper Joy were in charge of the arrangements. They had set up a schedule of functions similiar to those in Walla Walla, and these enabled all of the Spokane area trustees and overseers as well as a number of alumni to meet Dr. Anderson. After the completion of this schedule, our committee went into executive session to compare impressions and talk about the next step. The members of the committee unanimously agreed that Anderson had fully measured up to the expectations we had derived from his vita papers and letters of recommendation. Then the question was, What next? Some one—Mr. Easton, as I remember it—spoke up and said: "If Dr. Anderson meets all of our criteria and we are all agreed that we think we would like to recommend him, are we under any obligation to interview the other four?" To this I replied that I had not yet communicated with any of the others, thinking that I should not make commitments in advance of our meeting with Dean Anderson. The committee approved my decision to wait for further instructions.

Then followed a discussion of the propriety of making a decision in favor of Dean Anderson right now or waiting until the other four top men had been seen and interviewed. Somebody asked if we were obliged to spend an additional two thousand dollars to pay the travel expenses of the other men if we were already satisfied with the one we had seen. Of course the answer to that was obvious. We were not bound by any instructions or regulations which obliged us to do anything other than exercise our best judgment on every question that came before us. Then a motion was made and passed that we ask Dean Anderson to come before the committee again. After an hour or more of plying him with all sorts of specific questions, he was excused and we went into executive session again. Every member of the committee was more satisfied than before that Dean Anderson was the right man for the job. A motion was made and passed that the committee recommend his appointment, and I was asked to draft a letter to that effect for submission to the Board of Trustees. After some changes and corrections, the committee approved this draft, and I was authorized to have it properly typed and signed for presentation at the next meeting of the Board. We did not tell Dean Anderson of our action or reveal our action to any one but the

Board of Trustees. It was up to the Trustees to ratify or reject our recommendation, and we did not want to be accused of trying to force their hands. If they had rejected our first recommendation, we were prepared to continue the interviews until we had gone through all our list of prospects. After a month or so the Board of Trustees approved our recommendation and offered the position to Dean Anderson.

I have gone into some detail in describing the appointment of Winslow S. Anderson, because in later years certain disgruntled persons started the story that his appointment was a trumped-up affair. The only thing which might lend color to such a fabrication was our failure to interview the other four top-flight candidates. Probably we should have taken the time and spent the extra money necessary to do this. Maybe our minds would have been changed and maybe not. Maybe one of the others would have made a better president than Dr. Anderson and maybe not. But at any rate we could not have been charged with giving Anderson a "special break." Of course nobody made that charge at the time of the Anderson appointment. We got nothing but compliments then. Five years later, when Anderson became the subject of controversy, it was easy to convince the uninformed that he had been railroaded into the job.

My opinion, for whatever it may be worth, always was and still is that Winslow S. Anderson was a devoted and able president of Whitman College. As his successor in office, I can testify from first-hand knowledge that he left the College in much better shape than he found it. My opportunities to observe Winslow Anderson in action were as good as anyone could have had. Under him, as under Penrose, Clemen and Bratton, I served as a dean and department head. I transacted all sorts of business with him, conferred with him at length countless times, traveled with him, and frequently enjoyed the hospitality of his home. I saw him at his best and at his worst, but the worst did not appear until after his tragic affliction with a brain tumor.

The years of Winslow Anderson's administration included World War II and the post-war deluge of male students under the G.I. Bill. I don't believe we would have found a man who

337

would have made a better war president than Winslow S. Anderson. I know several highly reputed college presidents who did not do nearly as well as he. President Anderson conducted the negotiations and set up the contracts under which Whitman secured the two naval training units which were officially designated as V-5 and V-12. He not only handled all of the complex dealings, financial and other, with the Department of the Navy and the commanding officers on the campus, but he also, at the end of the war, effected the final settlements on terms which left Whitman College thousands of dollars to the good. Not all colleges were similarly successful in their dealings with the War and Navy departments. President Anderson was equally shrewd and equally successful in his dealings with Veterans' Administration under the terms of the G.I. Bill. Whitman could have lost its shirt in these transactions, but it ended up with a shirt that was both whole and clean. In speaking of these matters I have direct personal knowledge, because it became my duty to follow through and carry many of them to final termination. In addition to the success of his transactions with the Navy and the Veterans' Administration, President Anderson's most valuable and lasting contribution was the Student Center Building. He was chiefly instrumental in raising the funds for this building and was almost exclusively responsible for its planning and construction.

On the educational side, President Anderson had little opportunity to do anything constructive. It was wartime. All but a tiny handful of Whitman's men were in the Navy programs, and nobody wanted to think of curricular reforms until after the war. Reform for girls alone would have been a mess anyhow. Nevertheless, Dr. Anderson did try to initiate a movement for the introduction of a general education program at Whitman. I was a member of the committee appointed to study and report on that proposal, and I well remember the many hours of aimless talk in which we engaged. Dr. Anderson might have needled us more than he did, but I doubt if this would have done much good. He was likewise greatly hampered by war conditions in his efforts to effect needed changes in faculty organization and personnel. The one big change of this kind that he did succeed in bringing about brought him a peck of trouble. I refer to the forced resignations of the two Borleskes—"Nig" and "Mig."

I had no part in the Borleske business, but I did have a ringside seat and did not miss much that went on. I heard Borleske's side from Borleske, Anderson's side from Anderson, and the Trustee-Overseer side from several members of both boards. I do not intend to burden these pages with a repetition of the dismal details of that sad affair, which ended with the dismissal of both Borleskes by action of the Board of Trustees with approval by the Board of Overseers. My final conclusion was that the Borleskes made it impossible for the Board of Trustees not to fire them. If those two unshrinking violets could have curbed their tongues and kept themselves out of the public eye long enough for an anti-Anderson reaction to set in, I think they would have been invulnerable. But that would have required the Borleskes not to be the Borleskes.

The only reason I mention the Borleske rumpus at all is that it was during this clawing match that I first noticed symptoms of mental deterioration in President Anderson. I did not attach too much significance to these symptoms at the time, but no one as closely associated with President Anderson as I was could have failed to notice that he was inordinately garrulous, indecisive, and debilitated. I thought this indicated weariness and worry, and I took it for granted that, given a few weeks of rest, he would quickly bounce back to his normal self. But he did not.

In the academic year 1947-48, the first after the dismissal of "Nig" Borleske, President Anderson got his first chance to have his own way with the athletic program. I could not help noticing, for he talked with me much about athletics, that he seemed to be possessed of an obsession to eclipse anything Borleske had ever done. Without consultation with any one at Whitman, official or otherwise, he proceeded to handpick a head coach to succeed Borleske and also an assistant coach. Then he proceeded, with equal independence, to give these two men carte blanche with the athletic budget and also authorized them to hand out a large number of athletic scholarships. In respect to the athletic scholarships he made a serious mistake, one that certainly would have cost him his job if he had lived.

There was a long-standing rule at Whitman, one made by the Board of Trustees on recommendation of the faculty, that all scholarships and other grants in aid must be awarded by vote of the faculty committee on student aid. I was chairman of this committee by appointment of President Anderson, but he did not submit any request for athletic scholarships to this committee or give me the slightest inkling of what he was doing. I think the reason for this was that he expected to get the money outside the College budget and thought it was nobody's business but his own. If he had lived, he might have done this and no one would have been the wiser. That was not like the Winslow Anderson I had known so well, and I am glad I did not discover it until after his death.

As the year wore on I became increasingly aware that Dr. Anderson's mental condition was not up to par, but I still did not realize that he was mortally ill, nor did anyone else. On account of the unauthorized actions and other inexplicable behavior, some members of both boards began to lose confidence in President Anderson. At their commencement meeting in 1948 both boards gave him rather a rough time. Although they had no present intention of dismissing him, they did tell him that a president could not regard himself as having permanent tenure and that it might be prudent for him to keep that in mind. This was a great shock to Dr. Anderson, though it was not made public and was not made a matter of record in the proceedings of the two boards.

Following commencement, 1948, it chanced that I had to transact a great deal of business with President Anderson, mostly pertaining to the Division of Social Sciences of which I was the dean. I well remember our first conference after commencement. Dr. Anderson had great difficulty in holding himself to the business at hand, which was the filling of a faculty vacancy. He rambled from one thing to another and finally asked me if I had ever had trouble with my eyes. I replied that I had never had any eye trouble that simple refraction could not correct. Then he told me that he was having dizzy spells and double vision and had decided to have Dr. Ralph Stevens check his eyes. Some days later he told me that Dr. Stevens had found nothing wrong with his eyes but suggested that he go to Portland where he might obtain an X-Ray examination that would show whether there was any such complication as brain tumor. Dr. Anderson followed this suggestion, and when he returned from Portland he showed me several X-Ray photographs that had been taken in the Portland clinic. He said the Portland doctors assured him that these pictures revealed no trace of a brain tumor. He was in high spirits because he was sure he would soon be on the mend. All he needed, he said, was rest, and that he proposed to have right away. He had purchased a new automobile, and he was planning to give it a good workout on a long vacation trip to Crater Lake and environs.

When he got back from his vacation Dr. Anderson was worse rather than better, and soon found himself unable to make it to the office every day. Several times I had to go to his home to transact business with him. About this time I became involved in circumstances which caused him much distress. Out of a blue sky I received an offer to teach at the University of Washington in the year 1948-49. Francis G. Wilson, the professor of political theory there, was going to the University of Illinois for a year, and I was asked to replace him. I knew everybody in the political science department at the University of Washington so well that it was easy to deduce what was in the offing. If Wilson remained at Illinois (which he did) and I gave a good account of myself at the U of W, I would be first in line to succeed him. That would have been to my liking, because it would have meant an opportunity to specialize in political philosophies. So I went to Dr. Anderson's home one day when he was well enough to see me and asked him to recommend that I be granted a leave of absence for 1948-49. He was reluctant to do it; in fact, he begged me to withdraw the request and reject the Washington offer. He thought it would be impossible to find a replacement for me before the opening of the first semester, and if he did find a replacement, he feared people would misinterpret my taking a year off as an expression of dissatisfaction with him.

He finally did agree to present my request to the Board but would not promise to recommend its approval. I thereupon decided to do some talking in my own behalf. I had interviews with Frank Baker and Herbert Ringhoffer, the two Trustees then resident in Walla Walla, and told them that if I could not have a leave of absence, I would resign and accept the Washington offer anyhow. Although it was only for one year, I was fairly sure that it could be converted into a permanent appointment. Both Frank and Herb urged me not to resign and expressed the hope that I would decide to remain at Whitman. Then I got a little peeved and said that if they were so anxious to keep me at Whitman, they had better start thinking about making it worth my while. I would not stay if Whitman would not immediately pay me a salary commensurate with what the University of Washington had offered. I went back to President Anderson and delivered the same ultimatum to him. In less than a week my terms had been met and I had declined the Washington offer. Perhaps I should have been more noble and sacrificial, but after twenty-three years of deferred expectations at Whitman, I had no desire for more of the same.

President Anderson's condition grew worse by the day. He conceived the idea that bad teeth might be the cause of his trouble, was X-Rayed, and had two or three suspicious teeth extracted. This did not help. By September he was unable to transact business either at home or at his office. Around the first of October he was taken to the St. Mary Hospital for several days of observation and laboratory tests. I visited him while he was in the hospital and was shocked to see how much he had failed in the few days since I had seen him last. The hospital observations were inconclusive. Dr. Anderson returned home and was bed-ridden most of the time. One day in late October Mrs. Anderson called me on the telephone and said she was at her wits end. She had done everything she could think of except take Winslow to the Mayo Clinic. What did I think about that?

342

I urged her to get him there as soon possible, and she replied that I had given her the advice she wanted to hear.

In less than a week she had him in the Mayo Clinic at Rochester, Minnesota, where an exploratory operation was performed. The findings were inconclusive, but Dr. Anderson sank rapidly after the operation and on November 3 he passed away. The post-mortem operation disclosed an inoperable tumor embedded under the pituitary gland. This explained everything. The Mayo specialists were of the opinion that this tumor had been enlarging rapidly in the past two years. It was easy now to understand why the Winslow S. Anderson of 1947 and 1948 was so different from the man who had completely captivated us in 1941.

The Next President

The death of President Anderson precipitated a crisis. For more than a year Dr. Anderson had not been himself and had allowed some things to get badly tangled, and for the last five months he had been out of his office most of the time. Scores of decisions that should have been made had been postponed, so there was a large and growing backlog of unfinished business. To the last, Dr. Anderson had been so sure of his recovery and so determined not to admit his incapacitation that he had delegated no real authority to anyone. He had not even designated anybody to preside in his absence at meetings of the faculty and the Board of Deans. It was not necessary for the faculty to meet very often but the Board of Deans had to meet once a week. On account of unfilled vacancies in the Board, there were only three deans left—Armstrong, Haigh, and I. We formed the habit of meeting informally, without a presiding officer, but were never sure how far we could go in acting on the various questions which were put up to us.

When the notice of President Anderson's death on November 3 was received, it was evident that matters would quickly go from bad to worse if the Trustees and Overseers did not take immediate steps to give the institution a chief executive. Realizing this, Mr. D. F. Baker, president of the Board of Trustees, telephoned Judge James Alger Fee, chairman of the Board of Overseers, and asked for suggestions. The outcome of this telephonic conversation was that Judge Fee agreed to appoint a committee of Overseers, including himself, who would come to Walla Walla and meet with the Board of Trustees on November 20.

In the intervening seventeen days there was all sorts of wild speculation as to what would be done about a successor for Dr. Anderson. Both Mr. Baker and Judge Fee asked me if I would allow myself to be considered, and at first I said no. But when they asked what alternative I had to suggest, I was stumped. I did not want the job, but I had no candidate to offer. One afternoon Mr. Baker came to my office and spent an hour or more bearing down on the point that this was unlike any previous situation in which the office of president had become vacant. This was an emergency, he said, in which time was of the essence. Somebody had to take the reins in hand right now or a disaster would occur. We did not reach any agreement, but Frank asked me if I would be willing, in case I should be invited, to appear before the meeting of Trustees and Overseers on November 20 and talk things over with them. I said I would do that, provided it did not involve any commitment on my part. Frank said it was just between him and me; he was not even sure that the joint meeting would follow his suggestion that they have a talk with me.

About four o'clock on the afternoon of Saturday, November 20, 1948, I received a telephone call asking me if I could come to the meeting immediately. I could and did. After the customary amenities had been concluded, Mr. Baker, as chairman of the combined meeting, told me that they had spent all day trying to reach a satisfactory decision on the presidential vacancy and were now ready to offer me an appointment as acting president. Would I accept? I replied immediately that I would not. I said I might hesitate about the presidency, but I had no hesitation at all about the acting presidency. I went on to say that an acting president always has two strikes against him and in the present situation things were so fouled up that the third strike

344

would be called before he could get his bat off his shoulder. Then I asked if they would consider a counter-proposal, and they indicated that they would.

For several days I had been thinking about the emergency and my obligations relative thereto. After much weighing of factors and circumstances, I made up my mind that I would accept the presidency if I could get it on my own terms, and I had decided on some unusual terms. In explaining these, I said to the meeting that there was every reason why they should hesitate to make me president and every reason why I should be reluctant to take the job if offered. They had no reason to suppose that I had any special qualifications for being president and I had no taste for the kind of responsibilities that would be thrust upon me. However, I did recognize that Whitman was confronted with a grave emergency, and it might be that there was temporary need for a president who knew the College inside out, as I certainly did. Then I proposed that they appoint me president for a definite term of two years. If I were any good, I ought to be able to get things fairly well straightened out in two years. After that I would automatically and happily bow out of the picture and return to my teaching and writing. Meanwhile they would have two years to search for a permanent president, and ought to be able to find someone who could handle the job far better than I. After some discussion, my counter-prosposal was unanimously approved; I was elected president for two years with the privilege of resuming my former status at the end of that time; and a committee was chosen to begin at once on the search for a permanent president.

Since there was to be a memorial service for President Anderson on Monday, November 22, and since I among others was to speak at that service, the members of the meeting agreed that the public announcement of my appointment should not be made until November 23, and it was also agreed that nothing would be said about my appointment being limited to two years. It was left for me to announce this at such time as I thought most expedient. At the memorial service I paid tribute to Dr. Anderson without its being known to any except board members who had attended the meeting on November 20 that I was his successor in office. This five-minute eulogy, which I incorporate hereafter, said what I hoped the world would remember about Winslow S. Anderson.

IN MEMORIAM—WINSLOW S. ANDERSON

To all men alike is not Nature's way. It is given to some to live long and to others to live briefly. It is given to some to live dynamically and to others to live passively. It is given to some to live notably and nobly, transcendently and triumphantly, while others pass their days in futility and failure.

In the sealed book of personal fate, Winslow Anderson was not allotted a great span of years, but in all other respects he stood among the favored few to whom Nature gives in abundance. As though to compensate for the brevity of his life, he was endowed with exceptional qualities for living and achieving. His vitality, his energy, his capacity for unremitting labor, his tenacity of purpose, and his perceptiveness of actuality spared him the need of longevity for the accomplishment of great things.

We who have been his colleagues and co-workers well know how ably he labored and how well he wrought. We know that we are indebted to him for much that we now enjoy of material well-being and professional satisfaction. We know that he labored for us more than for himself, and that he sought to build for us, as for himself, a future rich with opportunity for greater values and finer services. We know that he stood behind us in our aspirations and our dreams, and that he wished us ever higher aspirations and loftier dreams. We know that in our dealings with him there was naught of pettiness, malice, or bigotry; nothing but integrity, sincerity, sympathy, and good will.

We shall not forget Winslow Anderson, and this is not the final expression of our high regard for him and for his services to us and to Whitman College. A man of his quality does not live in calendared time alone, but in the endless sequence of fruitions insured by the intensity of his devotion, however early curtailed, to the service of his fellow men.

PART V

PRESIDENT OF WHITMAN COLLEGE, 1948-1959

XXI. GETTING STARTED

The First Six Weeks

If not the hardest, my first six weeks as president certainly were the most frustrating. This was not so much because of their being the first as because of a fortuitous combination of circumstances which almost tied me hand and foot. Many things that had gone undone were now crying for attention, and I was ready to give them all the attention they demanded, but I had no secretary, not even a qualified stenographer. Mrs. Grace Lazerson, Dr. Anderson's secretary and also secretary to his three predecessors in office, had resigned three weeks before I took office. She had not been replaced because there was no president to do the replacing. A very conscientious woman had been employed to sit in the office and answer the telephone. She could type a little, but could not take dictation, knew nothing about the files, and was totally uninformed about past or pending business. I could not begin to function as president until I had a competent secretary.

Good secretaries are never easy to find, and my task was made more difficult by the fact that Mrs. Lazerson's salary was too low to compete for anything but junior grade typists. So the first thing I did was to add $600 a year to the salary, and the next step was to find out what was available in Walla Walla. At this juncture fortune smiled upon me. Several persons, including Mrs. Lazerson herself, had suggested Miss Winifred Dunphy, then principal clerk in the county welfare department. I went to see Miss Dunphy. She was interested, but wanted time to think it over. I did not blame her for that, but when she said that even if she decided in favor of the Whitman position, she could not start until the first of January, 1949 I came close to telling her to forget the whole thing. She had to give her present employer one month's notice, and I did not see how I could wait that long. For a while I debated getting on the telephone and seeing what I could do in Spokane, Seattle, or Portland, but after a second talk with "Winks" I decided to wait for her.

This was one of the wisest decisions I made as president of Whitman College. I am sure that I could not have found her equal anywhere, and I know that she made me a much more efficient president than I could have been without her. She was more than equal to every task I gave her, and she seemed to be able to do everything I needed done. Most of the time she was way ahead of me, anticipating the next step and planning things for me. I could delegate almost any duty or responsibility to her and be sure it would be done promptly and well. Her high intelligence made it easy to trust her with complex and difficult responsibilities, and I quickly ceased to worry about anything I had delegated to her. She was a perfect buffer between me and the scores of people with whom I had to transact business, and she had that rarest of all secretarial virtues—the ability to speak discreetly and tactfully without conveying wrong impressions. After "Winks" and I had worked together long enough to be a team, I found that I could be away from my office for days and weeks at a stretch and still be in constant touch, if need be, with everything important that was going on at Whitman. She knew exactly what to relay to me, what to dispose of herself, and what to hold until my return.

But in the six weeks that I had to wait for this paragon of secretaries, I could do only those things which were possible without secretarial assistance. One of these was to take the initiative in putting through an administrative reorganization of the faculty and the other was to try my hand at soliciting money. The latter was perhaps premature, but when I looked at the current-gift income for 1948 my heart sank. By the first of December it was apparent that if nothing more were done, the "take" for the year would not exceed $27,000 for invested funds and $8,800 for current expenses—both all-time lows. It might be possible by some pre-Christmas solicitation in Walla Walla to bring these figures to more respectable proportions. So I donned my smoked glasses, took my tin cup and made a number of mendicant calls on business and professional people in Walla Walla. I did not get a penny that year, but some of my calls did produce gifts in subsequent years. At any rate I had the satisfaction of doing in my first six weeks in office the one thing I knew how to do about raising money, namely, to go out and ask for it. My conscience was clear and my courage picked up, because I knew I would be able to screw up my determination to see that job done more persistently than it had ever been done in the past.

Reorganization

Administrative reorganization had become immediately imperative because my advancement to the presidency had left the Board of Deans with only two members—Charles J. Armstrong, Dean of Administration, and Frank L. Haigh, Dean of Basic Sciences. President Anderson a few years before had abolished the offices of Dean of Men and Dean of Women and had failed to replace the late W. R. Davis as Dean of Letters and Arts. A two-man board of deans could not function, and I did not want to fill the two vacant deanships. For one reason, there was a dearth of material for those jobs and, more important, I thought it most opportune right then to bring about a complete overhaul of the administrative machinery. After incubating a few ideas about what might be done, I set up a series of discussion sessions with the two remaining deans, and we three finally hammered out a reorganization plan for submission to the faculty. At a meeting on November 30 this plan went before the faculty and was approved without a dissenting voice or vote. It was put into effect immediately, and at the end of the year in my first annual report to the two governing boards, I described the new plan in the following words:

Although the new organization does not materially depart from the pattern of its predecessor, it has simplified and centralized many operations of the Faculty which were formerly vested in independent standing committees. It also transfers to the newly created Faculty and Administrative Councils most of the functions formerly reposed in

353

the Board of Deans. The Faculty Council is composed of five teaching members of the Faculty who do not hold administrative positions. The members are elected by the Faculty and are directly responsible to it. The Faculty Council acts as a preconsidering, advisory and recommending agency for the General Faculty. The chairman of the Faculty Council is the Dean of the Faculty, who is also responsible for co-ordinating the work of the five curricular divisions of the Faculty. The Administrative Council acts under the chairmanship of the Dean of Administration and is composed of the directors of the various administrative services of the Faculty. The Administrative Council deals primarily with matters of routine operation rather than matters of policy.

More than a year ago the Faculty voted to increase the number of curricular divisions from three to five, but it had not been expedient to put this action into effect immediately. In connection with the reorganization outlined above, the two new curricular divisions were set up and put into operation. Thus the curricular divisions of the Faculty at the present time are: I. Social Sciences, II. Literature and Language, III. Basic Sciences, IV. Music and Art, and V. Health and Physical Education.

Each of these divisions annually elects its own chairman, and the Dean of the Faculty exercises general supervision over the five divisions through their respective chairman. One result of the new divisional organization is that the academic work of the Conservatory of Music is now fully incorporated with the curriculum of the College, and education in the field of music is conducted as an integral part of the College program.

I was incorrect in saying that the new organization did not "materially depart from the pattern of its predecessor." In the long run it was a radical departure from the old organization, but I was writing at the end of the first six months when that was much less apparent than it is today.

354

The new organization scrapped the administration structure which had been established under President Clemen in 1934. In a previous chapter I have told of the part I had in that. In a sense, in 1948, I took the lead in putting my own baby to death. However, it was a baby which had outgrown its usefulness and needed to be put away. President Anderson had not liked this system, but had taken no steps to change or abolish it. Instead, he had set up alongside it a parallel organization of standing committees, which he appointed. Most of these committees duplicated in one or more functions work hitherto belonging to the Board of Deans, and the result was a good deal of both diffusion and confusion of responsibility. It may have been President Anderson's intention ultimately to supplant the 1934 organization with a faculty committee system headed by a dean of the College, but if so, he never got around to it.

When I came into office the 1934 organization was badly crippled and the parallel committee organization had been in a state of suspended animation for six months or so by reason of President Anderson's illness. In was transparently clear that the best way to attack the problem was to sweep the boards and make a fresh start. Obviously, a new mechanism with a new central cog was urgently needed, and it seemed to me that this should pivot on the faculty rather than on the office of president. In all matters having to do with pedagogics, both as to policy and administration, I thought the faculty should bear the responsibility. For the implementation of this principle, the Faculty Council was created. The reorganization legislation specified that this body should consist of five members of the faculty who held no administrative title or position. One member was to be elected each year for a term of five years, and upon the expiration of his five-year term a member was ineligible for re-election until one year had passed. These requirements were designed to accomplish three results: (1) insure that power and responsibility would rest in the hands of members chosen from and by the teaching faculty; (2) insure stability and continuity of membership, and (3) insure a constant in-put of new blood and afford opportunity for many members of the faculty to serve on the Faculty Council. The same purposes and results were sought by abolishing the office of divisional dean and requiring the faculty of each division annually to elect its own chairman and secretary. So, whether it was acting by divisions or as a whole, the faculty was in full control of the machinery for making and executing educational policy.

The Dean of the Faculty was made presiding officer of the Faculty Council, with power to vote only in case of a tie. It was his duty as presiding officer to prepare the agenda and expedite the transaction of the business of the Faculty Council; it was also his duty to coordinate the work of the Faculty Council and the five divisional faculties. In the interest of further coordination, it was provided that the President of the College, the Dean of the Faculty, the Dean of Administration, the Registrar and such other administrative officers as the Council might name should sit with the Faculty Council as *ex officio* members. This meant that the principal officers of administration were always present for consultation, but had no right to vote and no right to participate in deliberations except as desired by the Council itself.

The new machinery for managing the co-curricular activities of the College were of comparable character. The Dean of Administration had general supervision over these and was assisted in an advisory capacity by the Administrative Council, which consisted of the directors of such agencies as the Office of Student Affairs, the Placement Service, the Food Service, the Student Center, the Whitman Theater, the Infirmary, and the Housekeeping Service. The President of the College was *ex officio* a member of the Administrative Council but did not regularly attend the meetings of that body. Previously all such agencies had been operating in almost complete detachment from one another, though all were directly responsible to the president of the College. The new organization served to keep them in contact with one another and effected coordination where that was necessary.

Because it tied things together better than before, the new organization was more centralized, but because it also created various areas of independent authority and action it was at the same time more decentralized. It was also, I believe, more thoroughly democratic than any previous organization plan at Whitman. Its chief virtue from my standpoint was that it forced a constant face-to-face confrontation of the policy-making and policy-administering officers of the College and obliged them to perform their duties in the open view of all concerned. In my thinking it also had the virtue of fostering and developing the kind of leadership on both sides of the fence which relieved the president of the necessity of trying to be an Argus-eyed supervisor of everything that was going on. In the years since 1948, evolution has changed the system in many ways, some for the better and some for the worse, but I doubt very much whether the faculty would ever vote to do away with it.

There were other organizational changes that I would have initiated in November, 1948, had there been any chance of their being adopted. The most important of these was the unification of the Bursar's Office and the Treasurer's Office. The former operated on campus and the latter down town, and the collaboration between them was rather ineffectual. The opportunity came a few years later to locate both offices side by side in the Whitman Memorial Building and link them together as interacting parts of one business organization. This was not as spectacular, but in some ways it was more important to the welfare of the institution than the reorganization of the curricular and co-curricular machinery of the College.

From Two Years to Eleven

By its own terms, as I have previously explained, my tenure as president was to expire at commencement, 1950, by which time, it was presumed by the terms of my appointment, a permanent president would have been chosen. Expecting to step out in 1950, I was in a good deal of a hurry to get certain things done before that time. But as things turned out I served as president for eleven years, and retired voluntarily at commencement, 1959. I could have gone on several years longer if I had chosen to do so.

Mr. D. F. Baker, President of the Board of Trustees, was chairman of the committee which was supposed to find my successor. He had appointed the committee under a resolution of the Board of Trustees which stipulated that he should be its chairman. I took it for granted that the committee was at work and made my plans accordingly. At the annual meeting of the two governing boards, in 1950, I called attention to the fact that my appointment was about to expire and said I was ready to step out. Thereupon Mr. Baker spoke up and said there was no one to take my place, as his committee had never had a meeting and had nothing to report. I was then asked if I would be willing to continue, and I replied that I would go on for another year. A motion was then made and passed that I be reappointed president for the year 1950-51. When the end of that year came, I once more called attention to the forthcoming vacancy in the office of president. Mr. Baker then said that his committee still had not met and probably never would.

I was then offered a permanent appointment but declined it with thanks. I said I would be willing to continue on a year-to-year basis, provided it were clearly understood that the governing boards reserved the right to drop me at the end of any year and I reserved the right on my own volition to quit at the end of any year. To make this more than nominal, I insisted that the question of my reappointment be submitted for action at every annual meeting, and it was. I was re-elected every year from 1950 to 1958, and refused re-election in 1959.

At first glance this would seem to be an awkward and instable basis for collaboration between governing boards and their chief executive, but I liked it and the Trustees and Overseers seemed to accept it as one of my pardonable peculiarities. I liked it because I always knew where I stood. Every year I either got a vote of confidence or I did not. If I did get the vote of confidence, and I always did, I felt that I was in a stronger position to push forward with future plans. Had I ever failed to get the vote of confidence, I would have gladly given up the office of president and gone back to teaching. A college president has to row upstream most of the time, and if he has to row in uncertainty as to whether he has the unqualified support of his governing authorities, his job will be impossibly difficult. I did not love being president enough to want to continue against odds of that magnitude.

Being on a one-year basis did not make much difference in the way I conducted the office, but it did have one result that I did not bother to explain to any one. That had to do with the president's house on the campus. Mrs. Anderson and her daughter Shirley quite properly had been allowed to remain in the president's mansion to the end of the year 1948-49. Since my appointment was to expire in 1950, Elnora and I decided that it would not be worthwhile to occupy the president's home for one year only. Every year thereafter the same question arose and we arrived at the same answer. Since we would always be temporary tenants, we did not want to make an investment in furnishing the president's mansion and did not wish to put the College to the expense of making the alterations we would want if we were to occupy the house. So I told the Board of Trustees that we preferred our own home, which was true for the most part, and that the College needed the building more urgently for dormitory use than for a president's residence, which was also true at that time. There were times when we would have been in a bad jam if we could not have used the president's house to take care of the dormitory overflow.

If I had known in November, 1948, that my two years would stretch into eleven, would I have accepted the appointment? It is hard to answer that question retrospectively, but from what I can recall of my thinking and feeling in the fall of 1948, I am inclined to believe that I would not have taken the presidency under those circumstances.

XXII. MATERIAL THINGS

The Financial Record

My appointment as president was not hailed with expressions of confidence from any quarter. There was no reason why it should have been. I myself looked upon it as a stop-gap appointment, so did the governing boards, so did most of the faculty, and so likewise, I am sure, did most of the alumni and other friends of the College. No one expected me to do anything more than avert a serious crisis, and the very least of all expectations was that I would be able to do anything to better the financial condition of the College. In respect to fund-raising I would have heartily agreed with this estimate of my potential as a president. I had had only one brief experience with fund-raising and this had been a distinctly small-scale affair. I had not had the kind of training that seemed to bear any relation to fund-raising, and I just naturally disliked asking people for money. I did not consider myself a halfway good salesman for any cause or commodity.

But in all other aspects of finance I knew I was well trained— far better than was generally realized. In previous portions of this book I have told of my two years with the New York Bureau of Municipal Research. In my work with that pioneer institute of public administration I had received theoretical instruction and practical experience in corporate finance, both public and private, that could not have been excelled anywhere in America. I had no worries about such things as budgeting, purchasing, accounting, funding, and property management because I had been through the mill in those matters. But the mill did not include fund-raising, and at the Trustee-Overseer meeting when I was elected I frankly said that I knew nothing about fund-raising and could make no promises in that regard except that I would work hard at the job. Working hard was the sum-total of what I knew about raising money, and I did intend that my two years should include every exertion I could muster in trying to get money for Whitman College. I did live up to that intention, not merely for two years, but for eleven.

The last official financial report before I became president was made on October 14, 1948. My own last report was rendered on June 30, 1959. In tabular form the principal showings of these two reports are as follows:

	October 14, 1948	June 30, 1959
Total invested funds	$1,469,606	$4,979,403
Total Plant funds	546,245	2,561,286
Total indebtedness	188,000	None
Annual income	649,037	1,150,995
Annual expenditures	596,299	1,147,707
Average faculty salary	3,368	6,640
Average administrative salary	2,720	4,954

The magnitude of these gains might suggest that I was a finanical wizard, but I was not. Any of my predecessors could have been a better money-getter than I, if he had so desired. All of them had good success in obtaining gifts when they worked at the business of money-raising, but they did not often work at it. They chose to be occasional and spasmodic rather than persistent and regular fund-raisers. President Penrose said to me more than once that he thought it was a mistake to be always asking for money. He thought it irritated people and turned them against you. The smart thing to do, he said, was to wait until you were in serious need or had something to dramatize. Then you could really appeal to their emotions; then they would readily open their purses and make substantial gifts. That was exactly the principle he followed, and I think he sincerely believed he was right. Presidents Clemen, Bratton, and Anderson held the same conviction and followed the same practice in fund-raising. When they put their shoulders to the wheel all four of the presidents I have just mentioned had no difficulty in raising goodly sums of money, but their shoulders were so seldom at the wheel that the cumulative result of their labors never grew large.

I detested fund-raising, but I could see that it was Whitman's greatest need and that if the president of the College did not work at it incessantly and unremittingly there was little hope of getting much done. All of my predecessors had been given financial development assistants whose sole work was to carry on active and continuous financial solicitation in behalf of the College. None of these assistants was successful enough to justify his employment. There were several reasons for this, but the chief one, in my judgment, was that the president almost completely erased himself from the fund-raising scene, turning the whole responsibility over to the assistant and taking little part himself until there was a "big push" to be effected. It seemed to me that my only chance of large success in fund-raising lay in keeping the "big push" going all the time, and that was a job that I personally would have to spearhead. No financial secretary, director of development, or other aide to the president could supply the necessary overall leadership to keep financial solicitation going on day after day at an effective pitch. So I took upon myself the responsibility for making the wheels go round. There was not a single day in my eleven-year tenure in which I did not do some work on financial promotion, and many days I did little else.

It would be entirely misleading to convey the impression that I personally did most of the work, for I did not. I had abundant help and wonderful help, but I alone had the responsibility of seeing to it that all of the help was efficiently used. I was the one who had to see that there were no slowdowns or letdowns, that all the loose ends were tied together, that all things fell into place at the right time. To use a football analogy, I was a strategy-planner and signal-caller rather than the ball-carrier, and consequently had to be always on top of the play. Most of my help was volunteer help, which came from the members of the two governing boards, from scores of Whitman alumni, from friends associated with various trusts and foundations, from many business corporations and from well-wishers of Whitman College in all walks of life. Like of all my predecessors, I had a financial assistant much of the time, but unlike them I did not use him for direct solicitation work. I found that I could accomplish far more through volunteer solicitors or direct solicitation myself than by delegating this work to a lieutenant.

Getting volunteers proved to be far easier than I ever would have imagined. When I needed help, which was most of the time, I simply asked for it and it was invariably offered. Resort to high pressure methods was not needed and probably would have failed if tried. My objective was a full-scale solicitation every year, conducted in such a way that all persons on our prospect list received at least three invitations to make a contribution to Whitman College. This objective was always attained, and the results were invariably good. In years when we had special projects, such as Anderson Hall and the Penrose Memorial Library, a special committee was set up to spearhead this particular solicitation, but this was not necessary for the regular annual solicitations. In order to counteract the feeling that repeated annual solicitation was going to the well too often, I made repeated use of the following rationalization: "Every year you and virtually every other citizen of the United States are going to be solicited for gifts. All kinds of organizations and institutions will ask you for money, and you will give to some and not to others. You have that freedom of choice. In exercising that freedom, we hope you will include Whitman in your plans for annual giving, doing as much as you reasonably can each year. By doing this systematically, you will be able in total to help Whitman more largely than would otherwise be possible."

This rationalization was highly successful in the regular annual solicitations, but for the large special gifts necessary for such projects as Anderson Hall and the Penrose Memorial Library direct person-to-person solicitation was needed. Some of this I did myself, but a great deal of it was done by loyal volunteers who happened to be in a better position than I to say the right word at the right time. There seemed to be an unfailing supply of zealous individuals on whom I could count as a committee of one to solicit funds for Whitman College. Even with such wonderful help as I had, a college president is not likely to have much success in getting large gifts if he does not know where to look for them. In this respect I was specially fortunate. "Leads" and "tips" by the score rained down upon me like the fabled manna from heaven, and a surprisingly large number of them paid off. I tried to follow through on every bit of information that came to me, and in doing this I also had the help of many loyal volunteers. To such assistance I can ascribe the following large gifts which came to Whitman between 1948 and 1959:

The Sarah Harris Johnson Trust	$861,877
The Nathaniel and Bessie Usher Fund	371,799
The Ford Foundation Fund	325,593
The Henry and Lorene Copeland Fund	153,320
The Howard J. Knott Trust	123,086
The Carleton and Carolyn Kelley Fund	110,848
The William and Harriet Grimshaw Fund ..	110,000
The Edward A. Paddock Fund	60,564

The foregoing were the largest, but in the range from $5,000 to $25,000 there were many others. I remember, for example, the Grant S. and Etta S. Bond Fund, the William S. and Ella S. Clark Fund, the Arthur F. Douglas Fund, the Sarah Delaney Jenkins Fund, the Metcalf Memorial Fund, the Elbridge and Mary Stuart Fund, and the Guy M. Underwood Fund. I could describe the details by which all of the smaller as well as larger gifts were secured for Whitman, but that would only serve to particularize what I have already said about my dependence on the help of loyal volunteers.

Making Whitman Depression-Proof

Whitman's financial problems could not all be solved by raising money. Something also had to be done to stabilize the annual operation income. This came from four principal sources—annual gifts to current expense, the earnings of invested funds, tuition fees, and charges for board and room in the dormitory facilities. All of these were subject to much fluctuation. Least stable of all were the annual gifts to current expense. It was so difficult to anticipate the amount of these that in the past they had been budgeted by sheer guesswork. Since the guess was often excessive, that item of the budgeted income usually fell short, sometimes with disastrous results. I had seen that happen during the depression and hence was keenly aware of the harm it could work. After much reflection, I concluded that there was only one sure way to budget annual contributions safely, and that was to refrain from budgeting them until you had them actually in hand. To accomplish that, I asked the Board of Trustees to make a rule that all gifts to current expense should be held one year before being spent, or, in other words, should not be budgeted in the fiscal year in which they were received. The Board complied with this request. For that year we tightened our belts and spent none of the current expense gifts. The next year this accumulation of gifts went into the budget, and from that time forward we knew to the exact penny how much our expendable income from annual gifts would be. We never had to guess again. Of course, we did have to adjust our spending according to the annual variations of gift income, but we could tell in advance just exactly how much adjusting would be necessary on this account.

I think I must have had an obsession about the dangers of financial depressions to private colleges. I had seen and experienced enough adversity caused by depressions to impel me to do everything within my power to render Whitman depression-proof. So the next thing I sought to make accurately predictable was endowment income. There was enough variability in the earnings of our invested funds to throw budget estimates badly out of line. To overcome this, I asked the Board of Trustees to allow me to set aside surplus funds until I had accumulated an amount approximately equivalent to one year's income from the College endowment. When that had been done we would impound the endowment income for one year and use the surplus in its place. The Board granted this request. It took several years to hoard enough surplus to do the job, but in the spring of 1958 we had enough to impound the endowment income for 1958-59 and budget the surplus in its place. Then we budgeted the 1958-59 endowment income for the fiscal year 1959-60, and from that time forward it was possible to know a year in advance the exact amount of endowment income which could be budgeted. As in the case of the gift income, the annual expenditures had to be adjusted to the yearly fluctuations of endowment income, but it was an adjustment that could be made without the slightest bit of guessing.

I had a desire to do the same kind of job on tuition income and dormitory charges, but it would have taken several more years of penny-pinching to bring that about, and I had already announced that I would retire in 1959. So I did not undertake to accumulate funds for the purpose of impounding the necessary one year of income from those sources. If that could have been done, it would have rendered Whitman College completely depression-proof. As it is, I would say that Whitman, though not fully depression-proof, is sufficiently deficit-proof to ride out almost any depression that is likely to occur. With one-fifth of its annual income definitely known and actually in hand and the remaining four-fifths coming from student enrollment, a readily ascertainable and measurable source of income, it ought to be possible to avoid calamitous deficits.

Budgeting and Deficit-Financing

Deficit-financing is not solely the result of defective estimates of income; loose practices on the expenditure side of the budget can be equally responsible. The estimating of expenditures should be just as accurate as the estimates of income, and there should be a positive control of spending procedures that will keep expenditures absolutely in line with income. One thing I had been forced to learn from A to Z in the New York Bureau of Municipal Research was the making and administration of budgets—school budgets and city budgets in particular. With this background, I could not help perceiving, long before I became president, what was wrong with budgeting at Whitman. They had the cart before the horse. It had been the practice for many years for the bursar, together with the president to put together an estimate of expenditures for the forthcoming year. This was done mostly by taking the past year's expenditures as a base and guessing how much more or less would be needed for the ensuing year. When these estimates were totalled, the bursar and the president then tried to scratch up enough income to equal the expenditures. What they usually did was to take an average of income of the preceding three years from all sources, and if that did not prove sufficient, they would balance the budget by estimating that enough gifts would be received the next year to offset the deficit. Sometimes the gifts came in, but more often they did not.

The first thing I did with respect to budgeting was to reverse the order of estimating. Before there was any consideration of expenditures, the treasurer and I made a careful and conservative estimate of income for the next year and agreed that we would not submit a budget with expenditures in excess of that amount. Then I set up a budget committee consisting of myself, the two deans, the treasurer, the business manager, and the secretary to the president. As president, I acted as chairman and coordinator of this committee. Each of the other members was responsible for getting estimates of expenditures from division chairmen, department heads, directors of offices, and other officials placed under his jurisdiction. I insisted that all such estimates be supported by documentary proof that they were based on a most careful investigation of needs and costs. We did not allow anybody to guess that it would cost $500 to buy a certain piece of equipment; he was required to cite catalog prices. We did not allow a professor to guess that he would need 100 hours of student labor; he had to explain specifically how he proposed to use the labor. By this means we not only discouraged padding but secured reliable information by which we could intelligently trim the estimates of expenditure if they exceeded our expected income.

It did not take long for this tightening of budgetary procedure to produce results. Despite the fact that the annual expenditures of the College were doubled during my eleven years as president, we did not end a single year without a sizable surplus. For 1958-59, my final year, the surplus was $84,316.12. This was typical—less than some years and more than others, but big enough to give us plenty of unearmarked working capital. Some thought these annual surpluses were by-products of good luck, but there was no luck about them. With our controls over income and expenditures, we could not miss having a surplus at the end of the year. The only question was how large it would be.

Elsewhere I have mentioned the Whitman bond issue of $495,000 for the construction of the heating plant and Lyman and Prentiss halls. Although this had been refinanced in 1936-37, bonds in the amount of $188,000 were still outstanding when I became president. These were sold to be amortized 1959, and the amortization costs were about $20,000 a year. Fred Wilson, Treasurer of the College, and I begrudged every penny we had to budget for this debt service. When we discovered that the bonds were callable before maturity, we began to figure the angles to determine whether it would be advantageous to exercise that right. Our conclusion was that we could save both money and trouble by calling the bonds. By mutual understanding we began to tuck away surplus funds for that purpose. By 1952 we had accumulated the needed amount and got permission from the governing boards to go ahead. At a total cost of $133,530 we retired all of the outstanding bonds, thus releasing $20,000 a year for current use. If it had not been for our airtight budget system, I doubt if it would have been possible to save the money to lift this millstone from our necks. Since 1952 Whitman has been entirely debt free, and I can see no reason why it should ever again need to encumber itself with indebtedness.

Buildings and Grounds

One who did not see the Whitman campus during the 1920's and 1930's cannot even imagine how dilapidated everything was. When President Clemen spoke of "Roman ruins" he was not exaggerating very much. The whole physical plant was terribly in need of rehabilitation in 1934, and President Clemen tried immediately to do something about it; but neither he nor his successor, President Bratton, was able to lay hand on enough money to make much headway against the forces of neglect and deterioration. The financial resources of the College were so limited that there was little to spare for the betterment of buildings and grounds. During President Anderson's administration the acute financial stringency had eased somewhat. President Anderson was able to find money to care for some of the most urgent plant needs, including the construction of the

Student Center, the first new building since 1926. But it was still impossible to carry on a thoroughgoing program of rehabilitation. There just was not enough money to go around.

One of my most gratifying experiences in the office of president was to inaugurate and carry through a complete job of plant rehabilitation. Altogether, during my eleven years, the sum of $777,417 was spent for the rehabilitation of existing buildings and grounds. Of this sum, $525,504 went for various kinds of reconstruction and $251,913 went for new furnishings and equipment. Our total outlay for rehabilitation was $231,172 in excess of the aggregate capital value of the plant when we started our renewal program. I use the word "renewal" advisedly, for it describes precisely what was done. The old buildings were completely overhauled—given new foundations, new floors, new roofs, new wiring, new lighting, new plumbing, new plastering, and in most cases new decor and new furnishings. We tried to replace the old and outworn with the best we could afford in the way of materials, workmanship, and equipment. I think we succeeded in indefinitely prolonging the useful lives of such buildings as Whitman Memorial, the Conservatory, Billings Hall, Reynolds Hall, Lyman Hall, and Prentiss Hall. With proper maintenance there is no reason why they should not be doing useful service when the grandchildren of the present generation of Whitman students come to college.

Whence the money for this rehabilitation job? We never had a special solicitation to raise money for this purpose. Practically all the money we used for plant rehabilitation came from the same source the money used to retire the bonds and put our gift income and endowment income on an absolutely determinable footing. In short, it came out of surplus, and we achieved these annual surpluses through rigorously administered budgetary procedures. I often regretted that it was not possible to use more of these surpluses for educational purposes, but Whitman had fallen so far behind in money and material things that it was imperative to devote most of our surplus funds to the mere task of catching up.

Incredible as it may seem, there was no new construction on

the Whitman campus from 1926 to 1947, a span of twenty-one years. Never before in its entire history had Whitman College gone that long without some sort of new construction. This long drought was broken in 1947 when President Anderson brought the Student Center to completion. This building filled a longstanding need, but other longstanding needs were just as urgent yet seemingly far from realization. In my first annual report, I discussed these in the following language:

From time to time in the past, comprehensive plans have been prepared for future buildings on the campus. Never have we been able to approximate the realization of any of these plans and most of them have been quickly forgotten. Therefore, instead of emphasizing the total future building needs of the College, I prefer to single out three which are almost indispensable if the College is to continue to operate at reasonable efficiency. First on the list is a new library building. If the recent earthquake had been as severe in Walla Walla as it was on the Coast, the Whitman library building probably would have tumbled to ruin. Reynolds Hall is not only spatially inadequate for library purposes, but is becoming structurally dangerous. We have come to the point where we cannot allow the library to grow much more without jeopardizing the safety of those who use the building. I sincerely hope that the members of the Board of Trustees and the Board of Overseers will overlook no opportunity to help Whitman secure the funds needed for a new library building in the very near future.

Next in point of immediate urgency I would place the construction of a new girls' dormitory to complete the housing plans made at the time Prentiss Hall was built. We were sorely pressed for space to house girls when the College enrollment was half its present size. Today we are forced to crowd twice as many girls into the same space as supplemented by such temporary annexes as College House, Green Cottage, and the

President's House, all of which are unsuited to modern dormitory purposes. We clearly face the alternative of drastically reducing our enrollment of girls or providing additional dormitory space for them in the not distant future.

Third in order of urgency is the building of a new gymnasium. The present gymnasium was built when the College had less than 300 students. We are now obliged to use it for over 500 men and 300 women. To say that this precludes the possibility of anything approaching a satisfactory program of athletics and physical education is putting the case mildly indeed.

When I wrote those words in May, 1949 Whitman College could scarcely afford to build a birdhouse. I knew that some persons were saying that I was indulging in pipe dreams. But it seemed to me that if we were ever going to accomplish those results we should begin talking as though we meant business at once. Some persons took pains to remind me that it had been something of a struggle to collect all of the pledges for the Student Center, and advised me to wait a while before launching any more building projects. I had to agree with these advisers that the outlook for a new library, a new gymnasium, and a new girls' dormitory was not exactly bright, but I decided, nevertheless, to keep harping away on basic building needs. Every year my annual report and almost every speech that I made about Whitman College repeated, reiterated, and restated my remarks about new buildings so many times that people must have thought I was laboring under an obsession. Perhaps I was.

Makeshifts

The very best I could do in the spring of 1949 was to alleviate some of our worst space headaches with a makeshift arrangement. Just at that time the United States Government was dismantling the McCaw General Hospital, a war-emergency constellation of frame buildings located on the grounds of the Veterans' Hospital in the west end of the city nearly two miles from the campus. As a means of clearing the site as rapidly as possible the Government was offering to give away buildings to any non-profit organization which would move them off the hospital grounds. Four of these had special interest for us. They had been built and used for nurses dormitories and would be easily adaptable to corresponding uses on the Whitman Campus. They were much more solidly constructed than most of the jerry-built barracks put up by the Government during the war. Competent builders whom we employed to examine them were of the opinion that they should have a useful life of fifteen more years. After getting estimates on the cost of moving, resetting, and otherwise adapting these four buildings for College use, I asked the Board of Trustees to appropriate $50,000 for this purpose. For the expenditure of this sum, I expected to get two dormitories, a faculty office building, and a campus theater.

The Board was somewhat hesitant about putting this much money into frame buildings, and I did not fault its judgment on that score, but we were so hard up for space that I finally said that we had a choice of two solutions. One was the removal of the McCaw buildings to the campus and the other was to curtail enrollment in the amount of some 200 students. Our enrollment that year was 866, and we were woefully short of dormitory space, classroom space, and office space. Lyman and Prentiss Hall were full to overflowing and so were our three small annexes. Whitman Memorial was a rabbit's warren of classrooms and offices. Faculty members could not have individual offices; two to four would be crowded sardine-like into one little cubby-hole partitioned off from a classroom. All of the classes for Divisions I and II and part of those from Division III met in Memorial Building, and there were so many classes for so few rooms that it was almost impossible to set up a workable schedule of classes. Since these were conditions and not theories, the Board granted my request. In the summer of 1949 the four McCaw buildings were moved to College property on the west side of Penrose Avenue. The total cost of the project was $47,500, and in my annual report for 1949-50 I made the following comment on the benefits already realized.

As a result of this outlay we have four substantial buildings which have greatly eased the pressure for space. Two of the buildings have been used as dormitory annexes for women and have proved very satisfactory. The third building has been used as a faculty office building, and has supplied the members of the faculty with more and better space than was available to them in the cramped quarters of the Whitman Memorial Building. The fourth was remodeled to serve as a campus theater. For many years the Dramatics Department has been working under the serious handicap of having no place to store equipment, costumes, and other materials; no rehearsal space; and no auditorium for small performances. For a small outlay we have provided a theater which meets all of the essential requirements for the teaching of dramatics and the presentation of dramatic and musical performances on the campus.

Fifteen years proved to be a low guess for the useful life of these four buildings. As I write these lines in 1963 all except the theater, which burned, are still in use after fourteen years of yeoman service to Whitman, and they are in good enough condition to serve some useful purpose for several years more. The net earnings from the two dormitories have been more than sufficient to repay the orginal costs of removal. Much as I have always disliked stop-gap arrangements, I have been obliged to recognize that this one was fully justified.

The next stop-gap construction job was described as follows in my report for the year 1951-52:

The acute danger of fire and also of structural collapse in Reynolds Hall was sharply highlighted in my annual report a year ago. To avert these hazards the Trustees last summer authorized the construction of a fireproof stackroom as an annex to the present building. This structure was finished before the end of the first semester. By gradual stages since then the major part of the library collection of books, documents, and papers has been moved into the annex. This temporarily solves the problem of fire and structural collapse, but it does not solve the library problem. We need a new building as much as ever.

This Reynolds Hall annex is the one serious eyesore that I left on the Whitman Campus. This I have always regretted, but could see no other choice at the time. A new library building seemed decades away, and there was increasing evidence daily that the walls and beams of Reynolds Hall would not carry the weight of 60,000 books and 110,000 documents much longer. We dared not procrastinate. I have always regarded the $12,000 we sank in that hideous concrete box as insurance rather than an addition to the plant. Still it did meet an urgent need and serve a useful purpose for several years. It did safely house our priceless collection of books and documents until we got the Penrose Memorial Library, and since then it has rendered useful service as a classroom. Nevertheless, I hope the time may come when it will be given an honorable discharge and be removed from the scene.

Anderson Hall

I hated to give anything priority over a new library building, but in 1953 we were suddenly faced with a non-postponable crisis in the housing of women students. During the war Lyman House had been occupied by the Navy V-12 unit, and when that use ended, Lyman was converted into a dormitory for freshmen women. This was continued until the fall of 1949, when Lyman was restored to its original function as a dormitory for freshmen men. This was made possible by the acquisition of the McCaw buildings, two of which, as I have already related, were used as dormitories for women. Still there was an overflow of women students, and to provide dormitory space for them we rented a section of the Odd Fellows Home and christened it College House. Immediately there were so many complaints from the parents of girls resident in College House that we made

374

a quick switch by which the women were brought back to Lyman and the freshmen men shifted to College House and the two McCaw dormitories, which we had named Davis and Jacobs respectively. This makeshift satisfied the parents of girls but not the parents of boys. However, we were prepared to live with it until we could come up with something better, when, unexpectedly, in 1953 the Odd Fellows notified us that they would not renew our lease of College House for 1954-55. They had decided to tear the building down and use the site for a new building devoted to their own needs.

This spelled big trouble. Within one year we had to find ample housing for at least one hundred students or reduce the College enrollment by that number. The latter would have been a calamity, but the former presented a problem that could be solved only by constructing a new dormitory. There was no rental space available for a hundred students anywhere in Walla Walla or vicinity. Our dilemma was presented to the Board of Trustees at the regular meeting in March, 1953, just a few days after the Odd Fellows had given us notice of non-renewal. The Board voted to form two joint committees of Trustees and Overseers to take the lead in the effort to provide a new dormitory. One committee (composed of Henry J. Copeland, F. Lowden Jones, W. Lawrence Minnick, and Donald Sherwood) was to conduct the financial drive and the other (composed of Clarence Braden, Harold E. Crawford, Herbert Ringhoffer, and W. L. Teague) was to be responsible for the planning and construction of the building. The president of the Board of Trustees, the president of the College, and the bursar were made *ex officio* members of both committees. Mr. Crawford donated his services as architect for the proposed dormitory. Both committees began an immediate series of meetings and prepared recommendations for the annual joint meeting of the two governing boards on May 30. The financial committee recommended that we proceed at once to raise funds for the new dormitory, and the construction committee presented tentative plans which it asked to have approved as the basis for construction bids as soon as sufficient money should be available. The recommendations of both committees were promptly adopted.

Several years earlier, Mrs. Agnes H. Anderson of Seattle had made the College a gift of $165,000 with the stipulation that it be used in the construction of a dormitory for women. It had been held in suspense for two reasons: (1) during World War II building materials for private construction were not to be had; (2) the amount was insufficient to underwrite as large a building as Whitman needed. It was providential, however, that it was on tap and readily available in 1953. It gave us a wonderful running start on the total amount of $450,000 which the construction committee's estimates placed as the cost of the building we wanted. Instead of having to raise $450,000, we needed only $285,000, and our financial committee did such a bang-up job that we were able to call for bids in the fall of 1953.

It was decided to locate the new building south of Prentiss Hall, where the original Whitman College athletic field had been. It was also decided that instead of separate kitchen and dining facilities in the new building, we would double the capacity of the existing facilities in Prentiss Hall and serve both dormitories with one operation. This required a separate contract for the construction of an annex on the east side of Prentiss. These two construction jobs were completed without a hitch and both the dormitory and the enlarged food service facilities were ready for use on the opening day of College, September 13, 1954. The total cost of both was $435,461, nearly $15,000 less than had been estimated for the dormitory alone.

Since the late Mrs. Anderson was the largest donor and the new dormitory would have been impossible without her gift, it was named in her honor. It was planned to house 150 freshmen women, and most of the planning was done by a committee under the chairmanship of Miss Miriam Wagenschein, Director of Student Affairs for Women. Associated with her were graduate and undergraduate members of all of the women's social groups on the campus, a professor of art, a professional

376

interior decorator, and the purchasing agent of the College. Harold Crawford, the architect, and I often sat with this committee, but as far as possible we let the committee make all of the important decisions. This was not because we lacked ideas of our own, but because we thought first consideration should be given to the ideas of those who had had living experience with dormitories for women. If it had been a dormitory for men, we doubtless would have spoken our opinions more emphatically. I am glad we let the women have what they wanted, even though what they wanted may not have been the right thing. What Harold and I wanted might have been far worse. There is only one thing I know for certain about dormitories, whether for men or women, namely, that nobody has ever been smart enough to build one that was completely satisfactory to its successive generations of occupants and administrators.

The Penrose Memorial Library

Year by year the deficiencies of Reynolds Hall as a library became more unbearable. By 1955 it had become clear that if we could not have a new building, it would be necessary to add another ugly annex as well as spend a large sum to renovate the interior of the old building. In the March, 1955, issue of *Facets*, a semi-occasional news bulletin put out by my office, I described the library predicament as follows:

> The other evening I told a group of alumni that Whitman College has one very black eye. A first-rate college cannot long remain first-rate if its library is slipping down hill, and ours is. Reynolds Hall in its heyday was a pretty good dormitory for women, about as good as they came in the early 1900's. But if it has any redeeming features as a library building, I have not heard of them. The library migrated to Reynolds in 1935 from an old shack abutting Memorial. Nobody supposed that twenty years later it would still be trying to make do with an old parlor as a stack room, an old

377

dining hall as a reading room, an old kitchen as a periodicals room, and old student quarters for every purpose from storage to offices.

"Make do" cannot do the job much longer. Pretty soon we will have to stop buying books, even accepting gifts. No place to put them. Fire is a constant hazard and serious threat, and there is a lot of good old resinous fir in Reynolds that would make a blaze to remember. A library is for students to use. Our students cannot all use the library without stepping on each other's toes or sitting in each others laps. There is not room for more than a third of them to be in the library at one time.

I was making remarks of that tenor wherever I went in the spring of 1955, and in the Trustee's meetings and regional Overseers' meetings I bore down harder than anywhere else. I warned them that when the annual meeting came I would present them with a choice—either to go all out at once for a new library building or pour thousands of dollars into a patch-up job on Reynolds. I carried out this threat, and pointed out that no matter how much we might spend on Reynolds Hall, we could never convert it into a library facility that any accrediting agency would commend. After a general debate on the question, it was moved and passed that we proceed at once to raise money for a new library building which should be named the Penrose Memorial Library. Harold E. Crawford was appointed architect for the building, and Donald Sherwood and Harper Joy were named co-chairmen of the Gifts Committee.

As part of the solicitation program I wrote and published in November, 1955, an eightpage brochure in which there was a laudatory sketch of Dr. and Mrs. Penrose, an explanation of Whitman's critical need for a new library building, a description of the proposed Penrose Memorial building, and some detail as to our financial prospects and objectives. With respect to the latter I said in part:

In 1936, by the will of Edward D. Baldwin of the Class of 1906, securities worth about $66,000 were bequeathed to

Whitman College on condition that they be used to help build a Penrose Memorial Library. Final settlement of the Baldwin Estate was not obtained until 1942, by which time, owing to World War II, it was impossible to build. Various circumstances, including the Korean War, caused further delays. However, the Baldwin Fund was kept intact and judiciously invested. It is now worth more than $200,000. With this as a starter, the Trustees and Overseers are moving forward to raise the additional funds needed to bring the Penrose Memorial Library into reality. Members of the two boards themselves have already subscribed upwards of $175,000 to this end.

Thanks to the leadership of Donald Sherwood and Harper Joy, the money came in so speedily and generously that we were able to begin construction early in March, 1956. In *Facets* I reported this event as follows:

> After losing several bouts to the weather gods, we finally had a formal ground-breaking ceremony for the Penrose Memorial Library on March 2. It rained, but we defied the weather and went ahead.

On March 1, 1957, one year lacking a day from the date of groundbreaking ceremonies, we moved into the Penrose Memorial Library. I declared a holiday on the campus, and students and faculty organized themselves into a gigantic taskforce which literally piggybacked every book, pamphlet, and other item from the old library building to the new. My joy in that occasion was much heightened by the fact that the Penrose Memorial Library was more than completely paid for before we moved in. Our estimated cost for the building fully equipped had been approximately $600,000. We were able to do the job for slightly less than $500,000. Including the liquidated Baldwin Fund our total cash available for the construction and equipment of the Penrose Memorial Library was $529,630. Having finished the job with an overage of some $30,000, we decided to use $10,000 of this amount as a construction reserve to pay for things that might have been overlooked in the original planning. The balance of nearly $20,000 was given to the library for the purchase of basic books, *i.e.,* important books and sets of books that had been passed by in former years on account of lack of funds and space.

In the case of the Penrose Library, as with Anderson Hall, I did my best to let the library staff make the controlling decisions as to floor plans and service facilities. Miss Ruth Reynolds, Librarian, was made chairman of the planning committee, which, in addition to members of the library staff, included members of the faculties of Divisions I, II, and III. The architect the business manager, and I were ex officio members of this committee. Subject to the limitations of our funds and our building site, we tried to give the library and faculty people what they thought would best serve their own needs and those of the College. The result was very pleasing to some people and less so to others, but that would have ensued no matter who did the planning or what kind of building resulted from it.

The Science Building

In August, 1957, five months after we moved into the Penrose Library, I started beating the drums for a new science building. In the issue of *Facets* for that month I said:

> If I could get a million dollars, Whitman could have a new science building. If a new science building would do proportionately as much to serve the needs of science instruction in the future as Billings Hall has done in the past, American industry can ill afford to let Whitman go without the necessary million dollars. Scientists trained in Billings Hall have added enough to the earning power of American industry to pay for scores of buildings for the teaching of science. But you and I know that American industry is not so constituted as to make long-shot investments in education. If I ever get the million dollars, I am going to have to beg for them and beg hard.

One reason for this remark was that I had learned from experience that *Facets* was read by many people who were not on our mailing list and I felt certain some of these might become interested in a new science building for Whitman College. We had reached the point where we had to make a choice between trying for a new science building or settling for some sort of makeshift. There were two possible stop-gap solutions, either one of which might have enabled us to get along for several years without a new science building. One was to construct an annex to Billings Hall, which, according to my estimates, could be done for about $100,000. The other was to spend about the same amount refurbishing Reynolds Hall and move one or two of the sciences into that building.

Shortly after College opened in the fall of 1957 I met with the faculty of the Division of Basic Sciences to discuss these various possibilities. I told them candidly that if they would accept one of the makeshift solutions, they could have their additional space in a year's time, but if they insisted on a new building, they might have to wait six or eight years. It would take at least a million dollars to construct a suitable science building, and I knew it would take much longer than a year to raise that sum of money. It would not come as easily or as quickly as money for Anderson Hall and the Penrose Library. Without a dissenting word or vote, the faculty of Division III went for all or nothing. They said they would rather wait a dozen years than accept either of the stop-gap plans I had offered. I did not try to dissuade them, because I thought their preference was right, provided they could manage with Billings until a new building could be financed and built. They thought they could, and I deferred to their judgment.

Our best hope for quick money in large sums was to secure a grant from one of the big educational foundations. I felt sure there was a possibility of getting substantial help from several of these. In fact, off the record, I had been told by officers of some of the leading foundations that they would welcome applications from Whitman for grants in aid for a science building. However, there was only one foundation which made a practice of assuming the total cost of a building, namely, the Olin Foundation. If we could get a grant from this foundation, it might not be necessary to spend several years accumulating a fund made up of small gifts. So, with the approval and collaboration of the science faculty, I decided to file an immediate application with the Olin Foundation. Correspondence with the officers of the Foundation encouraged me to make haste. I appointed a faculty committee under the chairmanship of Professor Glen J. Woodward, and, with the assistance of this committee, I was able to submit our application to the Olin Foundation on November 27, 1957. In my annual report the following commencement, I commented on this action as follows:

> Should this application prove successful, our problem will be solved. Should it fail, we will be under the necessity of seeking other sources, no doubt many other sources, for there is little likelihood of finding a single donor, individual or corporate, from whom so large an amount could be expected.

Everyone who has dealt with the big educational foundations can testify that they are all alike in one respect: they can't be hurried. They take their own sweet time in making decisions, no matter how urgent the need of the applicant. I was sure we would not get a reply from the Olin Foundation in less than a year, and we did not. I made use of various corporate connections that might conceivably expedite action on our application, but none were successful. I did not want to withdraw the application without knowing whether our chances were good or poor, but I could not get a hint one way or the other. The only thing I could do was to keep the Olin application alive but at the same time take steps to establish a science building fund to which interested persons might make contributions. My recollection is that this fund had reached four or five thousand dollars when I retired in 1959. Thus the science building job was left to my successor to finish, and I have been thrilled and delighted at the way he responded to the challenge and with the great success he has achieved.

Additions and Acquisitions

When the science faculty plumped for a new building rather than a temporary palliative, it was my intention to use the money I would have invested in Billings or Reynolds, or both, to do something toward enlarging and modernizing the gymnasium. I had enough money on hand to make a good start and felt sure that it could be doubled or trebled with no great effort. Unfortunately, cirumstances forced my hand in other directions. One of these circumstances was a crisis in the operation of the Student Center because of insufficient space for the book store, for group meetings, and for the storage of necessary supplies and inventories. To remedy this critical situation, we added, in the summer of 1957, a south wing to the Student Center Building. By enclosing the open terrace on the south and excavating a full basement beneath, we gained enough space to keep the Student Center operation on an even keel for a few years though not enough for a permanent solution of its space problems.

The second circumstance that forced my hand was the burning of the Whitman Theater on March 13, 1958. Our insurance coverage was ample to rebuild the theater "as was." But by spending more money for a redesigned and enlarged theater, it appeared possible to provide a facility which would serve both the Department of Dramatics and the whole campus community far better than the original theater building could. This was brought before the Trustees and Overseers, who thought it the wise thing to do and authorized me to go ahead with a new theater building. The outlay for this project absorbed so much money that I had to forget about the gymnasium. In a way I was glad to be relieved of the responsibility for the gymnasium. I had not been able to see eye to eye with any of the physical education people on that. My ideal of a physical education plant for Whitman was a gymnasium for women situated south of Anderson Hall and an appropriate enlargement of the old gymnasium for the exclusive use of men. But the physical education people talked me out of this. In their opinion it was sheer folly.

In *Facets* for December, 1956, I made this announcement:

A new dimension has been added to the campus of Whitman College through the purchase of the Louis F. Anderson property. Other new dimensions are also in prospect. The College hopes to acquire other properties adjoining the campus, and has already purchased two in the block across Boyer from the Conservatory of Music. The plan is to enlarge the campus sufficiently to meet all modern needs and still preserve the beauty and spaciousness for which the Whitman campus has long been noted.

The Louis F. Anderson property and its beautifully colonnaded mansion had long been sought by the College. For a long time it seemed to be taken for granted that it would be bequeathed, but I never believed that because I remembered a violent falling-out between the Andersons and the Board of Trustees at a time when a deal for the purchase of the property almost went through. After reading a copy of the letter the Andersons wrote to the Board, I had no hope that either would ever bequeath their property to Whitman College. In fact, I feared that they might not even be willing to sell it to Whitman. About all I could do was to keep reminding them that there was a new order of things at Whitman, and that all the surrounding circumstances were different than when the first deal fell through. I had known both of them so well for so many years that I could do this without offense. After Professor Anderson's death, Mrs. Anderson became more agreeable to the idea of selling, and in the summer of 1956 she asked the College to make an offer. After a brief round of negotiations an agreement was reached whereby the College would buy the property subject to the right of Mrs. Anderson to occupy it on a rental basis as long as she wished. In order to raise the cash for the Anderson purchase, the College sold to the Roman Catholic diocese the tract of land now occupied by the De Sales High School. Whitman had been holding that property for thirty years. Once there had been a dream of using it as the site of a new athletic field and gymnasium, but those plans never worked out. Finally, I asked our athletic and physical education people for a conclusive judgment of its value for that purpose. Their answer was entirely unfavorable. They said it was the last place they would want to locate a new athletic plant. Then I recommended that the Trustees sell it.

I also recommended that in addition to the L. F. Anderson property certain other properties adjacent to the campus be acquired as soon as possible. Some of these were acquired before my retirement. Several others have been bought since.

XXIII. WORKING WITH THE FACULTY

The Faculty Attitude

It is said that no man is a hero to his valet. With equal truth it could be said that no president is a hero to his faculty. This would be true, perhaps even more true, if the faculty chose its own president. Faculties are inclined to take a dim view of presidents not so much because they dislike presidents as persons as that they hate the power embodied in the president's office. Most college and university presidents do have a good deal of power—never as much as the faculty members imagine, but always enough to lend plausibility to their imaginings. Most presidents exercise their power with moderation and justice, but most faculties find this hard to believe. Faculty people don't like to be coordinated, don't like to work in teams, don't like to comply with rules and regulations, don't like to function as organization men. One of the president's principal jobs is to see to it that faculty members do a lot of things that go against their grain. Most presidents do not enjoy this task at all, but it is natural for faculty men to take it for granted that the president takes delight in throwing his weight around.

Since the Whitman faculty had not been consulted or in any way represented in my selection as president, I could not assume that I was "the peoples' choice" or anything of the sort. I had never made any special effort to cultivate faculty members or done anything much to give offense to any of them. As a matter of fact, my career as a Whitman professor and dean had not been faculty-oriented. I had done my job to the best of my

385

ability, but I had no specially close friends or professional associates on the Whitman faculty and I was so much involved in off-campus activities that I sometimes felt more at home in that work than in my Whitman duties. Aside from chaperoning student parties, Elnora and I never had become involved in social life at Whitman. Nearly all of the friends we "partied" with and visited back and forth with were townspeople. This had come about in a perfectly normal and natural way. When we first came on the Whitman faculty we were so much younger than most of the professors and their wives that neither we nor they tried to make close friendships. There was mutual cordiality and correctness, but no closeness. On the other hand, we had many opportunities to make warm and constant friendships with townspeople of our own age group, and we made full use of these opportunities. As the years went by, our friends among the townspeople continued to be our best friends, and we found little occasion to seek friends on the faculty.

Perhaps the foregoing will help explain why the faculty attitude toward my appointment as president was not conspicuously enthusiastic. I was not one of them, really; few of them knew me well enough to have definite opinions; and, since they did not know what to expect, they expected nothing of any consequence. In a way this worked to my advantage, because I did not have to live up to any anticipations or advance notices. On the other hand, since I was an indeterminate quantity in their minds, they naturally did not look to me for leadership.

One of the first things I had to do was to assert leadership. Earlier in these pages I have described the reorganization plan which was adopted in my first two weeks as president. Fortunately for me, the need for reorganization was so obvious and so urgent that no opposition developed. Under the new organization the role of the faculty was much enhanced. Not only was the jurisdiction of the faculty extended; ten important positions in the new organization were filled by faculty balloting. This meant more opportunity for faculty participation and faculty eminence in the affairs of the institution. My stock rose accordingly—rose higher than it should have, because a good many faculty members seemed to gain the impression that the new president would be an easy-going executive.

I did not think of myself as either easy-going or hard-nosed. I sincerely wanted the faculty to be a more active and vital factor in the operation of the College, but there were certain matters that I thought should be given over to the faculty and certain issues on which I was prepared, if need be, to do battle with the faculty. In some of these particulars I had a good deal of trouble with the Whitman faculty members and they with me.

Salaries

When I hear college professors described as selfless idealists who care nothing for money, I wonder where I have been all these years. If there are any people who fret and fume more about salaries than the brethren of the faculty, I have not met them. Three things, commonly, are wrong with every professor's salary: (1) It is too low. (2) High or low, it is not as much as he is sure he is worth. (3) It is less than one or more of his colleagues, no more deserving than he, are getting. I had not warmed the presidential chair more than a few weeks when my education with respect to faculty salaries began in earnest. It began with individuals who came asking for salary increases. Sometimes they just asked and hoped. Sometimes they asked and argued. And sometimes they asked and threatened. To all these suppliants I said in substance the same three things: 1) That it was my intention to pay the highest salaries the budgetary resources of Whitman College would permit. (2) That it was my intention to fix salaries on the basis of merit, *as determined by me.* (3) That I would never increase a salary as the result of any pressure, threat, or duress. To everyone who complained about his salary, I made it clear that I would sooner accept his resignation than give him special treatment. If he had, or claimed to have, the offer of a higher salary elsewhere, I always advised him to take it, at the same time telling him that I would rather replace him than compete for him.

It was not long before I got the reputation of being a tough nut to crack. Although I was not striving for such a reputation, I was not sorry to have it. It spared me many a painful interview. It also helped me gain a freer hand in dealing with the salary problem than I would have had with the reputation of being a "soft touch" on salary matters. In setting individual salaries, I was determined to have a free hand, not because I wanted to dominate but because divided responsibility in that particular would inevitably end in turmoil and chaos. On that score I had to do battle with certain members of the Board of Trustees as well as members of the faculty. Certain members of the Board argued that it was the right of the Board to fix every salary paid by Whitman College. I conceded that they were right from the standpoint of law, but maintained that they were wrong from the standpoint of sound institutional practice. How could they expect the president to function as chief executive if every employee were impelled to go over his head and appeal to the Board in salary matters? They said this would not happen because the Board would back the president in carrying out its salary determinations. And I replied that the correct way would be for the Board to back the President's salary determinations, because the president was in a better position to make fair and realistic determinations. My contention was that the Board should adopt a salary scale to which the president should strictly adhere, but the individual salaries paid under that scale should be conclusively determined by the president. It was finally agreed to do it that way, but I had to put my foot down and refuse to do it their way. Some members of the Board were never convinced that I was right, but went along because they did not want to fire me.

Certain members of the faculty advanced the proposal that all salaries be fixed by the Faculty Council or a special faculty committee. I absolutely refused, and the Board backed me. The dangers of faculty salary-fixing did not have to be explained to the Board members; they could sense those dangers without half trying. I even refused to share the responsibility of fixing salaries with the deans and division chairmen, because I feared it would cause more headaches than it would cure. In making appointments and promotions I took counsel with the deans always, and often with the division chairmen, and almost invariably followed their recommendations. But when it came to salaries, I was convinced that the sole responsibility should be on the president. I repeatedly said that it was far better for the morale of the institution to have a single scapegoat and far better for everybody concerned to be able to pinpoint the responsibility for salaries on the one officer of the College who could not pass the buck. I still think I was right. There were times when I had to take a beating on account of salaries, but I think the beatings would have been more and worse if the grievances had been magnified by going through committees or subordinate administrative officials before centering on the president.

With respect to general salary scales it was easy always to be on the side of the angels. In my first annual report I asked for funds to increase salaries, and managed to eke out enough for a two per cent increase across the board. There were so many demands for money that the best thing I could hope to do was to lift salaries a little bit every year. I was successful in doing this, and in 1954 I made a progress report in the following words:

Five years ago the average full-time salary at Whitman was $3,368 for the academic year; the same average for 1953-54 is $4,320. Obviously we have been making progress. Unfortunately the salary scale was too low five years ago. What we have accomplished in the past five years is more in the nature of catching up than getting ahead.

Catching up was our principal job throughout the whole range of Whitman affairs. I was accused, perhaps justly, of moving more slowly in respect to salaries than with other catching-up jobs. Two years later, however, I was able to report greater progress. The following is what I had to say:

The budget for 1956-57 includes a substantial amount for salary increases. Under this budget, Whitman's outlay for salaries and wages will be 87 per cent more than it was eight years ago. It is a pleasure to report this progress, because it reflects salary increases and not an increase in the number of employees.

I had not yet made proportionate progress in rehabilitating the physical plant or underpinning the financial security of the College, but it was hard to explain that clearly. People could see with their own eyes what was being done in plant improvements; they could read about such financial transactions as calling the bonds and building up reserve funds; but what went into the pockets of a faculty member was known to him alone, unless he chose to disclose it. When I reported a salary gain of 87 per cent in eight years, the news, though gratifying, was an abstraction for most people, faculty members no less than others.

In 1956 I asked the Trustees and Overseers to set a minimum of $5,000 and a maximum of $10,000 as definite and immediate salary goals for Whitman College. The boards complied with this request, and I began looking for the additional $50,000 of dependable annual income necessary to achieve those goals. This proved to be less difficult than I had anticipated, and at commencement, 1958, I was able to announce that the $5,000-$10,000 salary scale would go into operation on July 1, 1958. At the same time I made the following comment:

A report published by the United States Office of Education on March 4, 1958, gives the average minimum and maximum salaries for private colleges and unversities as $4,230 and $7,360 respectively. In the same report the average minimum and maximum salaries for tax-supported institutions are given as $5,110 and $8,350. The Whitman minimum and maximum salaries for 1958-59 will be some $900 greater than those for private institutions generally and will compare most favorably with those for tax-supported institutions. Ten years ago the minimum faculty salary at Whitman was $1,800 and the maximum was $3,750.

The fact that our 1958-59 salary scale was better than the average for private institutions and substantially the same as the average for tax-supported institutions did not mean that Whitman salaries were as good as they should be and would certainly need to be in the future. But it did mean that we were no longer at the rear of the procession. We had moved up into the front ranks, and our next job would be to move up to being consistently as good as the best.

It often seemed to me that the more progress I made in boosting faculty salaries the more bitterly I was accused of favoritism. Possibly it is true that people are more likely to resent fancied discriminations in good salaries than in poor ones. I would not know about that, but I do know that there were just as many discriminations when Whitman salaries were disgracefully low as when they were raised to respectable levels. Discriminations of some sort are unavoidable, no matter what the salary scale. No two faculty members are equal in merit or worth to an institution, and whether one tries to differentiate on the basis of quality or to treat all the same, inequalities of some kind are bound to result.

I chose to differentiate on the basis of quality and openly said I did not intend to treat everybody alike. This, necessarily, made me the final judge of quality but I offered time and again, in the presence of the faculty, to be guided by any objective system of evaluation and rating the faculty could agree upon. I went even farther and appointed a representative faculty committee to study personnel evaluation and rating systems and present recommendations to the faculty. In spite of several nudgings from me, this committee never made a report. Every time I called for their report, the reply was that the committee was not quite ready. What I suspected was that so many disagreements had arisen within the committee that no report would ever be forthcoming. None was prior to my retirement.

The accusation that I played favorites was true, I always tried to favor the faculty members and other employees whom I judged most deserving from the standpoint of the value of their services to Whitman. Some of these were people I liked and others were people I disliked. Some of those I liked most as individuals I did the least for, and some I could hardly stand as individuals I did the most for. These discriminations were based, of course, on my own value judgments. My value judgments were not infallible, and I never allowed myself to imagine that they were. I did believe, however, and still do, that as president I was in a better position to evaluate all aspects of a faculty member's worth to the College than any other officer or than any group or committee. Not only did I have more sources of information; I also had better means of knowing how easy or difficult he would be to replace. Insisting upon exclusive authority in the fixing of individual salaries was insisting upon the right to be autocratic. I had no illusions about that, but I think there are some things that can best be settled autocratically. The whim of a committee is no less whimsical than the whim of an autocrat, and it can throw a great deal more sand into the gears of an organization. And there is no more damaging sand than grievances over salaries. I thought it better for the chief executive to be the only one accountable for such grievances, because he should be better able to cope with them.

Tenure

The most sacred of the several sacred cows worshipped by college professors is tenure. Faculty people commonly construe tenure to mean the right to hang on to a job as long as they wish, coupled with a correlative right to quit whenever they choose. They feel they should have their bread buttered on both sides, and this perquisite they treasure even more than money. Security is the greatest of all faculty passions, the one for which most professors are ready both to fight and to starve. If forced to choose between salary and security, they give security the highest priority. Furthermore, they make assumptions regarding security that they would not think of making as to salary.

Having been a Whitman faculty member twenty-three years before I became president, I knew full well that no tenure regulations of any sort had ever been adopted by the governing boards, the faculty, or any combination of the two. What I did not realize was that most faculty members thought they had full rights of tenure regardless of the lack of any express legislation. They took it for granted that tenure was an inherent and inalienable right that belonged to them just because they were college professors. If asked to supply a legal basis for this, most would have answered that it was implied in their contract of employment with Whitman College. It had not been the practice of Whitman to enter into formal written contracts with its faculty members, and the only evidence of any agreement, express or implied, was to be found in the exchange of letters by which the hiring was effected. After an exhaustive reading of all the files of correspondence with the faculty members then employed by Whitman, I came to the conclusion that there was not the slightest basis for implying a promise of tenure. No one had been promised anything more than an initial appointment at a stated rank and salary. From time to time, in most cases, rank and salary had been changed, and such changes might be interpreted as reappointments, but certainly not as grants of permanent tenure.

It seemed to me that the tenure situation at Whitman was badly in need of clarification. Almost any time a tenure issue might pop up and cause unnecessary trouble. I talked the matter over with the two deans, Haigh and Armstrong, and they fully concurred that something should be done. I had access to a good deal of literature on the subject of academic tenure, and from this I distilled a tentative set of rules and regulations which I proposed to submit to the Board of Trustees. The two deans and I had several meetings in which we went over my proposals with great care. At last we agreed on ten rules which seemed to cover the ground well enough. I presented these to the Board of Trustees and they were promptly approved. As soon as this had been done I sent every member of the faculty a letter enclosing a copy of the tenure by-law which the Board had enacted and said that the next step would be to establish the actual tenure status of all members of the faculty. Every member was invited to confer

393

with me, go through the correspondence in his file, and thus determine exactly how the Board's tenure regulations applied in his case. This touched off a minor hubbub in the faculty. I was charged with destroying academic freedom, violating long established rights of tenure, and planning wholesale dismissals from the faculty. Some of the more impassioned professors did not hesitate to accuse me of an intention to use these tenure regulations as implements to effect a purge. The half-moribund Whitman chapter of the American Association of University Professors then injected itself into the situation as the champion of faculty rights. Its officers called upon the national secretary of the AAUP to institute an investigation of me and Whitman College. However, they made the mistake of including a copy of the newly adopted Whitman tenure regulations, and the reply they got from their national secretary was to the effect that these regulations were entirely conformable with the principles the AAUP had always advocated. They should have been, for that was one of the sources from which I took my ideas.

Having failed to get me indicted by the AAUP, certain of the busybody members of the faculty tried to turn the Board of Trustees against me. Instead of asking me to present the Board a formal request for reconsideration of the tenure regulations, individual faculty members sought out certain Walla Walla members of the Board of Trustees and filled their ears with distortions of the truth. This forced me into a skirmish with the Board. I took the position that the proper channel of communication between the faculty and the Board of Trustees was the president. Unless the president had refused or failed to transmit to the Board any representations from the faculty, it was improper for faculty members to do so and improper for Board members to receive such communications. I had not refused or failed, because I had not been asked to transmit any communication from the faculty to the Board. We had rather a hot argument about this in one of the Board meetings, but the majority of the Board voted to support me. The faculty agitators were then informed that the correct way

394

to proceed would be to get the matter before the Faculty Council and ask that body to address a communication to the Board of Trustees.

When the issue came before the Faculty Council, it soon became apparent that there was no objection to the tenure regulations *per se.* The real reason the soreheads were so sore was that they had not been consulted in advance. In my judgment there would have been just as big an uproar if no steps had been taken until faculty opinion had been entirely placated. Under the charter of the College the Board of Trustees is given supreme authority over all appointments and removals, and is not obliged to consult anyone. Consequently no legal rights of the faculty had been disregarded. If any injury had been done to the faculty it was an injury to their pride. This was evidenced by the fact that the long discussions in the Faculty Council brought forth only one specific request, namely, that a joint committee of Trustees and faculty members be selected to consider the tenure regulations. I agreed to transmit this request to the Board of Trustees, and did so at the next meeting. The Board appointed two of its members and asked the Faculty Council to choose two faculty members to meet with these gentlemen. I arranged the time and place of the meeting, attended long enough to introduce the faculty men to the Trustees, then left the joint committee to its own devices.

As reported back to the Board, the meeting was described as brief and pleasant. The faculty members had no fault to find with any of the tenure regulations, but recommended an additional rule providing that any faculty members who had not been given permanent tenure by the end of their sixth year of service should be given notice that at the end of the seventh year they would either be given permanent tenure or be dropped from the faculty. The Board agreed to enact this additional regulation, and this brought the furore over tenure to a sudden end. Except for the six-year rule, the tenure regulations as originally drafted by the two deans and me were unaltered by so much as even a comma. They are now embodied in Article V of the By-Laws of Whitman College, which, because of its historic significance, I quote immediately hereafter.

ARTICLE V

Section 1. All appointments to the teaching faculty of Whitman College shall be made by the Board of Trustees on recommendation of the President of the College.

Section 2. In every case the initial appointment of a person as a member of the Faculty shall be for term of one academic year, regardless of the rank given the appointee.

Section 3. Appointments at the rank of assistant, associate, instructor, and lecturer shall always be for the term of one academic year and, except as provided in Section 6 below for instructors, shall be renewed only by appointment for one academic year.

Section 4. Except in the case of an initial appointment to the Faculty, all appointments at the rank of assistant professor may be for a term of two academic years and at the rank of associate professor for a term of three academic years. Upon the expiration of their respective terms such appointments may be renewed, but such renewals shall be subject to the provisions of Section 6 below.

Section 5. Except in the case of an initial appointment to the Faculty, all appointments at the rank of professor shall be for indefinite tenure. Indefinite tenure means that the appointment shall not run for a fixed term or period and shall be terminable only as hereinafter provided.

Section 6. Persons holding the rank of associate professor, assistant professor, and instructor may be given indefinite tenure by vote of the Board of Trustees at any time, but any such who have not been given indefinite tenure prior to the end of the sixth year of their service shall at that time be notified in writing whether they will be given indefinite tenure at the end of their seventh year of service; and in the event that indefinite tenure be not given, such persons shall not be continued in the service of the College beyond the end of their seventh year of service.

Section 7. Regardless of the status of his tenure, any member of the Faculty may be suspended or dismissed by the Board of Trustees for any of the following reasons: (1) conviction of an infamous crime, (2) misconduct reflecting seriously upon the College or upon the character and reputation of the person involved, (3) being a member, associate, or supporter of any organization or group which gives allegiance to a foreign power or strives to undermine or overthrow the Government of the United States by other than constitutional means.

In every case of proposed dismissal for the foregoing reasons, the accused shall have the right to a hearing by the Faculty Council or a specially elected committee of the Faculty, and the report or recommendations of the Faculty Council or special committee shall be received and considered by the Board of Trustees before final action is taken. However, a faculty member so accused may be suspended without pay by the President pending the aforesaid hearing and final action by the Board of Trustees.

Section 8. Regardless of the status of his tenure, every member of the Faculty shall be subject to retirement at the end of the academic year in which his sixty-fifth birthday shall occur. An affirmative vote of the Board of Trustees shall be necessary in order to continue the tenure of such a member beyond the academic year above specified and such continuance shall be for one academic year at a time. The Board of Trustees shall have authority to terminate by retirement the appointment of any faculty member who by reason of mental or physical disability shall have become unable to perform the duties for which he was appointed.

Section 9. Appointments to administrative offices such as director, dean, or any other non-teaching position shall carry no rights of tenure either definite or indefinite.

Section 10. No tenure regulations shall apply to part-time members of the instructional staff regardless of title, nor shall they apply to any person not holding the title of professor, associate professor, assistant professor, or instructor.

Under the by-law the tenure status of every member of the faculty was established, and each was notified by letter exactly where he stood. All new members of the faculty, as soon as they took up their duties, were given a copy of the tenure regulations and told exactly how they would be applied. By supplementing this procedure with a system of records which showed at a glance the tenure status of every faculty member, it was easy to avoid misunderstandings as to rights of tenure. It was my practice at the outset of every academic year, usually around the first of July, to send every member of the faculty a letter stating his salary for the year forthcoming and reciting also his current tenure status. Except for the six-year rule, adopted at the request of the faculty, no tenure questions arose during my remaining years as president. And the trouble with the six-year rule was not really tenure trouble but seventh year trouble. A teacher finishing his seventh year with the sword of certain dismissal hanging over his head was not good for the College either educationally or morale-wise. I tried to avoid such contretemps by effecting terminations before the end of the sixth year, but there were a few unfortunate cases in which I was caught off base. In one of these cases both the Dean of the Faculty and I recommended permanent tenure at the end of the sixth year, but were reversed by the Board of Trustees because certain members of the Board raised objections on grounds about which we had failed to secure any information. Another case turned on the technicality concerning a leave of absence. Did it or did it not count as one of the six years? The Board ruled that it did. In still another case, the deans and department heads on whose advice I mainly relied reversed themselves at the eleventh hour, forcing me to recommend against a faculty member whom I would have given permanent tenure without hesitation. These, however, were minor difficulties. In the main, our tenure regulations worked admirably, and, after a short cooling-off period, even the most virulent opponents were reconciled and satisfied.

There is always the question of whether the same good results could not have been obtained without a fight with the faculty. I think not. Actually, I did not have a fight with the whole faculty. Most of the faculty took no part in the affair. A little coterie of faculty politicians thought they saw an opportunity to stir up trouble. They would have done the same no matter what tactics I adopted, and I feel that my tactics of confronting the faculty with a *fait accompli* were well adapted to the situation. By that method I forstalled obstructionism, and got quick and complete results.

Personnel Problems

If I were asked to name the most disagreeable work I had to do as president, I would answer without a moment's hesitation that it was the hiring and firing. It seems to be a common supposition that in normal times there should be little annual turnover in the personnel of a college faculty. If that be true, I never encountered any normal times. I doubt if there is such a thing. I cannot remember a time at Whitman or elsewhere that some special reason could not be found to explain the high rate of faculty turnover. In my eleven years as president of Whitman, the special reasons were the aftermath of World War II, the Korean War and its after-effects, and the sharp decline of college enrollments in the 1950's owing to the low birth rate of the depression years. My annual faculty turnover ranged between ten and fifteen per cent, which meant that I had from six to a dozen vacancies to fill year after year. There were self-appointed critics, especially in the faculty and the student body, who thought this was excessive and blamed me for it.

The basic causes of the annual turnover were death, retirement, resignation, non-renewal of appointment, and dismissal. I was not held accountable for the deaths, but I was sharply criticized for enforcing the retirement rule literally and strictly.

Of course it was up to the Board of Trustees to make the final decision in every case of retirement. It was my duty to bring each case before the Board, and I did. The Board usually asked me for a recommendation, and in deciding what to recommend I took into account the welfare of both the professor and the College. There were some instances in which a replacement was so obviously needed that I tipped the scale in favor of retirement. There were others in which I was in doubt, but did not always vote no. In one of these cases I asked the retiree to continue on a half-time basis for a year, and he refused, saying it was all or nothing for him. Then, after I had replaced him, he changed his mind and wanted to continue. When I told him it was too late, he accused me of bad faith and told every one he could that I had brutally tossed him out.

Resignations were few and far between. Truly voluntary resignations were scarcer than hen's teeth. I recall only two or three in my entire eleven years as president. Every year, however, there were what I allowed to appear as voluntary resignations. Every year there were expiring appointments that I refused to renew. Unless they had been given permanent tenure, instructors came up for reappointment at the end of one year of service, assistant professors at the end of two, and associate professors at the end of three. In such cases, a denial of reappointment had the same effect as a forced resignation, but I never called it that. Almost invariably the faculty member involved chose to represent it as a voluntary resignation, and I never took the trouble to contradict him. As far as I was concerned, it was enough that our records showed that he had been denied reappointment. If he could save his face by telling the world he had resigned, that was all right with me. I had to deal with four cases of summary dismissal on grounds enumerated in Section 7 of Article V, but none of the accused wanted a hearing as provided in that By-Law. Consequently these, too, appeared to the public as voluntary resignations.

Nearly every case of non-renewal was a headache for me. There is nothing harder than to tell an unsuccessful person that he had performed so poorly that he cannot be kept on the payroll. He always thinks he has done a good job, and that somebody, usually the president, "has it in for him." Whether or not a teacher has done a good job is difficult to prove by objective evidence. Nearly always the issue narrows down to a matter of opinion. I never formed my own opinion of a faculty member without first consulting the deans, division chairmen, and department heads best situated to know about him, and in most cases I was able also to get a fairly good reading of student opinion. But when I called the man in to give him the bad news, I took pains not to implicate anyone else by name. I simply told him that my opinion, based on a careful and conscientious effort to ascertain the facts, was that he had not made good and therefore would not be reappointed. This enabled him to place all the blame on me and remain on a friendly footing with his faculty colleagues. It was not, however, because of a martyr complex that I "took the rap," but because I had asked for confidential opinions about the man, and if I did not respect those confidences, they would not be forthcoming another time.

It is always easier to put up with mediocrity than to prune it out, and a president is often tempted "to let things ride," but this is a perilous practice. My paramount aim in filling faculty vacancies was the progressive upbuilding of the quality of the Whitman faculty. For that reason I felt that it was as much my duty to make vacancies as to fill them. In dealing with faculty members not on permanent tenure, I felt I owed them no obligation to carry them on if I could find a replacement of superior quality. With that policy in mind I measured the person who was up for reappointment by certain criteria of excellence which I thought realizable for Whitman. In establishing bases for these criteria I interviewed scores of applicants all over the United States, visited and established personal contacts with the staff members of the leading university and commercial teacher placement bureaus, wrote hundreds of letters, and made uncounted personal calls. Every year I made an extensive hunt for superior teaching talent. Judging by the number of individuals whom I both hired and refused to reappoint, my batting average was not high. Only about a third of those I hired were good enough by my own criteria, to reappoint. Whether this was comparatively a high or low score I do not know, as I have never seen any data by which to rate myself. Maybe I did too much weeding, but I hoped to leave behind me a stronger faculty than I found when I became president.

Such rigorous weeding might not have been necessary if I could have made more rapid progress with the salary schedule. If I could have started with something approximating the salary scale of 1958-59, it would have been possible during my tenure as president to have recruited for Whitman some of the finest young teaching talent in America. It was available—at a price. If I had not been obliged to put so much money into plant rehabilitation and financial stabilization, it would have been possible for Whitman to match salaries with the best. For a college as isolated geographically as Whitman it is transcendently important to be able not only to match, but if need be, to overmatch the best. Ambitious young academicians in this day and age generally prefer to be located in or near great metropolitan centers, and prefer to serve in institutions likewise located. Because of opportunities for professional specialization and other career satisfactions, they also are inclined to prefer large universities over small colleges. It is not easy to convince the embryonic professor that he can make a great career in a small college located in a far northwestern city with an oddball name. Money offers the best means of overcoming his initial reluctance to take a job at such an institution as Whitman, and not money in the form of salary alone, but for travel funds, research facilities, sabbatical leaves, and other special advantages. The small college which will put most of its eggs in the basket of faculty compensation can look forward to an assured future.

Another personnel problem that I had to reckon with was that of promotions, Faculty people are paradoxical in this respect. Much as they detest regimentation in other respects, they want an escalator system of promotions—one by which they will progress regularly, by assured stages, from the bottom to the top. The governing boards of Whitman College did not believe in that sort of automation, and neither did I. Although they approved a salary schedule arranged by academic ranks, they refused to approve automatic promotion from one rank to the next. They said all promotions should be on the basis of merit, and not on the basis of having served at a given rank a stated period of time. Being in agreement with this principle, I moved some men upward much faster than others, for the sole reason that I thought they had proven themselves better qualified. This made some people happy and others quite unhappy, but I thought it was doing a favor to Whitman College.

The Business of Education

I would like to be able to write a lengthy account of my achievements in leading the faculty to great accomplishments in the business of education. I must confess, however, that in this responsibility of a college president I think I was a failure—in fact, almost a total bust. Try as I would, and did, I was unable to wheedle, bribe or drive the faculty into any new departures in educational concepts or practices. In the daily routine of instructional and co-curricular administration, I tried to run a tight ship, and apparently succeeded. Our machinery worked well, and the regular grist of the mill was promptly and efficiently handled; but there was no reaching for the stars. Most of our faculty seemed mortally afraid of innovation. Although it began before I became president, I had an active hand in getting the faculty to experiment with an unorthodox system of grading, but it was so non-conformist that they eventually went back to the old A, B, C, D letter-and-grade-point percentage game, which is more abstruse than abacadabra itself. But it was familiar, and hence beloved of faculty men all over the land.

I was instrumental in bringing about a complete codification of faculty legislation, which was very much needed, but did not mean anything educationally. I also sideswiped the faculty into a general revision of the rules of probation and dismissal for academic deficiencies, which likewise was much needed, but had no bearing on the quality of education at Whitman. Time and again I made revolutionary educational proposals. The faculty always listened courteously, sometimes discussed my proposals with seeming interest, but never budged a fraction of an inch from its long-established moorings. I decided that I was not cut out to be an educational leader.

XXIV. WORKING WITH THE GOVERNING BOARDS
Whitman's Dual System

In a previous publication (*Five Centennial Papers,* March, 1959) I wrote at some length about Whitman's dual board system. In one of those essays I dealt at length with the origin and development of the dual system and commented on its basic structural and operative features. No matter how elaborately constituent documents may prescribe and direct, human institutions such as Whitman's dual system are always more than they appear to be on paper. There are unwritten as well as written constituents. The essay in my *Five Centennial Papers* had much less to say about the former than the latter. One of the unwritten features of the dual system that cannot be discerned from a study of any of the basic documents is the role of the president of the College in the operation of the dual system.

The president of Whitman College is no longer a member of the Board of Trustees and is only an ex officio member of the Board of Overseers. He is not legally a member of any of the committees of either board, and may be excluded from their meetings. From a reading of the Charter, the Constitution, and the By-Laws of Whitman College, it is easy to conclude that the president is virtually a cipher as far as the work of the two boards is concerned. The actual truth, however, is that the success of the dual board system with all of its committee ramifications is more dependent on the president of the College than anyone else. The president has no legal authority or responsibility to serve as the connecting link between the two boards and supply executive leadership to both, but no one else can do so. If the president fails to perform this pivotal function, the dual board system works like a broken-down jalopy.

None of the documents provides that the president shall attend all meetings of the two boards, shall sit with all of their standing committees, shall prepare the agenda and initiate most of the business for such meetings, shall follow through and put into effect the actions taken, shall keep all their records, shall supply all their secretarial assistance, and shall do most of their fact-finding. But if the president did not do these things, the work of the two boards and their committees would soon grind to a halt. Because of their dependence on him as well as what they can do for him, the two boards offer the president splendid opportunities for promotional work. I knew before I became president that my predecessors, for reasons particular to each, had not made the most of those opportunities. President Penrose, the creator of the dual board system, did not exploit it much after the failure of the Greater Whitman campaign and following his blindness was unable to keep in touch with both boards. President Clemen tried to use the Board of Overseers to upend the Board of Trustees. President Bratton's ill-health made it impossible for him to carry the around-the-clock travel and work schedule necessary to get the most out of the dual board system. President Anderson had made a promising start with both boards when mental difficulties incidental to his affliction with a brain tumor caused him to lose the ground he had gained.

To a greater degree than any of my predecessors, I was equally responsible to both boards. The entire Board of Trustees and a committee of Overseers including the chairman, two vice chairman, and three leading members had taken joint action in appointing me to succeed President Anderson. I felt that I needed the full support and collaboration of both, and I was sure there was a far larger potential of service in both than had ever been realized. The first necessity, as I saw it, was

405

to get both boards really activated. Both had become rather pedestrian and apathetic. Not only did they need to be livened up; they needed to have vital and challenging work to do. Without asking permission, I assumed the prerogative of setting up agenda for the meetings in such a way as to speed up the transaction of routine business and allow ample time for the consideration of important questions of policy. To effect this result, I resorted to such well-known expedients as memoranda, reports, digests, and graphs which could be distributed in advance and thus curtail the time needed to get a meeting into full swing. Whenever the discussion wandered, as it often did, I would make use of my *ex officio* privileges, not to add to the discussion, but to ask a question or toss in a reminder which might have the effect of getting things back on the main line again. In addition to keeping things moving, I also strove to inject into every meeting a spirit of gayety and good feeling. As president, I usually had a chance to set the tone of the conversations, especially when I acted as host at luncheons and dinners connected with their meetings.

At every meeting I made an effort to bring up one or more important things that would come up for consideration in the next or some future meeting. The result of this was to awaken interest in what lay ahead and keep the members' minds on Whitman in the intervals between meetings. Another thing that helped enormously in activating the boards was to see that the members received ample public recognition for their services. In Whitman publications this was easy, and I saw to it that they featured our board members at every opportunity. We also found it possible to plant a good many stories in the hometown newspapers of the board members, and this gave them not merely a sense of personal importance but a feeling that working for Whitman was important too. The Board of Trustees responded more promptly to the livening up process than the Board of Overseers, which was to be expected, because the Trustees had from six to ten meetings a year and the Overseers only one. I soon realized that something had to be done to bring the Overseers together more often, and in

1950 I proposed a regional plan of organization for the Board of Overseers. In my annual report for 1949-50 I described this as follows:

The plan for the regional reorganization of the Board of Overseers . . . is not designed to change the essential character and functions of the Board. On the contrary, its purpose is to maintain the present composition of the Board but to break it down into regional subdivisions, each of which will be so organized that it can function as a unit. Each regional subdivision is to be headed by a vice chairman of the Board of Overseers and thus would be provided with leadership representing and speaking for the Board as a whole. It would not be permissible for the regional subdivisions acting separately to take actions or make decisions which would be binding on the Board. Their primary purpose would be to discuss, consider, and review matters in advance of the regular meetings of the Board and thus make possible a more efficient preparation for the regular annual meetings and also to provide greater opportunity for participation in Board affairs by members not regularly able to attend the annual meetings. It is also believed that one or two meetings of each regional subdivision throughout the year would tend to generate and maintain greater and more continuous interest in and understanding of the work of the College.

The regional plan was adopted and put into operation at once. Regional organizations were established in the Walla Walla area, the Portland area, the Puget Sound area, the Spokane area, and the New York area. Later I began to have Overseer meetings in Washington, D. C., and looked forward to one in Southern California and one in the San Francisco Bay area. It was my practice to attend a meeting of the Overseers in each region at least once a year and oftener when possible. The regional chairman was in charge of these meetings, and I was present primarily to make reports, answer questions, and explain projects and programs under consideration. In performing these duties I tried to make the regional meeting as nearly a business meeting as possible. Although a regional group of Overseers could not make decisions binding on the Board of Trustees or the Board of Overseers, it could pass judgment, raise questions, and make recommendations, and I encouraged this. It not only gave them opportunity to render practical service to Whitman but led many to make a special effort to attend the annual meeting at commencement time. Furthermore, those who attended the annual meetings were well briefed in advance on the business which was to come up.

I give the regional plan credit for a great revivication which took place in the Board of Overseers. Never since the Board was originally founded by President Penrose in 1908 was there such interest, enthusiasm, and spontaneous activity on the part of its members. In scores of ways they were highly helpful to me. They gave me money, they got money for me, they supplied me with invaluable tips on sources of money, they got me entree to people and places I could not have managed for myself, they gave me invaluable suggestions and ideas, and they kept me from making many a bad mistake. Whenever I had work to do in an area having a regional group of Overseers, no matter what kind of work I might be engaged in, I knew there was power and influence behind me that could multiply my effectiveness many times.

At the annual meeting of the Board of Overseers in 1956 I suggested another organizational innovation. This was the establishment of a permanent executive committee. In the past it had been taken for granted that the Board of Trustees would serve as an executive committee for the Board of Overseers, but this expectation had not been realized, and the regional groups of Overseers were in need of a kind of coordination that the Board of Trustees could not supply. For several years I tried to supply such coordination, but it was not truly a presidential job. Owing to the increased volume of business transacted both in the regional and the annual meetings of the Overseers, there was need for a standing committee, which could be convened at any time, to speak and act for the whole Board if need be. As president, I could transmit matters from region to region, and from a regional group to the Board as a whole, but there were times when it was inexpedient to await the results of such roundabout methods. There was no way that I as president could get prompt action in the name of the whole Board without convoking the whole Board, and that was seldom feasible more than once a year. Realizing, this, the Board readily approved my suggestion, and the first executive committee was established in 1956. It proved invaluable in various ways, particularly in preparing the agenda for the annual meeting, analyzing and reporting on the preliminary budget reviewing and advising on administrative reports, and preconsidering and coordinating recommendations from the regional groups.

In the three years that I worked with the executive committee of the Board of Overseers I came to regard it as an essential mainspring in the operation of the Board. It was the central organ which united, energized, and regulated the entire process of Overseer participation in the work of the College but without in any way dictating or dominating. I also give it credit for doing much to put the Overseers into parity with the Trustees, which was the original intent of the dual plan.

By reason of more or less accidental usage, the members of the Board of Trustees had largely taken over the running of the show in meetings of the Board of Overseers. Although the constitution of the College made them only ex officio members of the Board of Overseers, with no right to make motions and no right to vote and the right to speak only by courtesy of the chairman, the Trustees had fallen into the habit of doing most of the talking, making most of the motions, and actually voting just as though they were full-fledged Overseers. There was no malice in this. Most of the Trustees were former Overseers and felt wholly at home in Overseers' meetings. Very few had ever read the constitution, and the same was true of the Overseers. It seemed natural to the Trustees to jump into the act in an Overseers meeting, and it never occurred to them that they were stealing the show. Because of their more frequent meetings and closer contact with the business details of College operation, they knew so many of the answers that they could not resist the temptation to take over. Some of the Overseers used to ask me if they were expected to be anything more than an echo of the Board of Trustees. That question never was asked after the Overseers' executive committee began to function. Very quietly and tactfully, the executive committee planned and presented the agenda and the Board chairman conducted the meeting in such a way that it was obvious that the meeting belonged to the Overseers, and that the decision would be made by that Board.

Owing to the fact that Whitman's charter was granted by the state legislature and that the charter explicitly prescribes the structure and powers of the Board of Trustees, no change in that Board can be made without an act of the legislature. The charter says that there shall be nine members, and this number cannot be changed without the approval of the legislature. The same is true of most of the procedure and powers of the Board of Trustees. It is necessary to be very careful to follow the charter. Since the charter neither created nor authorized an executive committee, it is doubtful whether the Trustees may legally have one. This is not a serious deficiency, because most of the time this board has no need of an executive committee. It is generally easy to get a quorum of the nine members and to meet often enough to transact most business without any committees. Once in a while, however, it was necessary to get a quick authorization or a quick answer. Then we usually polled the Board by telephone and ratified the vote at the next meeting. But this did not take care of situations which required complex documents such as leases and deeds to be examined, and other matters of technical nature. To meet these difficult, though rare, situations, my suggestion was that the Board establish a *de facto* but not *de jure* executive committee, which could meet on call at a moment's notice and make decisions which would be moved and regularly voted at the next meeting of the Board. This worked very well in an occasional tight situation.

The Joint Committees

Except for three joint committees, there has been little or no overlap in the organization of the two boards. In three areas of common concern, however, it has been found highly useful to establish a standing committee made up of members of both boards. These are the finance committee, the farm committee, and the buildings and grounds committee. All three are now established by and their respective powers and duties are set forth in Article VII of the constitution of the College.

The finance committee should more properly be called the investment committee. Its history goes back to the beginning of the College and possibly even to the founding of the Seminary in 1859. Originally, of course, it was solely a Trustee committee because there was only one board. But when the Board of Overseers was created, it was given equal representation on the finance committee. The principal duties of this joint committee are, subject to board approval, to manage the investments of the College in stocks, bonds, mortgages, and other securities. It also handles investments in city real estate, but not in farm lands. I attended all meetings of the finance committee and was accorded all privileges except that of voting. The same was true of the treasurer of the College. I cherish my experience with the finance committee as much as anything I did as president of Whitman College. I used to say in all seriousness that any man who could get Whitman's finance committee to serve as his investment counsel could not help becoming a millionaire. I know that the growth of Whitman's portfolio in my years as president was as much attributable to money-making investments as to gifts, and they were investments with negligible risk. Whitman was more than fortunate to have the services of such men as Harper Joy (chairman), D. F. Baker, Donald Sherwood, Arthur Lee, Lowden Jones, Clarence Braden, and George Yancey, who spent so many devoted hours in the work of the finance committee.

The farm committee was established in 1949 to relieve the finance committee of the responsibility of managing the farm properties of the College. This action grew out of discussions which arose in the finance committee itself. For many years the only management the College farms had received had been the approval of leases by the Board of Trustees and the collection of rents by the treasurer. Whitman then owned eight farms

411

with a gross acreage of 3,625. This was big business of a highly specialized variety, and specialized management was needed. The finance committee was not expert in the field of farm management, nor was the Board of Trustees or the treasurer. It seemed to me that the solution of the problem was right before our eyes, namely, a farm committee to handle Whitman's farm investments just as the finance committee handled the other investments. This discussion resulted in action by the Board of Trustees, which provided for the establishment and appointment of such a farm committee. The treasurer, the president of the Board of Trustees, and the president of the College were made ex officio members of the committee, and the chairman of the farm committee was made a member of the finance committee, thus linking these two vital committees in a collaborative relationship. Though it had an independent status so far as farm operations were concerned, the farm committee reported to the finance committee and also to both governing boards. It would be quite as hard to overpraise the farm committee as the finance committee. In ten years from its establishment it tripled the valuation and doubled both the acreage and the annual income of Whitman's farm properties. The farm committee members to whom Whitman owed deep gratitude for this achievement were Clarence Braden (chairman), Henry Copeland, Ed Tucker, and Lester Robison.

The committee on buildings and grounds began as an *ad hoc* committee of the Board of Overseers and functioned only for one annual meeting. From year to year, however, there was such a large carry-over of committee personnel and business that it began to seem like a standing committee. At first its duties were not clearly defined. It always made an annual inspection of the buildings and grounds, reported its finds to the Board, and sometimes made recommendations. From 1926 to 1947 there was no new construction and precious little in the way of maintenance and repairs, and this almost put the committee on buildings and grounds out of business, there being no business for it to do. However, when we became involved in the major rehabilitation and new construction programs which I

412

have described above, it was necessary to have a new kind of buildings and grounds committee—one which would go on year after year as a joint committee of both boards and thus would be able to initiate and carry through large-scale and long-continuing plans of plant betterment. Appropriate legislation to establish such a committee was enacted, and the new committee began its work with the construction of Anderson Hall in 1953. As in the cases of the finance committee and the farm committee, the committee on buildings and grounds merits the highest praise. The individual members to whom most of the praise should go are W. L. Teague (chairman 1953-56), James Hill, Jr. (chairman 1956-59), James Hill, Sr., Howard J. Knott, Roy V. Peringer, Parker Barrett, Henry Copeland, Harold E. Crawford, John C. Lyman, Richard McKay, and George B. Woodward.

Board Personnel

No one could have had finer personal and official relationships with the two boards and the three standing committees than I had. No one could have had greater loyalty and cooperation. No one could have asked for more interest in the business of the College, and no one could have expected to get so much more than he asked. I do not mean to intimate that all was sweetness and light, that there were never any jarring notes to disturb the general harmony. There were differences of opinion within the boards, between the boards, and between the president and each board and committee. These differences were vigorously, sometimes vehemently, expressed, but never malignantly. There never was a broken friendship, never a resentful resignation. In fact, there were almost no resignations, and that itself came to be something of a problem.

By the requirements of the charter and the constitution of the College, certain specified officers of both boards had to be elected each year. Chief of these were the president, vice president, and secretary of the Board of Trustees and the corresponding officers (chairman, vice chairman, and secretary) of the Board of Overseers. Long before my time as president it had become the almost invariable practice to re-elect the same persons to the same office year after year as long as they continued on their respective boards, and this usually was for life. With respect to any responsible office, annual tenure is usually too brief and life tenure far too long. Our boards had gone clear off the deep end against annual tenure—so far that they had completely lost the refreshing vigor of occasional rotation in office. This was not a matter that could be brought up by the president of the College, though it concerned the president of the College more than anyone else. By private conversations with individual members of each board, I tried to bring about a realization of the growing danger of dead wood. There was a little talk in both boards at nominating time, but they never got around to doing anything. Nobody made any competing nominations, and nobody refused renomination and re-election.

Neither did they get around to doing anything much about the parallel problem of filling membership vacancies. The constitution sets the term of a Trustee as three years and of an Overseer as five years. In both boards the terms are so rotated that only a third in the case of the Trustees and a fifth in the case of the Overseers expire each year. Both boards are empowered to fill all vacancies in their own membership, and it became the fixed habit to fill the annually occurring vacancies by re-electing the same persons year after year. The only chance of getting new blood came as the result of death or resignation. During my eleven years the input of new blood in the Board of Overseers was proportionately much greater than in the Board of Trustees, but in my judgment it was not enough in either board. I tried by indirection to bring this matter under consideration in both boards, but had no success.

XXV. THE PUBLIC RELATIONS JOB

Travel

One of my first decisions was that I would have to be a traveling president. This decision was not by preference but by necessity. The last ten years of his presidency Dr. Penrose had

414

been incapacitated for travel, President Clemen never really got going on a travel program, President Bratton's health had curtailed his travel to a minimum, President Anderson had tried to travel more than his predecessors but wartime restrictions and failing health cut him down. For twenty-four years the president of Whitman College had not been in circulation, had not visited the people and places necessary or important in building up a modern public image of Whitman College, had not really worked at the job of public relations outside of Walla Walla. There was a tremendous lot of catching up to be done in the travel department, more than there was time to do unless I started immediately and kept at it year after year as consistently as I could.

My appointment book for the year 1949 records me as being in Spokane from January 16 to 23, in Seattle from February 6 to 12, in Portland from February 27 to March 5, in San Francisco from March 27 to April 2, in Moscow (Idaho) from April 12 to 14, in Wenatchee from April 16 to 18, in New York from June 5 to 11, in Washington, D.C. from June 12 to 17, in Seattle again from August 12 to 19, in Spokane again from November 4 to 6, in Portland again from November 13 to 15, in Eugene (Oregon) on November 17, in Spokane for the third time from November 20 to 25, and in Richland on December 14. This was fairly typical of my travel schedule year after year. Some years I did a bit more and some a bit less, but I never failed in any year to cover a large part of the United States. I managed every year to make the main centers of population (Chicago, Boston, New York, Philadelphia, Washington, San Francisco, Los Angeles, and all of the major cities of the Pacific Northwest). In addition I managed, if not every year, at least every other year, to go to lesser cities in the Northwest such as Boise, Yakima, Tacoma, Spokane, and Twin Falls. Except for steamships, I used every mode of travel available— planes, trains, buses, and private automobiles. For long trips I preferred going by rail because of the opportunity for work or relaxation, as I might choose, en route.

Like all college presidents, I soon discovered that running a road show and a home show at the same time could have moments of strain and crisis. There were times when I feared I might be overdoing the road show at the expense of the home show, but as I reflect upon the matter from the vantage point of retirement, I am inclined to think I should have done more rather than less traveling. It took four or five years to become reasonably proficient at the travel job. Though I did far more traveling than any previous president of Whitman, every trip seemed to generate more unfinished than finished business. It was my job to stir up the unfinished business and, if possible, see it through to completion. I might have done both more successfully if I had given more time to travel. I can imagine now that it might have paid vastly greater dividends (not monetary alone) if I had held more regional Overseer meetings, more alumni meetings, more special committee meetings, and managed more personal interviews. I feel sure I should have spent more time cultivating the great eleemosynary foundations. Most of my efforts with the foundations were brought to bear on the General Education Board, the Ford Foundation, the Alfred P. Sloan Foundation, the George F. Baker Foundation, the Crown-Zellerback Foundation, the General Foods Foundation, the International Nickel Foundation, and the Olin Foundation. Whitman received grants from several of these, but there were dozens of other foundations that I never found time to visit.

One chore that consumed endless hours of my travel time was interviewing applicants for faculty positions at Whitman. This work was done mainly in New York, Chicago, Seattle, San Francisco, and Los Angeles. There were days when it seemed that I could find time to do little more than sit in my hotel room and receive one applicant after another. Though I did not begrudge this time because of the importance of building a strong faculty at Whitman, there were times when it intruded on other work of equal importance. If I had planned more time away from the campus, my travel work might have been more fruitful, but what of the home show? I have a feeling that I did not give enough time to that, either.

The Constitution of Whitman College explicitly states that the president "shall have general responsibility for the welfare and advancement of the institution and of all its relations with the public." I was happy to have it thus laid on the line, even though the constitution was merely stating an inexorable fact. In every college and university in this country the main responsibility for public relations falls on the president. This necessarily follows from the fact that the president controls most of the sources of news, most of the channels of news dissemination, and most of the money available for publicity purposes. It is also more true of the president than any other officer of an American institution of higher education that he *is* news even though he may make no effort to create news. The president is in the public eye more than anyone else, and he can get public attention more readily than anyone else. If a college or university is not well presented in the news of the day, the fault is more likely to attach to the president than any one else.

I was aware of the news responsibilities of the president long before that office fell to me, and I had had previous experience with news media methods which I could use to get a running start on my news tasks at Whitman. In connection with my field survey work with the New York Bureau of Municipal Research, as Supervisor of the Training School for Public Service, and as a civic and political operator in Cleveland and Walla Walla, I had learned a good deal about making headlines, planting news releases, and dealing with reporters and publicity agents. Never before, however, had I been responsible for the totality of an institution's news, good, bad, or indifferent. That job I had to learn by trial and error.

The first result I sought to achieve was a continuous stream of news emanating from Whitman College—big news, little news, and news of every other magnitude. The main thing, it seemed to me, was a constant outpouring of news. I was aware that not all the stories Whitman put out would be used by newspapers and broadcasters, but I thought that a large output of news stories of every conceivable kind would probably get us the maximum number of acceptances. This seemed so good an arithmetical probability that it was the policy we decided to follow. When I became president, the Whitman news service was on a part-time basis. As soon as possible I put it on a full-time basis with Mrs. Helen Bragg, an exceptionally competent professional, in charge as director. She had a far better nose for news than I and had an unusual sense of touch and timing when it came to getting news stories in the hands of papers and broadcasting stations which would use them to the benefit of Whitman College.

As I have said before, our first aim was volume. This we got immediately. In my third annual report I did a bit of boasting, as follows: "To those who have felt that Whitman is not as much in the news as could be desired, it will be satisfying to know that during the year 1950-51 the Whitman News Service has issued 2,452 news releases to newspapers, wire services, and radio stations. . . The coverage of these news releases has included every activity of the College." Eight years later I reported in somewhat more specific terms, noting that the News Service had put out that year 1,115 general releases to newspapers, radio stations and TV stations, 1,128 sports releases, special stories to 312 hometown papers, 147 picture releases, and 236 special stories for Walla Walla papers alone. We tried for national as well as local and regional acceptance for our news releases, and were twice successful in making *Time* and once successful in getting editorial recognition in *Life*. This was the first time in Whitman history that the whole country, and the Pacific Northwest in particular, had been bombarded day after day, week after week, and year after year with news from Whitman College. The volume principle proved its merit. We did not hit the target every time, actually not a third of the time but we got Whitman in the news more often and more favorably than would have been possible any other way.

Constituency-Building

There is much more to public relations than just pumping out news releases. One of the most vital public relations objectives of a private college is the upbuilding of a supporting constituency —a large and widely distributed multitude of people who are specially interested in it and specially able to work for it and give it backing. I do not refer to financial backing alone, for that is sometimes less important than other kinds of backing. A college needs all-around backing, and a private college which lacks such a supporting constituency is bereft indeed. From its earliest years Whitman College had a constituency, sometimes a very good one and other times much less good. Whitman's first constituency was built mainly in the Congregational church. When Whitman went nonsectarian in 1908 it lost much of its hold on this constituency. The Greater Whitman Campaign of 1908-12 had two major objectives: (1) to raise $1,500,000, and (2) to build a new, broader, and stronger constituency. Neither was realized.

From 1912 to the end of his administration in 1934, President Penrose was ambivalent on the constituency problem. There were times he seemed to assume that the constituency sought in the Greater Whitman Campaign had been realized, and as long as the original personnel of the Board of Overseers remained, there was some justification for this. Within ten years, however, there had been so many changes of membership that it no longer reflected any of the constituency objectives of the original Board of Overseers. During the final fifteen years of President Penrose's tenure, Whitman had no constituency other than the personal constituency of Stephen B. L. Penrose, and as he grew older this was an ever-diminishing constituency. Presidents Clemen, Bratton, and Anderson all recognized that one of Whitman's greatest needs was a bigger, better, and more dependable constituency, but, for various reasons that I need not go into, none of these presidents was able to do much to bring that about. I did have an opportunity to attempt some large-scale constituency-building and directed a major part of our public relations endeavors to that end.

Certain categories of people were indispensable building blocks for the kind of constituency Whitman needed. One category that was rapidly growing in numbers and needed to be much more firmly and actively identified with the College was made up of alumni, former students, and the living parents of both. Another category was made up of members of the educational profession, such as high school principals, teachers, and counselors and college officers and faculty members, all of whose esteem could be of great value to Whitman. A third category consisted of business and professional leaders with a partiality for private enterprise in education. A fourth category was composed of the leading figures in the great charitable foundations giving aid to education. A fifth included prominent figures in government and public affairs. A sixth embraced three or four liberal religious denominations whose members preferred that their sons and daughters attend a non-sectarian college. We undertook a program of public relations aimed at drawing as many of these people as possible into a Whitman constituency.

There was not any royal road to success, and our success at best was only partial. Nor was there anything new or original about our methods. To bind alumni, former students, and interested parents more closely to Whitman, we used such time-tested methods as personal visits, reunions, special parties, publications, and news letters. I tried to get around each year and greet as many as possible in person. For the parents especially, we formed parents' clubs in the large centers of population, with provisions for life membership. We worked with these clubs in planning special meetings and social functions, and I made a point of attending all of these gatherings I could.

The other categories were not so easy to reach, and most of that job fell on my shoulders. I wrote letters, made speeches by the dozen, made personal calls, and attended scores of conventions. One thing I did not do was to go around bragging about Whitman or begging people to give us a lift. My propaganda, if such it was, had to do mainly with the role of the truly independent college, one not beholden either to church or state. I never failed, however, to point to Whitman as a good example of an independent college and mention what we needed to become an ever better example.

For all categories we made large use of written and printed communications. We tried in every way to enlarge our mailing list, and sent our communications to every one on the list. One of our most successful publications was a little four-page bulletin that I named *Facets of Whitman College*. Having none too great success with cumbersome mimeographed letters and reports, I came to the conclusion that something more sprightly and readable would be a better attention-getter. *Facets* was planned with that in mind. It was designed as a sort of four-page newspaper column which could be mailed in a letter-size envelope with one folding. Every issue was filled with brief, pungent paragraphs of information and comment, the paragraphs being separated by timely quotations or relevant pen-and-ink drawings. The big idea was first of all to trap the eye of the reader and then appeal to his mind. I did all of the writing for *Facets* and Kenneth Hupp, then asisstant to the president, did the drawings and supervised the typography.

Facets was sent to every person on our mailing lists, and it was not long before we became aware that it was actually getting several times that amount of circulation. It went to the original addressee and then apparently was passed from hand to hand throughout whole families, offices, and organizations. In this way copies of *Facets* found their way into channels of nation-wide publicity, and quotations were lifted from *Facets* by leading newspapers and magazines, including the very famous *Time* magazine. As an attention-getter, *Facets* exceeded all expectations and paid handsome dividends in publicity, if not in cash, and I think I could show that it also brought in some substantial cash contributions.

Another means by which Whitman reached a national audience was the management audit done in 1953 by the American Institute of Management of New York. This survey was an incidental outcome of a regional Overseers' meeting in New York in the spring of 1953. The late Arthur E. Douglas, then president of the Hotel Statler chain, was vice chairman of the Board of Overseers for the New York region. A few months earlier the American Institute of Management had made an efficiency audit of the whole Statler organization, and the published report had excited widespread comment. During the Overseers' meeting I happened to drop the remark that it would be wonderful if an AIM audit, or something like it, could be done for Whitman College. Art Douglas immediately spoke up and said he thought it might be possible. He was well acquainted with Jackson Martindell, president of the American Institute of Management, and said he had heard Martindell express interest in doing an audit for an institution of higher education. As soon as the meeting adjourned, Art got Mr. Martindell on the telephone and arranged for the three of us to lunch together the next day.

It did not take long for Martindell, Douglas, and Maxey to reach an understanding. Martindell really did welcome the opportunity to do a management audit of a college, and was ready to do the job during July and August of 1953, provided mutually satisfactory arrangements could be made. There was no trouble about arrangements. Martindell was willing to do the audit without cost to Whitman other than secretarial assistance for himself while he was on campus and summer housing for himself and family. I agreed to those terms and also obligated the College to purchase enough copies of the AIM report to supply our entire mailing list. It was understood that my promises would have to be ratified by the Board of Trustees, but I anticipated no difficulty about this, and there was none.

It was easy to provide suitable housing for the Martindells that summer. The President's mansion was then being used as a dormitory and would be vacant all summer. We merely cleaned it up, refurbished it some, and made the Martindells at home. The secretarial assistance for Mr. Martindell was mainly supplied by my office, and I drafted the services of our business office and principal administrative officers to act as research assistants for him.

Mr. Martindell began by presenting a list of one hundred questions for which we were to produce correct answers. This questionnaire covered every important aspect of the organization and operation of Whitman College. I assigned each question to the official or staff member best qualified to dig up and supply the kind of answer Mr. Martindell wanted. Quite a number of the questions I reserved to myself, since the information could be found only in the files of the president's office. When all the answers were turned in to me and compiled as a report, I turned this over to Mr. Martindell and arranged for him to have a personal conference with everyone who had supplied an answer. In this way he could probe beneath the surface of our report and verify any points of doubt. In order that Mr. Martindell might familiarize himself with the way in which Whitman's dual board system worked, I arranged for him to attend meetings of the Board of Trustees, the Finance Committee, and of the regional Overseers in Spokane, Portland, and Seattle. Altogether I believe he came as near to seeing Whitman at work from the inside out as it would be possible for an outside observer to do in six weeks.

In late August Mr. Martindell returned to New York and put his central office staff to work on the data he had collected at Whitman. Using this material, his staff produced a tentative audit report. In October Mr. Martindell flew to Walla Walla with the first draft of the proposed report, and this was checked and rechecked in the light of questions raised by his New York staff. In December, 1953, the American Institute of Management published its *Special Audit No. 116 (Whitman College)*. Copies of this went to everyone on the Whitman mailing list and the AIM mailing list, which, of course, meant nationwide circulation Because it was the first thing of its kind, if for no better reason, it engendered nationwide interest. For the first time an American institution of higher learning had submitted itself to critical examination by spokesmen of the world of business.

The American Institute of Management judged Whitman by the same criteria it had used in its management audits of business concerns, and its final report on Whitman was couched in the language of business, as distinct from the language of professordom. For this very reason the Whitman audit got more attention in business circles than it would have received if it had emanated from academic sources such as an accreditation committee or an educational foundation. In the realm of higher education the AIM report on Whitman College was viewed as a novelty, but thousands of business men read it as a realistic comparison of management in higher education with management in business. The high rating that Whitman was given by the AIM did us no harm in educational circles and did us much good in business circles. I feel sure that it was a factor in Whitman's being placed on the preferred list of several large corporate donors. It was also highly gratifying to thousands of Whitman alumni to have their alma mater so generously praised by a nationally eminent organization in the field of scientific management. Of course, there was adverse criticism as well as praise, and this was good for us, too. We needed to add up both the pluses and minuses. Otherwise, how could we see ourselves as others saw us?

Public Events

A college president is expected to squeeze every drop of publicity value out of public occasions such as convocations and commencements. I accepted this as my duty and did my best to discharge it well. I never did particularly enjoy it. Convocations at Whitman did not offer as much opportunity for publicity as commencements. President Anderson tried, with indifferent success, to make more out of the convocations. Traditionally, Whitman had only one convocation a year namely, the fall convocation at the opening of the first semester. President Anderson sought to make a big show out of this and also out of the winter convocation which he instituted for the second semester. For reasons I need not go into, the winter convocation idea did not take root at Whitman. It might have had a better chance if it had not been introduced during the war years when everything on the Whitman campus was abnormal. It seemed to make everybody happy when I discontinued the winter convocation. As for the fall convocations, I found them useful in getting local publicity, but I never succeeded in getting regional or national attention for any of our fall convocations.

Commencements make news rather easily. There is always a lot of speechifying at commencement time, and it is not hard to get commencement speakers who are themselves newsworthy and know how to make a newsmaking speech. I made an effort at every commencement to get speakers of this kind. I invited clergymen of national repute to deliver the baccalaureate sermons and men of national stature as business men, professional men, scholars, and public servants to deliver the commencement addresses. Sometimes I hit the jackpot with two outstanding speakers at a single commencement, and I never failed to have one who landed us on the front page of the Monday papers. Several of these speeches were taped and rebroadcast by leading radio stations.

Conferring "kudos" in the form of honorary degrees is another way of milking publicity out of the commencement weekend. In the selection of honorary degree recipients I always had one of three objectives in mind, and sometimes had all three in mind at the same commencement. First, I sought to bestow honor on persons of such high repute and achievement that Whitman would shine in reflected glory. Second, I sought to give due and deserved recognition to the accomplishments of Whitman alumni. Third, I sought to pay tribute to persons who had rendered uniquely valuable services to Whitman College. I felt that I could justify every honorary degree awarded during my presidency on one of these grounds, and more than a few could be justified on all three grounds.

At two commencements I resorted to an innovation which proved to have extraordinary publicity values. In 1955 I conferred the honorary degree of doctor of science upon six Whitman graduates who had won national distinction as scientists. No other honorary degrees were bestowed that year, and the entire commencement program was centered on the six scientists and their onetime major professor at Whitman, Benjamin H. Brown. At commencement, 1956, I awarded the honorary degree of doctor of laws on seven lawyer alumni of Whitman—six judges and one professor of law. The news engendered by these two commencements helped a great deal in dispelling the preconception of many people that Whitman was merely a little freshwater college in an out-of-the-way western town. I had plans to make the 1957 commencement or some later one a special occasion for honoring women graduates of noteworthy achievement, but I dropped this idea like a hot potato when I discovered that certain of the ladies I had in mind were pulling wires to get themselves favored.

A college president is called upon to make more speeches than anyone should. No public speaker, not even a Demosthenes or a Cicero, who holds forth as often as most college presidents think they must can make sense all of the time. He really is batting a high average if he makes sense half the time. On the other hand, if he can recognize genuine opportunity when he sees it, he should be able to deliver a few speeches of which he need not be ashamed. During the years that I was president of Whitman College I made scores of speeches, on scores of subjects, in scores of places. I can remember speaking at college and high school commencements and assemblies, at chambers of commerce, at Rotary, Kiwanis, and various other service clubs, at all sorts of dinners and luncheons, at numerous conventions, at political science meetings, at Phi Beta Kappa programs, and other functions too numerous to mention. Being an experienced public speaker with fluency always on tap, I usually made a good impression. But I seldom had anything important to say, and most of those speeches were quickly forgotten by my hearers and also by me. In my eleven presidential years I made only three speeches that gained a nationwide hearing, and each of these was a speech with which I took a great deal of pains.

On June 9, 1950, I was the guest speaker at the Inland Empire Dinner of the American Newcomen Society. The dinner was held at the Davenport Hotel, and the attendance came from Eastern Washington, Northern Idaho, and Western Montana. From the circumstances of my invitation, I gathered that I was expected to discourse for half an hour or so on a topic relevant to higher education and perhaps put in a polite plug for Whitman College. But I decided against doing this. It seemed to me that here was a heaven-sent opportunity to re-tell before a widely representative audience the great story of Marcus and Narcissa Whitman. I had hoped that such an opportunity would come

426

my way, but feared it never would. Nobody had really told that story in a dramatic way since Dr. Penrose's early days at Whitman, and much had been added in the way of historical documentation since then. I read all of the available new material and embodied my conclusions in a speech which I rewrote two or three times. My last step in preparation was to commit this speech to memory so perfectly that I could roll it off my tongue as though the performance were entirely extemporaneous.

The Newcomen Society Dinner was a posh, black-tie affair, with a lavish menu which had been preceded by an equally lavish cocktail hour. There were a number of preliminary toasts (fifteen-minute speeches) before I was called upon. As I began speaking I could discern that my audience was mellow but weary, so I decided to do some old-fashioned spell-binding. Making use of every oratorical trick I had learned in forty years of public speaking, I told the Whitman story in a way that resulted in a standing ovation when I finished. Charles Penrose of Philadelphia, who was master of ceremonies and senior vice president of the Newcomen Society for North America, immediately asked for a copy of my manuscript, saying that he wanted to publish and distribute it as a distinguished Newcomen address. This he did. The speech was set up, printed, and bound as a pamphlet by the Princeton University Press. The Newcomen Society distributed several thousand copies of it, and I gave several hundred to Whitman College, which has used them from time to time in public-relations work.

In the spring of 1951 I was invited to contribute a radio speech to the Columbia networks nationally broadcast series entitled *This I Believe*. The invitation came through my good friend and former student, Edward P. Morgan, who was the producer of this series. Edward R. Murrow was the announcer. Thirty or more supposedly representative American leaders were asked to take part in this series. Each speaker was allowed three minutes and thirty seconds to discourse on the topic "This I Believe." His speech was recorded and the Columbia Broadcasting System then distributed these disks to affiliated local stations all over the United States. The local stations programmed the speeches to suit their own convenience. I got enough reactions from listeners to know that my speech was heard at various times all over the Columbia network. Here is what I said in my three minutes and thirty seconds:

Philosophers have long surmised and modern science seems on the verge of proving that the key to the understanding of our universe is creative force forever creating the future from the present and the past. *This I believe,* and I further believe that the uniqueness of man lies in his possesion of unmeasured creative power.

This creative power is man's to use according to his own judgment as to ends and means. But it is not a power which man may refuse. Willingly or not, every man who lives must assume the role of a creator, for by doing nothing he begets results just as surely as by doing much.

So I am convinced, and I believe, that the most important thing for individuals, for groups, and for nations is to develop ideals by which the innate creativeness of each and all may be guided to greatness rather than to pettiness, to ever-unfolding excellence rather than to inferiority and depravity. Ideals are not *given* to man; he has to *create* them. And by creating ideals, man gains a truly transcendent power—the power knowingly to behave like a beast or a god or anything between.

By the ideals they create and their effective creativeness in the pursuance of those ideals, the individual, the group and the nation will take rank in the supreme reckonings both of man and of God.

Because I believe these things, I strongly believe in the United States of America and the American way of life. Admitting all of our failures and making allowance for all of our false boastings, I still believe that there has not yet appeared on this earth a form of society richer in exalted ideals than the United States or more successful in translating ideals into actuality. Thomas Jefferson once said that the mission of America was not to spread American ideals throughout the world, but to give the world a convincing example of what those ideals could accomplish here in America. That I believe America has done, not perfectly, but impressively—so impressively that all the world is aware of the dimensions of our achievement.

I believe that America can far surpass its past example of creative ideals at work. We have not yet, even here in America, fully exploited the possibilities of putting every man on his own with freedom and opportunity to became a greatly creative individual. For Thomas Jefferson that was the most fundamental and sacred of all American Ideals, the one from which he would never retreat.

Jefferson knew that creative individualism, properly fostered and safeguarded, could place America in the forefront of the nations of the world in the quest of the good life. Looking backward, we know that Jefferson was right. Looking forward, we see that the major task of our time is to manage the tremendously regimentive forces of mass production, mass living, and mass politics so that there will be ample security not alone for the material needs of the individual but for the creative genius which abides in us all. We shall not accomplish this by universalizing those kinds of security which stifle creativeness. *We must never kill the incentive to create.* Whatever the cost, we must give it room and stimulation, and, above all, higher and higher ideals to reach for. Only thus can we preserve and perpetuate the greatness of America's creative service to the world.

That was my creed in 1951; it is still my creed as I type these lines in 1963. Like all believers, I have not been able to be a living example of what I have believed. Nevertheless, the believing has been enormously worthwhile.

429

The speech of mine which received most national recognition was the commencement address which I delivered at Whitman on May 29, 1955. This was the commencement at which the six great scientists were given honorary degrees. Departing from precedent, I chose to make the commencement address myself that year rather than have an outside speaker. There were special reasons for this decision. The honorary degrees were to be conferred on the six scientists not alone to honor them but also to honor the memory of the late Professor Benjamin H. Brown, who had been the major professor of all six when they were students at Whitman. There were things I wanted said about Professor Brown and about the teaching profession in general that I thought no one else, including all six of the scientists, had as good a background for saying as Chester Maxey. This may have been egoism, but it was also realistic. I wanted a particular job done; I knew exactly what the job was and how it should be done. There was no one else to whom I could turn for that particular assignment.

I entitled my speech "The Work of the Teacher," and tried to work out a neatly capsuled summary of the basic qualities and abilities necessary to the making of a great teacher. Although I prepared the speech with a particular occasion and audience in mind, I took pains to give it a literary quality that might attract a wider range of interest. It was an easy speech to deliver, and the response from the commencement audience was good. Our news service sent copies of the speech to the customary press bureaus and wire services, and through these channels the speech found its way into the hands of the editors of *Life* magazine. I did not know this and was just as surprised as anyone when my speech was favorably featured in *Life's* leading editorial on June 20, 1955. In part this editorial said:

> On thousands of school and college campuses, under elm and maple, palm and pine, the massed and mortared youth of America has been getting its last formal advice. Every commencement orator tries to say something new, true or useful. Some succeed. * * * At Whitman College in Walla Walla, President C. C.

Maxey voiced some thoughts on what a good teacher should be. He must be a scholar but more than a scholar, his mind "a fountain, not a reservoir." He must know how to fix the student's vagrant attention through an "intellectual ascendancy . . . which instructs but does not enslave." He must be a model "in every utterance and every deed . . . Even though he may prefer it the back seat is not for the teacher . . . When there is something to be done which street corner literacy unaided cannot accomplish, (the teacher) is drafted for service and for a leadership which only men of high education can supply." The teacher must be a free man. But "the greater his freedom from external compulsions the more exposed he is to the subtle tyrannies of his own personal Pharisaisms. He will not overcome these merely by professing high ideals. Every day of his life he must work hard, far harder than other men to widen his knowledge, dethrone his prejudices, and rectify his judgments." Dr. Maxey's rigorous standard applies to the educated man in any calling. And because that standard has been set, and is here and there maintained, there was a sense of hope and purpose on the American campus this June.

This citation in *Life* resulted in so many requests for copies of the speech that we had it printed and issued as a bulletin of Whitman College. As such it received wide distribution. Some college presidents asked for enough copies to supply all of their faculty members.

Making speeches is but one of the public relations responsibilities of a college president. Another, which can be even more burdensome, is that of being a "joiner." A president is expected to accept membership and take part in the activities of many organizations of a civic or semi-civic nature. Since I had been doing this all my professional life, it was not necessary to step up the pace very much when I became president of Whitman. There were some, however, that I might not have taken on if I had not felt it to be a sort of presidential duty.

XXVI. MISCELLANY

Multi-Ring Circus

If he ever thinks of college presidents at all, the man on the street corner is likely to imagine them as bookish highbrows who eke out their days and nights in an unreal world of thoughts and theories. To those who see him from afar, it is inconceivable that a college president should know anything or have anything to do about such practical affairs as running a farm, operating a business, or directing a governmental agency. How can there be anything practical about education, except, of course, the inculcation of knowledge?

I often wished, when I was president of Whitman, that I had more time for the world of ideas and were obliged to give less to the world of deeds. I often wished also that all of my proudly practical friends might have been obliged to follow me around long enough to discover the kind of work I actually did. They would have gone crossed-eyed watching the multi-ring circus I had to keep going, and going right as far as possible every day of the year. Few businesses are as complex as a private college, and none demands a mastery of more varied problems of management. A college president may gain his job by reason of his reputation and achievements as an educator, but if education is all he knows or can do, he will not last long as a college president.

As president of Whitman College I was responsible for seeing that upwards of a dozen different kinds of business were carried on properly and successfully. It was my job to pick subordinates with know-how in many different fields and had to direct and supervise them all in the performance of their duties. If anyone fell down on his job, I was the one who had to answer directly to Whitman's governing boards and indirectly to her constituency as well as the general public. Everybody could see that I was in the education business, head over heels; but not many could perceive that I was almost as deeply involved in the farming business, the property management business, the hotel and restaurant business, the retailing business, the investment business, the fund-raising business, the contruction business, the hospital business, the personnel placement business, the entertainment business, and various others.

It was not necessary for me to be a farmer to discharge my responsibility for the management of Whitman's 3,625 acres of crop land. I had the help of a committee of eminently successful farm operators, but I had to know enough to understand what they were doing and why. I had to form judgments as to whether their policies were right not only for the immediate present but for the long years ahead. I had to keep in close contact wtih them, attend all their meetings, visit all the farm properties, talk with all of the tenants, and be informed enough about leases, mortgages, various kinds of farm insurance, fertilizer programs, and governmental farm policies and programs to do the coordinating and communicating that was necessary to integrate our agricultural operations with our other business activities.

It was not necessary for me to be a realtor to meet my responsibility for the proper management of Whitman's city properties. I could rely on expert help in that business, too; but I had to know enough about titles, rentals, mortgages and other aspects of the realty business to keep track of what our treasurer, business manager, and special committees were doing in that regard. Keeping track was not simply for the purpose of seeing that they did right; it was even more for the purpose of enabling me to use the authority of my office as helpfully to them as possible.

It was not necessary for me to be an experienced hotel man to supervise the housing and feeding of some five hundred persons a day. I had splendid assistance in that area, but I had to be in close and constant touch with what was going on. It was not merely that I was solely responsible to the governing boards for the expenditure of some $200,000 a year in our housing and feeding operations, but that I was equally responsible to the patrons (the students and their parents) for the quality of board and room they received at Whitman.

It was not necessary for me to be an experienced retail merchant to discharge my responsibility in connection with the operation of the fountain, snack bar, and book store in Whitman's Student Center. The manager was an exceptionally capable business man. But there was an outlay of $80,000 a year in that operation, and I had to know all the whys and wherefores, because I had to correlate that with the other food services and also be able to explain to the governing boards just where every penny went, in case they should want to know.

It was not necessary for me to be an investment banker to discharge my duties with respect to Whitman's $2,500,000 portfolio of stocks and bonds. As I have said earlier in this narrative, the Whitman Finance Committee was made up of investment experts. But it was my duty to attend every meeting of this committee and be fully informed regarding every sale or purchase made. Why? Because I, as president of the College, was more likely to have to answer questions about our investments and investment policies than anyone else. The big foundations always direct their questions first to the president, and so do most of the business corporations that help support higher education.

I did not have to be a trained and professional fund-raiser to meet my responsibilities in getting money for Whitman. But I found out one thing very soon, which was that no professional fund-raiser could replace the president. The people who give large sums to colleges would much rather deal with the president than with a professional fund-raiser, and they nearly always insist on doing so. Professional fund-raisers helped me in carrying on financial campaigns and sometimes took much of the drudgery off my shoulders. But they never relieved me of any of the responsibility and sometimes made the responsibility a mite heavier by making mistakes that I had to correct.

I did not have to be an architect or building contractor to discharge my duties in connection with the construction of the three new buildings which were added to the Whitman plant in my eleven years. But it was my duty to learn enough about architectural practice and building construction to see that suitable plans were prepared, suitable contracts drawn, and effective check-ups made at every stage of each job.

The fact that Whitman had to have an infirmary put me in the hospital business, and there were potential dangers involved in that operation, both medical and legal dangers, that obliged me to keep the infirmary under close supervision all the time. The fact that Whitman had a theater and a conservatory of music put me in the entertainment business, and, though financially speaking these were not large operations, they involved a multitude of details that I had to keep under control. The same was true of the placement service, the library, the activities of the student association, and several other activities which kept Whitman buzzing all the time.

In the multi-ring circus I have just described, education was supposed to be the big center ring and get most of the attention. I gave a great deal of time to educational policy and even more time to educational administration, but always with at least peripheral vision on all the other rings.

Religion at Whitman

There were sanctimonious souls who said I was a godless college president, and blamed me for an alleged decline of religious emphasis and activity on the Whitman campus. I never bothered to answer any of these accusations, nor did I make any effort to foster a religious revival at Whitman. I had known about religion at Whitman since 1908, and I remembered that even then, way back in my freshman year, I learned in the Wilbur Memorial Methodist Church that Whitman was a godless college and that most of the professors were atheists. They taught evolution, didn't they? And wasn't that proof enough that they were atheists?

When in later years I began to delve into Whitman history I learned that the first president of Whitman College to be accused of irreligion was the first man to hold the office, Alexander J. Anderson. Indeed, it was the savage and unrelenting criticisms of the Congregational clergy which led to the nervous breakdown that caused Dr. Anderson to resign. President Anderson was not an ordained minister, and the Congregational clergy said, therefore, that he was unfit to be the president of a Christian college. They said he gave courses in religion he was incompetent to teach and held him responsible for the alleged spread of irreligion on the campus. After making life so miserable for President Anderson that he decided to resign, the Congregational clergy had their way. President Eaton was an ordained minister of the Congregational Church, and the Congregational clergy liked him very much; but the Congregational laymen on the Board of Trustees did not, nor did the Congregational members of the faculty.

President Penrose was also an ordained Congregational minister, and I think no Whitman president ever had more brickbats thrown at him by incensed religionists than Dr. Penrose. In some quarters he was denounced for having transformed Whitman into a non-sectarian college; in other quarters he was denounced for teaching unorthodox doctrines, including evolution, in his courses on religion; and in still other quarters he was denounced for countenancing and supporting religious freedom at Whitman. One of my most cherished memories of Dr. Penrose, and this goes back to my freshman year, was being encouraged to think for myself in religious matters and being given to understand that the reasons for my beliefs were more important than the beliefs themselves. In his later years President Penrose was held responsible, incorrectly, for the discontinuance of compulsory chapel at Whitman. All he did was to appoint a committee to study the problem. It was by vote of the faculty that required chapel was abolished.

President Clemen was likewise a Congregational minister, and it was during his brief regime that the required courses in Bible and philosophy of religion went out of the window. This was by action of the faculty with President Clemen's hearty approval. President Bratton was an Episcopalian laymen and President W. S. Anderson joined the Congregational church after he was inaugurated president of Whitman. All we knew about his religion when he was elected was that he called himself a Protestant, and he was asked no questions about religion by the two Congregationalists and two Episcopalians on the recommending committee. As I later found out, he was a renegade Baptist who thought it would be good politics to join the Congregational church. I never could see that it helped him in any way. President Anderson made one important contribution to religious activity among the students, and that was to foster the establishment of the annual Campus Conference on Religion. This was extremely popular among the students and also with many members of the faculty, but it was far more an intellectualizing than a spiritualizing force.

My policy with respect to religion at Whitman was to maintain the status quo. I thought we had nothing to gain by either re-emphasis or de-emphasis. I knew of no viable methods of re-emphasis and had no interest in further de-emphasis. The religious problem as I found it on becoming president had two faces. One of these had to do with religion in the curriculum and the other with extra-curricular religious activities and affairs.

As I have already noted, all required courses in religion had been made elective a dozen years or more before I became president. Nobody, including the professors of religion and philosophy, wanted to restore any of these requirements or establish new ones. There was an emaciated department of Biblical literature in Division II and a similarly undernourished department of philosophy in Division I. One of my first recommendations was that we establish a full scale department in each field. This recommendation was quickly approved by the governing boards and put into effect. For three years thereafter we had more offerings in both religion and philosophy than ever before in Whitman history. But in 1951 the decline of enrollment owing to the combined effects of the low birth rate during the depression and the increase of the armed forces in the Korean War resulted in a temporary setback. Owing to circumstances irrelevant to this particular discussion, we lost our philosophy professor in the middle of the year and our religion professor at the end of the year. Because of the dual emergency and need for retrenchment, I employed a man to teach both religion and philosophy—a half schedule of each—as Dr. Penrose had done for so many years. This arrangement continued until 1954, when I again employed a full-time man in philosophy and began looking for a full-time man in religion. The Reverend Franklin R. Elliott of the First Congregational Church of Walla Walla had been doing part-time teaching in religion, and had done so well that I was not in a hurry to replace him. I mention these details merely to support the point that nothing was done in my administration to de-emphasize religion in the curriculum.

As for extra-curricular activities in religion, only three were being carried on at Whitman when I became president. These were the voluntary chapel services, the Campus Conference on Religion, and the Young Women's Christian Association. The chapel program was on its last legs. Nobody wanted to return to compulsory chapel, not even the professor of religion, and nobody knew how to insure attendance at the voluntary chapel services. With my full approval and cooperation, several expedients were tried, and all of them failed. The students would not come to chapel to hear speakers, they would not come to hear music, and they would not come to take part in devotions. A dozen was a big turnout, which was just enough to make chapel ridiculous. The man who finally tossed in the towel, said it was no use to try any longer, was not the president, but the professor of religion. I thought he was right and still think so.

The Campus Conference on Religion had my full approval and cooperation, but I insisted that it be entirely student-supported and student-managed. From memories of my own student days, I was convinced that nothing would kill the CCOR quicker than for the administration or the faculty to take a hand in it. Every year that I was president the students managed to raise enough money to stage a lively and disputatious program of religious discussions. These did not always make their elders happy, but they stirred up more interest in religion than the chapel services ever had been able to do.

The program of the Young Womens Christian Association ran along in my administration exactly as it had done in all previous administrations. Whatever the young ladies requested in the way of cooperation they got, but they were more interested in welfare work and social service than in religion per se. When I was a student at Whitman, I belonged to the Young Men's Christian Association, but that organization expired during World War I, so I am told, and no effort was ever made to revive it.

I am sure that a number of good people leaped to the conclusion that I must be undermining religion at Whitman because I was not active in any church. Elsewhere in this autobiography I have explained how that came to be. Technically, I remained a Methodist, but did not care to resume active membership in that church. Since no other church ever appealed to me enough to draw me into its fold, I preferred to remain a Methodist at large. Of course there are Christians who take churchism to be the essence of Christianity. If I read the New Testament correctly, the founder of Christianity did not take this attitude toward the established ecclesiastical institutions of his time. Since Whitman College was de-churched under President Penrose back in 1908, I did not feel out of place or ill at ease in serving as its president. Nor do I recall any instance of embarrassment on my part or that of anyone else because I was an ecclesiastical maverick. It could be that God absented himself from the Whitman campus during my regime, but we were richly blessed with human godliness just the same.

The Team

There is a much repeated saying that no man is an island, which, like many a neat aphorism is not universally true. In some callings a man can have as much insularity as he wishes. Writing is such a calling, so is research and so to a large extent is teaching. But, if there is any one calling above others in which one cannot have the slightest insularity, it must be that of a college president. No man alone could ever begin to run the multi-ring circus that I have described earlier in this chapter. From the moment he takes office, a college president must rely upon a team—a large and complicated organization—to take him to his goals. The most he can claim for himself is to have been instrumental in the success of the team.

Knowing how much I owe to team work, I cannot close this account of my eleven years as president without giving credit and paying tribute to the principal members of my team. I cannot begin to mention them all, and there may be some of whom I am unaware, whose names I never learned. Nor can I mention the many who, for various reasons worked with me less than five years. I would not trust my memory on that. However, I do want to list the names, in several categories, of the persons who were with me most of my presidential years and contributed most to the accomplishments of those years.

It would take a volume of many pages to enumerate in detail the contributions of every person named. Some made their principal contributions in money, some in service, some in both money and service. Some made important contributions in special knowledge and know-how, some in wise counsel, some in exertion of personal influence. Some made invaluable contributions in zeal and loyalty, some in dependability and diligence. Some made great contributions in performance far beyond the call of duty. Many, and I wish it were possible to specify their names, made contributions overlapping all of the particulars just mentioned.

By virtue of the constitutional structure of Whitman College, the presidents immediate superiors and most necessary supporters are the members of the Board of Trustees. I had a wonderful Board of Trustees. I doubt if any president of Whitman ever had a better one. To the following persons who served on the Board of Trustees during my administration, I feel a debt of special gratitude: D. F. Baker, Roy R. Cahill, Mary Jewett Gaiser, James S. Johns, F. Lowden Jones, Harper Joy, Howard J. Knott, Arthur T. Lee, John C. Lyman, Herbert Ringhoffer, Donald Sherwood, and Park Weed Willis.

Under Whitman's dual system, the Board of Overseers is responsible for general policies and broad objectives. None of the major projects carried to completion during my administration would have succeeded without the effective collaboration of the members of the Board of Overseers both collectively and individually. Of the members serving during my administration, I want to acknowledge a special debt to each of the following: Clarence Braden, Robert H. Brome, Henry J. Copeland, Ralph Cordiner, Harold E. Crawford, Arthur F. Douglas, William O. Douglas, Stanly A. Easton, Ralph P. Edgerton, Jonathan W. Edwards, James Alger Fee, Kenneth E. Fry, David W. Gaiser, Paul Garrett, J. Gordon Gose, Howard C. Graham, John J. Gurian, James Hill, Sr., James Hill, Jr., Nard Jones, Judd D. Kimball, J. Ernest Knight, Richard KcKay, A. H. Meadowcroft, Russell Miller, W. Lawrence Minnick, Robert L. Moore, Arthur H. Morgan, Edward P. Morgan, Charles D. Ogden, Grace Farnsworth Phillips, Roy V. Peringer, Robert L. Ringer, W. L. Teague, Hall Templeton, Bertram B. Warren, Kathryn Wilson, and George R. Yancey.

During my years as president there were about a dozen officers of administration who functioned as deans or directors of services. In a way these constituted the president's cabinet. Certain of those rendered services that were invaluable to me. In particular I would mention the following: Rodney W. Alexander, Charles J. Armstrong, Helen Bragg, Winifred Dunphy, Alta Glenny, Paul Harvey, Paul J. Jackson, Vern E. Kinsinger, Almira Quinn, Robert R. Reid, Ruth S. Reynolds, David Stevens, W. L. Stirling, Robert R. Thomsen, Miriam Wagenschein, and Frederick C. Wilson.

Citations for services of special value to the president should go to the following members of the faculty: Robert B. Burgess, J. Jerry Fogarty, Thomas D. Howells, Leo C. Humphrey, Frederic Santler, Robert L. Whitner, and Glen J. Woodward.

Similar citations should go to the following who served as secretaries, members of the housing staff, or the buildings and grounds staff: Ann Coleman, Blane Craigie, Mabel Dillard, Maude Garfield, Pearl Hall, Frank Jorgenson, William Jorgenson, Frances Mayer, Mae Saling, Karl Schwarz, Helen Struthers, Vicki Toppano, Lucile Walton, and Mabel Watrous.

A number of persons who at the time had no official connection with Whitman rendered services of incalculable worth to

441

Whitman College. I feel a great personal obligation to the following: Mr. and Mrs. Grant S. Bond, E. L. Casey, N. A. Davis, Mr. and Mrs. Carleton N. Kelley, Mrs Harriet Grimshaw, Mr. and Mrs. John G. Kelly, Mrs. Sarah Harris Johnson, Reno Ransom, Lester L. Robison, Eugene Tausick, Ed Tucker, Nathanial V. Usher, and Robert J. Williams.

PART VI
RETIREMENT 1959-?

XXVII. FAREWELL TO WHITMAN

Planning for Retirement

Kirtley F. Mather has written that "comparatively few people look forward to retirement with unalloyed pleasure." I must have been one of the comparatively few who did not look upon retirement as a wasteland but as an opportunity. In my young manhood I began to think about retirement and look forward to it as a time when I would have all the freedom I wanted. I even began to think about how I would make use of such unrestricted freedom, and conceived some plans which I found very helpful when my time of retirement finally came.

Having sponsored Whitman's retirement rule and applied it to others, it was certainly up to me to observe it strictly myself, and I did. In 1955 when I became sixty-five years of age, I so informed the governing boards, pointed out that the rule applied to me, and stated that I was ready to comply with it. Both boards urged me not to retire, but I pointed out that the rule applied to me, and stated that I was ready to comply with it. I also pointed out that the rule was self-operating and specifically said that an affirmative vote of the Board of Trustees should be necessary to continue an employee beyond his sixty-fifth year. Such a vote was immediately forthcoming, and I agreed to go on from year to year until June 30, 1959. I declared that I would not under any circumstances continue beyond that date.

One of the reasons I agreed to serve four years more was the Penrose Memorial Library. At commencement, 1955, we were just getting started on the financial drive for that building, and I had an ambition to see that project through to completion both financially and structurally. I feared that if I retired before the library drive got into "high" there might be a slowdown which would be fatal to its success. Another reason for deciding to stay on the job a while longer was the fact that several major gifts for other than library purposes also seemed just around the corner. Negotiations with respect to these were going on through my office and were in fact mostly in my own hands. They might have been carried through to success regardless of my retirement, but there was a chance that they might not. I thought I ought not to force that risk upon Whitman College. Whether my staying on as president had anything to do with it or not, it is a fact that in the very next year (1955-56) Whitman received gifts aggregating $810,352.

A third reason for my willingness to postpone retirement a few years was the discovery, rather fortuitously in a way, that my health was so good that two insurance companies (Penn Mutual and Massachusetts Mutual) were eager to bet a half million dollars that I would not die in office. Thereby hangs an interesting little tale. The same two companies, through local representatives, had tried to talk the Board of Trustees into insuring the life of Winslow Anderson for a half-million dollars just a year before he died. The Trustees thought the premium was too steep, and so refused the deal. When the same insurance men approached the Trustees with a proposal to insure me for a half-million with the College as beneficiary, the Trustees were sufficiently interested to ask me if I would be willing to take the necessary physical examinations. I readily agreed, as it meant getting my annual check-up free. Two of Walla Walla's leading medicos, one representing each company, gave me the works and I came through without a single question mark against me. The Board then decided that if the examinations showed me to be a prime risk for the insurance companies, I would be a poor risk for the College at a preminum of some $25,000 a year. So they refused to take out the policy. But the results of the examinations freed me of all worry about health as a factor in staying on the job after sixty-five.

I selected 1959 as my retirement year mainly for sentimental reasons. Whitman would be observing its centennial in that year, and I felt that there would be a sort of poetic propriety in closing a chapter of my life simultaneously with the ending of the first century of life for the institution. Another sentimental

446

reason was that I had been the executive officer in charge of Whitman's seventy-fifth anniversary program and wanted the unique distinction of also directing the one-hundredth anniversary. The theme-song of the seventy-fifth had, perforce, been poverty, and I wanted my swan song to be one of prosperity. However, I did not have the nerve to set up a comparison between the condition of the College in 1934 and 1959. I merely compared 1959 and 1948.

One never knows when he reaches the point of diminishing returns so far as his contribution to the success of an organization or institution is concerned. Nobody else knows, either, until his deficiencies are glaringly obvious. I wanted to retire with the score still in my favor, and I hoped 1959 would not be too late. I thought we could finish the library and a certain amount of fund-raising by that time, and that would clear the way for my successor to start with a clean sheet. Things actually moved a bit faster than I had anticipated, and I could have stepped out a year or two earlier and have left everything in good shape. But I had set my retirement for 1959 and I carried on up to my last day in office just as though I would be on the job the rest of my days.

Probably I could have continued a few years longer. Physically and mentally I was in excellent condition, and everything seemed to be going my way. Furthermore, I was not tired in mind or body, but I was tired of the job. The chief reason why I was tired of the job was that I wanted to do something else. I could still do the work, but it had become a bore. I was chained to a routine that would be essentially the same routine tomorrow and tomorrow and tomorrow as long as I should be president. If I had to live a routine, as most of us do, I wanted it to be my own and not one dictated by circumstances largely beyond my control. Furthermore, I was not at all worried about what I would do with my time in retirement. I had financial security, an ample income for life, and I had every possible freedom of choice as to what to do after retirement. If I wanted to resume teaching, I knew that would not be difficult. If I wanted to write, I had more projects in mind

447

than I could finish if I lived to be a hundred. If I wanted to travel, I could. If I wanted to dabble in politics, I had the time and the means. If I wanted to play around with gardening, I had as good a half-acre for that purpose as any one could want. If I wanted to try my hand with the stock market, I had means enough to keep me well occupied and still not jeopardize my principal. And if I wanted to do nothing but loaf around, I had everything necessary to make the life of a sluggard enjoyable. So I chose to retire with no reluctance whatever, and never for a moment have I regretted that decision.

In connection with my thinking about retirement I reached a firm conclusion that I would sever all but the most nominal connections with Whitman College. This was a totally unemotional decision based on the conviction that the greatest disservice a president emeritus can do to his successor and to his college is to hang around the campus sopping up gossip and offering a sympathetic shoulder to weepers and wailers. I had seen more than enough of that sort of thing in the dozen or more years that Dr. Penrose lived on the campus after his retirement as president. Dr. Penrose did not mean to be constantly looking over the shoulders of his successors in office, but, being on the campus every day, he simply could not help it. Talebearers ran to him and he listened. Sometimes he expressed opinions. It never occurred to him, I am sure, that these opinions might be grossly distorted in transmission from ear to ear via the campus grapevine. I was determined that I would not provide the slightest justification for anyone ever to say that I put any stumbling blocks in the way of my successor. The only way I could be sure of this was to divorce myself from Whitman affairs and absent myself from the campus most of the time.

With respect to my successor in office, I was determined to be as neutral as I could possibly be. I did not want to appear to be for him or against him, because either attitude might handicap or hurt in some way. No man can transmit either his popularity or his unpopularity to another, but if he tries to do so, he can be sure that his failure will result in some kind

448

of trouble. I was asked to take part in the selection of my successor, but refused. I was urged to issue public statements endorsing him, but refused. I was urged to volunteer my good offices and personal counsel in getting him started on the job, but refused. The only thing I would and did say was that IF AND WHEN HE SHOULD ASK ME, I would be glad to give him any information or judgment he might think worthwhile. Otherwise, I would keep silent, and I would not take it amiss if he never asked me anything. I had been free to make my own mistakes as president, and I wanted my successor to enjoy the same freedom.

The Centennial Year

So far as the regular work of my office was concerned, the year 1958-59 was little different from any other. I had set the date of my retirement as June 30, 1959, because that date marked the termination of both the fiscal and the academic years for Whitman College. It seemed to me that a transition from an old regime to a new one could be most easily accomplished at that time. But I did not change my routine, postpone anything, or slack off in my work, and I remained in my office and at work until 5 P.M. of the last day. Why not? There was no reason to hold a wake of any kind just because I was retiring.

A few additional labors were occasioned by the centennial program, but these were not personally burdensome to me. In the fall of 1958 I appointed a special committee to plan and carry through the program of events for Whitman's 100th anniversary. This committee was composed of Professors Frederic F. Santler (chairman), Rodney W. Alexander, Thomas D. Howells, Kenneth E. Schilling, and Robert L. Whitner. Being ex officio a member of this committee, I met with it from time to time and kept in touch with all plans and arrangements. A very impressive series of special events was programmed.

The first of this series was the Centennial Convocation, held on the evening of February 23, 1959, in the Walla Walla High School Gymnasium, the only auditorium in the city with sufficient seating capacity to accommodate the crowd. This convocation was a well-balanced combination of pomp and circumstance, exemplified by the academic procession in resplendent costume, and a musical and narrative dramatization of the history of Whitman College. The narrative was written by members of the Centennial Committee and was read by Professor Alexander, one of the members of the Committee. The reading was interspersed with correlated musical selections by the Whitman Choir and a specially organized brass ensemble. Following the narrative were three speeches—an introductory speech by me, a response in behalf of the alumni by Mr. Earl Dusenberry, president of the Whitman Alumni Association, and a response by the Honorable Albert D. Rosellini, governor of the state of Washington. My little speech was mainly in the historical vein, and since it was the last formal speech I made as president of Whitman College, I incorporate it here:

This convocation is the first of a series of public events in the observance of the centennial of Whitman College. In behalf of the students, the faculty, the administrative staff, and the official boards of the College, I have the privilege of extending a cordial welcome to the people of Walla Walla and the entire Northwest to share these events with us.

Strictly speaking, what Whitman is commemorating this year is the 100th anniversary of a corporation. The Whitman Seminary, though chartered in 1859, could offer no instruction until 1863, and was intermittently closed and reopened until it expired in 1882. But the corporation did not expire. It has been in continuous existence from the moment Governor Gohlson signed its charter on December 20, 1859 to this very hour. In 1883 its charter was amended, giving it additional powers and privileges, but its corporate existence was not at all interrupted by those amendments.

This corporation, whose legal name is the Board of Trustees of Whitman College, was created by a special act of the territorial legislature of Washington in response to a request from Elkanah Walker, George H. Atkinson, Elisha S. Tanner, Erastus S. Joslyn, W. A. Tenney, H. H. Spalding, John C. Smith, James Craigie, and Cushing Eells, who were designated to be the first members of the Board of Trustees.

The initiative for this act came from a group of private citizens, but the incorporation could be accomplished only by a sovereign enactment of the government of Washington Territory. Thus it may be truthfully said that Whitman College as it is today is as much the handiwork of public authority as of private enterprise.

The charter itself makes clear what the territorial legislature had in mind. The charter states that this corporation shall be a "body politic and corporate." That wording makes it clear that the legislature intended to create and did create a legal entity which would be something more than a purely private corporation and something less than a fully public corporation. Lawyers call such corporations quasi-public corporations. Scores and scores of such corporations have been created under the laws of Washington, but I dare say there is only one in existence today which has been continuously active for one hundred years, namely, the Board of Trustees of Whitman College.

Whitman College could not have been brought into being without the aid and authorization of the territorial government of Washington, and Whitman cannot fittingly observe its centennial without the participation of the government of the State of Washington.

It is a matter of extreme gratification to us that the 36th legislature of the state, now in session at Olympia, has already participated through the enactment of a joint resolution of appreciation and congratulation.

We are highly honored tonight by the presence of the chief executive of Washington, who has come to Walla Walla to participate in this convocation as a distinguished guest and featured speaker. Later in the year we are to have the privilege of welcoming to our midst the chief justice of Washington.

Ladies and gentlemen, it is a distinction and a pleasure on this historic occasion to present the Honorable Albert D. Rosellini, Governor of Washington.

Governor Rosellini's address was nicely tailored to the occasion and was impressively delivered. In felicitous phrases he extended official greetings, lauded Whitman College, and commented on the historic significance of the centennial observances. Earl Dusenberry was equally pleasing in voicing the interests and feelings of the alumni. The other participants in this Centennial Convocation were the Reverend Franklin R. Elliott, who offered the invocation and pronounced the benediction; Professor David Burge, who composed and directed the musical numbers performed by the brass ensemble; Professor Stanley R. Plummer, who played the organ; Professor Kenneth E. Schilling, who directed the choir; and Professor Rodney W. Alexander, who was the narrator of the four-part Whitman saga. Quite as much as the speakers, these participants enhanced the memorability of the convocation.

The other featured events of our centennial program were three public lectures by nationally distinguished scholars, a memorial service at Waiilatpu (site of the original Whitman mission), a centennial banquet held on the evening of May 30, and the centennial commencement exercises held in the campus amphitheater on May 31. The first of the three lectures was held on March 30, the speaker being Dr. Edward L. Tatum, Professor of Biology at Stanford University and winner of the Nobel Prize in medicine in 1958. His subject was "A Century of Progress in Genetics," and he talked so far over the heads of the audience that everybody knew he must be a great scientist. The second lecture came on April 20, and the speaker was a Whitman graduate, Dr. Walter H. Brattain, a staff member of the Bell Laboratories and a Nobel laureate in physics in 1956. His subject was "Man and the Universe: How Much Does He Know?" Dr. Brattain also dealt with scientific subject-matter, but was far more to the taste of the audience than Dr.

Tatum. The third lecture was given on May 11, and the speaker was Dr. Howard Mumford Jones, Professor of English and onetime Dean of the Graduate School, Harvard University. His lecture was entitled "On Yon High Eastern Hill," and was a beautiful exposition of the values of a liberal education. These lectures served the purpose of symbolizing the academic stature and embellishing the national reputation of Whitman College. My only function in connection with them was to act as master of ceremonies.

The memorial service at Waiilatpu consisted of musical numbers by the College choir and a talk on the historical significance of Marcus and Narcissa Whitman by Robert L. Whitner, professor of American history of Whitman. The featured speaker of the centennial banquet was the president of the University of Washington, Dr. Charles E. Odegaard who made an erudite and interesting address on the interrelations of public and private institutions of higher education. I was called upon for some remarks and spoke extemporaneously for about ten minutes. I had no vital message to leave behind, and used my time mostly to express gratitude for the cooperation I had received in my years as president of Whitman.

The centennial commencement exercises fell on my sixty-ninth birthday. The baccalaureate speaker was the Reverend Russell B. Staines of Seattle, a Whitman graduate of 1933 and a former student in my classes. The speaker at the graduation exercises was the Honorable Frank P. Weaver, Chief Justice of the State of Washington, a longtime Beta brother and personal friend of mine. Both speeches were of high quality and well suited to the occasion. In connection with the degree-granting there was one irregularity, the result of an amiable conspiracy against me on the part of the faculty and the Board of Trustees. They tried to keep it from me until the last moment, but, since I was in charge of the program, they could not execute the plot without my consent. The plot was to award me the honorary degree of Doctor of Humane Letters. I acquiesced, not because I thought I specially merited this particular honor, but because so many of my coworkers seemed to think I did.

Such in brief were the formal events of the centennial program. To me, and I believe to others, they were simple, yet fitting and impressive. It was my own decision that there should be much less fanfare than I had put into the seventy-fifth anniversary observances in 1934. That was a year in which Whitman needed fanfare to bolster its courage. I felt that fanfare would be out of keeping with the spirit of Whitman in 1959. In connection with my retirement there were many pleasing social events which Elnora and I shall always cherish in our memories. One was a dinner given in our honor by the girls of Anderson and Prentiss Halls, another a dinner given for us by the Gamma Zeta Chapter of Beta Theta Pi, still another a dinner in our honor by a group of Yakima alumni who made a special trip to Walla Walla for this purpose, yet another a luncheon in our honor by the Walla Walla Chamber of Commerce, and finally the farewell dinner on the evening of June 30 by the administrative staff of the College. We received many gifts and other tokens of appreciation from the Trustees, the Overseers, the Faculty, the Associated Students, and many other individuals and groups. We were almost overcome by the plenitude of honors and gifts heaped upon us, and we agreed between ourselves that we had been honored much in excess of the usual amenities of retirement.

XXVIII. OLD MAN MAXEY

Breathing Spell

If there is any truth in the common saying that a man is as old as he feels, I was still a young man when I retired. I was sixty-nine years of age and in superb physical condition. I had not experienced any of the characteristic infirmities and disabilities of old age, and at the time of the present writing (August, 1965) I still have not. Every year I have gone through my annual check-up without a single question mark against me. I have had enough physical vigor and stamina to do all of the manual labor involved in the care of half-acre of lawn, flowers, and vegetable garden. I have had enough mental energy and concentration to grind out hundreds of pages of typescript and to do quantities of reading, both for professional and pleasurable purposes.

But one thing I discovered soon after my retirement was that there is such a thing as growing old without feeling old. One day it dawns on you that all of your onetime cronies are gone, that you can count real contemporaries on the fingers of one hand, that no matter how you feel about yourself other people regard you as old. Until I retired I had been too busy with a multitude of things to realize that I was gradually getting to be like "The Last of the Mohicans," a survivor of a bygone era. Forever in the future I would be Old Man Maxey. Nothing could ever change that.

This was no particular shock to me, but it did take a breathing spell of six months or so to map out in my mind the kind of life that Old Man Maxey, with plenty still on the ball, might best strive to make for himself as a senior citizen. One thing I decided rather soon was to stay off the academic treadmill. When President Armstrong of the University of Nevada (he was my former vice president at Whitman) invited me to accept a lectureship at that institution, I declined with sincere thanks. After forty-two years of college teaching and administration, it was hard to develop much enthusiasm for more of the same. I was well enough known in my own profession to secure desirable teaching or lecturing appointments in a number of places, but I wanted, for a while at least, to be completely my own man.

Some people wondered why I did not make a trip around the world or otherwise use my new freedom for travel. They did not realize that I had been traveling constantly for eleven years, and hated the sight, sound and smell of planes, trains, hotels, and motels. Travel was something that had to be scheduled, and I was determined, for a while anyhow, to be completely emancipated from schedules. Every day, as it suited my fancy, I would make or unmake a pattern of life. This did not mean being idle; it just meant being uncommitted.

455

After a few months of this relaxing irresponsibility, I settled upon three major pre-occupations for the years ahead, however many or few they might be. One of these had to be writing. All of my profesional life I had been a writer on the side. In such time as I could snatch from other work I wrote books and articles, but I had never had a chance to put writing foremost in my life. Now I had that chance, and I determined to make the most of it. My second major pre-occupation, if the opportunity arose or could be made, would be public affairs. All my life I had avoided being an academic recluse by being active in politics and civic affairs. If I could continue that kind of activity in my old age, I could still live on the banks, if not navigate the middle, of the stream of life. And my third major pre-occupation for retirement was to be money-making. Although I had not been exactly a failure in that respect, my freedom of action had been much restricted by the necessity of the exercise of caution to safeguard to the utmost the financial security of my wife and children. That necessity no longer existed; I was now free to see what I could do by dabbling in the stock market.

Re-learning to Write

For eleven years I had been divorced from the regular and rugged grind of manuscript production. Had I lost my touch or not? Non-use of skills sometimes rusts them out, but I did not believe this had happened to me. As president of Whitman College I had been writing something all the time—letters, memoranda, reports, brochures, and the like. I thought this would be enough to keep me in practice as a writer. But it wasn't. The first shock was to discover that I had lost most of my speed on the typewriter and with the loss of speed, naturally, a considerable loss of ability to compose while typing. And it had been so many years since I had tried to compose in longhand that it was a totally lost skill. My first task, therefore, was to recapture as much as possible of my former proficiency on the machine. Right away, in July, 1959, I began hammering away on a series of essays that I called *Afterthoughts*. These had to do with educational matters, particularly those specially appertaining to a college president.

By forcing myself to work on the typewriter from three to four hours a day I soon got my finger coordination back into the old groove but it took much longer to recover my ability to think directly into the machine through my fingertips. Between the first of July, 1959, and the first of June, 1960, I wrote seventeen essays on such topics as "The Liberal Arts," "The College and Its Faculty," "The Administration," "The Athletic Situation," and "How Not to Raise Money." In total, the seventeen added up to about 60,000 words of manuscript which was so far inferior to my past professional standards that I decided the only thing to do was to put it away in the pickle barrel and let it soak for an indefinite time. Some time I might rescue it from the brine and work it over. It was not all dross but none of it was fit for publication in its present form. However, the exercise, physical and mental, of working a year at nothing but writing began to show results. I began to compose fluently again, and to find the typewriting machine an aid instead of an impediment.

The next writing I attempted was in the field of political theory. Between July, 1960, and August, 1961, I did first and second drafts of a 55,000-word volume entitled *The Higher Powers: A Politico-Ecclesiastic Treatise.* This dealt with the history and ideologies of statism and ecclesiasticism. I had to research it as well as write it, and this forced me back into the kind of work I had done in writing my *Political Philosophies* a quarter of a century before. I could have done nothing better calculated to revivify my powers as a scholar and writer. Without being told, I could feel myself recovering my former stride. *The Higher Powers* was a great improvement over *After-thoughts,* but I decided to keep it in cold storage for a time.

Next I turned to autobiography. Once I had vowed that I would never write an autobiography, but the longer I lived the more reason I saw for recanting that vow. I was constantly being asked questions about past events and circumstances which I had assumed were matters of pretty general knowledge, at least in Whitman circles. I would say to people "You know how it was" or "You remember so and so," and then suddenly be pulled up short by the realization that some of them had not even been born at the time of the events referred to. Finally it dawned on me that I could answer some questions that no one else could, and that no one ever would if I did not. Then I would think of the thousands of letters and papers I had written on matters pertaining to Whitman College, how scattered these were and how difficult it might be for any future historian to make sense out of them without some sort of road map to guide him. So I decided to put together some sort of narrative that could be termed an autobiography.

Between August, 1961, and June, 1962, I did first and second draft manuscripts of an autobiography to which I gave the title *The World I Lived In*. This ran to about 150,000 words. Between June, 1963, and January, 1964, I did a third draft of this, and in 1965, I gave it another going over. It was not my intention to write a minutely exhaustive autobiography. I had kept diaries only in a few short periods of my life and I had failed to keep copies of anything like all of the letters and papers I wrote. I did have enough documentation, however, to write a fairly well connected account of how my years have been spent and to explain, from my point of view, many of the events and circumstances in which I have been involved.

From July, 1962, until the end of June, 1963, I worked on a book that I had begun before I became president of Whitman. As explained earlier in this book, I had an agreement with one of the major publishing firms to do a book on political parties. This fell through, by mutual agreement, when I became president. One day in 1962, looking over the three chapters I had written, it occurred to me that I had something there which could be built up into a book of contemporary importance. I went to work on it, and by July, 1963, had finished the second draft of a manuscript entitled *Bipartisanship in the United States*. This manuscript of 145,000 words I decided was the best thing I had done since *Political Philosophies*. As soon as I finished it I started peddling it around among the publishing firms. It was accepted by the Caxton Printers Ltd., was published in February, 1965, and is now generally available in bookstores and libraries throughout the United States.

City Politics

On a warm afternoon in July, 1960, I was visited by two gentlemen representing the Walla Walla Chamber of Commerce. They were Fred Schneiter, the manager, and Jerry Cundiff, chairman of the public affairs committee. The purpose of their call at my house was to ask me if I would preside over a contemplated meeting of representative citizens to stir up interest in the forthcoming election of the first city council under the manager plan. The Chamber of Commerce proposed to sponsor such a meeting in the hope that it might help bring out a good slate of candidates for the council. I thought this a worthy enterprise and readily agreed to serve as chairman of the meeting, which was held the following week.

The meeting assembled in the large conference room in the Chamber of Commerce building, and was attended by some twenty citizens selected to represent all walks of life in Walla Walla. My job was to sit at the head of the table and keep things going smoothly, which was not at all difficult. After much talk the group came to the unanimous conclusion that about the best thing the Chamber of Commerce could do to arouse interest in the councilmanic election, which was to be held on September 13, would be to promote a public forum luncheon with a prominent out-of-town speaker. Such a luncheon, it was thought, might draw a large crowd, focus public attention on the forthcoming election, and get a goodly amount of space in the newspapers. Everybody agreed on this, and it was also decided to invite Mr. Tom Bostic, Yakima's first mayor under the manager plan, to be the speaker. Then Mr. Schneiter turned to me and asked if I would act as master of ceremonies at the luncheon, and I replied that I would.

The forum luncheon was scheduled for early August, just prior to the first day of filings for the new city council. Mr. Bostic accepted our invitation to be the principal speaker, which was fortunate indeed for us. He was a prominent young business man, the owner of radio and television stations in Yakima, Pasco, and Lewiston, and had been strikingly successful in getting the manager plan off to a good start in Yakima. My assignment as master of ceremonies of the luncheon involved three responsibilties: (1) some explanatory opening remarks, (2) the introduction of Mr. Bostic, and (3) conducting a question-and-answer session following Mr. Bostic's speech. In my opening remarks I explained the procedure necessary to file for the council in the forthcoming election and made a strong plea for good citizens to put aside their personal preferences and become candidates for the council. Tom Bostic made just the right kind of speech for the occasion, told about Yakima's experience with the manager plan and strongly seconded my plea for a large turnout of candidates. The question-and-answer period cleared up a number of uncertainties and gave me an opportunity to reemphasize the importance of running for the council.

The forum luncheon had drawn a large crowd, had been given front-page treatment in the newspapers, and had been publicized on all the radio stations, but it looked for a while as though nobody was going to respond to our appeal and run for the council. At the end of the first week of filing only five candidates had signed up, barely enough to constitute a quorum of the council. If the voters were to have any range of choice at all, there should be at least two candidates for each of the seven seats, and more would be better. At this juncture people began to stop me on the street and telephone me at home, saying they thought I ought to become a candidate. This put me on the spot. I had done more spouting in public about the importance of running for the council than any other citizen of Walla Walla. I had chairmaned both meetings designed to encourage people to run, and everybody knew that I had plenty of time to give to public service. People told me that if I would file, many others would be stimulated to follow my example. Finally I said that if fourteen candidates had not filed by the end of the second week, I would file the following

Monday morning. There were not fourteen at the end of the second week and I did file the next Monday morning, and before the end of the filing period there was a total filing of twenty-five. Having accomplished my purpose, I was tempted to withdraw, but it was too late then. At the election on September 13, 1960, I was one of the seven elected to seats in Walla Walla's first city council under the manager plan. The other six were Clarence Anderson, Lawrence E. Cousins, Mabel Groseclose, Franklin Hanson, Harold R. Holm, and Harold Jackson. All were persons I knew quite well and fully respected and trusted. All were strong proponents of the manager plan, none represented any special interests, and none had any personal axes to grind. All were holding public office for the first time, including me. I had dabbled in politics more than any of the others, had been a congressional candidate once, but had never been elected to office.

The councilmen-elect were notified by the city clerk that the oath of office would be administered on September 28, the day of the final meeting of the old city commission. After a bit of more or less spontaneous telephoning among ourselves, an agreement was reached to the effect that it would be a good thing if we could have a sort of pre-inauguration caucus. Accordingly, I invited all of the members-elect together with Royce Lawrence, the city clerk, and John Reese, the city attorney, to my house for coffee on the afternoon of September 25, which was a Sunday. Among the matters we thought needed talking over before we took office were what to do about an administrative head pending the choice of a city manager, how to proceed in the search for a city manager, what to do about the 1961 budget, which would be up for adoption on October 4, what kind of procedure to follow in our own deliberations, and what to do about electing a council chairman, who under the law of the state would become *ipso facto* the mayor of the city. Mr. Lawrence briefed us on the budget and Mr. Reese on the third-class cities law under which Walla Walla had elected the manager plan.

After Mr. Lawrence and Mr. Reese left the meeting, the

councilmen-elect got their heads together to make preliminary decisions on matters that would confront us immediately after our inauguration on September 28. It was suggested that we immediately choose a chairman and then formally elect him after we were sworn in. To avert any possible embarrassment to any one present, I made the suggestion that we dispense with formal nominations and elections. Instead of that, I proposed that each of us, without any mention of names or any discussion, write on a slip of paper the name of one councilman other than himself whom he would prefer for chairman. If the result of this utterly secret ballot gave a majority to any member, we would declare him chairman and formally elect him on September 28. If, however, no one received a majority on the first count, we would then proceed by the same method to choose between the two highest on the first ballot. My suggestion was accepted, and I was chosen chairman on the first ballot.

On taking the chair, I suggested that we first try to agree upon a method of conducting the business of the city during the period necessary to find a city manager. It was quickly proposed and carried that we ask Royce Lawrence, city clerk, to serve as manager *pro tempore* and that I, as spokesman for the council, would go to the city hall every day to do whatever trouble-shooting might be needed. It was also agreed that I, speaking in the name of the council, would send a letter to every city official and employee explaining how we proposed to proceed pending the hiring of a city manager and asking their cooperation in these temporary arrangements. It was further agreed that as soon as we were installed in office I would announce the appointment of three temporary committees—one to make recommendations on the pending 1961 budget, one to formulate permanent rules of procedure for submission to the council, and one to screen applications for the position of city manager.

Everything went smoothly on September 28. We were duly sworn in; I was immediately elected chairman and mayor; the appointment of the three committees was announced; Mr. Lawrence was named temporary manager; and then, having

462

secured its approval in advance, I read the following inaugural statement in behalf of the council:

With the approval of the city council I wish to make this brief inaugural statement.

First, I am sure that I express the feeling of every member of the council in extending sincere thanks to Mr. Hereford, Mr. Saunders, and all members of the city administration for the cooperation and courtesy shown to us in the period between our election and inauguration.

Second, I believe every member of the council would want me to say to the people of Walla Walla that our chief concern is the welfare of the whole city and all of its members. The members of this council do not represent any special interests or groups, and do not favor East Side, West Side, North Side, South Side, or any other section of the city. The members of this council will be just as considerate of individuals as of groups or organizations, and expect to provide the means whereby individuals may communicate with the council just as readily as groups and organizations.

Third, all members of the council agree that our main concern is the future and not the past. We are not going to embark on a wholesale program of repealing past ordinances and enactments. We are not going to reopen every question and reargue every issue. We are not interested in changing what has been done in the past unless the change is important in solving current and future problems.

Fourth, we are all united in the purpose not to transact any business of transcendent importance until we shall have secured a well qualified city manager to head the professional services of the city.

Fifth, we are in the process of considering applications for the position of city manager. Upwards of forty applications are now being scrutinized, and more are being received every day. If it were necessary, we could fill the position of city manager, at a moment's notice, but we feel that it is important to take ample time to screen the applications thoroughly. We have, accordingly, appointed Mr. Royce Lawrence, city clerk, to serve as manager *pro tem.* Until a permanent appointment is made, Mr. Lawrence will coordinate the routine operations of the city government and will be in constant touch with the city council. We are confident that these temporary arrangements will work out satisfactorily.

As agreed in advance, our temporary budget committee was composed of Messrs. Holm and Jackson, our rules committee of Messrs. Cousins and Hanson, and our manager application committee of Mrs. Groseclose and Mr. Anderson. At the request of the council, I took on two special assignments. One of these I have already mentioned—daily troubleshooting at the city hall. This was as much to help Mr. Lawrence as to help the council. It could be easily foreseen that the temporary manager might have some tough decisions to make, and I was given authority to speak in the name of the council in backing his decisions. As it worked out, he and I had a conference at 10 A.M. every day, and I made any decisions that might be giving him trouble. He was authorized to say that the decision was mine and therefore the decision of the council. Throughout the months of October and November, 1960, I went to the city hall every day and fielded the tough ones. This was not hard for me; every day for eleven years I had been making equally difficult decisions as president of Whitman College. My hide was tough and the barbs caused little pain. But one result of my two months as the voice of the council at city hall was that many people gained the impression that I had the council wrapped around my finger. That I stepped out of this voice role as soon as the city manager took office did not change their minds. The original impression seemingly could not be erased.

The second special assignment given me by the council had to do with the physical arrangements and facilities of the council chamber. Many changes were needed to accomodate the new system of government. For more than fifty years Walla Walla had been governed by a commission of three members, whereas the newly elected council had seven members. In addition to the seven council members, facilities had to be provided for the city clerk, the city attorney, the city manager, possibly an assistant manager, and members of the press. The small table around which the three commissioners had convened obviously would not do for the new council, nor would the old arrangement serve any better for the additional and regular administrative functionaries who had to attend council meetings.

After a good deal of trial-and-error sketching, I went to the council with a tentative semi-circular scheme of seating for the council members. On a raised platform, each at a separate desk the members of the council would sit in a semi-circle facing the audience, the mayor in the center and three councilmen to each side. Seated off the platform behind a straight row of desks facing the council would be the city manager in the center, flanked on each side by the clerk, the attorney, and any others needed for council business. Behind this row of desks, separating it from the audience, would be a railing with gates at each extreme. In short, what I proposed was a legislative chamber rather than a committee room. The council approved this plan, and the city's department of public works carried through the work of remodeling and refurnishing. I supervised this work in behalf of the council.

In the same connection I made another recommendation which the council approved and put into effect. This was the purchase and installation in the council chamber of synchronized loud speaker and tape recorder systems. This was viewed as an unnecessary innovation at the time, but I insisted that no modern legislative body could take the risk of not having tape-recorded archives of everything said by its own members and also everything said by officials and private citizens who might appear before it. I maintained there was no sound reason why anyone should object to that and every reason why it was desirable for the protection of all involved in council proceedings. I finally won out and the installation was made.

The loudspeaker system enabled everyone in the room, auditor, officer, or councilman, to hear every word uttered in

465

council proceedings, a matter of paramount importance. The tape recording system not only made records which could be played back, in case of doubt, for everyone to hear as often as desired, but records which could also be transcribed verbatim and typed or printed as documents—100 per cent accurate documents. The first dividend returned by the new installation was correct minutes. After a few meetings with the tape recorder as a rectifier, there was never any need for additions or corrections to the minutes, no need to rely on anyone's memory of what had been said or done. If it had been legally possible, we could have dispensed with the reading of the minutes altogether. Our new sound installation was also a complete protection against misquotation outside as well as inside the council chamber. If a councilman, administrative official, or private citizen should claim that he had been misquoted in the press or in grape-vine reports about town, it took only a few minutes to settle the question beyond all possibility of question or doubt.

I think it is true that tape recording had much to do with speeding up the transaction of business in council meetings. Nobody, including myself, could possibly be as discursive and windy with the tape reeling off before his eyes as without this constant reminder that *tempus fugit*. It became rare for the council to be in session as long as an hour. Some dear souls objected to this as steamrolling business through, but actually it was the result of time saved by the elimination of drooling and rambling. Nor was there any curtailment of freedom of speech. We did not hold the watch on anybody, but everybody became more conscious of time.

Mayor

As a general rule the mayor in city manager government is pretty much a figurehead. Sometimes he is facetiously called a "toothless tiger." Being well aware of this, I assumed that my principal job as mayor of Walla Walla would be to preside over council meetings. Therefore, I was genuinely surprised to discover that there was much more to the job than I had anticipated. Presiding at council meetings proved to be one of my lightest burdens. Although the city manager statute of the State of Washington gives the mayor very few powers, it does lay upon his shoulders a great many duties. He is made chairman of the finance committee, consisting of himself, the city clerk, and the city treasurer; and this committee is responsible for the investment of all city funds. He is likewise made chairman of the board which administers the firemen's health, accident, and pension funds. State law makes him an *ex officio* member of the city-county airport board. So I had many regular meetings to attend. By special invitation, I also attended meetings of the park board, the personnel board, and other municipal bodies.

The state law required that the police and fire departments report certain occurrences immediately to the mayor, which often means that they may have to rout him out of bed or call him out of a party or meeting. This happened to me several times. There is not much the mayor can do about the emergencies reported to him, but the law requires them to be reported just the same. The law also requires the mayor's signature on all ordinances, resolutions, and contracts made by the council; he must also sign the minutes of the council, the finance committee, and the pension board. In addition his signature is required on all bonds sold by the city. I well remember a day spent in signing some 500 bonds which had been voted to finance the modernization of the city's sewage disposal plant.

Besides these and other legally imposed duties, the mayor is expected to be the city's official greeter, handshaker, welcomer, and social spokesman. He is invited to speak at conventions, luncheons, dinners, and other gatherings. He must make an appearance at cocktail parties, smokers, exhibitions, and scores of other functions. I kept close track of my schedule for 1961, and when I added them up at the end of the year the notations on my appointment calendar showed that I had attended 144 official meetings and sixty-one non-official ones, which signified that the "toothless tiger" was busy if nothing else. For all of this "busyness" I received the same salary as every other councilman—five dollars per regular council meeting, not to exceed two meetings per month said the state law, and this was subject to a deduction of 3½ per cent for Social Security, which as a retired person I was already drawing. The council tried to vote extra compensation for the mayor but found that it was forbidden by state law.

City Problems

As I have already mentioned, the first major problem of the council was to get the best man we could for city manager. The outgoing commission had budgeted a salary of $12,000 for the manager, and we felt that it would be good policy to adhere to that if possible. As soon as we began interviewing we became aware that it would take long and diligent searching to get as good a man as Walla Walla should have for that salary. Altogether our searching committee sifted through more than seventy applications and selected twenty of them as being good enough for consideration by the entire council. After several meetings spent in going over the credentials and other papers of the twenty, the council picked ten whom it wanted to interview in person. As mayor and council chairman, it fell to me to issue the invitations and carry on the incidental correspondence by mail, telegraph, and telephone to get the ten candidates to Walla Walla. When the council had finished these ten interviews, it picked two men as being the best of the ten. I was empowered to offer the appointment first to Mr. George Smith, assistant city manager of Tacoma, and if he did not accept to Mr. Leland F. Kraft of Wichita, Kansas, recently city manager of Wood River, Illinois. On the basis of their supporting papers and impressions made in their interviews with the council, it was a toss-up between these two men. Smith was given the first refusal of the job solely on the ground that he had experience in the State of Washington which might prove specially helpful in Walla Walla. Having an offer of the managership at Yakima at the same time he received our offer, Smith decided in favor of Yakima, and our offer then went to Kraft, who accepted. It was my opinion after a year and a half of official association with Mr. Kraft, and is still my opinion, that the council did Walla Walla a very good turn in appointing him. He was excellently trained in the city manager program at the University of Kansas, had several years of experience as an assistant manager and city manager, and had the qualities of tact and common sense which are specially needed in a small, conservative city such as Walla Walla.

Even for the writer of these lines, who had a finger in most of the municipal pies between September 28, 1960, and April 15, 1962, it would be insufferably tedious to go into much detail in describing the city business transacted between those dates. There were, however, a few matters of special prominence, which tested the mettle of the council and gave the manager occasion to prove his worth. I shall briefly review a few of the more important of these.

The first hot potato the new city government had to handle was tossed in our laps by the Board of Education. For two or three years the school board had been the storm center of a furious controversay over the location of a proposed new high school building. The big question was whether there should be a new building on a new site or a remodeling and enlargement of the old building on its existing site. In the face of a storm of objections, the Board of Education decided on a new building on a new site, but did not specify where the new site would be. Several possibilities were mentioned. The city was the owner of a ten-acre tract of undeveloped land on South Howard Street which had been acquired for eventual development as a city park. But the city had no immediate plans, nor any money, to carry out this project in the near future.

The school board cast an envious eye on this tract, deeming it the best possible location for the new high school, and offered to buy it from the city. This started a controversy in which the council had no real interest and did not want to become involved, but could not escape. The Board of Education was entitled to a yes-or-no answer, and either answer was loaded with trouble for the council. The people who lived in the vicinity of the Howard Street tract were violently opposed to having it sold to the school board for a high school campus, said the city had pledged itself to develop a park there, and would be guilty of a betrayal if it allowed the property to be used for any other purpose. On the other hand, the strong partisans of a new high school on a new site demanded that we sell the property to the school board, saying that it was our duty to all the people of Walla Walla and to future generations of Walla Walla youth to make this property available for educational use.

There was an advisory board of park commissioners which had existed for many years and had always been consulted on matters pertaining to park and recreational facilities. The council decided, correctly and properly, that it would take no action until the school board's offer had been referred to the park board for an advisory opinion. Instead of cooling things down, this seemed to heat them up. One group of citizens thought we should have by-passed the park board, and another thought we were trying to put the park board on the spot because we were afraid to make a decision. Several of the school directors thought we were trying to show them up in a poor light. But we waited, nevertheless, until we got a report from the Board of Park Commissioners. This recommended in the strongest terms against the sale of the property to the school board and proposed that it be immediately developed in whole or in part as a city park. Thereupon, without waiting to see what the council would do about the park board's recommendations, the school board withdrew its offer to buy. There was nothing now for the council to act upon.

This inaction pleased nobody. The residents of the Howard tract area were glad not to have the property sold to the school board but disappointed that the council took no action of the recommendation for its immediate development as a park. The champions of the new high school were displeased because they thought, incorrectly, that council action had forced the school board to withdraw its offer, which was entirely untrue.

The council never even took a tentative vote on the sale of the property to the school board. The basic question the council had to decide was not whether to sell to the school board but whether to sell at all. That was the question on which the council asked the advice of the park commissioners. The school board withdrew its offer before the council had a chance to discuss the negative recommendation of the park commissioners, but nobody understood that, apparently. A good many of the pro-school board people accused me of swaying the council against the school board's offer. All the swaying I did was to express the opinion, which was unreservedly shared by every other member of the council, that we should not consider the school board's offer until we had made a decision, independently of that offer, whether or not to retain the property and develop it as a park.

The next hot potato was vice; specifically, gambling and prostitution. Our legal duty in those regards was simple and clear. The state law prohibited both gambling and prostitution, and prescribed severe penalties for violations. It was the legal duty of the prosecuting attorney of the county to enforce these laws, and it was the city's duty to give him full cooperation. City ordinances did not ban gambling and prostitution, but made it a misdemeanor for anyone to use or permit the use of any structure owned by him for gambling or prostitution. For many years it had been the deliberate policy of the city government to shut its eyes to violations of its own anti-vice ordinances as well as the state law. Certain licensed businesses, such as taverns, pool halls, cigar stores, and hotels were allowed to run card rooms, punch boards, and other forms of gambling. Certain licensed lodging houses were allowed, under police supervision, to operate as houses of prostitution. Since this *laissez faire* policy was made effectual by indifference and silence on the part of the city commission and the police department, the public was not well informed on the actualities of the situation. There were all sorts of rumors, and there was also much evidence of highly selective enforcement. Violators who did not keep in the good graces of the police and the city commission had the book thrown at them, while the favored violators flourished with impunity.

One of the first questions City Manager Leland F. Kraft brought before the city council was law enforcement. He wanted to know and the chief of police wanted to know whether to pursue the old *laissez faire* policy or to crack down. The council unanimously agreed that there was only one honest and honorable answer to that question. The law was on the books and should be rigorously and faithfully enforced. If there was to be a policy of toleration, it should be accomplished by repealing the law rather than ignoring it. The council members were not trying to stamp out sin or start an anti-vice crusade, but each had taken an oath to uphold and enforce the law—all of it, not just selected portions—and to vote for non-enforcement would have been to repudiate the oath of office.

The decision of the council raised a howl of protest. I was visited at home one evening by a self-appointed committee consisting of a tavern owner, a beer distributor, a punchboard middleman, a novelty manufacturer, and a large farm operator. All were men I knew pretty well personally, and they presumed on long acquaintance to advise me that I did not know the score. Since I had been in college work all my life, they were sure I did not understand that in the realm of practical affairs one had to make concessions to reality. I told them that I would make one big, broad concession to reality. If they would prepare and sponsor an ordinance to repeal the city's anti-gambling and anti-prostitution ordinances, I would not only introduce it in the council but would also vote for it. But they would have none of that. They did not want the law repealed; they just wanted it ignored. That, they said, would be best for everyone. Furthermore, they even accused me of knowing "damn well," as they phrased it, that there was not a "China-man's chance" that a repeal ordinance would pass, and that I had proposed it just to show them up. They left about midnight, still convinced that I was naive, but also of the opinion that I was an s.o.b.

At the next meeting of the council a delegation of leading

business men appeared and urged the council to reverse itself on gambling and prostitution. Most of them were retail merchants of high standing in the community. In the group were two former presidents of the Walla Walla Chamber of Commerce and a former chief of police. Nearly all were good churchmen and some were church officials. Many, if not all, were engaged in lines of retailing which could and maybe did, profit somewhat from the trade of the houses of prostitution and their inmates and patrons. Thanks to our tape recorder I can quote verbatim samples of the opinions of these eminently respectable citizens.

The former chief of police explained how he had dealt with prostitution:

> Prior to the time when I took over here, we had thirteen places in Walla Walla. When I left we had three, but believe me those three were taken care of and every police officer on the beat knew who was there and when they came, and if they left we sure knew that.

A former president of the chamber of commerce mourned the prospective loss of business as follows:

> From the financial standpoint it looks to me like we have chased $300,000 out of town, and we sure need the business. I mean this is the amount of money they spend here in a year's time.... And taxes going the way they are, we certainly need the business, and I think it is better to have it controlled and supervised by the medical profession here in town to the point that it has been than to have it as it is.

Another former president of the chamber of commerce wanted us to wink at violations:

> We feel that closing the houses was a very bad move for the community. In this country we accept a degree of law with a degree of enforcement. We have parking tickets, but we give courtesy tickets. We have laws against gambling but we have bingos and bazaars and various things that are

just as illegal as some other things, but we allow them for the good of the community.

An active leader in veterans organizations said:

I don't honestly believe you can stamp out the houses or the business they are engaged in. If you think at this moment you haven't got people in this town who are in the business, I think you would be really surprised. As you know, I was raised in Walla Walla, and this is something we have always had here. I thought nothing of it, the same as other people, and at the same time, looking back on it, we had no serious problems.

These were typical samples. A dozen or more leading business men spoke in the same vein, but the council refused to back down. The houses of prostitution were closed down and the professional gamblers put out of business, but there was no disaster, economic or otherwise. None of the taverns, rooming houses, or pool rooms went into bankruptcy or failed to renew their licenses and conform with the new requirements. The newspapers reported that the Christmas trade that year was the best in the entire history of the city, and the public utility services (water, electricity, gas, and telephone) reported that more people moved into town than moved out. It was said, however, and perhaps with some truth, that the gamblers and prostitutes merely moved out beyond the city limits and bestowed their special blessings on the suburban areas. If so, the board of county commissioners and the prosecuting attorney ignored them, which, of course, was no business of the city council. In the city boundaries, perhaps for the first time in the history of Walla Walla, the law was strictly and honestly enforced. But this added nothing to the popularity of the city council.

The council's second big success in stirring up snarling animals resulted from the enactment of Walla Walla's first dog-leash law. This was an issue which the council inherited from the outgoing city commission. There had been a good deal of agitation on this subject for some years, and the commission decided to have an advisory referendum before taking any action. This referendum was on the ballot at the same election in which the seven members of the new council were chosen. However there was very little public discussion of the matter, and not one of the twenty-five candidates for the council took a position on it. It could be regarded, therefore, as a completely uninfluenced referendum. When the ballots were counted, it was found, to every one's surprise, that the people had voted 3,800 to 1,640 in favor of a dog-leash law. Since the council had been elected at the same time as the advisory vote, we had no choice but to take it as a mandate from the voters. It was our duty to follow through and give the people some kind of dog-leash ordinance.

We did not move fast enough to please the pro-leash people, and the anti-leash people, though they had lost the election overwhelmingly, came before the council with astounding arguments that the people did not mean what they said when they voted yes in the referendum. Very wisely, the council delayed action to give the manager and his staff time to make a thorough study of dog-leash legislation in other cities. This took five months, but enabled us to come up with a much better draft than if we had leaped before looking. In fact, one of the drawbacks of the manager's initial draft was that it was too good. By that I mean that it tried to embody everything that had been found good in other cities, and as a result it contained so many assailable provisions that it would be hard to get any united public support for it. After we had argued and argued in the council over one feature and another without making much headway, I sat down one afternoon with a red pencil, a pair of scissors, and a paste pot and did major surgery on the manager's draft. My theory was that the paramount thing was to get the dogs off the streets, and I cut out of the draft everything that did not bear directly on that. When I offered my draft as a substitute for the manager's draft, the council quickly accepted and passed it. In the manager's draft there were things that even the pro-leash people could differ about; in my draft there was no basis for quibbles and little to make difficulty in enforcement. It took a year or so for the public to get used to the leash law, but after the second year even the anti-leash people were reconciled to it.

Not everything the council did in its first year and a half touched off emotional reactions. In the case of most matters of major importance, just the reverse was the case. Despite the fact that we gave them every possible bit of publicity and almost begged people to attend the briefing sessions and final sessions when they were under consideration, the general public paid so little attention that a majority of the voters never gave the council or the manager credit for any of these accomplishments.

A good example of what I am referring to was our water resources study. In January, 1961, the council authorized the city manager to employ an approved firm of consulting engineers to make a reconnaissance study of the feasibility of city participation in the Mill Creek reservoir project which had been proposed by the United States Corps of Engineers. It took some months to complete this study, but when it was finished Walla Walla got far more than a report on the practicability of participating in the Mill Creek storage project; over and above that it got a blue print for the development and utilization of its water resources for the next fifty years.

Nobody patted members of the council on the back for this. We gave it all the build-up we could in the press and other channels of publicity, but it just would not sink into the public mind. Much the same fate attended another project of vital importance to the city. This was the enlargement of the city's sewage treatment plant to accommodate the increasing volume of industrial wastes originating in Walla Walla's three large food processing plants.

The old sewage plant, built in 1927 and enlarged in 1952, had become unequal to the growing demands made upon it. The processing plants as well as the city were up against a real dilemma. If they could not discharge their waste fluids into the city sewers, they would have to close down and go elsewhere, at a tremendous loss, of course, both to themselves and the people of Walla Walla. There was a further complication in the fact that the state pollution control commission had ruled that these cannery wastes had to be purified before they could be released into Mill Creek, the carrier of the city's sewage effluent.

This ruling made the city eligible for a federal grant in aid for stream purification. The council, therefore, authorized the city manager to apply for a federal grant of $172,860 and at the same time empowered him and the city attorney to enter into negotiations with the three food processing firms and certain irrigation districts and water users associations which would be affected by the contemplated improvement. These negotiations were successfully carried through. The food processing firms entered into an agreement with the city under which the city, with the federal grant plus a bond issue of $435,000, would pay for the improvement and carry through the completion of the project. The bonds were to be made redeemable in series extending over a period of twenty-seven years, but the processors agreed that as each year's installment of bonds came due they would pay to the city an amount sufficient to cover both interest and principal. As a result of these negotiations and transactions, the city got a sewage treatment improvement costing a total of $607,860, which at the end of twenty-seven years will have been entirely reimbursed by the processing companies. We tooted our horn shamelessly about this, and had something to toot about, but the public was unimpressed.

On the evening of May 27, 1961, some small boys turned in a false alarm which resulted in the worst accident in the history of the Walla Walla fire department. The alarm was answered, as it should have been, by pumper trucks from stations One and Two, which were supposed to go to the scene of the fire by different and non-intersecting routes. By a mixup that has never been satisfactorily explained, these two pumpers, running at fifty miles per hour, collided at the intersection of Third and Poplar. One fireman was instantly killed and four were seriously injured. Both pumpers were wrecked beyond repair. In a moment the city had lost two-thirds of its pumping capacity. In the face of a major conflagration, our fire department would be virtually helpless. It would take at least $50,000 to buy new pumpers, and the city did not have that amount of available cash lying around. A little interfund borrowing was possible, but not enough to meet the need. Orders had to go in immediately if new pumpers were to be delievered in three to five months. Hence, there was no time for a bond issue or a special tax levy. The finance committee as well as the council struggled with this problem, and finally hit upon the following solution: (1) to issue tax anticipation warrants in the amount needed, (2) to sell these warrants to the fireman's pension fund, and (3) later authorize a tax levy to redeem the warrants from the pension fund. All of these steps were quickly taken, and the city was soon in possession of two new and greatly improved pumpers. All of these transactions were carried on in public meetings and fully reported in the press, but the public never understood or appreciated how the emergency had been met. In fact, there were rumors to the effect that the council had been bribed by the manufacturing company which won the bid to supply the new pumpers. This I know because I was on the receiving end of telephone conversations in which such accusations were made.

Other Constructive Enactments

Undoubtedly the most important piece of legislation enacted by the council during my term of service was the Subdivision Control Ordinance passed in July, 1961. I am almost tempted to say that this ultimately may prove to be the most important ordinance enacted by the City of Walla Walla in more than fifty years. Walla Walla never before had taken such a step. From the first incorporation of the municipality in 1859 down to the enactment of this subdivision measure in 1961, there had been no comprehensive and uniform regulations governing such matters as platted additions to the city, street specifications, utility provisions, and many other matters vital to the physical layout of the city. Everything was higgeldy-piggeldy. Each real estate developer made his own deal with the city authorities and complied, perhaps, with the terms and conditions they laid down. But the city authorities seldom made sure that their stipulations were consistent with past usage or soundly conceived for the future. Even more seldom did they do any rigorous checking to insure strict compliance with the requirements they had laid down. As to such things as lot sizes and shapes, street widths and surfacing, street names and numbers, parking strips, subsurface utilities, sidewalks, and scores of similar matters, the Walla Walla scene mutely but eloquently testifies to years of virtual anarchy. Not so evident to the naked eye, but equally a result of the same anarchy, is the fact that millions of dollars have gone down the drain unnecessarily because of substandard additions to the city. There is some reason also to suppose that fat profits have redounded to the not-so-ethical developers and builders.

Early in January, 1961, the council announced its intention to enact a tight and comprehensive ordinance providing rules and regulations for city approval of all future subdivisions, plats, dedications, and the like. The city manager was instructed to undertake the preparation of such an ordinance, and was advised in that connection to work in conjunction with the city's department of public works, the city planning commission, the real estate board, and the building construction committee of the chamber of commerce. It took six months of meeting after meeting, hearing after hearing, draft after draft to whip out an ordinance acceptable to all of these interests. But when that tedious and exacting job was finished and the ordinance came before the city council for final enactment the council chamber was entirely vacant save for members of the council and administrative officials. Not a single citizen was present to approve, object, or even watch. This ordinance had been given maximum publicity treatment, but nobody seemed aware that anything important was going on.

In November, 1960, even before we appointed a manager, the city was offered an apportunity to buy one, and maybe two, tracts of land comprising part of the Veterans' Hospital Grounds. The two tracts aggregated about ninety-five acres, all within the city limits. On one tract an immediate bid was necessary, and, since we did not yet have a city manager, I was asked by the council to assume the responsibility of conducting the negotiations and filing the necessary papers with the General Service Administration. When the second tract became available, the manager was on hand to do this work. For about half of its appraised value, the city bought a parcel of land of priceless importance to its future development. The council voted to set aside these two adjoining tracts for development as a public park and to name it Fort Walla Walla Park in commemoration of the fact that the third United States Army garrison of that name had embraced that land. Fort Walla Walla Park, inside the city limits, had potential uses that could not be had anywhere else within twenty miles of the city. It has been developed already for use as a trailer park, a diversified picnic area, a horseback riding area, a hiking area, a camping area for boys', girls', and other youth clubs and organizations. The old Fifth Cavalry cemetery is located within the bounds of Fort Walla Walla Park, and it is hoped some day to place near the cemetery a suitable building for a museum of local history. By citizens who thought the money should have been spent on the city's other parks, the council was severely criticised for the outlay needed to acquire Fort Walla Walla Park, but if the council had not done this, future generations could justly damn it for sheer stupidity.

In common with most cities, Walla Walla had a street problem that was growing more acute every year. All over the city pavements were disintegrating, and most of the arterial streets needed widening as well as repaving. The new city council addressed itself to this problem at once, and discovered, also at once, that there was not much that could be done right away. The chief difficulty was the lack of money to do the job. The city's public works department estimated that an outlay of not less than $2,000,000 would be necessary to take care of the arterial streets alone, and if all of the secondary streets were to be restored, ways would have to be found to provide many times that amount of money. A 1961 state law provided for a fund-matching deal (75 per cent from the state and 25 per cent from the city) for arterial streets in all Washington cities. Under this we were able to make some progress on the improvement of East Isaacs and Roosevelt streets, but the city's revenues were so restricted that we could not put up matching money for more than one or two blocks a year. The only possible way of getting enough money to enable the city to match the state in a comprehensive arterial improvement program was by means of a bond issue, and that would require a popular referendum. However, we knew it would be folly to try to pass a bond issue without first completing all of the preliminary planning, engineering, and cost studies necessary to inform the voters on what they would be voting. The council instructed the manager to proceed at once with this preliminary work, which required two years to finish.

Perhaps the loudest controversy that arose during my service on the council was the enactment of the budget for 1962. Throughout 1961 we had been obliged to operate on the budget handed to us by the retiring city commission, which we soon discovered was predicated on deficit financing. For many years it had been the practice of the city commission to set up a compilation of proposed expenditures and then to proceed to "guess-timate" enough income to equal or overbalance the proposed expenditures. There was a certain amount of tax income that could be accurately estimated, but the rest of the estimates were largely grabbed out of thin air. If this guessing fell short and real income fell below "guesstimated" income, the commission merely issued interest-bearing tax-anticipation warrants to cover the shortage. If then the anticipated tax income failed to materialize, the commission issued and sold general obligation refunding bonds in the amount of the deficit, which was really nothing but converting floating debt into funded debt without really wiping out the deficit at all. Year after year the funded debt of the city grew and absorbed more and more of the city's current revenues for amortization costs. Some day the piper would have to be paid, but the honorable commissioners did not expect to be around when the day of reckoning came.

When the city manager government was installed in Walla

481

Walla in 1960, a total of $415,000 in refunding bonds was out-standing. This represented the accumulated deficits of I know not how many budget years—money still to be paid out for dead horses. The council was determined to stop deficit financing of that sort, no matter how many toes might be stepped on. Individually and collectively, we were opposed to it in both principle and practice. We also decided that the way to stop it was not to taper off, but to halt the practice instantly and totally. If it were necessary to levy additional taxes in order to provide the needed revenues we were fully prepared to take that step. This was the crux of the controversey over the 1962 budget.

By drastic retrenchments and rigorously accurate estimating, we found it possible to cut the total expenditures of the city for 1962 to a figure $18,847 below those carried in the 1961 budget, but even this saving was not enough to enable us to avoid additional taxation. If the council had not been deter-mined to give every city employee a modest salary increase, it would have been possible to skin through without increasing taxes, but there had been no salary increases at city hall for three years; morale had suffered, and the city was in danger of losing many of its best employees. We decided to make the people of Walla Walla dig up enough more taxes to finance the salary increases and also a few indispensable capital outlays. We hoped these extra taxes might be temporary, and we levied them in such a way as to spread the burden as widely and fairly as possible. The means we chose to this end were an increase in water rates, an increase of the electric utility gross revenue tax, an increase of the telephone utility gross revenue tax, and an increase of the gas utility gross revenue tax. The utility companies, of course, merely passed the additional levies on to their customers, but they howled bloody murder just the same. So did everybody else, because everybody was hit. It made no difference that nobody was really hurt.

In connection with the hearings on the budget I got in bad with the Chamber of Commerce committee on taxation. Council briefing sessions and regular sessions were wide open to the public, and any citizen or group of citizens could appear and be heard without let or hindrance. Dozens of people did this in connection with the budget controversy, but the Chamber of Commerce committee asked for the special privilege of meeting in private with the members of the council, behind closed doors. I being the chairman of the council was asked if I would arrange such a meeting. Thereupon I blew my stack and told the chamber brothers that as far as I was concerned city business was public business and would be transacted in public. The other members of the council might do as they pleased individually, but I would not use my position as mayor to arrange a secret meeting with the chamber or anybody else. That put a quietus on the matter. The other members of the council took the same stand, and the Chamber of Commerce committee was forced to make appearance at an open meeting of the council. I thus incurred the wrath of all the members of the chamber committee. It seemed that they had been accustomed in the past to have private sessions with the city commission whenever they wished, and thought they were entitled to that privilege with the new council.

Defeat

When the council took office on September 28, 1960, its tenure of office was beclouded by a tricky action of the outgoing commission. Instead of setting the election of the council for the first Tuesday in March as required by state law for city elections, the commission set the election for the first Tuesday in September. The commission justified this on the ground that it would save money to combine the city election with the state wide direct primary election. But the real reason was that the outgoing commissioners wanted to draw their salaries five months longer.

The state law governing manager-plan cities stipulated that the four councilmen receiving the highest number of votes in the first election should have four-year terms and the three others two-year terms. Thereafter, every two years, either three of four council vacancies would occur. Our attorney assumed that this would apply to the September election in which we were chosen, but was unsure whether our terms should be dated from March or September. He asked the attorney-general of the state for a ruling on this point and got a response which really mixed the pickles. The attorney-general declared that the September election of the council was irregular and not in conformity with state law. Therefore, he said the council members elected at that time were *de facto* but not *de jure* councilmen, and hence were not entitled to the tenure of office prescribed by the city-manager law. In order to make things valid, it would be necessary to vacate all seven of the councilmanic positions as of the first Tuesday of March, 1962, and re-elect a new city council at that time.

Meanwhile, the state legislature, always a Meddlesome Mattie in municipal affairs, had inflicted a wholly new system of election on Washington cities. The practice for many, many years had been that city councilmen were elected either by wards or at large, as prescribed either by state or their own homerule charters. The new law, enacted by the 1961 legislature, required all city councilmen to be elected by position and specified how this was to be done. Each councilmanic position was to be given a number, determined by lot, and candidates must file for one and only one of these according to its official number. In other words, you filed for Position No. 1, Position No. 2, or Position No. 3, and so on, and were on the ballot in that form. If more than two persons filed for a particular position, a primary election must be held in February to eliminate all but the two highest for each position. Then, in the final election, each voter was privileged to cast a ballot for one candidate for each position.

In spite of its theoretical merits, this system of election had some glaring defects. For instance, if the voter liked both candidates for Position No. 1 and despised both candidates for Position No. 2, he was put in the anomalous position of being obliged to help defeat a man he wanted and help elect a man he did not want. And, of course, this could be true all the way down through the three, four, or seven positions, as the case might be in any election. It did no good for the voter to abstain from voting on a position both of whose candidates were unacceptable to him, because his abstention was bound to have the effect of enhancing the weight of the votes that were cast for this position. Under the general ticket plan as formerly in vogue in Walla Walla and other Washington cities, the voter was able to go through the entire list of candidates and pick out those who suited him most exactly. He also was able, by abstention, if he were chiefly interested in helping one or two candidates, to withhold assistance to the rivals of his favorites.

In consequence of the attorney-general's ruling, all seven members of the council had to decide whether to run again in March, 1962. In a private caucus we talked it over. I said I had decided not to run again; then all the others said that if I didn't run, neither would they. The city manager and the city clerk, who were there by invitation, begged us all to run again, and there were some persuasive arguments on their side. If we all declined to run, that surely would give the impression that we had lost confidence in the manager and perhaps in the manager plan itself. And if some ran and others did not, it might give the impression that we were in disagreement among ourselves, which was far from the truth. After much soul-searching we came to the conclusion that it would be best if we all ran again. I finally said that if everyone else felt that way, I would put aside my personal preferences and stand for re-election along with the other six.

Since we now had to file for numbered positions, we drew lots to determine which would be which. I drew Position No. 1, which was bad luck in a way because it misled many voters into supposing that I was running for mayor again, which of course was impossible under our state law. This was explained again and again on the stump and in the newspapers, but the incumbent mayor was running for Position No. 1, and no amount of factual dissemination could overcome the belief that the man elected to Position No. 1 would be the next mayor.

Since there were more than two filings for all but one of

the seven positions, a primary election had to be held on the first Tuesday in February. All of the incumbent councilmen were renominated and one opponent for each man was also nominated. I polled the smallest vote of any of the seven renominated councilmen and did not need spectacles to read the handwriting on the wall. It was clearly evident in the primary election that Maxey was the principal target of the opposition. The idea seemed to be that getting rid of Maxey would change everything at the city hall. Maxey was supposed to be running the show down there and the rest of the council were just puppets. Nothing could have been sillier or farther from the truth. It was my duty to preside over council meetings, to act as the titular head of the city government, and to be the city's official spokesman on many occasions, but everything I did was under the authority of the council.

An uninformed observer watching me preside over the council meetings could have gained the impression that I was dominating the proceedings, for I did run the meeting. But that is a presiding officer's job. If the chairman does not run a meeting, not much business is likely to be done. As the result of a lifetime of experience in presiding over meetings, I was thoroughly familiar with parliamentary law and usage and knew how to keep things moving. This I did. At every meeting I saw to it that the council completed its agenda, and that its own rules as well as general rules of parliamentary procedure were strictly followed. This was exactly what the council wanted done and praised me for doing, but it had nothing to do with questions of policy. On questions of policy there were frequent differences of opinion, and the voting was not always unanimous. On roll-call votes, my name was always called last, which meant that I could not change the result unless there was a 3-3 tie before my turn came. On viva voce votes, aside from stating questions, putting motions, and calling for the vote, my voice was joined with others. There was no way that I could have overawed or browbeaten the council no matter how hard I might try.

But my opponents had convinced themselves that getting

Maxey out of the picture would change everything at city hall. All seven of us filed for re-election, as I have said, but none of us did any campaigning—halfway hoped we would not be re-elected. The man who ran against me for Position No. 1, Dr. Bradford, did no campaigning either, but most of the other candidates, though they were running against other members of the council, did their campaigning against me. An opposition committee, led by certain druggists, tavern owners, jewelers, restaurant operators, and disgruntled ex-city employees, was formed to conduct the campaign against Maxey. This committee published and distributed from door-to-door throughout the city a twelve-page pamphlet in which they promised everything which might attract votes and paid their respects to me in the following words:

> The council is composed of seven members, who elect one of themselves to hold the office of mayor. His proper function is NOT that of a puppet-master, who leads the rest of the council around. It is NOT that of a dictator who refuses to allow any citizen his voice in public council meetings. His function is properly that of representing the city as a councilman, to welcome visiting officials and conventions, together with presiding smoothly over council meetings. He should be suave, diplomatic, and reasonably uncontroversial.

I did not bother to answer this tirade either publicly or privately, but in certain respects I regarded it as complimentary. To be denounced in my seventy-second year as a puppet-master and dictator certainly could be taken to mean that my enemies did not regard me as senile. In some way I must have accomplished the amazing feat of making the "toothless tiger" look dangerous. I would much rather be damned for that than be praised for being "reasonably uncontroversial."

The election took place on March 13, 1962. Of 12,000 eligible voters in the city only about 4,000 cast their ballots in the councilmanic election. In other words, two-thirds of the city electorate did not care enough about municipal affairs to go to the polls and express themselves. The one-third who did care re-elected five of the incumbent councilmen and defeated two—Hanson and Maxey.

That the 13th of March proved to be a bad day for mayors all over the state. Nearly every mayor who ran for re-election that time was defeated, including Tom Bostic of Yakima, who was universally recognized as one of the outstanding business and civic leaders of the Pacific Northwest. In Walla Walla, the opposition got rid of me with ease, but in reality lost the election. By concentrating on me, they failed to eliminate a majority of the council. After the election the five re-elected council members closed ranks and took pains to see that the two new members of the council were kept safely handcuffed. Of course no one likes to be defeated, but I was not very sorry to be relieved of my councilmanic and mayoral responsibilities. I had already accomplished much more than I had in mind when I filed for the council in August, 1960. Then my only purpose had been to stimulate others to file. In addition to accomplishing that, I had helped lay the guide lines for the new regime, had participated in the crucial decisions of the transition period, had helped choose the first city manager, and had been influential in shaping the organization and methodology by which the business of the council would be transacted for many years to come.

Other Civic Activities

Defeat for re-election took me out of local politics but not out of civic activities. In July, 1962, I was elected president of the Walla Walla Symphony Society. I served two terms of one year each in that office, concluding my tenure as of June 30, 1964. Though not a musician myself, I had long been interested in musical affairs. My wife had been a professional musician for many years; also my daughter Marilyn. I knew that the Symphony Society was in need of a little trouble-shooting at that particular time and I had time to give for such a purpose.

The Symphony Society's troubles were not serious, but might become so if certain changes were not made. The changes most urgently needed had to do with budgeting and management of funds, the retirement of certain committee chairmen, and the introduction of new blood into the board of directors and other official positions. My job was to effect these changes with a minimum of travaille for all concerned. To do this I had to attend a great many board meetings, committee meetings, and personal conferences. The first thing was to modernize the Society's constitution and by-laws which dated back to 1907, and had been pretty generally ignored for a long time. On my recommendation, the Board of Directors established a committee to deal with this problem. I worked with the committee all through the year 1962-63 and was much gratified when on June 4, 1963, a new constitution and a new set of by-laws were adopted and put into effect.

The next most important thing I had to do in 1962-63 was to help break in the new executive secretary. For the first time in its long history the Symphony Society employed a paid secretary in that year. It was my responsibility to give the secretary all necessary counsel and support, and also to determine to a considerable extent which particular duties she would take over. This required quite a little doing in 1962-63 but in 1963-64 the executive secretary had things so well under control that an occasional telephone conversation sufficed to keep things going smoothly. In 1962-63 it fell largely to me to bring about new appointments in the following positions: treasurer, chairman of women's committee, chairman of booking committee, chairman of finance committee, and three vacancies in the board of directors. In 1963-64 no such changes were necessary. One further thing that fell to me in 1962-63 was to collaborate with the treasurer and the executive secretary in changing the accounting procedures of the Symphony Society and installing for the first time a budget system.

I had little or nothing to do with the artistic achievements of the Walla Walla Symphony Orchestra, although such matters were largely talked over in board meetings and I sometimes participated in those discussions. Nor could I claim direct credit for the fact that more Symphony Society memberships were sold in 1962-63 than ever before and still more in 1963-64. These peak achievements were mainly due to the work of the campaign chairman, the publicity chairman, the finance chairman and their respective committees. All I did was to try to keep them all happy and enthusiastic.

The Marcus Whitman Foundation was another civic activity which occupied me in my retirement years. I was one of the original incorporators of this nonprofit corporation, which had been established back in 1949 to help promote and finance the campaign for a statue of Marcus Whitman in the United States capitol building at Washington, D. C. With the success of that campaign, the Marcus Whitman Foundation normally would have gone out of existence. But there were tag ends of business to carry on for a number of years, a certain amount of money in the treasury had to be invested and accounted for, and various historical functions and occasions in which the Whitman name and fame should have some kind of agency support. So the Marcus Whitman Foundation was kept alive. When I retired as president of Whitman College, I tried to resign from the board of the Marcus Whitman Foundation. The board asked me to reconsider and urged me to stay on, saying that I was one of the few original incorporators left and therefore they wanted me to be a life member. Since there were only two or three meetings of the Marcus Whitman Foundation each year, I could not say I could not spare the time. So I agreed to continue, but dodged all duties except attending board meetings.

In Early September, 1963, I was asked to be a member of a so-called citizens' committee on street improvements. Earlier in this chapter I related what the city council did in 1961 to initiate a program of street improvements for Walla Walla. Having secured a planning loan from the Housing and Home Financing Agency of the United States Government, the council authorized the use of this loan to employ the eminent engineering firm of Stevens and Thompson, Portland and Seattle, to make a comprehensive study of all aspects of Walla Walla's street improvement problem. The Stevens and Thompson report was received on August 5, 1963, and the city council immediately asked sixty-one representative citizens to serve as an advisory committee on the question of what should be done in pursuance of this report. I attended the first meeting of this committee and was nominated for chairman, but withdrew my name. There were two reasons for this, and modesty was not one of them. My first reason was that I did not want to take on as much work as the chairmanship would involve, and the second was that I had been a member of the council when the Stevens and Thompson study had been authorized and thought it would not look quite right if I should later serve as chairman of a citizen's committee to evaluate this report. I did, however, agree to serve as chairman of one of the subcommittees of the committee of sixty-one.

My sub-committee was called No. 4 and consisted of about a dozen people, both men and women, who were sincerely interested in the street problem and also proved to be grand people to work with. The Stevens and Thompson report was divided into twenty parts called phases, each of which dealt with a particular combination of primary and secondary arterial streets. Each sub-committee was asked to examine and reach conclusions as to every one of the twenty phases and then file a report with the general chairman. This required regular meetings for about two months. I not only presided at the meetings of Sub-Committee No. 4 but drafted all three of the reports which it submitted to the general chairman. When all of the sub-committees had finished their work, the general chairman called all of the sub-committee chairmen together for the purpose of trying to whip out a consensus that would fairly well reflect the composite opinion of the sixty-one members of the general committee. This was not easy, and the general chairman's final report was far too composite to be accurate. But the council accepted it, nevertheless, as the best guide to public opinion it could get, and subsequently voted to put on the ballot in the municipal election of March, 1964, a bond issue proposal embodying, as nearly as they could approximate it, the action favored by the citizens' committee on each of the Stevens and Thompson street improvement phases. This bond issue failed to pass.

Scholarly Activities

In addition to the writing of books I had always carried on such incidental scholarly activities as doing book reviews for the professional journals, writing articles, and delivering lectures on topics of special interest. During my eleven presidential years I had little time for such activities. After retirement I was able to resume them on a modest scale. Each year after 1959 I did two or more book reviews for the *Annals of the American Academy of Political and Social Science*. The books assigned to me for review were neither textbooks nor popular treatises but highly technical and specialized works based on recent research. This was good for me—kept me abreast with some of the newer developments in my own profession and also forced me to exercise critical faculties which had not been used for some years.

In May, 1962, I accepted appointment as a contributing editor for the *Dictionary of Political Science* to be published by the Philosophical Library of New York. The subjects assigned to me for ten to seventy-five words of definition or description for each were: Michael Bakunin, Bishop Jacques Benigne Bossuet, Brook Farm, Corporative System, Darwinism, Evolution, Greek Catholic Church, Horace Greeley, Code of Hammurabi, Icarianism, Iron Law of Oligarchy, Jesus, Harold J. Laski, Sir Henry Maine, Roberto Michels, Monism, Moses, Robert Owen, Vilfredo Pareto, Roman Catholic Church, Friederich Karl von Savigny, Social Darwinism, Socrates, Theocracy, Tradition, Traditionalism, and Utopianism. This assignment was intellectually fascinating. In several of my books, especially in *The American Problem of Government* and *Political Philosophies*, I had written something on most of these topics, but in these works I had not faced the challenge of condensation to not more than seventy-five words without sacrifice of basic information as well as accuracy. To meet this test I was obliged to review many of my own writings and also consult those of many other authoritative scholars. It was a profitable experience for me. The *Dictionary of Political Science* was published in 1964, and I was gratified to discover that the editor-in-chief had accepted all of my contributions without change.

After I left the office of mayor, I did not do a great deal of public speaking, and that was the way I wanted it. As mayor I had done far more public speaking than I would have preferred and most of it was purely piffle. I was much gratified, therefore, in the spring of 1964 to accept an invitation to return to Whitman College as a visiting professor and deliver a series of lectures the second semester each year. The title of my series for 1964 was "Religion and the Rise of Nationalism," for 1965 it was "The Political Dilemma of the Colored American," and for 1966 it was scheduled as "Liberal and Conservative Political Thought." This brought me back to the campus in a capacity that did not make great demands on my time and energy but brought me many social and intellectual satisfactions. All this without any detriment to the full enjoyment of retirement.

Farming

Most of my life I have been to some extent a tiller of the soil. I was brought up that way. Not only did I work on farms belonging to various members of our family, but did farm work right at home in the town of Ellensburg. In my boyhood most families in town kept chickens, a cow, two or three horses, and maybe a pig or two, and also grew a vegetable garden. For shade trees we planted mostly fruit trees, and therefore always had fruit to grow and harvest. The only period of my life when I was completely detached from the soil was when I lived in New York and Cleveland, eight years in all. When we moved west in 1925 we bought a farm in the Spokane Valley and operated it for eight years before we sold it. Most of my summers during that time were a combination of writing and farming.

In Walla Walla I managed to grow some flowers and vegetables nearly everywhere we lived, and when we bought land and built the house where we now live I found myself the proprietor of a half-acre farm. This was in 1939. Since then I personally have done all of the lawn work, all of the pruning and trimming, all of the digging and cultivating, all of the planting and harvesting—all of everything that had to be done in the growing of grass, flowers, fruits and vegetables on a half-acre tract. This has required me to engage in vigorous manual labor from one to two hours every single day. If you have enough diversification, there is more real work for a man on a half-acre such as mine than on 1,000 acres of wheat. I have enjoyed doing this work, and I believe it has contributed much to my continued good health.

I have experimented with nearly every kind of shrub, tree, flower, fruit, and vegetable which can be grown in the Walla Walla climate. I have had some great successes and some whopping failures. And the failures have been more interesting than the successes. Every year I have an almost complete failure in something as common as cabbage or tomatoes that I have grown successfully for years. Then I spend the time until the next planting season trying to figure out what happened and why. Thus I have learned much about the vagaries of Mother Nature—one thing in particular that has been good for me as a political scientist. I have learned, and learned well I hope, the lesson that you cannot force Nature beyond a certain point, which sometimes is very hard to find. Time and again I have found it advisable to lay off and give Time and Nature a chance to do their inevitable work. I might have been a better political scientist if I had learned this lesson earlier in life.

Profit and Loss

I may have given the wrong impression in saying, earlier in this narration, that one of my major preoccupations in retirement would be the making of money. I did not need to make money in retirement, as our retirement income was quite

494

sufficient to our needs. My remark had reference to the fact that I had always been interested in certain methods of making money, especially the stock and bond market. This interest, however, was not simply one of profit and loss; it was far more an interest in playing games with the American economy. Prior to retirement my participation in such games had been circumscribed by the fact that I was always up to my ears in competing activities and interests which seemed to have more imperative claims upon my time and attention. After retirement I was free to give as much or as little attention to the securities game as I might wish, and I took advantage of this freedom.

I had no desire to speculate just for speculation's sake, but I did want to try out some theories. As a result of some years of observation and study, and also from the experience of sitting with the investment committee of Whitman College for eleven years, I developed some ideas about profit and loss in securities investments. I came to believe that some, if not all, of these ideas were valid in every day's market, year in and year out. In other words, I concluded that there were always good "buys" and poor "buys" no matter what the general state of the market, and no matter what the reading of the Dow-Jones average. After retirement I was in a position to test my ideas on a limited scale with my own funds, and I did so.

I started a program of stock and bond investments in January, 1960, which enabled me to pick and choose rather freely. The outcome at the time of this writing, which is November 1965, has been very gratifying both as to income and capital gains. The profits have been substantial and the losses negligible. It goes without saying that the psychological satisfactions have been correspondingly agreeable. I have even allowed myself to fancy that if I had chosen a business career instead of one in education, I might perhaps have accumulated a goodly store of wealth.

But I do not regret the choice I made. If one could set up a profit-and-loss statement on such a thing as an academic career,

I believe mine would evidence a great accumulation of wealth not reckonable in dollars and cents. The academic life has been a good one for me and good also, I hope, for the world I lived in.